A Dictionary of
Sri Lankan English

First print : October 2007
Second print : March 2009
Third print : February 2011

ISBN 978-955-50542-0-1

Published by:
Michael Meyler
www.mirisgala.net

Digital Artwork by Prem Kumar @ Spot Digital Graphics
Printed by Samayawardhana Printers

A Dictionary of
Sri Lankan English

Michael Meyler

Edited by Dinali Fernando and Vivimarie VanderPoorten

Illustrated by Anura Srinath

CONTENTS

FOREWORD

In describing the growth of languages, linguistic historians have outlined certain stages through which a living language seems to develop as it moves from being merely a spoken dialect to a medium capable of recording and communicating all forms of human activity, in both speech and writing. One of these stages involves the growth of the word stock as the language expands, and attempts to make this increasing vocabulary accessible to all users of that language. The tool that makes vocabulary accessible is the dictionary, and the creation of a dictionary contributes towards the next important stage – standardization, and the acceptance of that language as a viable medium of formal communication.

These stages of linguistic development are readily observable in modern languages such as French and English. Thus, in the case of English, it was the development of dictionaries such as that of Dr Samuel Johnson in the eighteenth century and the Oxford English Dictionary in the nineteenth century that have helped to make British English the language it is today. It is also a recognized fact that American English owes much to the efforts of Noah Webster and his monumental "American Dictionary of the English Language" of 1828.

It is against this backdrop that we need to set the "Dictionary of Sri Lankan English" by Michael Meyler. In recent times, English has re-surfaced in Sri Lanka as a major mode of education and social development. The language today is of interest to politicians, employers, employees, parents, teachers, students and the general public across the country. Its presence is proclaimed through the media and through advertising where it is often inter-twined with the two major mother tongues of this island. It is heard everywhere – in the speech of young people and of those not so young, in all Sri Lankan communities. All these users shape the language, bringing into it Sri Lankan habits, customs, expressions, interests and experience. The language has expanded to an all-purpose mode of contemporary communication, and is now ready for its next stage of development. The

"Dictionary of Sri Lankan English" is a timely contribution towards this stage for it attempts, as Webster did, to introduce "uniformity and accuracy" to the multicultural vocabulary of Sri Lankan English.

This "Dictionary" is indeed in the "Great Tradition" of lexicography for it is the work of one man working mostly alone, for a long period of time – twenty years. With commitment and a little help from his friends, Michael Meyler has taken advantage of his experience as a teacher of English and a lexicographer, and of his position as an informed outsider, to create a work that "describes the way English is used in Sri Lanka". It charts the social and cultural nuances of the words and phrases that we use, nuances that we as Sri Lankans are scarcely aware of. It pinpoints Sri Lankan usage of grammatical structures and compares it with British usage, vividly demonstrating that our English is distinct in a number of ways. It reflects and illustrates Sri Lankan phonology, reinforcing the notion that our variety of English is a variety with its own features. In short it is indeed a dictionary and not a mere glossary.

Michael Meyler himself notes that the work is by no means comprehensive. The "Dictionary of Sri Lankan English" is however an important contribution to the development of English in this country. It serves as a testimony to dedication and sensitive lexicography, and as notice to researchers, teachers and all those interested in Sri Lankan English that much work lies ahead.

Ryhana Raheem
Post Graduate Institute of English
Open University of Sri Lanka

INTRODUCTION

Ever since I first came to Sri Lanka as an English language teacher in 1985, I have been fascinated by the way English is spoken and written here. This interest is partly the personal curiosity of someone with a general interest in languages, partly the professional interest of a teacher of English in Sri Lanka. One fateful day around 20 years ago, I was inspired to write down a couple of examples on the back of an envelope. I soon ran out of space on the envelope and copied my collection onto a few sheets of paper, which I later typed up on an old-fashioned typewriter.

Around 15 years ago I was introduced to the field of professional lexicography as a contributor to the Oxford Learners' Wordfinder Dictionary. At the same time I typed up a computerised version of my own dictionary. I was living in Edinburgh at the time, and Sri Lankan friends passed on old copies of the Sri Lankan Sunday newspapers which I scoured for examples. After joining the British Council in Colombo in 1995, I expanded the dictionary and added the quotations from published books. With the help of Dinali Fernando and Vivimarie VanderPoorten I was able to make extensive additions and corrections, culminating in this publication.

I see this as a work in progress, frozen in time by the practical considerations of publication. I am aware of a number of shortcomings. However, I hope that one of this book's strengths is the fact that my outsider's perspective, as a speaker and teacher of British English, gives me an insight into Sri Lankan English which is perhaps not available to someone who speaks it as their first language.

A Guide to the Dictionary

This dictionary aims to describe the way in which English is used in Sri Lanka. It attempts to define Sri Lankan English (SLE), and to promote the acceptance of SLE as one of the many established varieties of English as an international language.

An entry is included on the grounds that it is a feature of the English spoken by Sri Lankan speakers of English, and that it differs in some way from current "standard" British English. It does not include those features which are better defined as "common errors made by learners of the language". However, drawing a line between what should be included as an acceptable example of SLE, and what should be omitted on the grounds that it is an "error", is clearly a controversial issue.

Who is the dictionary for?

The dictionary should be of interest to anyone with a general interest in Sri Lanka and/or in the English language. Specifically, it is intended for the following groups:

- Learners and teachers of English in Sri Lanka, who need to be aware of the differences between SLE and "standard" British English. By avoiding linguistic jargon, I have attempted to make the dictionary accessible to learners of English as well as native speakers.

- Sri Lankan and foreign linguists and academics interested in the increasingly popular field of international varieties of English. Dictionaries have been produced of Indian English, South African English, New Zealand English and so on, but as far as I know, no one has yet attempted to compile a dictionary of Sri Lankan English.

- Foreigners living in Sri Lanka, for whom the dictionary will serve as a glossary of the language they hear around them, an introduction to aspects of the country's culture, and as a souvenir of their stay here.

What is Sri Lankan English?

The answer to this question is not as simple as it may seem. Even within a small country like Sri Lanka, and even within the relatively tiny English-speaking community, there are several sub-varieties of Sri Lankan English. Sinhalese, Tamils, Muslims and Burghers speak different varieties; Christians, Buddhists, Hindus and Muslims have their own vocabularies; the older generation speak a different language from the younger generation; and the wealthy Colombo elite (who tend to speak English as their first language) speak a different variety from the wider community (who are more likely to learn it as a second language).

The issue is further clouded by the number of different terms which have been coined to describe Sri Lankan English and/or its different sub-varieties: Standard Sri Lankan English? Lankan English? Singlish? Tamlish? Sinenglish? I have attempted to keep things simple by sticking to the term "Sri Lankan English", which I shall refer to as "SLE", and which for the purposes of this dictionary, I define as follows:

"Sri Lankan English (SLE) is the language spoken and understood by those Sri Lankans who speak English as their first language, and/or who are bilingual in English and Sinhala or Tamil."

I am aware that this is a broad definition which raises a number of questions. Some of these issues are discussed in more detail below.

What does the dictionary consist of?

The dictionary contains approximately 2,500 examples, listed alphabetically, of words and expressions which are characteristic of the English spoken in Sri Lanka. All of the entries in the dictionary contain some or all of the following features:

- the **headword**, written in **bold type**. Occasionally an entry will contain a related word, also in **bold type**, which is not thought to require a separate entry. Where there are two or more identical headwords, they are numbered, e.g. **moonstone** (1), **moonstone** (2). Sometimes an entry is followed by one or more supplementary headwords preceded by a box: □, e.g. **pol** is followed by □ **pol arrack** and other collocations of **pol**, even though according to alphabetical order these words would follow subsequent headwords such as **pola** and **polecat**.

- a pronunciation guide, written in the /phonetic font/ explained in the pronunciation section below. The pronunciation is given for non-

English words, and for English words where SLE pronunciation differs substantially from "standard" British pronunciation.

- a definition of the word, either a simple "translation" into standard British English, or a longer explanation. In many cases an illustration is also included.

- the derivation of the word, for non-English words, e.g. of Sinhala, Tamil, Hindi, Malay, Arabic, Dutch or Portuguese origin. Where relevant, it is mentioned if the word appears in the OED (Oxford English Dictionary), for example with a different spelling or definition. It is also mentioned if the word is used elsewhere, e.g. "(also India)". In this context "India" often refers loosely to the whole Subcontinent.

- **cross-references** to other entries, also written in **bold type**. There are three types of cross-reference: 1) words in brackets with the symbol =, immediately following the headword, e.g. **king coconut (= thambili)**, refer to another entry which has an equivalent meaning; 2) words in brackets with the symbol >, appearing after the definition, e.g. **molgaha (> vangediya)**, refer to other related entries, e.g. similar words, opposites, or entries which include a more detailed explanation or relevant quote or illustration; 3) words in **bold type** appearing within the text of the definition or notes, e.g. **milk hopper**: a **hopper** made with **coconut milk**.

- *example phrases and sentences*, written in *italics* and marked with a degree sign: ° Examples are included to illustrate the different ways a word or expression may be used, and the different contexts in which it may be found. Many of the examples are taken from authentic sources such as newspapers, magazines, advertisements, etc. Others were overheard on the TV or radio, or in real conversations.

- notes comparing Sri Lankan and British usage, preceded by the arrow symbol: → These notes explain differences in meaning in more detail, and also focus on certain grammatical and pronunciation features. In this context, as elsewhere in the dictionary, the abbreviations SLE and

BSE are used to refer to Sri Lankan English and British Standard English respectively.

- quotes from a selection of 30 published books (listed in full on page xxxiii). Each quote is preceded by the diamond symbol: ♦ and followed by a page reference, e.g. (AG 42) means the quote given comes from Anil's Ghost page 42.

The books represent a range of contemporary Sri Lankan writing. All are works of fiction (novels and short stories) published between 1982 and 2006, and set mostly or entirely in a Sri Lankan context. The authors are either Sri Lankan, or of Sri Lankan origin living abroad. The quotes are included merely to illustrate entries in the dictionary, not to act as a glossary for the books themselves or to make any judgement on their style or content.

Quotes have not been changed in any way, apart from a few cases where the original contains an obvious typographical error. Where the spelling of the target word differs from the spelling of the headword, this can be assumed to be either a variant or a non-standard spelling of the word. Three dots (...) show where a quote begins or ends in the middle of a sentence, or where words have been cut within a quote. "Double inverted commas" represent direct speech, colloquial language which the author has put into the mouths of his/her characters (perhaps consciously using what the author him/herself would consider incorrect English).

As well as helping to illustrate the meaning and usage of the headword, quotes also serve to reveal alternative spellings, and show when different authors (or their editors) feel it necessary to mark out certain "non-standard" English words by putting them in italics or inverted commas, or by including a definition of the word, for example in a footnote (marked with an asterisk *). Multiple quotes are included for particularly common words in order to emphasise their frequency, and to illustrate the different contexts in which they may be used.

Features of Sri Lankan English

The main features of Sri Lankan English are considered under the headings Words and expressions, Grammatical features, and Pronunciation.

1.　Words and expressions

SLE includes many non-English words, the majority of which are of Sinhala and Tamil origin. Others derive from Dutch and Portuguese, the languages of the pre-British colonial powers; from Hindi and other Indian languages; or from Malay and Arabic.

Many of the English words and expressions used in SLE are not found in British English: some of these may be unique to SLE, others may be found in other varieties elsewhere in the English-speaking world. Others exist in British English with a different meaning; sometimes this difference is obvious, sometimes it is more subtle. Others may be standard English words, but are characteristic of SLE simply because of the frequency with which they are used.

SLE includes a number of features characteristic of British colonial language which has fallen out of fashion in contemporary British English, including "Anglo-Indian" words which date from colonial times and are common to the whole Subcontinent. These words are considered archaic in British English, or are restricted to more formal contexts. Even in SLE they tend to be used more by the older generation.

One significant feature of SLE is a more marked difference between the written and spoken language than in standard British English. This distinction is perhaps a reflection of the gulf which exists in Sinhala and Tamil between formal written language and the everyday colloquial language. This helps to explain why the language of journalism and certain letter-writing conventions in Sri Lanka seem dated and overly formal to speakers of British English.

A large number of words (both English and non-English) refer to cultural and environmental aspects of Sri Lanka which may not be familiar to speakers of other varieties of English, such as animals and birds, plants and trees, fruits and vegetables, food and drink, and Buddhism and other religions.

There are a few cases where non-English words have been "Anglicised" by the addition of an English ending: for example the verb endings –ise and –fy on asweddumise and rasthiyadufy, and the English plural –s on nouns such as halmassas and karapottas.

There are also many common collocations (or combinations of words) which do not normally appear in a standard dictionary of English. Look up 'rice' in a British dictionary and you will find collocations such as rice bowl, rice paper, rice pudding. None of these appear in this dictionary: instead you will find rice belly, rice cooker, rice flour, rice mill, rice packet and rice puller.

The dictionary also includes abbreviations which are unique to SLE; common exclamations; and finally a host of idioms and other expressions which do not exist in British English, but which greatly enrich the language, helping to relieve the drudge of the lexicographer's toil, and hopefully to entertain the curious reader.

2. Grammatical features

The alphabetical arrangement of a dictionary does not lend itself to a detailed analysis of grammatical features. However, notes on a number of ways in which the grammar of SLE varies from standard grammar can be found within the pages of the dictionary. Many of these features are characteristic of informal colloquial language, and might not be considered acceptable in a more formal written context.

2.1 Verbs

Continuous forms tend to be more frequent in SLE, for example with "state verbs" such as have, like, want, know, think and understand, where the simple form would be more likely in BSE: "She's having a fever". This is particularly common in deductions after modal verbs such as must, might and may: "You must be thinking I'm mad", "You may be knowing them", "They might be not wanting to come".

Other modal verbs are also used differently in SLE. Can is used instead of could ("An important letter can arrive this week"), and vice-versa ("Application forms could be obtained from the secretary"); will is used instead of would ("I knew the car will be there"), and vice-versa ("We would inform you as soon as we hear").

The past perfect tense is used differently in SLE. It is commonly used to report something which the speaker did not experience first-hand, and which is therefore not being reported as absolute fact: "The robbers had escaped in a white van". In this case the simple past would be more common in BSE, unless it is introduced by a phrase such as "The police said that ..." or "It was reported that ..."; or else to show that one event happened before another: "When the police arrived, the robbers had already escaped".

Colloquial SLE is less strict than BSE in following the "sequence of tenses" in conditional sentences and hypothetical statements, e.g. after 'I wish'. The present tense tends to be used instead of the past tense ("I wish I don't have to go"), and the past tense instead of the past perfect tense ("If you went you would have enjoyed", "If only she didn't say that").

The verb 'like' is used differently in SLE. 'Do you like?' is used in offers to mean 'would you like?' or 'do you want?': "Do you like some more rice?" It can even be used without an object: "Do you like?" – "Yes I like." In addition, 'like' is often followed by the infinitive where the –ing form would be more likely in BSE: "I like to go for films". The same applies with similar verbs such as 'love' and 'hate': "I hate to cook".

Some other verbs which need an object in BSE are used without the object in SLE: "Can't believe!", "He told he will come", "I prefer if you don't do that". Others which are followed by a preposition in BSE are used without the preposition: "You better refer your dictionary", "What are you talking?". Others are used with a preposition in SLE but not in BSE: "Why don't you ask from your father?" Others are used with a different preposition: "How much did you spend for your car?"

Phrasal verbs also differ in a number of ways. Several phrasal verbs exist in SLE which are not used in BSE: "You've put on since I last saw you!", "He gets played out every time". Others are used in a different context ("He passed out from Peradeniya last year"), with a different meaning ("She came down in maths"), or in a different form ("He got down from the bus in Galle").

In some cases a verb which is a phrasal verb in BSE (such as 'put on' or 'throw away') is used without the particle in SLE: "I'll put a shirt and come", "Please don't throw my letter". In other cases a particle is added in SLE which would not be there in BSE: "She couldn't bear up the pain", "They're planning to bring down a specialist from the UK".

2.2   Nouns, articles, prepositions, adverbs

Certain nouns which are plural in BSE, are singular in SLE: "Can you lend me your scissor?", "I need to buy a new trouser". Others which are uncountable in BSE, are countable in SLE: "I'm thinking of buying a small land", "Do you have a paper I can use?"

Noun combinations such as 'card pack', 'English knowledge' and 'glass pieces', would be expressed as 'pack of cards', 'knowledge of English' and 'pieces of glass' in BSE. A combination such as 'beer bottle', 'curd pot' or 'matchbox' normally refers to the container (bottle, pot, box) as well as its contents (beer, curd, matches), while in BSE it would refer to the container itself, which may be empty. The full container would be called 'a bottle of beer', 'a pot of curd' or 'a box of matches' in BSE.

The definite article 'the' is omitted with the names of countries (UK, US, Maldives, Philippines), and with places (in office, going to temple). The indefinite article 'a/an' is omitted with numbers (hundred, thousand), and with quantifiers (couple, few, little, lot of). In the case of 'few' this can affect the meaning, since standard English makes a distinction between 'few' and 'a few'.

Certain prepositions are used differently in SLE: "We're waiting from morning", "He's 3 years younger to me", "She's very good in maths". The preposition 'of' is used after 'enough' and after 'how much', 'so much' and 'too much': "Is there enough of salt?", "How much of money do you have?"

Certain adverbs are also used differently: adverbs of time ("I'll do it after", "I saw him two months before"), and adverbs of place ("They must be waiting down", "Let's get some food from out").

A few words which are written as one word in SLE would be written as two words in BSE: "They're open everyday", "It's upto you to reply".

2.3 Word order

In questions, prepositions which are normally separated from the question word in BSE, often come at the beginning of the sentence in SLE: "From where did you get it?", "To whom did you give it?" This sounds rather formal in BSE, where these questions would more likely be expressed as: "Where did you get it from?", "Who did you give it to?"

A number of adverbial words and phrases tend to come before the main verb in SLE, while in BSE they would come at the beginning or end of the sentence: "They anyway won't come", "You at least must come", "I of course don't like it".

Other words tend to immediately follow the noun they refer to in SLE, while in BSE they would come in a different place in the sentence: "He speaks Russian also", "Tomorrow even we'll be open", "Tamil and Sinhala both". (See also the note on intonation in the section "Connected speech" below.)

2.4 Colloquial features

Many of the features already mentioned are characteristic of spoken language. Another example is the doubling of words in phrases such as 'small small problems' and 'hot hot hoppers'; in expressions like 'so so?' and 'can can!'; and in questions: "What and what have you been doing?", "Where and where did you go?"

Colloquial SLE is much more inclined to drop redundant grammatical items such as articles, pronouns, auxiliary verbs and the verb 'to be'. Well-known examples include phrases such as 'what to do?', 'how to go?', 'nothing to worry', and the ubiquitous question tags 'isn't it?' and 'no?' Similar economy of expression is seen in one-word utterances such as 'so?', 'how?', 'come!', 'sit!'; in time expressions such as 'day before', 'day after', 'early morning' and 'those days'; and in phrases such as 'fully worth', 'worst comes to worst', 'soon as possible'.

As mentioned earlier, verbs are often used without an object in SLE: "I don't like", "I don't think", "Can't believe!". In the last example the subject 'I' is also dropped. This omission of the subject pronoun is also found in expressions such as "Can't be!", "Can't help!", "Can't say!"; in short one-word answers ("Can you come tomorrow?" - "Can't!"; "Do we have any dhal?" – "Have!"); and in colloquial sentences like "Raining so no tennis", "Haven't any petrol".

3.   Pronunciation

The phonetic font used to show the pronunciation of words in the dictionary is my own. I hope that it is largely self-explanatory, although I am aware that it oversimplifies certain aspects of SLE pronunciation. Some of the symbols used are explained below using English, Sinhala and Tamil words from the dictionary as examples.

The font was originally developed as a way of writing Sinhala and Tamil phonetically, so there is a danger of implying that only Sinhala and Tamil sounds are used in SLE pronunciation. While it is true that Sinhala and Tamil sounds feature prominently in SLE, it should also be mentioned that this becomes more exaggerated among those who speak Sinhala or Tamil as their first language, and who are not necessarily as fluent in English as speakers of "standard SLE".

A number of features of SLE pronunciation are described below. However, pronunciation is one area where it is difficult to generalise, since every individual speaker pronounces the language differently.

3.1 Vowels

symbol	English example		Sinhala/Tamil example	
ɑ	uncle	/ankl/	amma	/amma/
ā	parcel	/pāsəl/	aachchi	/āchchi/
œ	carrom	/kœrəm/	ambul	/œmbul/
œ̄	jam	/jœ̄m/	mal lella	/mal lœ̄llə/
e	men	/men/	elle	/elle/
ē	lane	/lēn/	thera	/tērə/
i	iguana	/iguānə/	iddly	/iɒli/
ī	ekel	/īkəl/	seeya	/sīya/
o	office	/ofis/	pol	/pol /
ō	coat	/kōт/	poya	/pōyə/
u	put	/puт/	uluhal	/uluhāl/
ū	coolie	/kūli/	pooja	/pūja/
ə	hopper	/hopə/	Sinhala	/singhələ/
ə̄	Burgher	/bə̄gə/	verti	/vāтi/

There is a tendency in SLE to pronounce some vowels more "closed" than in BSE, which reflects the way Sinhala and Tamil vowels are pronounced. However, this is more exaggerated among first-language speakers of Sinhala and Tamil who do not speak "standard SLE". Indeed, this tendency is satirised by speakers of standard SLE when they refer to a "not pot" accent, pronouncing the English words 'not' and 'pot' with an exaggeratedly closed 'o'. Speakers of standard SLE will make a distinction between a more open 'o' in English words like 'office', and a more closed 'o' in Sinhala words like 'pol'.

In addition, the BSE diphthongs /ei/ and /əu/ tend to be replaced by the long vowels /ē/ and /ō/ in SLE. So the word 'lane' is pronounced /lēn/ and 'boat' is pronounced /bōт/. (Both these features are also characteristic of Scottish pronunciation.) This means that the distinction between 'boat' and 'bought' is less distinct in SLE than in BSE; but again, the distinction is made more clearly by speakers of standard SLE than by those who do not speak English as their first language.

Here are some other examples where vowels tend to be pronounced differently in SLE and BSE:

granite, marine, binoculars: the letter i pronounced /i/ or /ī/ in BSE, /ai/ in SLE

sponge, oven, worry, wonder: the letter o pronounced /a/ in BSE, /o/ in SLE (making 'wonder' a homophone of 'wander')

mis<u>chie</u>vous, <u>pan</u>try, <u>pa</u>rental, <u>pla</u>stic, <u>vi</u>deo: underlined syllable pronounced short in BSE, long in SLE

<u>air</u>port: BSE /ǣ/, SLE /eya/

3.2   Consonants

Most of the consonants are pronounced almost identically in SLE and BSE. The main exceptions are the following:

t	Thomian	/tōmiən/	thaaththa	/tātta/
т	tea	/тī/	chatti	/chaттi/
d	than	/dǣn/	duwa	/duwə/
ɒ	Dada	/ɒœɒa/	bandakka	/banɒakka/

The symbols /т/ and /ɒ/ represent the retroflex t and d, pronounced somewhat like the English t as in 'ten' and d as in 'dog', but with the tongue further back on the roof of the mouth. These sounds are common in Sinhala and Tamil, and this is how the letters 't' and 'd' tend to be pronounced in SLE.

The symbols /t/ and /d/ represent the dental t and d, pronounced with the tongue between the teeth. These sounds are similar to the voiceless 'th' as in 'think' and 'thought', and the voiced 'th' as in 'this' and 'that', but pronounced as "stops" rather than "fricatives". These sounds are common in Sinhala and Tamil, and this is how many speakers of SLE tend to pronounce the 'th' sound.

However, many speakers of standard SLE pronounce the English 'th' as a fricative sound just as in BSE pronunciation, while using the dental stops /t/ and /d/ for Sinhala and Tamil words such as duwa, thambi and thosai.

A similar issue arises with the pronunciation of the sounds /v/ and /w/. In Sinhala and Tamil (as in other Indian languages) there is only one letter covering both these sounds, and normally pronounced somewhere between the two. The failure to differentiate between the sounds /v/ and /w/ is a common feature of SLE pronunciation. However, it should be pointed out that many speakers of standard SLE do make a clear distinction between the two.

Here are some other examples where consonants tend to be pronounced differently in SLE and BSE:
husband: BSE /z/, SLE /s/
Asia: BSE /zh/, SLE /sh/
nephew: BSE /f/, SLE /v/
cease: BSE /s/, SLE /z/ (making it a homophone of 'seize')
healthy/wealthy: BSE voiceless 'th', SLE voiced 'th' or dental /d/
s(w)ord, clim(b)ing: the letter in brackets is silent in BSE pronunciation, but tends to be pronounced in SLE

3.3 Stress

There is a tendency in SLE to pronounce weak syllables more strongly than they would be pronounced in BSE. This affects the stress patterns in individual words and the rhythm of sentences.

A number of 2-syllable words are stressed on the second syllable in BSE pronunciation, but tend to be stressed on the first syllable in SLE. These include nouns (address, boutique, cassette, dessert, gazette, hotel, museum, papaw, police, rupee, sarong), verbs (translate, maintain, persuade, migrate, supply), words which can be nouns or verbs depending on the stress (convict, desert, progress, protest, object), opposites (increase/decrease, import/export, upstairs/downstairs), compounds (week-end, ice cream, best man, UK, US), and others (although, correct, hello, mature, unless, until).

Words ending in –et are pronounced /-ɪт/ in BSE, and /-əт/ in SLE: basket, biscuit, bucket, cricket, market, ticket, wicket.

Plurals and third person verbs ending in –es are pronounced /-ɪz/ in BSE, and /-əs/ in SLE: buses, wishes, houses, matches, judges, chances.

Past tense forms and adjectives ending in –ed are pronounced /-ɪɒ/ in BSE, and /-əɒ/ in SLE: landed, needed, started, excited, wicked, cussed.

A number of 3-syllable words are stressed on the final syllable in BSE pronunciation, but tend to be stressed on the first syllable in SLE, e.g.: nouns (afternoon, cigarette, engineer, lemonade, Japanese); verbs (understand, entertain, recommend, represent). Others are stressed on the second syllable in BSE pronunciation, but tend to be stressed on the first syllable in SLE (umbrella, vanilla, already, scientific, whatever, interior).

Negative words in which the negative prefix would be unstressed in BSE (except for special emphasis), but more likely to be stressed in SLE: unhappy, informal, immature, irregular, misunderstand, disappear.

Words beginning with an unstressed e- are pronounced /i-/ in BSE, but with a stronger /e-/ in SLE: enjoy, exam, expect, escape, environment, embarrassed.

Words beginning with an unstressed con- or com- are pronounced /kən-/ or /kəm-/ in BSE, but with a stronger /kon-/ or /kom-/ in SLE: computer, commence, complain, consult, convey, control.

Words beginning with an unstressed to- are pronounced /тə-/ in BSE, but with a stronger /тu-/ in SLE: today, tonight, tomorrow.

Words ending with an unstressed -a are pronounced /-ə/ in BSE, but with a stronger /-ɑ/ in SLE: camera, umbrella, vanilla.

Longer words often have a "primary stress" and a "secondary stress". In BSE the primary stress is usually towards the end of the word (second or third syllable from the end). In SLE the primary and secondary stress tend to be inverted, bringing the main stress forward to the first or second syllable. So certain words tend to be pronounced on the first syllable in

SLE (application, conversation, education, information, qualification, opportunity, university, probability, possibility); in others the stress tends to fall on the second syllable (pronunciation, association, examination, imagination, determination, responsibility).

"Shifting stress" in words such as advertise/advertisement and photograph/ photographer/photographic tends to be less marked in SLE, with a tendency either to stress the first syllable, or to pronounce all the syllables with a more even stress than in BSE pronunciation.

The following words contain one syllable which tends to be elided in BSE pronunciation, but pronounced in SLE: cam(e)ra, comf(or)table, diction(a)ry, lib(ra)ry, laborat(o)ry, rest(au)rant, secret(a)ry, veg(e)table.

Here are some other words where SLE pronunciation varies from BSE:
drawer: BSE /brō/, SLE /broyə/ (to rhyme with 'lawyer')
poem/poet: BSE /pəuim, pəuiт/, SLE /poyem, poyeт/
botany: three syllables in BSE, second syllable dropped in SLE ('botny')
flower/flour: homophones in BSE but pronounced differently in SLE:
/flavə/ and /flā/
warmth: one syllable in BSE, weak vowel added in SLE: /wōməth/
tuition: 3 syllables in BSE with the stress on the second syllable: /тyu'ishən/,
2 syllables in SLE with the stress on the first syllable: /'тyūshən/
vehicle: BSE /viyəkl/, SLE /vehikəl/

3.4   Connected speech

Words such as articles, prepositions, conjunctions and auxiliary verbs, which serve a grammatical function rather than carrying meaning, tend to be pronounced "weak" in BSE, often with the "schwa" vowel /ə/. These words are generally pronounced more fully in SLE. A simple example is to compare the weak 'and' in the BSE phrase "fish'n'chips" with the fuller 'and' in the SLE phrase "rice and curry". Similarly the weak 'of' in the BSE "cuppa tea" is likely to be pronounced more clearly in SLE: "cup of tea".

In SLE, as in BSE and in Welsh, Australian and South African English, the letter 'r' is not pronounced in words like 'mother', 'card' and 'earth', as it would be in Scottish, Irish, American and Indian English. In BSE, however, a final 'r' is pronounced if it is followed by a vowel, for example in the phrases 'mother_and father', 'here_and there', 'four_or five', 'you better_ask'. Interestingly, this "linking r" does not appear in SLE pronunciation. This means that the phrase 'sore eyes' is pronounced /sō aiz/, whereas in BSE it would be pronounced /sōr_aiz/.

Two examples of SLE intonation patterns are also worth mentioning. The first is well known: the tendency to end sentences in colloquial speech with the tag 'no?' spoken with a rising intonation. The other is the tendency to attach the word 'and' to the preceding word in lists: "Sinhala and ... Tamil and ... English", which in BSE would be pronounced "Sinhala ... and Tamil ... and English". A parallel can be drawn with Sinhala and Tamil, where the word 'and' is expressed as a suffix (Sinhala –y, Tamil –um).

A similar effect can be noted with the words 'also' and 'too', which (as mentioned above) immediately follow the word they refer to in SLE, in the same way as the equivalent suffixes in Sinhala (-t) and Tamil (-um): "He speaks Russian also", "I too was angry". In BSE these words tend to come at a different place in the sentence ('also' immediately before the verb, 'too' at the end of the sentence). The difference in word order also affects the intonation of the sentence.

The Seven Sisters

There are a number of issues which I have encountered in compiling this dictionary. I have called these issues - for no particular reason - the "seven sisters". I include them here in an attempt to explain the criteria by which items have been included in (or excluded from) the dictionary.

1.   Spelling conventions

Spelling, more than any other, is one area where dictionaries are expected to be prescriptive. We are so used to "looking it up in the dictionary" to check the correct spelling of a word. But how do you spell a non-English word which doesn't yet appear in any dictionary, and which is normally used only in spoken contexts?

This problem is illustrated in the very first entry, aachchi: A Sivanandan spells it two different ways in "When Memory Dies" ('aatchi' on page 240 and 'aachi' on page 342); Manuka Wijesinghe spells it 'achi' in her recent book "Monsoons and Potholes". But the spelling chosen for the headword is aachchi, and I have tried to be as consistent as possible by using the "double a" spelling in other words such as aappa, aasmi, maama, thaaththa, and the "double ch" spelling in achcharu, kachcheri, thaachchiya, thangachchi. This is thought to reflect the majority usage observed in other contemporary sources such as newspapers.

However, there is clearly a dilemma in attempting to strike a balance between being consistent in spelling conventions, and reflecting actual usage, which is far from consistent. The only consolation is that the English language, having historically absorbed words from so many different languages, already contains so many spelling inconsistencies that it can surely take a few more!

2.   The generation gap

Like any language, SLE is constantly evolving. The language spoken by today's younger generation is very different from the language inherited from the British at independence. On the other hand, many of the features of "colonial" English remain in SLE having fallen out of fashion in British English, which explains why some aspects of SLE seem outdated and formal to speakers of contemporary British English. Both languages have developed in their own different ways, and a number of factors have influenced the way in which SLE has evolved over the past 60 years.

Most significant perhaps was the "Sinhala only" policy which led to English being dropped as the medium of education in Sri Lankan schools, and the emigration of most of the Burgher community and many other first-language English speakers. This resulted in what most people would regard as a general "lowering" in the standard of English in the country. As Sinhala became the dominant language of education and government, its influence on SLE also increased. One result of this was a merging of English and Sinhala by bilingual speakers into the hybrid often referred to as "Singlish", which has become a significant feature of SLE.

The reversal of the isolationist policies of the 1970s, and the increasingly open-market attitudes of subsequent governments, resulted in greater exposure to contemporary British, American and Australian language and culture via educational and commercial opportunities. The growth of English-medium "international schools", exposure to foreign media and the internet, the growing expatriate community, and the return from abroad of many younger generation expatriate Sri Lankans, have all influenced the way people speak English.

The main aim of this dictionary is to reflect contemporary usage (corresponding roughly with the quarter century from 1980 – 2005). However, many older words and expressions are included – partly because this language is still being used by the older generation, also because the colonial and post-colonial years remain a significant period in Sri Lankan memory. This is reflected in the number of recent books set during that period (including several of the books from which I have taken quotations).

3.   Class distinctions

There are also significant class distinctions in the way people speak English in Sri Lanka. The stereotype "Colombo 7" family are likely to speak English as their first language, to send their children to international schools, to spend holidays visiting relatives abroad, and to be exposed to international English via the media, internet, etc. The English they speak is therefore likely to be closer to an international standard. They are also likely to have the ability to switch between "Sri Lankan mode" and "international mode" depending on the context they are in.

The further you travel - metaphorically, if not geographically - from "Colombo 7", the greater is the influence of Sinhala and Tamil on the English people speak. Many Sri Lankans can claim to be bilingual in English and Sinhala or Tamil, but there are degrees of bilingualism, and many people speak English as their second language. The result is that, as well as the many Sinhala and Tamil words which have entered SLE, there are also many grammatical features which would be considered errors not only by speakers of British English, but also by educated Sri Lankan English speakers.

One feature of the language spoken by bilingual English/Sinhala speakers is a tendency to switch freely between English and Sinhala in mid-conversation, even in mid-sentence. This is further compounded by the tendency of spoken Sinhala to include so many English words - a feature sometimes referred to as "Singrisi". As a result of this mingling of languages, it can be difficult to define exactly where the Sinhala ends and the English begins.

Recently this code-switching between English and Sinhala has become more fashionable - a development which has been picked up by a number of advertisers. This dictionary reflects this trend by including a large number of Sinhala words and expressions, but longer Sinhala phrases are avoided on the grounds that they are better described as examples of code-switching.

4. Sinhala and Tamil: striking the right balance

As the previous paragraph implies, Sinhala words feature more prominently in this dictionary than Tamil words. The main reason for this is simply that Sinhala is the majority language in Sri Lanka, spoken by so many more people, and politically so much more significant.

As a result of this imbalance, while many Tamil speakers are trilingual, speaking Sinhala as well as English, this is less common among Sinhala speakers, who are more likely to be bilingual and unable to speak in Tamil. For this reason Sinhala and English (but not Tamil) tend to be the "link" languages between different communities. Sinhala speakers can drop Sinhala words into their conversation and make themselves understood, while Tamil words are less likely to be understood by non-Tamil speakers. This helps to explain why Sinhala has had a much greater and more visible influence on SLE.

In addition, Sinhala speakers tend to merge Sinhala and English into a hybrid "Singlish" or "Singrisi" - using Sinhala loan-words in English and English loan-words in Sinhala, as well as code-switching regularly between the two languages. Tamil speakers may do the same thing amongst themselves, but they cannot do so to the same extent outside their own language community. Interestingly, this type of code-switching between English and Tamil appears to be more common in Tamil Nadu, where Tamil is the dominant language.

5. Indian English and Sri Lankan English: where to draw the line?

Another issue is the relationship between Indian and Sri Lankan varieties of English. Indian English has long been recognised as an established variety of English, and has been well documented ever since "Hobson Jobson" was first published in the 19th century. But "Indian English" is a hugely diverse language, incorporating not only the vast diversity of India itself with all its ethnic groups, religions and native languages, but also other countries in the subcontinent such as Pakistan, Bangladesh, Nepal - and Sri Lanka. As a result there is a tendency to think of SLE as being just a sub-variety of Indian English, an impression encouraged by the relative lack of documentary evidence of SLE as a separate entity.

Of course there is a big overlap between Indian English and SLE. Both varieties evolved from the English of the British colonials of the 19th century, and much common vocabulary developed to describe the common flora and fauna of the two countries. Another common factor is the existence of many Tamil words in both Indian and Sri Lankan English.

However, it is also striking how many differences there are between Indian English and SLE. It therefore seems to be valid to make a distinction between the two, while at the same time acknowledging their common features. Perhaps it is more helpful to see both of them as distinct but overlapping sub-varieties of a more general "South Asian English".

Another issue is the fact that so many Indian words have entered British English through the British Asian community. This dictionary includes many Indian English words which are commonly used in Sri Lanka, but others are omitted on the grounds that they are as much part of British English as Indian English or SLE.

A similar issue arises with Muslim words of Arabic origin which, as well as being common to the entire Muslim world, have also entered international English via Muslim communities in the UK and elsewhere in the English-speaking world. This dictionary includes Muslim words which are particularly common in Sri Lanka, while others are omitted on the grounds that they are part of international Muslim English.

6. British English and International English: which standard and why?

Why is British English chosen as the standard against which SLE is compared? So-called "standard British English" is only spoken by a tiny percentage of the English-speaking world, mostly concentrated in south-east England. It could be argued that a broader "international English" would be a more relevant standard with which to compare SLE.

However, unfortunately "international English" remains an elusive and ill-defined concept. Most of the best-known dictionaries and coursebooks are based on either "British English" or "American English". British English is the language from which SLE originally evolved, and it remains a widely accepted standard for English as an international language. It is still seen (rightly or wrongly) as a "model" to be aspired to by Sri Lankan learners of English, who need to be aware of the differences between SLE and "standard" English - particularly if they intend to sit for a foreign exam which will be marked by a non-Sri Lankan examiner.

7. Right and wrong: a descriptive or a prescriptive approach?

In deciding what to include in a dictionary of SLE, and what to exclude, one constantly comes up against the question of standards: Where do you draw the line between what is an acceptable example of SLE, and what is better described as an "error"? In contrasting SLE with "standard" British English, there is a danger that many readers will interpret this in terms of right and wrong, which is not the idea. On the contrary, the intention is only to describe the way the English language is used in Sri Lanka, without attempting to make any judgment on whether it is "correct".

However, merely by deciding to include a particular word, the compiler is inevitably bestowing it with a seal of acceptability. This dictionary includes many features of colloquial SLE which would be recognised as mistakes by teachers (and examiners) of standard English, and indeed by many speakers of standard SLE. Many of these features are marked "(coll.)" in the dictionary, showing that while they may be common features of the colloquial language, they would not necessarily be considered acceptable in a more formal written context. I believe that including such features is the best way to reflect the way that English is actually used in the current Sri Lankan context.

Acknowledgements

Two books published recently have helped to draw attention to different aspects of Sri Lankan English. The first, Knox's Words by Richard Boyle (Visidunu Prakashakayo 2004), draws on the author's research for the OED into words of Sri Lankan origin and how they have become absorbed into the English language. I am grateful to Richard for the access he has given me to his research for the OED, parts of which have appeared as the Concise Guide to the Anglo-Sri Lankan Lexicon serialised in the Sunday Times. I would also like to thank Richard for the enthusiasm he has shown for this project.

The second book is The Post-Colonial Identity of Sri Lankan English by Manique Gunesekera (Katha Publishers 2004), which describes the social and historical context of SLE, together with a detailed analysis of its grammatical and phonological features, and a glossary of 576 items. I would like to acknowledge Manique's book as a valuable point of reference in the latter stages of my research, and her glossary as the direct source of a number of items in this dictionary.

I would like to thank Professor Ryhana Raheem for the encouragement she has given, for reading the dictionary and giving valuable feedback, and for agreeing to write the Foreword.

Thanks also to Paru Nagasundaram who gave invaluable comments on the Tamil references; and to Ameena Hussein, Amy Hamlyn, Jim Ranalli and Julie Webber, who read through the dictionary at different stages and gave useful feedback.

Thank you to Gill Westaway for her interest and support; to other colleagues and students at the British Council who have taken an interest; and to the SLELTA committee and membership for their encouragement.

Thank you to those whose artistic and/or technical skills have shaped the design of this book: Anura Srinath who drew the illustrations; Adrian Neville and Rohan Titus; Prem Kumar for the computer wizardry; and above all to Nelun Harasgama for coming to my rescue and overseeing the final design.

Thanks also to Sonali who lived with it; to Lal and Steve for being there; and to Dushyanthi Mendis for always asking "When?"

My greatest debt however is to Dinali Fernando and Vivimarie VanderPoorten, who for want of a better term have been credited as the "editors" of this book. To a large extent the compilation of this dictionary has been a "one-man show", and I take full responsibility for any shortcomings. But thanks to Dinali and Vivi's invaluable input the result is undoubtedly far more authoritative than I could ever have achieved single-handedly. It was also much more fun. Thank you both for being so patient, for answering all those emails, and above all for making me laugh.

This dictionary undoubtedly contains many omissions, inaccuracies, inconsistencies and subjective judgements. Of course, like all dictionaries, it aspires to be comprehensive, accurate, consistent and objective. But human nature, and the nature of language, surely make this an impossible aspiration. I would welcome any feedback and comments at the email address below.

Michael Meyler
October 2007

michaelm@sltnet.lk
www.mirisgala.net

BIBLIOGRAPHY

The quotations given in the dictionary are taken from the books listed below, ordered alphabetically according to the abbreviations by which they are identified.

AG   *Anil's Ghost*: Michael Ondaatje (Picador 2000)

BTH   *Bringing Tony Home*: Tissa Abeysekara (author publication 1998)

CG   *Cinnamon Gardens*: Shyam Selvadurai (Penguin 1998)

CM   *Child in Me*: Sybil Wettasinghe (author publication 1996)

CP   *Colpetty People*: Ashok Ferrey (Perera Hussein 2005)

CU   *A Cause Untrue*: David Blacker (Perera Hussein 2005)

FB   *Funny Boy*: Shyam Selvadurai (Penguin 1994)

FSD   *The Far Spent Day*: Nihal de Silva (Vijitha Yapa 2004)

GC   *The Ginirälla Conspiracy*: Nihal de Silva (Vijitha Yapa 2005)

HC   *The Hamilton Case*: Michelle de Kretser (Vintage 2003)

JFT   *The Jam Fruit Tree*: Carl Muller (Penguin 1993)

July   *July*: Karen Roberts (Phoenix 2001)

KCS   *Kider Chetty Street*: Jagath Kumarasinghe (Sooriya 2005)

M&P   *Monsoons and Potholes*: Manuka Wijesinghe (Perera Hussein 2006)

MiP   *Murder in the Pettah*: Jeanne Cambrai (Penguin 2001)

MM   *Monkfish Moon*: Romesh Gunesekera (Penguin 1992)

OD   *Out of the Darkness*: Gunadasa Amarasekara
       (translated into English by Vijita Fernando) (Visidunu 2003)

OM   *Once, on a Mountainside*: Vijita Fernando (author publication 1995)

PMS   *Paduma Meets the Sunbird*: Nihal de Silva (Popsicle Books 2006)

Reef   *Reef*: Romesh Gunesekera (Penguin 1994)

REP   *The Road from Elephant Pass*: Nihal de Silva (Vijitha Yapa 2003)

RF   *Running in the Family*: Michael Ondaatje (Picador 1982)

SG   *The Sandglass*: Romesh Gunesekera (Penguin 1998)

SMS   *Swimming in the Monsoon Sea*: Shyam Selvadurai (Penguin 2005)

TT   *Once Upon a Tender Time*: Carl Muller (Penguin 1995)

WCS   *The Window Cleaner's Soul*: Lal Medawattegedera
       (author publication 2005)

WE   *At the Water's Edge*: Pradeep Jeganathan (South Focus Press 2004)

WMD *When Memory Dies*: A. Sivanandan (Penguin 1997)

YY   *Yakada Yaka*: Carl Muller (Penguin 1994)

Z   *Zillij*: Ameena Hussein (Perera Hussein 2003)

KEY TO THE DICTIONARY

The key opposite shows the main features of the dictionary and the symbols used to identify them. For further details, see the Guide to the Dictionary (pages xi-xiii).

For an explanation of the phonetic font used to show the pronunciation of words, see the Pronunciation section (pages xix - xxii).

For a list of the abbreviations used to identify the sources of the quotations, see the Bibliography (page xxxiii).

Other abbreviations used in the dictionary:

SLE   Sri Lankan English
BSE   British Standard English
OED   Oxford English Dictionary

adj.   adjective
adv.   adverb
coll.   colloquial
comp.   compare
esp.   especially
n   noun
nc   countable noun (a noun which has a plural form)
nu   uncountable noun (a noun with no plural form)
opp.   opposite
orig.   originally
prep.   preposition
v   verb
vi   intransitive verb (a verb which does not take an object)
vt   transitive verb (a verb which takes an object)

cross-reference to words
with the same meaning

headword

definition

derivation

pahana
/pahanə/ (= oil lamp, polthel pahana)
a lamp with a cloth wick soaked in
coconut oil: either a small clay lamp
which is lit in temples etc.; or a large
brass lamp which is lit on **auspicious**
occasions (weddings, opening
ceremonies, etc.) (Sinhala)

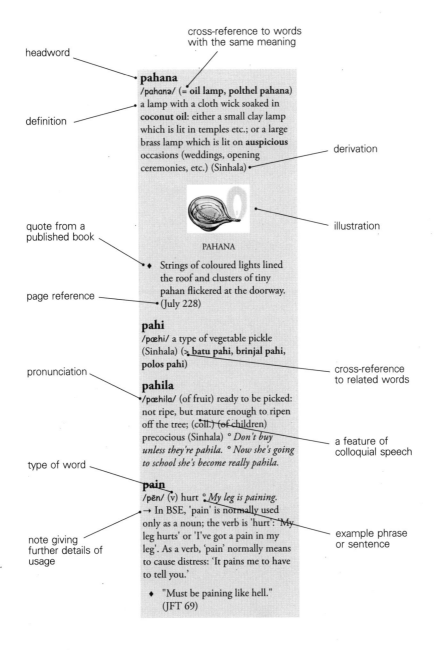

PAHANA

illustration

quote from a
published book

page reference

♦ Strings of coloured lights lined
the roof and clusters of tiny
pahan flickered at the doorway.
(July 228)

pahi
/pæhi/ a type of vegetable pickle
(Sinhala) (↘ batu pahi, brinjal pahi,
polos pahi)

cross-reference
to related words

pronunciation

pahila
/pæhilə/ (of fruit) ready to be picked:
not ripe, but mature enough to ripen
off the tree; (coll.) (of children)
precocious (Sinhala) ° *Don't buy
unless they're pahila.* ° *Now she's going
to school she's become really pahila.*

a feature of
colloquial speech

type of word

pain
/pēn/ (v) hurt ° *My leg is paining.*
→ In BSE, 'pain' is normally used
only as a noun; the verb is 'hurt': 'My
leg hurts' or 'I've got a pain in my
leg'. As a verb, 'pain' normally means
to cause distress: 'It pains me to have
to tell you.'

example phrase
or sentence

note giving
further details of
usage

♦ "Must be paining like hell."
(JFT 69)

A

aachchi

/āchchi/ granny, grandmother (Sinhala)
(> seeya)

- "Don't cry, *aatchi*, please," he pleaded. (WMD 240)

- "You know *aachi's* cousin, don't you?" (WMD 342)

- "Do you realise this wretched infant will make me an *aachi*?" (HC 129)

- Achi had a worried look on her face. (M&P 13)

aappa

/āppa/ (= hopper) a bowl-shaped rice flour pancake, a popular morning or evening meal (Sinhala; Tamil appam) (> pani aappa, paal appam)

□ aappa kade

/āppa kaᴅe/ (= hopper boutique) a small kade serving hoppers (Sinhala)

□ aappa thaachchiya

/āppa tāchchiya/ a small bowl-shaped pan used for making hoppers (Sinhala) (> thaachchiya)

AAPPA THAACHCHIYA

aarachchi

/ārachchi/ (dated) a junior clerk, esp. in government service; originally a headman (Sinhala/Tamil)

- … he was probably a senior peon or *aaratchi* in some government department. (WMD 205)

aasmi

/āsmi/ a type of sweet consisting of crisp, deep-fried strands of rice flour batter, folded in two and decorated with coloured sugar syrup (Sinhala)

AASMI

- The table is laid with kavum, kokis, athirasa, aasmi and combs of bananas. (July 52-3)

aatha

/āta/ (= anoda, custard apple) (Sinhala)

aaththa

/ātta/ grandfather (father's father) (Sinhala) (> seeya)

- "I saw her and Aththa only during school holidays." (M&P 63)

above mentioned

mentioned above, as mentioned earlier (more formal in BSE) (> undermentioned)
° *With regard to the above mentioned order, …*

A/C, a/c

/ē sī/ air-conditioning, air-conditioner, air-conditioned ° *Can you put the A/C?* ° *Does it have A/C?* ° *an a/c van*

- "AC or non-AC?" - "I think non-AC, dear," said Mrs. Sarath. (CP 97)

achcharu

/achchāru/ pickle; also used in the sense of a mess, a mixture, a pickle (Sinhala, from Malay) (> Malay pickle) ° *His family is a real achcharu!*

♦ "But what a real *achcharu* Uncle's family is." (WMD 76)

♦ ... all the onions in the *achcharu* ... (WMD 144)

♦ All they would say over and over again, and in nightmarish unison, was that they were a separate people who had, for five centuries, been mixed up like an *achcharu* (they laughed bleakly at their use of the Sinhala word for pickle) by European colonialists and now wanted to be returned to their pristine separateness in their pristine homelands. (WMD 324)

♦ When the pain first manifested itself Leela thought it was temporary, brought on by the green mango *achacharu* she loved and ate by the dishful. (HC 210)

actually

really, honestly ° *A: We're going to get married. B: Don't tell lies! A: Actually!* → In BSE, 'actually' = 'in fact', and is normally used to correct a mistake or to introduce some surprising information: 'Actually, my name's John, not Jeff'; 'She's on holiday actually'. When it comes at the beginning of a sentence in BSE, 'actually' is usually followed by a comma (in writing) or by a pause (in speech); this is not necessarily the case in SLE.

aday!, adai!

/aɒē/ (= **ado!**) hey!, wow! (Sinhala/Tamil exclamation)

♦ "Aday, ... this is not Jaffna, you know." (FB 94)

♦ "Aday, Soyza, you better watch out or I'll give you something," ... (FB 216)

♦ "*Adai*, von Bloss is coming in cricket boots." (TT 188)

♦ "*Adai*, Merril, fine one you are." (TT 195)

adigar

/aɒigā/ (dated) a chief minister in the **Kandyan** kingdom (from Sanskrit)

admit

take to hospital, admit to hospital (usually passive; more formal in BSE) (> **ward**) ° *Six people were admitted after the accident.*

♦ All were admitted for food poisoning ... (YY 108)

ado!

/aɒō/ (= **aday!**) hey! (Sinhala exclamation, usually restricted to men and often considered rude)

♦ *Ado*! He lifts up his hand palm stretched open as if to slap him. (MM 117)

♦ We had only gone a few yards beyond the van when one of the men called out, "Ado, Tiger." (FB 193)

♦ "*Ado*, boys, I need assistance here, ..." (CU 306)

♦ He screamed and shouted "Ado I will catch you, you bugger ..." (M&P 155)

adopt out

give (a child) for adoption ° *She has decided to adopt out the baby.*

advanced level

(= A/L) A level exam (> **ordinary level**)

♦ Since she had finished her Advanced Levels and begun university, they managed to meet more often, even attending a few parties together. (July 245)

♦ "It is obviously evident that the Tamil examiners have cheated by awarding excessively high marks to

Tamil Advanced level candidates."
(M&P 303)

aeli maeli

/ǽli mǽli/ (coll.) indifferent, lethargic,
wishy-washy (Sinhala) ° *No need to be so
aeli maeli about it!*

affair

relationship, love affair ° *They had an affair
for five years before they got married.* → In
BSE, an 'affair' often suggests an illicit
sexual relationship between two people who
are not married to each other (e.g. 'an extra-
marital affair'); in SLE it is often a more
innocent relationship or love affair between
two young people, with or without sexual
connotations.

after (1)

(coll.) (adv.) after that, later, afterwards ° *I'll
do it after.* → In BSE, 'after' is a preposition
which needs to be followed by a noun,
pronoun or phrase: after this, after that,
after lunch, after I go home, etc.; in SLE
it is also used as an adverb standing on its
own.

after (2)

(prep.) for (a period of time), for the
first time since (a point in time) ° *It was
the largest turnout after 20 years.* ° *Mr
Ariyaratne was visiting Jaffna after the crisis
in 1983.* (BSE: ... for 20 years, ... for the
first time since 1983)

♦ ... I saw the Co-op store with its low
flat-tiled roof after forty six years.
(BTH 50)

♦ "Wasn't it the first time you spoke
to Nimal after about six months?"
(OD 74)

□ after a long time!

(coll.) it's been a long time!, I haven't seen
you for ages!, long time no see! ° *The two
men met after a long time recently.*

♦ "How, Auntie Nellie, after a long time,
no?" (JFT 136)

□ to be after something

to have (just/recently) had or done
something ° *I'm after my lunch.* ° *He's
after a few drinks.* ° *You look like you're
after a swim.* ° *She's after a stroke.* ° *Is
your child after A/L's?* → In BSE, 'to be
after something' means to be looking for
something.

AGA

(= **Assistant Government Agent**) (> **GA**)
° *an AGA division*

agency post office

a private post office

aggala

/aggəla/ a type of sweet made with **rice
flour** and **honey** and shaped into balls
(Sinhala)

♦ Excess rice, left over from the meals
was sun dried, pounded finely and later
mixed with treacle and made into little
balls. This was *aggala.* (CM 13)

ah?

(coll.) eh?

♦ "Why you want to get all high and
mighty, ah?" (JFT 13)

♦ "So, what is this I hear, aah? Nobody
will play with my little daughter."
(FB 7)

♦ "What is wrong with the army, arh?"
(WE 77)

aiya

/aiya/ elder brother; can also refer to a male
cousin or any older boy (Sinhala) ° *Where's
your aiya?* ° *the aiyas in grade 5*

♦ Tell him Victor aiya has come.
(MM 64)

♦ "Ask Charlie aiya." (WMD 233)

♦ "Which one of you is aiya's girlfriend?" (GC 123)

♦ "All he said was, *Aiya will pay.*" (CP 56)

♦ "Jeevan Aiya, I want to talk to you privately, ..." (WCS 69)

♦ "Aiyo, Aiya was wondering why we didn't come?" (M&P 22)

♦ "Aiya, why can't we go inside the airport anymore?" (M&P 204)

aiyar
/aiyər/ (= **kurukkal**) a Hindu priest (Tamil); also **aiya** as a term of address (like 'father') (> **poosari**)

aiyo!
/aiyō/ (= **amme! ammo! apo!**) oh! oh no! oh dear! oh God! (Sinhala/Tamil exclamation, used to express anything from lighthearted banter to extreme grief) (> **aney!**)

♦ "*Aiyo* (Sinhala expression used in much the same way as *'anney'*), I don't know, Clarence." (JFT 10)

♦ "*Aiyo*, Mother, don't go." (JFT 109)

♦ "*Aiyo!*" Somebody else slapped his thighs and flung down his cards. (Reef 163)

♦ "Aiyo, sir, small problem, sir." (FB 172)

♦ "Amma," Balendran said gently. "It's over." - "Aiyo," she said. "Aiyo, aiyo." (CG 303)

♦ "Aiyoo, what a thing." (CG 340)

♦ "Aiyo, thaathi. Is it true? Did you lose?" (FSD 53)

♦ "Aiyo, I hope Aunt Wilhelmina or one of her friends doesn't pass by and see this." (SMS 152)

♦ "Never heard of the Kandy *perahera*, sir? *Aiyo*, famous touris' attraction, no?" (CU 55)

♦ "Aiyo! But those people are Christians no, they don't believe in karma." (M&P 16)

ajoutha
/ajūtə/ a type of card game (Sinhala from Portuguese)

♦ So they played two-handed Ajoutha and drank. (RF 127)

akka
/akka/ elder sister; can also refer to a female cousin or any older girl (Sinhala/Tamil)

♦ They were the akkas or big sisters of the village. (YY 81)

♦ Why are you in white, Akka, wear the pink Manipuri, after all it is a wedding, no? (OM 19)

♦ "Is *akka* here too?" (WMD 97)

♦ "Are you mad or something, akka?" (CG 17)

♦ "Imagine if akka got pregnant right after they were married." (CG 248)

♦ "I'll talk to akka about it." (SMS 124)

♦ "Aney, Akka, our daughter looked like this too no, you remember?" (M&P 26)

♦ Kusita no longer called me Akka as she had done prior to becoming a student at the international school. (M&P 312)

akki
/akki/ (= **akka**) (coll.) elder sister; can also refer to a female cousin or any older girl (Sinhala) ° *What did you get for akki?* ° *One of the akkis came to our class.*

♦ "Akki? Why should I call you akki?" (GC 146)

♦ "Akki, there, Nenda wants you to come for dinner." (M&P 369)

A/L
(= **advanced level**) A level exam (> O/L)

ala
/alə/ potato (Sinhala) ° *ala curry*

□ ala thel dala
/alə tel dāla/ potato fried with onions and chillies (Sinhala) (> **thel dala**)

♦ It was to be a traditional Sinhalese meal - yellow rice, brinjal pahi, ala thel dala, pickle and of course Enid's famous chicken curry. (July 18)

alavanguwa
/aləvanguwə/ a pointed iron rod used for digging (Sinhala; Tamil alavangu)

all
everybody, everyone, everything ° *All are scolding me.* ° *Did you bring all?* → In BSE, 'all' is generally used with a noun or pronoun: all the books, all my friends, all of them, etc.; it is less common standing on its own as in the examples and would normally be replaced in colloquial speech by 'everybody/everyone' or 'everything'.

♦ … and Father Romiel told all to kneel … (JFT 73)

♦ Champa came out running with two of the other girls. All were in tears and talking incoherently. (FSD 34)

♦ "They have no mother, no father. All are gone." (M&P 210)

♦ "All will want to buy for one rupee." (PMS 104)

all the time
always (word order, also **half the time**) ° *I am all the time telling him to be careful.*

♦ … the Latin lecturer was half the time away on a camping trip … (WMD 161)

♦ The monks were all the time trying to make out that the temples were in some sort of danger … (WMD 219)

♦ "In India they are all the time getting children when they are fourteen …" (M&P 301)

all what
all (that), everything (that) ° *The President listened to all what the UNP said.* ° *Tell me all what happened.*

♦ Diana and Heather said they knew all what mummy was doing … (YY 215)

almirah
/almaira, ælmaira/ wardrobe (Anglo-Indian, from Urdu via Portuguese)

ALMIRAH

♦ I wanted to turn out the almirahs, empty the drawers again, go through everything; … (MM 98)

♦ An almirah was carried off by four men to a clearing near the signals cabin. (JFT 150)

♦ We crossed to where the almirah and chest of drawers stood. (Reef 80)

♦ He goes to his almirah and unlocks it. That almirah is the repository of a great deal of pilfered goods, smuggled out of the port of Colombo. (TT 144-5)

♦ "There are some of my daughter's old dresses in the *almirah* and they should fit you." (WMD 353)

♦ Next to it was an intricately carved antique almirah of tamarind wood against the wall. (CG 102)

♦ The tall antique almirah was wide open. (July 65)

♦ Maud drew a bottle and two cloudy tumblers from a varnished almirah. (HC 144)

♦ On top of his almirah, there was an old suitcase. (SMS 191)

♦ What the Kumarihamy did not add was that lying at the bottom of her almirah was a letter from the LRC which had arrived two weeks ago, ... (CP 101)

♦ I knew where his wallet was hidden in the Almirah. (M&P 176)

alms-giving

(= **dane**) a religious ceremony, involving giving alms to Buddhist monks, or as charity to poor people, for example at fixed periods after someone has died

♦ "Then why didn't you come earlier?" - "How to? First, seven day almsgiving, then one month almsgiving, then the three month almsgiving." (M&P 71)

also

(word order) too, as well (> **too**) ° *John also was there.* ° *He speaks Russian also.* → In SLE, 'also' immediately follows the word it refers to: in Sinhala and Tamil, the equivalent is a suffix (-ut, -um) attached to the end of the word. In BSE, 'too' or 'as well' are more common, usually at the end of the sentence: 'John was there too/as well', 'He speaks Russian too/as well'. Note the different word order with 'also' in BSE: 'John was also there', 'He also speaks Russian'.

♦ "I am taking Dias-*mahathaya* to the observatory, you also come." (Reef 62)

♦ "And the patties also she liked?" (Reef 76)

♦ "I phoned around and checked the hospital also." (TT 202)

♦ "It happened when my mother died also." (WMD 32)

♦ "... if I didn't fall ill, my elder boy also would have been in the University by now." (OD 6)

♦ Keep her mobile phone also on the table. (FSD 109)

♦ "They must have brought outsiders also ..." (GC 54)

♦ "... sat in this dirty cane chair and drank tea also." (WCS 15)

♦ "... you can see him in the newspapers also, and on the TV in those ads." (WCS 33)

♦ "Will he give an injection for me also?" (PMS 226)

□ **also ... also**

(repeated in the same sentence) ° *Priya also came, Nalini also came.* → BSE: 'Priya came, and so did Nalini'.

□ **also ... not**

(= **too ... not**) not ... either ° *Sanjiv also didn't speak.* → In BSE, 'also' and 'too' are not used with negatives, 'either' is used instead: 'Sanjiv didn't speak either.'

♦ "And I couldn't come to see you, also." (WCS 30)

alu kehel

/alu kehel/ (= **ash plantain**) a green variety of banana used as a vegetable (BSE 'plantain') (Sinhala) (> **plantain**)

alu puhul

/alu puhul/ (= **puhul**, ash pumpkin)

aluwa

/aluwa/ a type of sweet usually cut into square or diamond shapes; there are several different varieties (Sinhala, from Arabic 'halva') ° *coconut aluwa* ° *rulang aluwa*

♦ ... *muscat* and *aluwa* that the servants had got from the sweetmeat seller. (WMD 125)

♦ "You'll like them, and the old lady makes some superb *aluwa*." (WMD 165)

♦ While talking to me he had helped himself to potato *aluwa*, milk toffee, *thala guli*, coconut rock and two cream horns. (HC 77-8)

ambalama

/ambələmə/ an open wooden structure used as a shelter for travellers (Sinhala; Tamil ambalam)

AMBALAMA

♦ Anil and Sarath and Palipana and the girl had reached and now sat within the square wooden structure of an *ambalama*, an oil lamp at the centre of it. ... It was a structure of wood, with no walls and a high ceiling. Travellers or pilgrims used its shade and coolness during the day. (AG 98)

ambalavi

/ambəlavi/ a type of mango (Tamil)

♦ She offered her husband a mango that Saha had brought from Jaffna. ... "Ah, ... there's nothing like an *ambalavi*, is there?" (WMD 36)

ambarella

/æmbərællə/ a type of fruit like a small, sour, green mango (hog plum or hog apple) (Sinhala) ° *ambarella chutney*

ambarenafy

/æmbərenəfai/ (coll.) squirm with embarrassment (from Sinhala verb 'ambarenava') (> **-fy**) ° *Can't you talk to a boy without ambarenafying?*

ambul (1)

/æmbul/ (adj.) sour, acid, sharp (Sinhala) ° *The mangoes are a bit ambul.*

ambul (2)

(= **sour plantain**) (n) a small yellow variety of banana (Sinhala) (> **plantain**)

ambul thiyal

/æmbul tiyal/ a dry tuna fish dish prepared with **goraka** (Sinhala)

am I right?

(a question tag used as a less common alternative to **is it?**, **isn't it?** and **no?**)

♦ "So your Madame is more important to you than your own family, am I right?" (M&P 201)

amma

/amma/ mother, Mummy, Mum (Sinhala/Tamil)

♦ *Amma* said we could go and buy a new saree. (MM 107)

♦ "I heard Amma and Appa talking about it." (FB 103)

♦ "Are you and *amma* going to Colombo?" (WMD 127)

♦ "You are sure to be spotted and Amma is going to hear about it." (CG 17)

♦ ... oh how I miss my amma's food he thought ... (Z 70)

♦ *"Amma, why are her legs full of spots?"* (WE 27)

♦ "Amrith, I'm going to tell Amma." (SMS 91)

ammamma; ammappa

/ammamma, ammappa/ grandmother (mother's mother); grandfather (mother's father) (Tamil)

♦ Ever since the news had arrived that *Amamma*, living with Daniel's uncle and aunt in Scarborough, was critically ill, ... (CU 299)

amme

/amme/ (coll.) an older woman working as a **servant** (Sinhala)

♦ She didn't feel comfortable with the others, the receptionist, librarian, secretaries, tea ammes and even some of the other lecturers, purely for linguistic reasons. (Z 41)

amme!, ammo!

/ammē, ammō/ (= **aiyo!**) (Sinhala exclamation)

♦ *"Ammo*,* if I go to say like that I'll get a kanay." (* *Ammo* - Oh, mother!) (TT 56)

ammi

/ammi/ (= **amma**) (coll.) mother, Mummy, Mum (Sinhala)

♦ "If you want one, ask your Ammi to bring you a sister from the hospital." (July 22)

♦ "Ammi, ... please don't send me away." (SMS 193)

♦ "I don't want to go to America Ammi, I want to stay here and study." (M&P 304)

amude

/amuᴅe/ loin-cloth (Sinhala)

AMUDE

♦ The backs of their swimsuits were like the amudés that farmers wore when working in the fields, a waistband with a strip of cloth which disappeared into the buttocks. (July 98)

amu miris

/amu miris/ green chilli (Sinhala) (> **miris**)

anamalu

/ānəmālu/ a long green variety of banana (Sinhala) (> **plantain**)

♦ Dinner was laid on the table, his glass of water and the aanamalu plantain he liked for dessert. (July 162)

♦ He flicked the butt out the window, and saw the glowing end bounce off one of the *anamalu* trees in a shower of sparks. (CU 48)

ancestral home

(= **maha gedera**) a family home, the home of one's parents or grandparents (> **walauwa**) → An 'ancestral home' suggests something grand in BSE, which isn't necessarily the case in SLE. It could be a grand house (a **walauwa**) or a more modest family home.

♦ He clung on to the large, rambling ancestral home, dreaming of the power and influence his family had once wielded, ... (WMD 243)

♦ I went through my ancestral home like a thief. (HC 52)

♦ ... and he had even been prevented from attending his father's funeral at the family ancestral home, in Kurunegala. (SMS 69)

♦ Mrs. Adonis's dead husband's ancestral home was dilapidated and wet. (M&P 122)

and

(pronunciation, e.g. in lists) ° *Tamil and | Sinhala and | English and | ...* → In SLE, 'and' tends to be pronounced strong ('rice and curry'), while in BSE it tends to be pronounced weak ('fish 'n' chips'). It also tends to be spoken with the word which comes before it, followed by a pause (|), while in BSE it tends to be spoken with the word that follows it, preceded by a pause ('Tamil | and Sinhala | and English'). The equivalent in Sinhala and Tamil is a suffix (-uy, -um) attached to the end of each word in the list.

□ ... and all

(coll.) ... and so on, etc.; also used to add emphasis (see quotes) ° *Don't forget to bring the plates and all.* ° *books printed in Hong Kong and all* → Less common in colloquial BSE, and can also mean 'as well': 'I brought a cassette and all.'

♦ "You know beyond the lagoon and all: Nilaveli, Kuchchaveli." (MM 83)

♦ "You think after getting engaged and all I can just go and find someone else?" (JFT 86)

♦ "What, from dynamiting and all?" (Reef 58)

♦ "Imagine implicating a child and all." (FB 75)

♦ "So all right, we know Sinhala because we have to talk to the dhoby and the baker and the boutique man and all." (YY 228)

♦ "So you saw his face and all?" (TT 54)

♦ "I get complaints from all the relatives saying they're going to clubs and getting involved with undesirable women and all, but what to do?" (July 328)

♦ "You saw him no, came in a beautiful vehicle. Smartly dressed. Was very nice and polite and all to me ..." (WCS 15)

□ ... and come

(coll.) go and ... (> **bring and come**) ° *I'll get the paper and come.* (BSE: I'll go and get the paper.)

♦ "I'll make a nice cup of tea and come." (YY 162)

□ ... and go

(coll.) before going (> **take and go**) ° *Let's finish our work and go.* ° *Why don't you eat and go?* (BSE: Have something to eat before you go.)

□ ... and them

(coll.) ... and the others (also US) ° *Rohan and them didn't come.*

♦ "See that was another thing Roswitha and them neglected." (M&P 233)

♦ "By the time uncle Tissa and them return with Rasitha, all this will be over." (M&P 344)

ande

/ande/ a traditional **Kandyan** system of leasing out paddy fields for cultivation, the fee being a share of the harvest (Sinhala)

♦ ... there were sections whose interests might be different, like the *andé* cultivators, ... (WMD 271)

aney!

/anē/ please! (Sinhala exclamation similar to **aiyo!**, especially used when asking or pleading for something) (> **sin!**) ° *Aney sin, no?* ° *Aney, you must come!*

♦ "*Aiyo*, nothing, *anney* (a Sinhala expression used loosely in conversation to express pain, dismay, loss or grief). Let go, Mummee, it's hurting." (JFT 9)

♦ "Don't, *anney*, suppose someone comes," ... (JFT 81)

♦ "*Aney* Missy, I haven't anything in return ..." (Reef 105)

♦ "Then what about school fees and piano lessons and the baby's milk and, *anney*, I don't know." (YY 127)

♦ "*Anney*, don't know, child, whole trouble is that Bunty is too soft-hearted." (YY 209)

♦ "Chee, Hemantha! Don't say things like that aney!" (July 75)

♦ "*Aney*, Themis, is your third leg any better than your second? Or have you got a permanent limp there too?" (CP 111)

♦ "Every rich person I know has some problem aney." (WCS 33)

♦ "Aney, I don't know Doctor, it felt like a lifetime ..." (M&P 12)

♦ "Aney there is no medicine for your foolishness." (M&P 169)

angampora

/angampora/ a traditional Sri Lankan martial art (Sinhala) ° *Angampora, a 2500 year old martial art, is still being practised in many areas.*

anicut

/ænikət/ an irrigation channel created by damming a river (Anglo-Indian, from Tamil) ° *Two drown in anicut while bathing*

° *The tank was, in ancient times, fed by an anicut across the Menik ganga.*

anna, annai

/anna, annei/ (= **aiya**) elder brother (Tamil)

♦ "Ratnam *annai* has come," ... (WMD 119)

♦ "Sit down, *annai*, you look tired." (WMD 339)

anoda

/anōda/ (= **aatha**, **custard apple**) (Sinhala)

antenna

/æntena/ aerial (also US, less common in BSE)

♦ It had a small Sri Lankan flag attached to its antenna, ... (FB 178)

♦ Ravi had been awake since a magpie robin stationed itself on the TV antenna on the roof and began its morning concert. (FSD 212)

anusasana

/anusāsana/ a sermon given by a Buddhist monk (Sinhala) ° *Mr Wickremesinghe and his wife Maithree listening to an anusasana.*

anyway

(word order) ° *They anyway won't come.* ° *It's anyway too late.* → In BSE, 'anyway' is one of a number of adverbs which normally come at the beginning or end of a sentence; in SLE, they often come between the subject and verb.

apale

/apəle/ (= **bad time**) an **inauspicious** period according to astrology (Sinhala) ° *I have an apale till the 16th of next month.* ° *First she met with an accident and then her child got dengue - must be having an apala time.* ° *My son had apala.*

apo!, apoy!

/apō, apoi/ (= **aiyo!**) (Sinhala exclamation)

♦ "*Apoi*, long time ago. How to remember all that?" (YY 32)

♦ "*Apo*, old, no?" (TT 213)

♦ "Apo, please don't ask for me again. I certainly don't want to be your wife in the next birth." (M&P 268)

♦ "Apo! Listen to this!" (M&P 277)

appa
/appɑ/ (= **thaaththa**) father, Daddy, Dad (Tamil); grandfather (Muslim Tamil)

♦ "Appa, who was that person who was killed?" (FB 60)

♦ "But you must get *appa's* permission first." (WMD 127)

♦ "Oh, so you are going to disobey *appa* and *amma*, are you?" (WMD 156)

♦ "I had an interesting talk with Appa this morning." (CG 53)

♦ "Come. We must talk to your appa." (CG 236)

♦ "Don't you understand what Appa's problem is?" (July 173)

♦ "My appa was a teacher … I suppose with his teaching and his private tuition, appa made a fair living." (REP 90)

♦ … *Appa* had retired, and was now learning how to cook. (WE 62)

♦ "Otherwise I'm telling Amma and Appa what happened." (SMS 178)

♦ "*Appa*, look! Look at the smoke from the wing!" (CU 359)

appachchi
/appachchi, appochchi/ (= **thaaththa**) father (in **Kandyan** Sinhala) ° *Amma would check our Sinhala books and Appchchi our English ones.*

♦ "Putha, he wants to buy some of Appachchi's music." (WCS 13)

appamma; appappa
/appamma, appappa/ grandmother (father's mother); grandfather (father's father) (Tamil)

apply
put, spread, rub on (e.g. paint or ointment) (more formal in BSE) (> **rub**) ° *Have to apply some cream, no?*

appreciate
(vi) appreciate something ° *I will appreciate if you can come a little early.* (BSE: I would appreciate it if you could come a little early.)

appu
/appu/ male **servant**; also grandfather (Tamil)

♦ The apu appeared with a tray. (HC 99)

♦ Devendra suggested tea and the appu, an old Tamil man in spotless white, took the order. (FSD 137)

araliya
/arəliyə/ (= **temple flower, temple tree**) frangipani (Sinhala)

ARALIYA

♦ … and wear araliya flowers in her hair like the other bridesmaids. (FB 6)

♦ I imagined them standing under an araliya tree, … (FB 44)

- The garlands of araliyas had come undone and lay broken and crushed on the ground. (FB 99)

- ... the araliya and jasmine flowers floating in carved, red clay bowls ... (CG 121)

- Araliya Gardens had been named for the abundance of araliya trees which grew in almost every garden. (July 13)

- Her hair was dressed with araliya flowers that perfumed her head with their scent. (Z 169)

- It had been Jacintha who'd rushed Tilak to hospital when he'd broken his arm, after falling off the Araliya tree in the back garden. (FSD 11)

- Araliya trees spread their branches over the stairs, providing shade. (SMS 187)

- Fortunately Seela and company under the Araliya tree diverted my attention. (M&P 239)

arangetram

/arangētrəm, ærəngētrəm / the first dance recital given by a student of **Bharatha Natyam**, marking the end of her apprenticeship (Tamil)

architect-designed

designed by a qualified architect ° *architect-designed house in Battaramulla*

arecanut

/erikənaт/ (= **puwak**) a type of palm tree; the seed is chewed with **betel leaves**, and so is also referred to as **betel nut** (OED areca; also India, from Malayalam via Portuguese) (> **betel, chunam**)

- Arecanut trees were cut down and split to make the temporary abode. (CM 81)

- "Arecanut," said one, ... pointing to a tall, thin, stately palm with a tuft of leaves and fruit at the top and all trunk below. (WMD 94)

- ... his grandmother, who was elaborately preparing her first chew of betel and arecanut for the day. (WMD 284)

ARECANUT TREE

- Its cordate leaves could be sold to the betel women who used them to wrap the small fragrant parcels of areca-nut parings and lime that constituted their trade. (HC 137)

- Sarpin Mama is seated on a bench grating an areca nut. (GC 87)

ariya

/āriyə/ pure, Aryan (with reference to the **Sinhala** race or language) (Sinhala, from Sanskrit)

- "Don't give me something in your fucking high flown *Aariya* Sinhala." (WCS 15)

- Instead of dinosaurs, whales and stuffed birds, this museum had a single exhibit of a blood stained Ariya Sinhala shirt and a blood stained Ariya Sinhala sarong. They had once been crisp white and freshly laundered. Before SWRD had been shot. (M&P 135)

armchair

(= **hansiputuwa, planter's chair**) a large rattan armchair with folding leg-rests (also called an **easy chair**) → In BSE, an 'armchair' suggests an upholstered chair.

♦ ... and two cane armchairs - *hansiputu* - and a sofa-bed by the windows. (MM 73)

♦ Mr. Karl was lying in an armchair in his verandah, fast asleep. (REP 106)

♦ But grandpa stays at home in his armchair, his arms and legs stretched on its extension arms, and he lights his pipe stuffed with tobacco. (KCS 118)

♦ Her arms, as heavy as an ordinary man's legs, hang limply over the sides of the armchair. (PMS 81)

arrack

/ˈæræk/ (= **coconut arrack, pol arrack**) a popular alcoholic drink distilled from **coconut toddy** (also India, from Arabic, Hindi, etc.) (> **gal arrack, old arrack**) ° *a shot of arrack* ° *an arrack cocktail*

♦ My father, for his part, roasted pieces of wild boar on an open fire to 'taste' with the special double-distilled arrack he had brought for Uncle Pathi. (WMD 212)

♦ "Give up this bloody arrack, man. Give it up." (SG 116)

♦ Anil found the arrack bottle and poured herself a glass, ... (AG 283)

♦ Mr Munasinghe fortified himself with several arracks before going to the station to fetch his wife. (July 61)

♦ "It would have begun with bottles of arrack for his cronies." (HC 290)

♦ ... a 375 ml bottle of arrack. (FSD 242)

♦ "It's time for my arrack and ginger beer." (SMS 62)

♦ With an ample supply of arrack on offer, people had better things to do. (WCS 60)

♦ Groups of young men sat at tables set up on the grass, drinking beer or arrack. (CU 39)

♦ After Thathi's departure, the card and arrack parties with the Maldive fish increased. (M&P 202)

as

when, as soon as ° *As I entered the room they left.* → In BSE, 'as' can be used in the same way, but 'when' is more common; 'as soon as' is used to stress that the two things happened at the same time. In SLE 'as' is more likely to be pronounced strong: /æz/; in BSE it is more likely to be pronounced weak: /əz/.

♦ "So now what to do? ... Sure to ask as I go back." (JFT 95)

♦ As Gunapala saw me walking to the window, he came running and shut it. (OD 145)

♦ As I saw that it was Wicks I was surprised and not too pleased. (OD 146)

as ever

(coll.) very ° *That child is forward as ever!*

ash colour

grey

♦ At the point at which the passage ended, there was an ash-coloured door. (WCS 44)

ash plantain

(= **alu kehel**) a green variety of banana used as a vegetable (BSE 'plantain') (> **plantain**)

♦ But she carefully washed the stone with a little water and poured the yellow coloured water into the ash plantain curry. (OM 29)

♦ Maud propped it against the bakelite salt-cellar while lunching on curried ash-plantain. (HC 159)

ash pumpkin
(= **puhul, alu puhul**) a variety of gourd used to make **puhul dosi** (**pumpkin preserve**)

ask: to ask from somebody
to ask somebody ° *You better ask from your father.*

♦ "I have asked this same question from myself several times recently." (OD 118)

ASP
Assistant Superintendent of Police

♦ The A.S.P. was impeccably dressed, his hair well-oiled, his moustache trim, and his khaki uniform well-pressed. (FB 127)

♦ Startled, Somaweera could hardly comprehend what the ASP had said. (OD 15)

Assistant Government Agent
(= **AGA**) a senior civil servant at local level (> **Government Agent**)

asst. supdt.
assistant superintendent (of an estate)

assure
(vt) assure somebody of something
° *Britain yesterday assured its strongest support for the Sri Lankan peace process.* (BSE: ... assured Sri Lanka of its strongest support)

as vaha
/æs vaha/ the evil eye (Sinhala) (> **kata vaha**)

asweddumise
/asvædumaiz/ to prepare land for paddy cultivation (clearing, levelling, terracing, etc.) (from Sinhala) ° *asweddumised land*

→ This word is a famous example of an Anglicised form of a Sinhala word, often mistakenly assumed to appear in the OED.

ata pass
/atə pās/ (coll.) educated up to grade 8 (Sinhala: ata = 8)
° *What can you expect from these ata pass fellows?*

atapirikara
/atəpirikərə/ alms given to Buddhist monks in the form of robes and personal items (Sinhala)

atasil
/atəsil/ the 8 Buddhist precepts which are observed as a form of religious vow, e.g. on **poya days** (Sinhala) (> **sil**)

athiraha, athirasa
/atiraha, atirasə/ a type of sweet made with **rice flour** and **honey** and deep-fried (Sinhala; Tamil athirsam) (> **aasmi**)

aththamma
/attamma/ grandmother (father's mother) (Sinhala) (> **aachchi**)

♦ Attamma's house had a long verandah, on one end of which was an arched window. (CM 15)

aththan
/attān/ brother-in-law (Tamil)

♦ "What's the matter with you, *aththan*?" Uncle Gnanam bit out the *aththan* as though to address my father as brother-in-law was itself a matter of shame. (WMD 169)

aththey
/attei/ (= **maami**) aunt (Tamil)

ati kukula
/æti kukula/ coucal, a large black bird with brown wings (Sinhala)

ATI KUKULA

at last

(word order) ° *Rex at last stopped the car.* → In BSE, 'at last' usually comes at the beginning or the end of the sentence.

at least

(word order) ° *You at least must come.* → In BSE, 'at least' is usually used with numbers, and comes before the thing it refers to ('at least 100 people'); in SLE it is also used in other contexts, and usually follows what it refers to.

atta flour

/ɑʈɑ̄, ɑ̄ʈɑ/ wholewheat flour (also India, orig. Hindi)

attached to

working for ° *I am attached to the Labour Department.* → In BSE, to be 'attached to' a department, etc. suggests being assigned there for a temporary period; in SLE, it suggests working there on a permanent basis.

attain age

(= **come of age, cross, grow up**) (of a girl) reach puberty (> **big girl**)

- ♦ "And don't make any plans for tomorrow because Gayathri has attained age, so they're expecting us round." (CP 141)

- ♦ "Has Karunawathie attained age, or you?" (M&P 235)

attend

go to (a school, etc.) (formal in BSE) ° *She is attending Ladies' College.*

atuwa

/ɑʈuwə/ a storage bin or silo used for keeping paddy; also a space above the **hearth** in a traditional kitchen used for storing vegetables, etc. (Sinhala) (> **vee bissa**)

- ♦ "They have a big house and coconut land and two acres of paddy. There is grain in the atuwa from Yala to Maha." (OM 28)

at what time?

what time? ° *At what time will you come?*

auntie, aunty

aunt; also a term of respect/affection used by a child to a woman or by a young person to an older woman, even if they are not related ° *Priya Aunty*

- ♦ … and even the canteen aunties were divided into two factions: … (FB 220)

- ♦ He could always look after Auntie, he said, in the evenings, … (WMD 57)

- ♦ "One of Denis's ancient aunties had a long rigmarole about a murdered planter." (HC 255)

- ♦ "I'll take you home once aunty gets back." (FSD 184)

- ♦ "They locked aunty in her room." (GC 255)

- ♦ "You must call me Aunty, dear. In Sri Lanka, that's how we address older people." (SMS 110)

- ♦ "Ah Rani dear, come and meet this nice Auntie and these Uncles," Mrs. B. said. (CP 121)

- ♦ "Aney, Putha open your eyes and look at your aunties." (M&P 26)

♦ "Aney aunty you are in a bad mood."
(M&P 275)

♦ "Go and ask that aunty for some
water," ... (PMS 136)

auspicious
lucky, favourable (day, time, etc. according
to astrology) (> **inauspicious**)

♦ ... she would have consulted her
astrologer. She wouldn't have
taken any risks! It must be the
most auspicious day of the month.
(MM 109)

♦ They wear their new clothes (in that
year's auspicious colour), keep their
radios on and (depending on the
auspicious time) wait for the New
Year to be announced. Although no
one really needs a radio because the
country explodes at the auspicious
time with the sound of fire-crackers.
(July 52)

♦ These particulars having been deemed
satisfactory, further consultations were
required to determine an auspicious
date for the wedding. (HC 125)

♦ A spokesman for the developer
announced that the opening ceremony
would take place at the auspicious time
of 11.07 a.m. on 7th July. (GC 321)

♦ Ammi placed the duty free television
set in an auspicious corner of the house
and looked at the roof as the first
sound of thunder roared across the sky.
(M&P 256)

♦ "He tells me that Sunday the 12th is
very, very auspicious. Any arrangement
made on that day is sure to be
successful." (PMS 267)

avurudu
/aurudu/ (= **New Year, Sinhala New Year,
Sinhala and Tamil New Year**) (Sinhala)

° *avurudu celebrations* ° *avurudu sale*
° *avurudu gifts* ° *avurudu sweets* ° *avurudu
games* ° *Tight security for Avurudu*

♦ Avurudhu is on the fourteenth of
April, but the rituals and ceremonies
begin on the thirteenth, which is
technically the Old Year. The special
Avurudhu almanac with its auspicious
times and auspicious colours is
published in the newspapers several
days before, to give people time to plan
their festivities and sew their clothes.
(July 52)

□ avurudu kumari
/aurudu kumāri/ a young girl chosen as a
beauty queen as part of traditional **New
Year** celebrations; also **avurudu kumaraya**
(Sinhala: kumari = princess, kumaraya =
prince)

□ avurudu pola
/aurudu polə/ a pre-**New Year** sale of
clothes, gifts, etc. (Sinhala)

AWW
(coll.) empty-handed, visiting someone
without bringing a gift (from Sinhala
expression 'ath wana wana' = 'swinging the
hands'; see quote for a variation: 'waving
the hands') ° *We're always going there AWW.*

♦ "*Apoi*, how to come like that, just
waving the hands? Must bring
something for Beryl even." (YY 152)

ayah
/āyɑ/ (dated) nanny (Anglo-Indian, orig.
Portuguese)

♦ The nurse or ayah in charge of our
cleanliness was a small, muscular and
vicious woman named Maratina.
(RF 138)

♦ ... Sheilah Mortimer who came with
an ayah and kept darting out of class

to ascertain that the ayah sat, waiting, under the tamarind tree ... (TT 20)

♦ In her first years, the baby - Anoja - would spend most of her time on her own or with a succession of gloomy, wizened ayahs. (SG 21)

♦ She handed her newborns over to an ayah, and took off for a week's shooting as soon as she could. (HC 172)

♦ Amrith could also hear the voices of his ayah and the cook in the corridor. (SMS 193)

♦ A week later his friend met her on the London flight flying first class, with the children and ayah in economy. (CP 145)

ayurveda

/āyurvēdə/ traditional indigenous herbal medicine; adj.: **ayurvedic** (Sinhala; Tamil ayurvedam; also India, orig. Sanskrit) (> **native medicine, native doctor, vedamahatteya, vedarala**) ° *ayurvedic medicine* ° *an ayurvedic physician*

♦ ... but by the time Gamini's father, Herath, was born, western medicine had overtaken *ayur-veda*. (WMD 243)

♦ Ayurvedic treatment had been mooted, consultations with leading gynaecologists in Colombo and London having failed to produce a result. (HC 104)

♦ ... mixed with the aroma of teas, spices, ayurvedic medicinal balms, ... (SMS 139)

B

baabath

/bābat/ tripe, a meat dish usually served with **pittu**, a **Malay** speciality (orig. Malay) ° *Ask anyone on Malay Street for the pittu and baabath shop and they'll point the way.*

baada

/bāda/ (n/adj.) bad luck, jinx; **inauspicious** (Sinhala) ° *Aiyo, it was a real baada trip.*

baappa

/bāppa/ uncle (father's younger brother) (Sinhala)

baas

/bās/ skilled labourer, handyman (carpenter, mason, plumber, mechanic, etc.); also the foreman of a team of workers (orig. Dutch = boss) ° *mason baas* (builder) ° *vadu baas* (carpenter) ° *paippa baas* (plumber)

♦ "Aiyo, Amma, ... just get this other roof-baas, for goodness' sake." ... "Gineris and his sons have always been our family baases, ... Besides, I don't trust these modern baases; ..." (SMS 61)

baba

/baba/ a baby or small child (Sinhala/ Tamil) ° *Cute baba, no?* ° *Don't wake the baba!*

♦ "But you would have been just a baba, then." (SG 156)

babbler

(= **seven sisters**) a small grey thrush-like bird which is often seen in noisy groups of around seven birds (> **demalichchas**)

♦ Then a babbler flew up in a jitter of leaves and all three deer vanished ... (HC 189)

♦ I had been watching some Babblers hopping about the hedge in front of the vehicle. They were called the seven sisters because they always moved about in small flocks, chirping noisily as they hunted for insect prey. (REP 335)

♦ Then a small flock of Babblers took off from a thicket and flew away with squeaks of alarm. (FSD 93)

back (1)

(= **before**) (adv.) ago (also US, less common in BSE) ° *two years back*

♦ That was thirty years back. (KCS 103)

back (2)

(n) (coll.) backside, bum ° *He just sat on his back and waited.*

♦ "*Chee*, see what she is doing. When she goes to the lavatory, washing the back with the left hand; and now putting it into our cake." (JFT 184)

♦ The right hand was used to eat rice and the left to wash the back. (M&P 51)

♦ The saronged man in trousers who had stroked Ammi's back in the bus ... (M&P 106)

♦ ... foreigners did not wash their backs. Period. They only used toilet paper and were unsuitable for marriage. (M&P 116)

♦ A swift kick in the back lifts each of them over the front steps and into the garden. (PMS 162)

back shot

(in **carrom**) a shot in which the **striker** rebounds off the far side of the board (> **carrom**)

back side

back (of a house, etc.) ° *I kept the car in the back side.* → In BSE, 'backside' = bottom, bum (SLE **back**).

♦ "Hullo, hullo, come, come. Beryl is in the backside. Sit, will you." (YY 136)

bada (1)

/baɖə/ (= **bundi**) (coll.) tummy, belly (Sinhala) ° *She's got a big bada.*

bada (2)

/baɖə/ fatso, nickname for a fat person (Sinhala) ° *She's a real bada.*

badapissa

/baɖəpissa/ (coll.) the youngest in the family (Sinhala) ° *So that means you're the badapissa?*

bad time

(= **apale**) an **inauspicious** period according to astrology (> **good time**)

♦ "People said it was my bad time, *senasura*, but I don't believe in all that nonsense." (WMD 78)

baila

/baila/ a popular style of dance music (orig. Portuguese)

♦ ... so they all thought at first that he was singing a Sinhalese baila. (RF 46)

♦ ... his name emerging in a street *baila* for a week or two. (AG 214)

♦ Even after they had had a few drinks together, Bala was the one who sang old songs and danced the baila, while Stanley drummed on the kitchen table with two wooden spoons. (July 5)

♦ The last day of circumcision was always the grandest with bands playing, baila dancing and secretive tombola played upstairs. (Z 131)

- They started soberly with Christmas carols, then to Irish ballads and finally to the inevitable Baila. (FSD 188)

- The music changes to something I recognize. Baila. The boys in the village sometimes dance to these tunes. (GC 128)

- A fast beat baila song bursts forth. (WCS 38)

- Then the Portuguese came and went. They left pol sambol and the Baila dance behind. (M&P 151)

- Jim Reeves gave way to Baila. Baila was for old lovers, not for young lovers like us. (M&P 294)

bakala

/bakələ/ (coll.) bow-legged (Sinhala) ° *Did you see the bakala walk?*

baka pandithaya

/bakə panɒitəya/ know-all (Sinhala) ° *He's a real baka pandithaya - has an opinion on everything.*

balal as

/balal æs/ (an expression to describe distinctively light brown or green eyes; Sinhala = cat's eyes) ° *Real balal as - must be having Burgher blood.*

balance

change, rest, remainder ° *You forgot your balance.* ° *He spends only half his salary and sends the balance home to his family.* ° *He banked three lakhs and spent the balance.* ° *Now the balance acreage is being axed.* ° *the balance books* → In BSE, 'balance' as a noun usually refers to the amount in your bank account (your 'bank balance'). It is less common in the sense of 'rest' or 'remainder', and is never used in the sense of 'change'. In SLE it is also used as an adjective as in the last example (BSE: 'the rest of the books').

- He said he had a thousand and asked for time, whereupon he was given a month to make good the balance ... (JFT 142)

- Miss Lawton, at Mary Sisler's insistence, would stay the balance of the weekend. (CG 215)

- I gave her the balance cash I had with me, two hundred rupees. (REP 57)

- I also had the pans and the balance of the smoked venison. (REP 139)

- Velaithan ate sparingly though, never too happy with flesh meals anyway, and I polished off most of the balance. (REP 150)

- ... in order to give the bank enough time to recover all its dues and credit the balance proceeds to Ravi's account. (FSD 100)

- "You wouldn't be able to lend me ten would you? You see I can lay my hands on the balance fifteen." ... "Here's five, and you'll somehow have to find yourself the balance." (CP 58-9)

- "I know how to find the balance money." (PMS 103)

balaya

/baləya/ a type of fish (skipjack tuna, bonito) (Sinhala) (> **blood fish, heaty**)

- It was explained that the Bala or Balaya (bonito) is very heaty. (YY 82)

baliya

/baliyə/ (coll.) a derogatory term for a woman who looks wild or unkempt or weirdly dressed; originally a type of **thovil** or exorcism ceremony (Sinhala) ° *Comb your hair, men, you look like a baliya!* ° *Real baliya she looked in that dress!*

ball-picker

(in tennis) ball-boy (> **pick**)

bana

/banə/ Buddhist sermon (Sinhala) ° *bana preaching*

- The temples would reverberate with bana ... (Z 23)

- "It must have taken you a long time to learn that - it is like the *bana* the priest preaches on a Poya-day," ... (WE 81)

bandakka

/banɒakka/ (= **lady's finger**) okra (Sinhala; Tamil vendikkai)

BANDAKKA

- He began to tend the kitchen garden, pottering around the aubergines and the *bandakka*, ... (WMD 44)

- ... and boiled *bandakkas* sprinkled with black pepper and salt (the poor man's asparagus, he called it). (WMD 123)

bandicoot

/bænɒikūt/ a very large rat (also India, from Telugu)

BANDICOOT

- I even went up on the roof to clear the gutters and make a big noise to chase away the bandicoot. (Reef 169)

- I well remember the incident of the dead bandicoot placed under my coverlet. (HC 29)

- He examined a bandicoot caught in a trap, a rat the length and weight of a cat, whose flesh, his grandmother assured him, tasted like suckling pork when curried. (HC 224)

- ... pythons that ate bandicoots in the dog's kennel ... (M&P 122)

- "I shall eat cake if there is no rice. But I shall never eat yam. That is what bandicoots eat." (M&P 183)

banian, banyan

/bæniən/ vest, singlet (also India, from Arabic/Portuguese) → Both spellings are given in the OED; but the tree of the same name is normally spelt 'banyan'.

BANIAN

- He wore a banyan over a crumpled sarong and scratched at his head as he walked. (MM 71)

- His banyan revealed a few strands of black hair on a narrow boyish chest. (Reef 22)

- He was wearing a sarong and a banyan. (FB 64)

- ... emerging in green-striped pyjamas and a banian that rolled up his belly, ... (TT 207)

♦ ... dressed in immaculate white verti and shawl and banian ... (WMD 6)

♦ ... tall and strongly built and dressed in a white gauze banian and a checked sarong; ... (BTH 52-3)

♦ Today, he wore a banian, the sleeveless vest people usually wore under their shirts. (July 131)

♦ "Do you know that such vests and banians are of immense value in this country?" (OD 58)

♦ He did not look too well and was lying down on his bed wearing a sarong and a banyan. (Z 64)

♦ A watchman dressed in a filthy banian and sarong trailed Sam through high-ceilinged rooms ... (HC 134)

♦ Martin, a short barrel-chested character in a sarong and sleeveless banian, ... (FSD.75)

barbet
(= **kottoruwa**) a small green bird with a large beak

♦ One of the spry barbets that flew about the garden developed an interest in Harry. (HC 228)

♦ Barbets, bulbuls, robins and orioles perch on the crowns of trees and shrubs ... (GC 316)

bar soap
a long bar of soap from which smaller pieces can be cut

♦ "I got some bar soap and a couple of tooth brushes." (REP 74)

base hospital
/bēs/ a main regional hospital (also Australia)

♦ From the base hospital at Polonnaruwa they would travel to peripheral

hospitals, where some of them were to live. (AG 228)

basket woman
(coll., derogatory) fishwife, loud-mouthed woman ° *screaming like a basket woman!*

bat: to bat away, bat on
(coll.) to slog away (at something), slog on (with something) ° *How's she getting on? - Oh, she's still batting away.*

□ still batting
(= **not out**) (coll.) still living, still going strong (cricket idiom) ° *95 and still batting!*

Bata slippers
(= **rubber slippers**) (brand name; coll. also **Batas**) (> **slippers**)

♦ That Enid in her poplin dresses and Bata slippers had rubies and sapphires and diamonds. (July 66)

♦ She changed her silver slippers for the Bata ones she wore around the house and went outside to the garden. (July 305)

♦ ... and I am proud of my new Bata slippers. (GC 9)

♦ "I don't want you coming like a beggar. No Bata slippers, please." (SMS 23)

batch
a group of students in the same year at university ° *He was in my batch at Peradeniya.*

♦ It is not surprising that Nimal always came first in his batch and passed his exams with the highest honours. (OD 132)

♦ Their batch had scattered all over the globe, a few to the States and others to England. (FSD 3)

batchmate

classmate, contemporary at university ° *He's one of my batchmates.*

- More visitors and Ravi recognized several batch mates he had not met since they left school, four years ago. (FSD 2)

- "Our batch-mates admire him for that," ... (GC 122)

- "And he said that he was a batch mate of yours at the University of Ceylon." (KCS 133)

bath (1)

/bāth/ (n) wash, shower, swim (> **river bath, sea bath, well bath**) → In BSE, 'having a bath' usually means getting into a bath-tub. In SLE, you can 'have a bath' under a shower, at a well (a **well bath**), in a river (a **river bath**), in a **tank**, or even in the sea (a **sea bath**). 'Having a bath' generally incudes washing your body (except in the case of a **sea bath**), and wetting your hair (a **head bath**); if you don't wet your hair, it is called a **body wash** or a **body bath**.

- What Vijay loved most, though, were the well-water baths, when he stood beside his father in his little sarong and had the water poured over him, bucket after bucket, ... (WMD 282)

- But Devi was returning from her bath at the well, ... (WMD 331)

bath (2)

/bat/ (= **rice, rice and curry**) (coll.) (Sinhala) ° *Have some more bath.* ° *We're having bath for lunch.*

bath curry

/bat kari/ (= **rice and curry**)

- ... Pearl's heart-warming *buth* curry. (SG 117)

- "Can't you Sinhalese manage without your buth-curry?" (FSD 148)

bathgulla

/batgullə/ (coll.) a person who loves to eat rice (Sinhala: gulla = weevil)

bath kade

/bat kaɖe/ a small eating place serving **rice and curry**, etc. (Sinhala) (> **kade**)

bath packet

(= **rice packet, lunch packet**) a **rice and curry** meal wrapped up to be taken away (> **packet, parcel**)

- She ate bath packets with her fingers and drank water from the tap. (Z 43)

bathala

/batələ/ sweet potato (Sinhala)

- "At least ask her if she eats *bathala*." (GC 15)

bathe

(vi) have a bath (also US) (> **bath**) ° *I was told not to bathe for three days.* → In BSE, 'to bathe' usually means to go for a swim for enjoyment, e.g. in the sea; it is also used transitively to mean washing e.g. a baby or a dog: 'Have you bathed the baby yet?'

- They made him bathe every day and wear fresh clothes. (OM 38)

- Velaithan had already bathed and changed into her 'day' kit. She always bathed before dawn, a practice that made me shudder. (REP 119)

- We bathe and bathe till our skin is wrinkled and pale. (GC 34)

- She normally bathed only once a week and I knew that she had bathed yesterday. (M&P 207)

bathroom

toilet (also US) ° *I need to go to the bathroom.*

☐ bathroom slippers

(= **rubber slippers**) flip-flops (> **slippers**)

batta (1)

/batā/ an extra allowance paid for going **outstation** on work (Anglo-Indian, from Portuguese)

- ♦ "But you're losing *batta**, no?" (* The extra outstation allowance paid to a government servant who stays out of home on a duty turn.) (YY 7)

- ♦ Pay was good and when laced with lashings of overtime and Sunday pay and overnight and outstation *batta*, Sonnaboy could bring home over a thousand rupees, which in the 1940s was princely. (YY 73)

- ♦ "That's his *bata* sheet. The principal has to sign it, so the inspector can claim his travelling and subsistence from the department." (PMS 70)

batta (2)

/batta/ hopscotch; also a home-made landmine (= **johnny batta**) (Sinhala)

- ♦ Hopscotch was a girl's game. Harry would have scorned it at home. Here he scoured garden beds for a smooth, flat stone. His *butta* landed in the first, second and third squares. (HC 230)

batta (3)

/batta/ (coll.) a short person; female: **batti** (Sinhala)

Batti

/bæti/ (coll.) Batticaloa

batu

/batu/ (= **vambatu, brinjal**) aubergine (US eggplant) (Sinhala) (> **thalana batu, thibbatu, elabatu**)

☐ batu moju

/batu mōju/ a **brinjal** pickle with **dry fish** (Sinhala) (> **moju**)

☐ batu pahi

/batu pæhi/ (= **brinjal pahi**) a pickle made with fried **brinjals** (Sinhala) (> **pahi**)

- ♦ Samare consciously bent down to serve himself and the blazer sleeve-edge smoothly dived into the tempered batu pehi. (WCS 59)

bayagulla

/bayagulla/ (coll.) coward, wimp (Sinhala: baya = fear, gulla = weevil) ° *Don't be such a bayagulla!*

b'day

birthday ° *Wish you a happy b'day.*

be: be on line!

(on the phone) wait a minute, hold the line

- ♦ "Please be on line," he was told, … (MiP 93)

beach boy

a boy or young man who spends time on the beach, e.g. a tout targeting tourists or a young male prostitute

beans: to give somebody beans

(= **scold**) to blast somebody, shout at somebody ° *She'll give you beans if she finds out.*

bear up

(= **cope up**) (vi/vt) bear something, endure something, cope with something ° *I can't bear (it) up any more.* ° *She couldn't bear up the pain.* (BSE: I can't bear it any more, She couldn't bear the pain.)

beat show

(= **musical show**) (dated) a live concert (> **show**)

bed rest

(n/v) staying in bed (when sick) (less common in BSE, and never used as a verb) ° *The doctor recommended a week's bed rest.* ° *I was told to bed rest for a week.*

♦ ... the doctors ordered complete bed rest for Prema. (WMD 58)

bed sheet

sheet (also US, less common in BSE)

♦ The bed-sheet is draped across our heads ... (GC 198)

♦ Nenda was counting the bed sheets the dhobi had returned after washing. (M&P 163)

bed tea

early morning tea in bed ° *At what time do you like your bed tea?*

♦ ... the conundrum that was still occupying him when the servant-boy came in with bed tea. (HC 116)

bedun

/bædun/ a fried dish usually of fish or meat (Sinhala) ° *beef bedun*

♦ ... fish koftas, fried squid in what was known as a *'bedun'* (a thick gravy sauce) ... (JFT 186)

beedi

/bīɒi/ a small cheap hand-made cigarette (Sinhala/Tamil/Hindi; also India)

BEEDI

♦ On one side a long smouldering wick hangs for customers to light their cigarettes and dry-rolled *beedis.* (MM 116)

♦ The driver was on his haunches, smoking a *beedi*.... He took a last puff and chucked the *beedi* away ... (Reef 81)

♦ He pulled out a tied bundle of beedis from a drawer and lit one, ... (AG 75)

♦ He found Herath leaning on his ancient taxi, reflectively smoking a beedi and waiting for his summons. (July 4)

♦ In the violet shade of a line of rickshaws a child sat on his heels, puffing on a *beedi*. (HC 211)

♦ An old man was seated ... staring at the road and smoking a beedi. (FSD 213)

♦ Those were the midday hours that Ramu used to lean against the wall of the Golden Pumpkin Hotel and smoke beedi after beedi. (KCS 171)

bee-eater

a small green bird, common in the dry zone

♦ The bird was a blur of green perched far in a tree - a bee-eater with its twin-wand tail and pirate patch eyes. (TT 115)

beeralu

/bīrəlu/ a traditional style of lace-making from the Southern Province (Sinhala, from Portuguese)

before

(= back) ago ° *two weeks before* → In BSE, 'before' would be used like 'earlier' to mean before a certain time in the past: 'We had seen them two weeks earlier/two weeks before'; but 'ago' or 'back' would be used to mean 'before now': 'We saw them two weeks ago/two weeks back'.

beli

/beli/ a green fruit with a hard shell and orange flesh (Sinhala) ° *beli juice*

BELI

♦ She would shake woodapples and bellis with a firm fist and she would squeeze avocados mercilessly. (Z 4)

☐ belimal drink
/belimal/ a drink made from the **beli** flower (Sinhala)

believe
(vi) believe something ° *Can't believe, no?* (BSE: I can't believe it!)

benumbed
numb (formal in BSE) ° *My leg is benumbed.*

bestman
/bestman/ best man (2 words)
→ Pronounced as two words in BSE, with the stress on the second word: /best 'mæn/. In SLE it is pronounced as one word, with the stress on 'best' and the second syllable pronounced weak: /'bestman/.

betel
/bīt(ə)l/ (= **bulath**) a combination of **betel leaf**, **arecanut** and **chunam** (lime paste), which is chewed as a stimulant (also India, from Malayalam via Portuguese) ° *The import of 'babul' betel - known to be widely used by schoolchildren - is to be banned.*

♦ He spat out his betel chew and looked back into the cart. (WMD 138)

♦ The toddy tapper squatted and pulled out his plastic bag, and they waited quietly until he had his betel chew firmly lodged in his cheek. (July 131)

♦ He paused to pop a chew of betel into his mouth. (July 153)

♦ The other servants settled on their haunches at a respectful distance from our camp-stools, chatting quietly over their betel. (HC 69)

♦ When the old woman walked away he spat very accurately, a scarlet betel jet that arced to earth an inch short of that green skirt. (HC 176)

♦ The cop was a middle-aged man with a broad, clean-shaven face and decayed, betel chewer's teeth. (REP 316)

♦ When Valli's mother would come home from work on the estate, dizzy from the sun, her gums dark with betel, ... (WE 29)

♦ Her lips are drawn back and teeth, betel-red, are bared like those of a rabid dog. (GC 66)

♦ Sinhala Only was for backwoods aristocrats who chewed betel and kept chickens. (CP 101)

☐ betel juice
the red liquid which is spat out by people chewing **betel**

♦ That worthy, whose mouth was always full of chewing betel leaf, jogged up, spat a stream of betel juice on a pile of sleepers ... (JFT 145)

♦ Her smiling lips were full and red with betel juice. (OM 45)

♦ She spat an enormous mouthful of betel juice in their general direction and vanished into the night! (OM 47)

♦ The man behind the row of blue and orange bottles spat out a slug of betel juice. (SG 276)

♦ He spat out a stream of betel juice, which streaked the sand like a splatter of blood. (July 118)

♦ ... trying to avoid touching the graffiti and betel juice stains on the walls. (Z 55)

♦ Her plump cheeks held wads of betel and her teeth were striped red with betel juice. (Z 123)

♦ With her mouth full of red betel-juice I have to say Agnes was beginning to look quite a bit like a tubercular vampire. (CP 111)

♦ "That's it," he says, spitting a stream of betel juice. (PMS 135)

□ betel leaf

(= **betel, bulath**) the leaf of the **betel** vine, used in the preparation of **betel**; also given as a sign of respect (e.g. to parents, teachers) on **auspicious** occasions (> **arecanut, chunam**)

♦ A well laden tray of betel leaves with accompaniments was always ready to be served. On it were spread out betel leaves, pieces of sliced arecanut, a small container called the *killotaya* for *chunam*, some tobacco and of course the nut cracker to slice the arecanut. (CM 11)

♦ "Hello Auntie," he greeted Prema and quietly placed a sheaf of betel leaf and arecanut in her hand. (WMD 53)

♦ Old people sat on their haunches and looked blankly ahead of them, chewing what little arecanut and betel-leaf they could lay their hands on. (WMD 229)

♦ At the various auspicious times, the family eats, pays homage to its elders and exchanges gifts of cash wrapped in betel leaves. (July 53)

♦ ... the feminine appearance, neither too dark nor too pale, too thick nor too thin, of the perfect betel leaf. (HC 213)

♦ The silvery hair falls forward as the old man bows his head to accept the sheaf of betel leaves. (PMS 87)

♦ In his hand he carries a customary sheaf of betel leaves to be given to the class teacher. (PMS 215)

♦ One by one the children offer the teacher a sheaf of betel held in both hands. (PMS 217)

♦ ... the leaves look exactly like betel, but the smell of pepper is unmistakable. (PMS 219)

□ betel nut

the seed of the **arecanut** tree, used in the preparation of **betel**

♦ Her breath smelled of onions and betel nut, a pungent, unpleasant combination. (July 250)

□ betel-stained

stained with **betel juice**

♦ He nodded at me; a betel-stained almost toothless grin slowly split his face. (MM 91)

♦ ... opening and shutting his betel-stained mouth over broken, yellowing teeth ... (WMD 366)

♦ Sure enough, when it was their turn the old man greeted her with a betel stained smile. (FSD 224)

♦ Her betel-stained mouth opens like a cavern. (PMS 199)

□ betel tray

a tray on which **betel** is served

BETEL TRAY

♦ First, the visitor was served hot tea in a glass. Then the betel tray was offered. (CM 11)

beti amba

/beTi ambə/ a small sweet variety of mango (Sinhala)

better

(coll.) had better (also US) ° *STC better be on the lookout.* ° *We better go now.* (BSE: We'd better go now.)

♦ "You better not let the parents see him like that," … (FB 50)

♦ "You better watch out too," … (SG 231)

♦ "You better sit down and prepare yourself for this." (CG 291)

♦ "You better replace those needles." (AG 131)

♦ "But Appa called and said he was coming to pick me up. We better wait for him." (July 337)

♦ "You better wash up and come." (FSD 96)

♦ "Well Mithra fellow, you better bring this girl back safe," … (GC 229)

♦ "Amrith, … you better come out. I mean it." (SMS 178)

♦ "I better get over to HQ and see what we can find out about the situ." (CU 379)

B/G

(= **G/B**) (in **marriage proposals**) Buddhist **Govigama** ° *B/G parents living in Colombo seek suitable parner for their daughter …*

Bharatha Natyam

/barətə nāṭyəm/ a traditional South Indian dance (Tamil)

BHARATHA NATYAM DANCER

♦ … a niece who was nineteen … and could do nice kolam and knew Bharatnatyam. (YY 45)

♦ … how her mother is forcing her to learn Bharata Natyam … (Z 26)

bheeshana time

/bīshanə/ the period of the JVP troubles in the late 1980s (Sinhala: bheeshana = harassment, intimidation)

bhikku

/bikku/ Buddhist monk (Sinhala) ° *the National Bhikku Front*

♦ The *bhikkus* droned for hours … (MM 115)

♦ It all depended on the *bhikkus* now. (WMD 222)

♦ "He has given the green light to the *bhikkus* and the bigots," … (WMD 227)

♦ "He seemed to live more like a don than a *bhikku*," … (SG 154)

♦ The bikkhu took their seat without thanks. (July 78)

bhikkuni

/bikkuni/ Buddhist nun (Sinhala)

bibikkan

/bibikkang/ a type of sweet rich cake made with **gram** flour, grated coconut and **jaggery** (Sinhala, from Malay)

- ◆ There was coconut cake called *bibikkan*. (CM 76)

- ◆ ... bibikan fragrant with the smell of cardamom and cloves, ... (CG 375)

bibili

/bibili/ (coll.) rash, spots, pimples, blisters (Sinhala)

bic

a segment of an orange or other citrus fruit

bicycle repair shop

(= **winkle**) (less common in BSE)

- ◆ ... Gamini had just returned from the bicycle repair shop with the good news that his bike had not been irreparably damaged. (WMD 252)

- ◆ We went past at least two bicycle repair shops. (REP 36)

big big

(coll.) big (usually with plural nouns) (> **small small**) ° *They're earning big big salaries.* ° *big big houses*

- ◆ "We will be in big-big trouble." (SMS 152)

big girl

a girl who has **attained age**, i.e. reached puberty

- ◆ Daughters were nice but needed dowries, big girl ceremonies and careful watching. (July 32)

- ◆ After all these months of being afraid she was a freak, of watching her friends having their 'growing-up' parties and listening to them discussing cramps and Kotex, she had finally joined the elite ranks of the big girls. (July 165)

- ◆ Loku, conscious now of her status as a 'big' girl, has a 'diya reddha', a length of thin material, wrapped modestly round her body. (GC 92)

- ◆ "I thought she would have at least come back now to see you being a big girl in your trouser suit." (M&P 238)

- ◆ "... I came when Lydia and Pam were here, then I came when Chooti became a big girl ..." (M&P 257)

big made

heavily built (> **small made**) ° *a big made girl*

- ◆ A big made fair girl, she was rather flabby, her face quite plump. (OM 27)

- ◆ Later on, another big-made man was constantly looking at the same wineshop ...(KCS 129)

big match

an annual cricket or rugger match between rival schools (e.g. the **Royal-Thomian**: Royal College vs. St Thomas' College) ° *big match fever*

- ◆ ... the boys of St Joseph's, who were St Peter's rivals and clashed with frantic regularity on every Big Match day (when the schools met at an annual cricket encounter) ... (TT 96)

- ◆ The most memorable days of the year were sports day, and the day of the big match, the cricket match, between us and St Peter's, the two 'premier' Catholic schools. It was not that our fixtures with the other schools were not bitterly contested, but this was in the nature of a family feud, nurtured carefully over the years on the lines of the Royal-St Thomas encounter. That of course was *the* big match, the battle of the elites, graced by the illustrious and the powerful, and elevated to a national event. (WMD 133)

big onions
(= Bombay onions)

bil, b-i-l
brother-in-law ° *Slain underworld leader's b-i-l abducted*

biling
/biling/ a small green fruit with a bitter taste, which grows from the trunk of the tree (Sinhala; OED 'bilimbi', from Tamil) ° *biling sambol* ° *biling chutney*

BILING

♦ ... *billing,* jak seed and coconut, ... (WMD 141)

billa
/billa/ bogeyman, an imaginary creature used to frighten children (Sinhala) (> **gonibilla**)

♦ They brought a *billa* - someone from the community with a gunnysack over his head, slits cut out for the eyes - to anonymously identify the rebel sympathizer. A *billa* was a monster, a ghost, to scare children in games, and it had picked out Ruwan Kumara and he had been taken away. (AG 269)

binna
/binna/ (in **Kandyan** law) a marriage where the groom goes to live with the bride's family (opposite: **deega**) (Sinhala) ° *... settled in a "binna" (marriage in which the bridegroom shifts to the bride's house) ... ° In contrast, the "binna" married wife commands great power in marriage.*

bio-data
CV (curriculum vitae) (US resumé)

bio-science
a set of subjects studied for A levels (botany, zoology, physics, chemistry) (> **commerce subjects**)

bioscope
(dated) cinema; also a derogatory term for an Indian or Sinhala **formula film**

♦ The neighbours applauded vigorously. This was better than the Bioscope. (JFT 25)

♦ Just two miles away there was the 'bioscope' and after the late show there were women there too. (OM 48)

biscuit
ingot ° *gold biscuits*

bit
(coll., derogatory) girl, girlfriend

♦ "I also wanted a bit like her." (OD 131)

♦ "Don't you know that bits like to have it inside for more than two seconds?" (CU 44)

♦ "Couldn' they just have shown us a picture of the bit?" (CU 106)

bite, bites
(n) a snack, usually accompanying a drink ° *Devilled prawns make a delicious bite.* ° *Shall we order some bites?*

♦ He always had a 'bite' to be consumed with the arrack. (YY 92)

♦ "Booze is cheap an' the bites are good." (CU 34)

bitter gourd
(= **karawila**) a type of vegetable with a bitter taste

♦ ... boiled rice, liver curry, bitter gourd. (Reef 83)

♦ He tried to speak to Rani from behind the bitter gourd creeper, ... (WMD 44)

♦ That afternoon the *nonamahatheya* herself came out of the house, carrying boiled rice, curried bitter gourd, salt fish and a rustling parcel done up in brown paper. (HC 169)

blachan, blachang
/blachang/ a prawn **sambol** (orig. Malay) (> **lamprai**)

♦ ... and a prawn blachan ... (JFT 186)

black gram
(= **ulundu**) a type of pulse used to make flour (> **gram**)

blackguard
/bləgāb/ (= **scold**) (dated in BSE, and more common as a noun) ° *They blackguarded me for driving too fast.*

♦ "Siya is always blaguarding her. He says it is because of her that we have no Maldive fish and the pol sambol tastes like tissue paper. Mrs. Adonis is always blaguarding her saying it is because of her that she has to die all alone in her house without any of her children, Ammi is always blaguarding her saying it is because of her that the headline on her palm is not travelling anymore and Magi and Nenda are always blaguarding her that it is because of her that we have no Podian." (M&P 190)

block (1)
traffic jam ° *There's a big block on Havelock Road.*

♦ None of that was of any help, as there seemed to be a serious block further up the road. (REP 334)

block (2)
plot (of land) ° *The land is divided into six blocks.*

block out
divide up, mark out (land) ° *Coconut land is being blocked out into 10-15 perch plots and sold for housing purposes.*

blood fish
any type of fish with red meat, esp. tuna (e.g. **balaya, kelavalla**)

blow off
/blō/ blow up, go off, explode ° *The bomb blew off without any warning.*

blowing
/blōing/ (n) wind, breeze ° *There was a strong blowing.* ° *While travelling the ventilators provide a blowing to the driver.*

blues: out of the blues
out of the blue ° *Each idea comes to Shiranthi out of the blues.*

boarded
boarding, staying in a boarding house (the passive form is dated in BSE) ° *He is boarded at Wellawatte.*

♦ To supplement his income he taught Sinhala to the sons of rich Sri Lankans who were boarded at British public schools. (CP 72)

boarding
(n) boarding house ° *They're looking for a new boarding.*

♦ The society ran a boarding for some of them ... (CG 57)

♦ "Where's this new boarding of yours?" (GC 227)

boards: to go on the boards
(of a play) to be performed ° *Indu Dharmasena's new play will go on the boards next week.*

bodhi pooja

/bōdi pūja/ a Buddhist religious ceremony (Sinhala) ° *We even had several bodhi poojas and made vows to various temples.*

- ♦ She is contemplating beginning a series of Bodhi Pujas in order to deviate the curse. (M&P 211)
- ♦ Following the sacrifice of the goat, it is advisable to do a Bodhi puja every Tuesday until the child reaches its fifth year. (M&P 315)

body parts

spare parts for vehicles (body panels, etc.) → In BSE, 'parts of the body' refers to the human head, arms, legs, etc.; 'body parts' suggests that they are severed from the body, e.g. as a result of a bomb blast or a gruesome murder. Neon signs advertising 'body parts' seem strange to speakers of BSE!

body wash, body bath

washing your body without wetting your hair (> **bath**)

- ♦ Ammi had no hot water for her body wash as the gas geyser had not been turned on. (M&P 58)

bokku

/bōkku/ culvert (Sinhala)

- ♦ Hemantha pilfered a whole pack of Gold Leaf from his father's cupboard, and even smoked one with the boys down by the bokku. (July 49)
- ♦ "There's nothing wrong with having a boyfriend, but I'll have no daughter of mine meeting men by bokkus." (July 255)

bola curry

/bōla/ a meatball curry (Sinhala)

bola folhado

/bola fiādo/ a type of layered cake, a **Burgher** speciality (Portuguese)

- ♦ ... and that intrinsically Portuguese sweet - the many layered cake which was a Burgher speciality: the *bola folhado* (pronounced Fi-a-dho). It is like a very rich Danish pastry ... (JFT 186)

bolanool man

/bōlanūl/ (dated) travelling salesman selling thread, cloth, pins, ribbons, etc. (Sinhala)

- ♦ Every few months a *bolanool* man called at the house, a Moor with a withered hand and a tin trunk carried on his head. (HC 203)

bo leaf

/bō/ the pointed leaf of the **bo tree** ° *in the shape of a bo leaf*

BO LEAF

- ♦ "Now the yellow borders represent Buddhism, the Bo-leaves are also Buddhism because Lord Buddha attained enlightenment under a Bo tree. A branch of this Bo tree was brought and planted here." (M&P 105)

bolla

/bōlla/ a type of fish (bigeye scad) (Sinhala)

bolt: to put the bolt, put a bolt

/bōlт/ (coll.) to bolt, do a bolt, run away

♦ "If saw this he put the bolt and won't come back." (JFT 47)

♦ "There Kelaart on the line with blood pouring and Dickson putting a bolt." (YY 168)

bomb

(coll.) (adj.) attractive, sexy

♦ Kamini Saverimuttu went to St Mary's and was what the boys called 'a bomb bit'. (July 74)

♦ "Looking bomb today," he would say, his eyes unashamedly roving over her curves. (July 75)

bombai motai

/bombai мoтai/ a sweet similar to candy floss (Sinhala/Tamil) ° *One may still come across a few Moors engaged in selling Bombai muttai ...*

Bombay onions

(= **big onions, B onions**) large onions
(> **red onions**)

♦ Lucy-*amma* was cutting onions, Bombay onions. (Reef 24)

♦ "Plenty of Bombay onions coming in." (WMD 138)

♦ Aunty Bundle ordered fifteen pounds of Bombay onions for the seeni sambal and onion sambal, ... (SMS 137)

♦ A strange pink shade gleams on Bombay onions. (KCS 163)

Bombay sweets

different types of Indian sweets (**boondi, muscat,** etc.)

♦ In the Bombay sweet seller's large circular tin container were three tiers. (CM 55)

Bombay toast

bread fried with egg and milk (US French toast)

bombili

/bombili/ Bombay duck (a type of **dry fish**) (Sinhala)

♦ ... buying *bombili* (the dried 'Bombay duck' - a thin eel-like fish that is found in abundance in Indian waters) ... (JFT 43)

bonbon

(Christmas) cracker

♦ Ammi drove the blue Hillman to Christmas decoration classes and learned to make Bonbons... My mother made quality Bonbons and Cargills Limited bought them all. Each and every Bonbon my mother made cracked when pulled. Inside the Bonbons she had metal whistles and plastic dolls imported from China. (M&P 108)

B onions

(= **Bombay onions**)

bookrack

bookshelf, bookcase

boondi

/būndi/ a type of sweet made with **gram** flour (Tamil; also India)

boot: to give somebody the boot

(coll.) to end a relationship with somebody; also **to get the boot, to be given the boot**
→ In BSE, to 'give someone the boot' is to kick someone out, e.g. of a job or a house; it is unlikely to be used in the context of a relationship.

♦ "What? She gave you the boot or what?" (TT 195)

♦ "So, have you got the boot?" (OD 112)

♦ "I gave her the boot, or rather, ... she gave me the boot." (CP 53)

BOP
(= broken orange pekoe)

Borah, Bohra
/bōra/ a member of a small Muslim community of North Indian origin

♦ It did not help that the Nagoda Mills, which had collapsed on her father's head, were owned by a Borah merchant. (WMD 306)

border villages
front-line **Sinhala** villages bordering traditional **Tamil** areas in the Northern, Eastern and North-Central provinces

bore
pierce (somebody's ear) ° *I decided to get my ears bored.*

boric powder
the powder used on the surface of a **carrom** board to make it smooth (> **carrom**)

boroa
/boroa/ **rulang** biscuits (Portuguese)

boru
/boru/ (coll.) false, fake, artificial (Sinhala = lies) ° *He's a real boru case.* ° *a boru organisation*

□ borukakul dancer
/borukakul/ stilt dancer (Sinhala)

BORUKAKUL DANCER

♦ ... no amount of rational explanation about stilts could lure him out to watch the *bora kakul* men dance. (HC 215)

□ boru part
(coll.) putting on airs (Sinhala) (> **part**)

♦ "But there was never any *boru-part* about him, you know. ... He was sincere. He didn't put on airs like the rest of them," ... (SG 11)

□ boru shok
/boru shōk/ (coll.) a false show of wealth (Sinhala) ° *All that jewellery? Just boru shok!*

both
(word order) ° *Tamil and Sinhala both* (BSE: both Tamil and Sinhala)

♦ "Yes, something about a breakout or riot and some prisoners being killed, Tamils and Sinhalese both." (WMD 368)

bo tree
/bō/ a tree found at all Buddhist temples, like the tree under which the Buddha attained enlightenment; also called pipal or Indian fig tree (ficus religiosa) (Sinhala) (> **bo leaf**)

BO TREE

♦ People were praying by the *Bo*-tree inside the temple square, ... (Reef 65)

♦ Together we made our offerings at the dagoba, shrine room and at the Bo tree. (CM 9)

♦ ... memories that came alive at Poson and Wesak and New Year's Day, when thousands of devotees made their way to the temple of the Bo tree which Sangha-mitta, the daughter of the Emperor Asoka, had brought as a sapling from India, two centuries before the birth of Christ, to inaugurate Buddhism in Lanka. (WMD 199)

♦ ... and the two roads met again just before another Bo tree - how come there are so many Bo trees along the old road especially where there was a junction of sorts? (BTH 17)

♦ The temple's huge white stupa gleamed softly in the morning sun, and the bo tree near by rustled in that peculiar way bo trees do - each heart-shaped leaf on its slim, long stem rustling individually as the breeze blew through. (July 91)

♦ The two families built a huge sand dagoba, a replica of the Kalutara one, and even found a small bo plant growing near the house, which they uprooted and solemnly stuck near their Bodhiya. (July 125)

♦ Lord Buddha had attained enlightenment under a bo tree in Bodhigaya in India, which was why every temple or shrine had one planted near by. No one was definitely sure, but it was said to be a criminal offence to uproot a bo tree. (July 125)

♦ As they were passing under the living arch thrown across the road by the bo tree at Kalutara, she lit another cigarette. (HC 145)

♦ Bo-trees grew from the cracks in the rocks, ... (SMS 188)

bottle

jar °*jam bottle* → In BSE, a 'bottle' is a tall, narrow container for liquids, while a 'jar' is for jams, chutneys, etc. In SLE, a 'bottle' refers to any glass container. Note also that in SLE a 'jam bottle' means a jar which is full of jam, while in BSE a 'jam jar' means simply the container itself, which may be empty. The same applies to a number of other words, e.g. 'milk bottle', 'beer bottle', 'matchbox', etc. In BSE these refer to the containers, while the full containers would be 'a bottle of milk', 'a bottle of beer', 'a box of matches', etc.

♦ ... a bottle of *seeni-sambol* ... (JFT 136)

♦ The jam bottle is opened. (KCS 102)

bottle gourd

(= **diya labu, labu**) a type of gourd used as a vegetable

♦ It took time but I found ... some bottle gourd and small green tomatoes. (REP 156)

bottle lamp

a kerosene/paraffin lamp made from a bottle

♦ The mud and wattle homes in our village were usually lit up at night with the simple homely bottle lamps. (CM 75)

♦ The dim light they had seen turned out to be a bottle lamp which had been placed on the floor in a corner. (July 149)

♦ The long hours of study by the light of a bottle lamp, ... (GC 7)

bottle man

a man who collects empty bottles and newspapers for recycling ° *Today one cannot sell old newspapers even for Rs 6/- per kilo to the bottleman.*

♦ 'Bottle men' had their field days, going around with baskets on their heads buying up all the empty bottles which they in turn resold. (JFT 189)

♦ Then there was the *bothal karaya*. ... That morning they had hidden themselves in the dense foliage of the tree till the bottle man was just passing the gate. (FSD 11)

bouchee, bouchee case
/būshi/ a small choux pastry snack with a sweet or savoury filling (orig. French)
° *chicken bouchees*

boundary wall
(= **parapet wall**) garden wall

♦ The shadow of the jam fruit tree lengthened slowly, falling across the boundary wall ... (JFT 62)

♦ ... and pitched his bicycle against the low boundary wall. (JFT 105)

♦ Today was Saturday, and after tuition, they usually spent a few hours sitting on her boundary wall and chatting idly. (July 87)

♦ Niresh signalled to Amrith and they leapt over the short boundary wall. (SMS 117)

♦ The boundary wall on both sides was a mere five metres away, ...(CU 464)

boutique
(= **kade**) a small shop or eating place (from Portuguese) (> **hopper boutique, tea boutique**) ° *We got our lunch from a boutique.* ° *He owns a small boutique on the Galle Road.* → In BSE, a 'boutique' suggests a small shop selling expensive fashionable clothes; in SLE it is the local corner shop selling everyday provisions and/ or cheap meals, etc. Note on pronunciation: This is one of several words which tend to be pronounced with the stress on the first

syllable in SLE, and the second syllable in BSE.

♦ We drive along Reclamation Street through markets and boutiques. (RF 65)

♦ ... the railway station, the rows of ill-lit boutiques. (TT 200)

♦ A New Town with boutiques and bazaars and bus-stops and small businesses had sprung up ... (WMD 199)

♦ ... and there was a boutique with a long verandah half enclosed by a counter painted in alternate strips of blue and white ... (BTH 13)

♦ He could see the lights from the boutiques and the buses. (OD 29)

♦ She bought her cigarettes at the boutique and lit the first one from the smouldering rope that dangled beside the entrance. (HC 175-6)

♦ Miriswatte was a small junction with a few boutiques and shops. (REP 320)

♦ ... Ravi took out the parcel of roti and curry they'd bought at an all-night boutique. (FSD 244)

♦ This boutique underwent refurbishing ... and Cheeta Aiya, the elderly owner of the boutique was keen that Samare ceremonially declare open the shop. (WCS 60)

♦ "He stopped here and asked me if I needed something from the boutique." (M&P 350)

bowser
a tanker carrying fuel, water, etc. (> **gully bowser**)

♦ "A refuelling bowser has arrived from the airport, and we can start supplying you." (CU 123)

box along, box on

carry on, get on OK (in spite of problems)
° *How are you? - Oh, I'm boxing along.*

box plan

theatre seating plan ° *Box plan available at the Lionel Wendt.* ° *All seats have been box-planned.*

box seat: in the box seat

in a commanding position (e.g. in a cricket match) ° *Trinity in the box seat* → This is one example of a number of idioms favoured by Sri Lankan sports journalists; also used in Australian English, but less common in BSE.

boy

young man (> **girl**); (= **houseboy, servant boy**) male **servant**

♦ Nimal, my boy, would see them in, ... (MM 29)

♦ The Railway permits no liquor to be sold on the premises but the 'boy' keeps the arrack in his den which he sells to the drivers. (YY 92)

□ the Boys

(= **Tigers, LTTEers**) (coll.) members of the LTTE

♦ "Yes, all the young people, the Boys as they are called, all they can talk of is armed struggle." (WMD 305)

♦ Once that policy is known, the villagers themselves are not going to take kindly to having their own 'boys' use them as shields... They will either get their 'boys' to go further afield to lay their ambushes, or they will sneak the info to us." (REP 62)

♦ They were known as 'the Boys'. The antiquated grievances of the Tamil people in the north were now represented by the Boys. The Boys

wanted nothing less than a separate state called Eelam. (M&P 260)

brake oil

brake fluid

brassiere

bra (dated in BSE)

♦ The Grama Sevaka came back with his wife, a large lady who wore a reddha and a lace blouse which showed a tattered black brassiere underneath. (July 297)

♦ We come to a stall with piles and piles of brassières. (GC 59)

breadfruit

(= **del**) a large green fruit used as a vegetable (curried, boiled or fried)

BREADFRUIT

♦ ... and occasionally the crash of an overripe bread-fruit falling through the thick leaves of that huge tree. (MM 71)

♦ He liked breadfruit too and always brought some home when the fruit was in season. But he always called them 'toe-crackers'. He found that after a spell of breadfruit the skin between his toes began to split. (YY 82)

♦ On the upper shelf were stored dried jak and breadfruit to be used in the rainy season. (CM 14)

♦ ... the disputed yield from a single branch of an overhanging breadfruit tree. (HC 41)

♦ "We had a breadfruit tree and a few coconut palms." (REP 103)

♦ She brings a large platter of boiled breadfruit to him, with white scraped coconut and a paste of red chillies mixed with lime. (KCS 121)

♦ She has a large garden planted with coconut, jak and breadfruit trees. (PMS 78)

□ **breadfruit chips**
chips made of deep-fried **breadfruit** pieces

♦ All day Soma went back and forth from the kitchen bearing fried breadfruit chips in a silver epergne ... (HC 161)

♦ She could picture me, sitting up in bed with my afternoon tea, the hot little plate of breadfruit chips by my side, ... (CP 106)

break
/brēk/ (coll.) pick (fruit, flowers, etc.) ° *Let's break some mangoes and eat.*

□ **to break off**
(vi) (of a couple) to break up, to split up ° *Mohan and Dilani have broken off.* → In BSE, a couple could 'break off' their relationship or their engagement (vt).

□ **to break a queue**
to jump a queue

□ **to break fast**
(of Muslims) to eat after fasting ° *They have to break fast at sunset.*

♦ "Come, ... we have one hour more before we break fast, let me tell you a story." (Z 177)

□ **to break rest**
to stay up all night without sleeping ° *I broke rest last night.*

♦ "See the sacrifices we are making for you. Going in hot engines ... breaking rest ... getting wet ..." (YY 112)

□ **to break your head over something**
to worry about something, get stressed about something ° *What's the point in us breaking our heads over this?*

□ **to put a break to somebody**
(= **put a line, put a cap**) (coll., dated) to chat somebody up, approach somebody with romantic intentions

breudher
/brūdə/ a type of cake, a **Burgher** speciality traditionally eaten at Christmas (orig. Dutch) ° *You can't appreciate a good breudher until you've tasted ours.*

♦ ... breudhers (a dough cake baked in a special ring mould with plums and sultanas and a traditional cake for Christmas breakfast) ... (JFT 26)

♦ And there must be the *breudher* for breakfast which is the rich Dutch yeast cake. Making a real Dutch *breudher* is another art Maudiegirl excelled in ... After the bread dough has been brought from the bakery, the *breudher* mixture is prepared. Ten egg yolks, mind, and the men are commandeered because the *breudher* needs a strong beating arm. ... So the *breudher* is also baked and there is a right royal spread with the family sitting down to a Christmas breakfast of *breudher* and cheese, ... (JFT 186-7)

♦ "If you don't like Breudher you could have given it to the servants." (Z 85)

bring: to bring something and come
to bring something (> **take and go**) ° *Remember to bring your book and come.*

♦ "Sit, sit, I'll bring and come." (JFT 181)

♦ "Tani, go tell Marie and her parents to bring their dinner and come." (FSD 187)

♦ Maybe Richard Koch would organize another "bring and come" party for them. (FSD 300)

□ **to bring something/somebody down**
(= **get down**) to bring/get something/ somebody from elsewhere (esp. abroad), import ° *The vehicles were brought down from Japan.* ° *They're planning to bring down 15 specialists from UK.* ° *A VIP son has brought down the latest Aston Martin sports car.*

brinjal
/brinjol/ (= **batu, vambatu**) aubergine (US eggplant) (Anglo-Indian, from Portuguese) (> **batu**)

♦ … the sound of a fan when someone throws brinjals at it, … (RF 77)

♦ … the piping hot rice with *dhal* and *brinjal* and fried fish and prawns, … (WMD 16)

♦ … beds of vegetables - brinjal, murunga, okra, pumpkin; … (CG 14)

♦ "Have some brinjals, this is my pride …" (AG 95)

♦ Dierdre fried the sliced brinjal and wondered why Enid's mother was such an unbearable snob. (July 20)

♦ … but in any case all the fried *brinjal* I could eat. (HC 49)

□ **brinjal pahi**
/brinjol pœhi/ (= **batu pahi**) a pickle made with fried **brinjals** (Sinhala) (> **pahi, lamprai**)

Bristol board
a sheet of plain cardboard (less common in BSE)

♦ "And asking for Bristol board and big box of Reeves." (TT 90)

Britisher
British person (also US)

♦ … the day when a heavily-jowled Britisher had actually got off the train, … (YY 6)

♦ The Britishers moved into India, … (TT 13)

broiler
battery chicken, a young chicken raised for broiling or roasting (less common in BSE) (> **curry chicken**)

♦ … and fifteen broiler chickens. (SMS 137)

broken orange pekoe (BOP)
a high grade of tea (> **pekoe**)

♦ He always drank lots of tea: estate-fresh, up-country broken orange pekoe tip-top tea. (Reef 76)

♦ They found him in the White Falls factory, running his fingers through a sample of Broken Pekoe, his pale eyes alight. (HC 99)

♦ This was part of his daily morning routine, along with a cup of Broken Orange Pekoe Ceylon Tea, … (CU 285)

bucked
(coll.) pleased, chuffed ° *Ruvini was highly bucked when I told her.*

♦ "Aren't you even a bit bucked that he is interested in you?" (GC 55)

bucket
a small bucket-shaped **Vesak lantern**

BUCKETS

bucketing

pouring a bucket of water (often dirty water mixed with garbage etc.) over someone's head (a common student prank during **ragging**)

♦ I have learned a new word today - bucketing. Why did these seniors inflict such misery on innocents like us? How can they possibly consider bucketing good fun? (GC 16)

♦ "We can fill some basins of water. Bucket them when they come." (GC 38)

bucket man

(= **latrine coolie**) (dated)

♦ One day he had borrowed Sonnaboy's bicycle, gone carousing, and when wobbling back the following morning, collided with a bucket man. (JFT 30)

bucket shop

betting shop → In BSE, a 'bucket shop' is a travel agency selling cheap air tickets.

♦ Her arms still flagged down strange cars for a lift to the Pettah market where she could trade gossip with friends and place bets in the "bucket shops." (RF 125)

♦ "Must have gone to the bucket shop as usual." (YY 13)

bucks

(coll.) **rupees** → In the US, 'bucks' is a colloquial word for dollars.

♦ "When you find him, tell the fellow he owes me five thousand bucks." (SG 274)

♦ "Look, Nira, my grandmother sent me ten bucks!" (July 73)

♦ "Let's face it, 15,000 bucks must be big money for that poor bugger." (WCS 12)

Buddha: the Buddha

/buddə/ Buddha (the article 'the' is omitted in BSE) ° *the teachings of the Buddha*

□ Buddha Sasana

/buddə sāsənə/ the Buddhist religion (Sinhala) ° *the Ministry of Buddha Sasana*

buffalo curd

(= **curd**) a milk product similar to yoghurt, made with buffalo milk

♦ For dessert there is buffalo curd and jaggery sauce ... (RF 137)

♦ ... other Galle delicacies which include excellent buffalo curd and treacle ... (YY 92)

buffalo grass

a thick variety of grass

♦ ... and thick tongues of buffalo grass grew everywhere. (MM 64)

♦ There we sat on a thick carpet of buffalo grass ... (BTH 32)

buffer

bumper (on a car) → In BSE, a train has a 'buffer', and a car has a 'bumper'.

buffet

self-service meal → In BSE, a 'buffet' is any meal where you serve yourself; in SLE it suggests something grander, e.g. at a hotel with a wide variety of dishes.

bugged; bugging

(coll.) annoyed; annoying ° *He's really bugging!* ° *She's so inquisitive, I'm getting really bugged with her.* → In BSE, 'bug' (vt) is used as a verb (with an object) meaning 'annoy' or 'get on your nerves' ('Don't bug me!', 'It's really bugging me'); in colloquial SLE it can also be used without an object, and the forms 'bugged' and 'bugging' can be used like adjectives.

bugger

(= **fellow**) (coll.) chap, bloke, guy (dated and more negative in BSE) ° *He's a harmless bugger.* ° *I scolded the bugger!* ° *Bugger didn't even turn up!*

♦ "Trouble is now these other buggers are playing up, no." (MM 134)

♦ "Bugger gets everywhere." (Reef 159)

♦ "Taught the bugger a lesson." (FB 168)

♦ "Where is the bugger?" - "What bugger?" - "Bugger in white." (YY 76)

♦ "These buggers are worse than our buggers," ... (YY 222)

♦ "… and these buggers can't even see that." (WMD 230)

♦ "Bugger died years ago." (SG 102)

♦ "This bugger is useless," … (CG 159)

♦ "I knew it would put the wind up those buggers." (HC 280)

♦ "… our buggers can't bat" … (WE 102)

♦ "This bugger missed a two foot putt on the seventeenth," ... (FSD 52)

♦ "This bugger is up to something." (GC 247)

♦ "Bugger has a camera with a big bloody zoom on it, and he's taking shots." (CU 180)

♦ "Buggers have been a bit touchy about terrorism lately." (CU 355)

♦ "I have nothing to tell that bugger." (M&P 64)

buggy, buggy cart

(dated) a small **bullock cart** used for carrying people (Sinhala bakki karatte)

BUGGY CART

♦ They would arrive around eleven in buggy carts pulled by bulls … (RF 40)

♦ … and many went in buggy-carts … and Viva lit crackers outside and startled the skittish bulls who nearly took off with the buggies. (JFT 51-2)

♦ This pleasant native doctor came riding in a handsome buggy cart. The brass lamps, bell and varous other fittings were highly polished. The bull drawing the buggy cart was jet black, with a cluster of jingling bells tied around its neck. The tips of the bull's horns too were covered wth shining brass fittings. (CM 54)

♦ They travelled by train from Panadura and hired a buggy cart to bring them through the village to our home. ... I still remember the overwhelming outburst of joy to see them alight from the buggy at our gate.(CM 77)

♦ Even the buggy in which Tissa and he had gone from the station to the village seemed somehow familiar, ... (WMD 20)

♦ Once a week, with a servant in attendance, our buggy cart carried me into the nearest town, several miles distant, for my elocution class. (HC 18)

♦ They were met by the blaze of too many lamps and the silhouette of a buggy crouching before the verandah. (HC 175)

bulath
/bulat/ (= **betel**) (Sinhala)

BULATH

♦ In front the zinc-topped counter is flanked by a betel box and stacks of heart-shaped green *bulath* leaves neatly stacked stem on stem, groove on groove. (MM 116)

♦ He went out to inspect their work and was particularly pleased with the discovery of a *bulath* vine, woven around the trunk of a *lovi* tree. (HC 137)

♦ He chewed slowly on his wad of *bulath* pushing it from one jaw to the other with his tongue. ... He spat out a long stream of *bulath* juice on to her feet. (WE 45)

bulbul
/bulbul/ (= **kondaya**) a small black bird with a crest on its head (also India etc., from Arabic)

♦ ... the arrows I tipped with flattened nails, fletched with *bulbul* feathers. (Reef 55)

♦ Birds favoured this tree, which housed a large pair of rat snakes at its roots, especially the barbet, the forest bul-bul, the leaf bird, the white-eye. (TT 114)

♦ ... bulbuls drinking at a tank ... (AG 227)

bullock cart
a cart pulled by a bullock and used for transporting goods, etc.

BULLOCK CART

♦ Already a bullock-cart was trundling its way to Wellawatte, ... (JFT 62)

♦ Until the family moved, in a procession of bullock carts, to Wellawatte, ... (TT 35)

♦ "Only, when I used to come as a young man to Jaffna, we had single bullock carts, now you have double bullock carts." (WMD 139)

♦ Now the car surged forward, nosing between a bullock cart and a colonnade of coconut trees. (HC 146)

♦ And a bullock cart rolls towards them. The bullock cart man beats the bull and shouts at it. (KCS 39)

♦ "Shall we hire a bullock cart to carry the prize home?" (PMS 251)

□ bullock cart pace
snail's pace, very slowly ° *Peace talks moving at bullock cart pace*

bull's eye
a fried egg

bulto
/bulʈo/ a type of hard boiled sweet made with **jaggery**

♦ The boutique sold a little of every thing from *Janatha Beedi* to *Gunasiri Bulto*. (WCS 60)

bun

bread roll (sweet or savoury) (> **short eats**) → In BSE a 'bun' is either plain or sweet, but not savoury.

bund

/banɒ/ dam, dyke, the wall of a **tank**; also the low mud dyke around a paddy field (Anglo-Indian, from Hindi) ° *Let's go for a walk along the bund.*

♦ The kabaragoya is in fact a useful scavenger and is now protected by law as it preys on fresh water crabs that undermine and ruin the bunds of paddy fields. (RF 73)

♦ Turning uphill they swayed up the road to the Nuwara Wewa bund … (YY 145)

♦ "What were you doing on the bund at this hour and without your clothes?" (YY 150)

♦ … and where the road crossed the narrow strip of paddy land must have been the bund of the now vanished tank. (BTH 49)

♦ Somaweera sat on the bund near the well and gazed at the field … (OD 62)

♦ "The road by the bund will be guarded. If we keep heading south on the by-roads, avoiding the bund, we will cross the rail track," … (REP 48)

♦ A bund bursts inside me and I feel tears pour down my face. (GC 158)

♦ Miss Kanthi takes them to her favourite spot by the bund for the environment lesson. (PMS 105)

bundi

/banɒi/ (= **bada**) (coll.) tummy, belly (Sinhala) ° *She has a big bundi.*

♦ "What? But you are newly-married, no? And your wife, young thing, no? and already getting a bundy." (JFT 139)

♦ "Sha. Pukka big bundy. Nice big baby for sure." (YY 138)

bungalow

a large house (Anglo-Indian, from Hindi) (> **circuit bungalow, estate bungalow, running bungalow**) → In BSE, a 'bungalow' is a small, modest single-storied house; in SLE, as in India etc., it suggests something grander, sometimes with two storeys, and often in the country (e.g. on an estate or in a national park). It can also be a place where people stay temporarily, e.g. on holiday or on official duty.

♦ … three of us and one servant rattle around this huge long bungalow … (RF 166)

♦ The bungalow is down a bumpy lane off the main coast road. (MM 89)

♦ The bungalow we had rented surpassed all my expectations. (FB 114)

♦ There is a bungalow 'boy' to see that drivers and guards are comfortably ensconced. (YY 92)

♦ The headmistress's bungalow was on Mission Road, the lane that ran by the school. (CG 90)

♦ It was the usual signal that a car was on its way to the bungalow. (HC 114)

♦ The old holiday bungalow had been a comfortable building of stone and timber, with a wide, open verandah at the front of it. (REP 155)

◆ They had left the bungalow just as the sun was rising. (SMS 195)

◆ The house was a two-storey construction and built in the style of a Dutch colonial bungalow. (CU 58)

□ **bungalow keeper**
the person employed to look after a **bungalow**

◆ But the gates were kept padlocked and the bungalow-keeper had orders to turn visitors away, ... (HC 147)

◆ I crawled into what must have once been the bungalow keeper's backyard and home garden. (REP 156)

Burgher

/bāgə/ (n/adj.) a member of the community of Sri Lankans of Dutch, Portuguese or other European descent (orig. Dutch); adjective (coll. and derogatory): **Burgherish** (> Dutch Burgher)

◆ The result was a hotch-potch that was, for convenience, classified as Burgher (from the Dutch 'burgher' or townsman). ... The Burghers found immense favour with the British because their mother tongue was English, ... It's hard to find a 'true' Burgher today. (JFT 27-8)

◆ "In those days, Burghers thought they were a cut above other Sri Lankans." (FB 80)

◆ "And since this is a celebration, we'll even ask that burgher bugger to join us." (July 16)

◆ Burghers emigrated in their droves to Australia and England to join relatives already there, becoming cinema ushers and cleaning ladies. (July 40)

◆ Emma had the unmistakable look of a Burgher, which only other Burghers recognize. (MiP 19)

◆ "Wilson could be a Burgher name. In fact you do look like a Burgher." (Z 139)

◆ Ravi noticed with amusement that there were no formalities in a Burgher household. (FSD 96-7)

◆ Various Burgher associations in the West contributed generously to the upkeep of the home. (SMS 163)

◆ With her Germanic surname and her fair-skinned Burgher looks she blended in well. (CU 104)

◆ The Burghers were the descendants of the European colonists who had first come to Sri Lanka in the seventeenth and eighteenth centuries. ... Sri Lankan Burgher families jealously guarded their colour, heritage and family names; ... (CU 107)

◆ "How do those half burgher people know of our Sinhala customs?" (M&P 233)

□ **Burgher girl**
a girl from a **Burgher** family ° 'A Nice Burgher Girl' by Jean Arasanayagam

◆ ... their brother, the eldest in that family too, had married a Burgher girl from Galle ... (OM 18)

◆ ... and the Burgher girls in their immaculate white uniforms ... (BTH 41)

◆ Dierdre looked in on them, muttered a quick prayer that they would marry good burgher girls and went off to bed. (July 49)

◆ Burgher girls sipping long drinks on the verandah, ... (HC 84)

◆ Ravi thought how strange it was that his mum had always warned Tilak and him about getting entangled with Burgher girls. (FSD 161)

buriya

/buriyə/ navel (Sinhala)

- "She'll chase me off and you'll have to marry one of those creatures with rings in the *buriya*." (GC 231)

buriyani

/buriyāni/ a rice dish cooked with meat (India: biriyani)

- Then comes the sweet smell of cooking buriyani ... (KCS 64)

buru anda

/būru ændə/ (= camp bed, donkey bed) a folding bed consisting of a piece of **gunny** on a simple wooden frame (Sinhala)

BURU ANDA

bus halt

(= halt) bus stop ° *Where is the nearest bus halt?*

- It never stopped at the bus halt, but a few feet away. (July 24)

- Buses ploughed past bus halts reluctant to stop ... (July 138)

- The authorities agreed to move the bus halt to some other spot. (KCS 29)

bush coat

a lightweight short-sleeved cotton jacket

bush shirt

a short-sleeved shirt worn outside the trousers and often worn on formal occasions

- I had tried to get rid of that yellow bush-shirt many times. (Reef 80)

- The sweat under his arms turned the light blue of his cotton bush shirt to a patchy dark blue. (July 4)

- He had begun the day clad in trousers and a bush shirt, ... (HC 70)

- I saw him lying there, in his office trousers and the khaki bush shirt. (M&P 167)

- My brother Rasitha got bush shirts in all sizes until the age of five. (M&P 324)

- The school inspector is a plump man in trousers and bush shirt. (PMS 65)

- ... the shopkeeper is smartly dressed in a bush shirt and clean white sarong. (PMS 161)

businessman

shopkeeper; also used to refer to any person who is self-employed → In BSE, a 'businessman' suggests someone who is wealthy, perhaps involved in more than one business; in SLE, it can mean something much more modest.

bus stand

bus station ° *the Pettah bus stand*

- Rickshaws had been hired to take the family to the Galle Road and the bus stand to the Fort. (YY 33)

- "Put him at the Mount Lavinia bus stand," ... (TT 142)

- ... going once in a while to see a film and meeting at bus stands after tuition classes. (July 73)

- A police car cruised by, slowing down to a crawl as it passed the bus stand. (July 290)

♦ "Pick up something simple and go over to the bus-stand." (REP 310)

♦ "The office van will drop us at the Pettah bus stand." (FSD 67)

♦ "I'll tell the driver to drop you at the bus stand." (GC 123)

♦ Finally Paduma decides that they've seen enough and leads them towards the bus stand. (PMS 147)

bust up
(vt) blow (money), spend recklessly ° *She bust up her full salary on the first day.* ° *Top officials busting up funds* → In BSE, to 'bust up' (vi) means to 'break up' (e.g. of a couple).

but
(coll.) (word order) (> **so**) ° *Tasty food. Lot of oil but.* ° *They lost in Colombo but.* → In colloquial SLE, 'but' and 'so' can sometimes come at the end of the sentence; this will never happen in BSE.

♦ "Are these genuine passports, but?" (CU 29)

butter
(v) butter somebody up, suck up to somebody ° *You have to butter them, no?*

butter cake
a plain cake made with butter, sugar, flour and eggs

♦ The butter cake is still hot from the oven, she warns us. I have never tasted homemade butter cake before. (GC 122)

butter fruit
avocado pear (also known in colonial times as 'alligator pear')

by
at (a point in time) ° *We'll be leaving by end of August.* → In BSE, 'by' as in the example means 'at or before'; in SLE it usually means 'at (not before)'.

by-heart
(v) learn by heart ° *We had to by-heart the whole poem.*

C

cabook

/kəbuk/ (= **kabook**) laterite, a reddish clay which becomes hard and is used as a building material (from Portuguese)

cad

(coll.) a womaniser; adj.: **caddish** (dated in BSE)

cadjan

/kæjæn/ dried palm leaves woven together and used to make roofs, fences, etc. (Anglo-Indian, orig. Malay) ° *a cadjan hut* → BSE pronunciation: /kæjən/

CADJAN HUT

- ♦ ... enjoying a panoramic view of the Indian Ocean and his plot of *cadjan cabanas*. (MM 82)

- ♦ ... a whistle of blue flame shot out and climbed the *cadjan* fronds. (Reef 17)

- ♦ Stout cadjan classrooms burn easily, ... (TT 111)

- ♦ On the Wellawatte bank was a colony of squatters in cadjan huts ... (TT 194)

- ♦ "The well's over there, ... behind the *cadjan* fence, ..." (WMD 14)

- ♦ The nights he spent slapping mosquitoes in a cadjan thatched shack. (OD 9)

- ♦ "Only the roofing is different, some have green sheets but mostly they are of cadjan or straw." (GC 306)

- ♦ ... a little piece of land left by his grandfather, where he literally camped out in a cadjan hut till the warehouse was built. (CP 181)

- ♦ ... the sea bar, a wood and cadjan structure built between the swimming pool and the beach, ... (CU 294)

cadju, cadjunut

/kaju/ cashew, cashew nut (Sinhala; also India, from South America via Portuguese) ° *devilled cadju* ° *cadjunut curry*

- ♦ "Cinnamon, or *cadju* or whatever." (MM 20)

- ♦ And *cadju* - cashew nuts - fresh from the countryside. (Reef 75)

- ♦ The wind moaned through the leaves of the cadju trees, ... (OM 3)

- ♦ Some played the cadju nut game on the gravel road. (CM 67)

cadre

/kāðə/ (nc) a member of a military or revolutionary organisation (e.g. the LTTE, JVP, etc.); (nu) staff, employees, esp. of a government institution ° *the movement of LTTE cadres into the Eastern Province* ° *Tiger gunman kills Karuna cadre in hospital* ° *university cadre* → In BSE, 'cadre' is normally restricted to the sense of a group of employees, soldiers, etc. with a particular role or rank ('officer cadre'), but even in this sense it is rarely heard. It is also used in the context of Communist countries to refer to a Party member or an official in a government or military organisation.

- ♦ Their cadres, especially the women, had perfected the art, or science, of suicide bombing. (REP 10)

- ♦ A uniformed cadre stood near the entrance and pointed to a long wooden bench inside. (REP 44)

♦ "Our cadres are poised to take control." (GC 340)

cage
/kēj/ a box or table on an official form ° *Give the relevant details in the cages provided.*

cager
/kējə/ basketball player (> **cueist, grappler, lifter, paddler, pugilist, ruggerite, scrabbler, shuttler, slicer, soccerite, spiker, sticker**) ° *a cager tourney* ° *Mercantile cagers on song, retain title* → There are a number of words for sportsmen and women which are popular with Sri Lankan journalists, especially in headlines, but which are not found in BSE.

cake structure
an artificial wedding cake made of polystyrene (also **kiribath structure**)

call: to call somebody for something
to invite somebody to something (a meal, party, etc.) ° *We forgot to call Nalini and them for the wedding.*

called as
(coll.) called ° *He likes to be called as Sam.*

camp
a public clinic or sports training programme ° *health camp* ° *eye camp* ° *blood donation camp* ° *rugger camp* ° *cricket coaching camp*

camp bed
(= **buru anda, donkey bed**) a folding bed consisting of a piece of **gunny** on a simple wooden frame

campus
university (> **varsity**) ° *He's a graduate of Peradeniya campus.* ° *She's studying at campus.* ° *Are you going to campus?* → In BSE, 'campus' is used in the limited sense of the buildings, grounds, etc. which comprise a university, and would normally be used with the article 'the'. In SLE it is much more common as a general word for university and is often used (like 'university' in BSE) without the article.

♦ … to hear a local or visiting South Asian writer read from a new book at the Kelaniya campus. (AG 228)

♦ She had started at Colombo campus last year and was apparently doing very well with her degree studies. (July 243)

♦ Somaweera remembered that there had been reports of trouble both in the Colombo and Peradeniya campuses. (OD 12)

♦ "Yes, I'd say we had a good time although politics on campus was a nuisance." (REP 105)

♦ Dr. Gunapala is new to the campus. (GC 135)

can (1)
/kæn/ (vt) cancel, abandon ° *I'm afraid we'll have to can the meeting.*

♦ His father … had suddenly decided to can the Royal College and pack him off to St Thomas' College in Gurutalawa. (TT 100)

can (2)
/kæn/ could, might, may (> **could**) ° *An important letter can arrive this week.*

□ can; can't
(coll.) yes (I can); no (I can't), etc. (> **have**) ° *Can you come tomorrow? - Can!* ° *Will you go and buy a pound of bread? - Aiyo, can't!* ° *She's a person who can't say can't to anyone.* → In SLE, 'can' and 'can't' commonly stand alone where BSE would require a full sentence with pronoun, etc. ('Yes I can', 'I'm sorry, I can't').

□ can't

it's impossible ° *Can't with these children!*

♦ "Can't with those boys, Mummy. Always putting their sticks and raising my dress in front of everyone." (YY 130)

□ can't be

it can't be true

♦ "Those people must have gone somewhere." - "Can't be. I heard them earlier in the morning." (Reef 28)

♦ "Is the MSD involved?" - "Can't be. The Minister has resigned." (FSD 194)

♦ "She said seven days from yesterday." - "Can't be, ... Holidays only started a few days ago." (PMS 207)

□ can't help

it can't be helped

□ can't say

I don't know, you can't tell, who knows?

♦ "Could it be something like that? But after all this time? Can't say, and I even dreamt of my father last night!" (OD 15)

canard

rumour, hoax, false report (orig. French) ° *President to expose opposition canards in parliament.* → This is one of several words favoured by Sri Lankan journalists, but rare in modern BSE.

candlestand

candlestick

canopy

soft top, folding roof (on a car)

cap: to cap somebody, to put a cap to somebody

(= put a break, put a line) (coll., dated) to chat somebody up, approach somebody

with romantic intentions ° *I saw him capping her!*

♦ "Why don't you put a cap to Therese?" (TT 195)

caparison

a decorated cloth worn by an elephant, e.g. in a **perahera**; (v) to wear a caparison ° *caparisoned elephants*

CAPARISON

♦ The magnificent tusker is caparisoned in a cloth of gold that shimmers in the moonlight. (PMS 245)

card pack

pack of cards

carpet

a tarmac surface on a road; (v) to surface a road with tarmac ° *a carpet road* ° *I didn't know this road had been carpeted.*

carrom

/kœrəm/ a popular game in which 2 or 4 players hit pieces like draughtsmen (called **men** or **dogs**) into pockets at the 4 corners of a square table, by flicking a larger piece called the **striker** (also played in India and other Asian countries) ° *carrom board* ° *carrom tournament* ° *carrom men*

♦ ... carom tournaments and tombola evenings. (YY 109)

♦ Rabot stared, then thumped the carom board and crowed till tears ran down his cheeks. (YY 212)

♦ ... when Carloboy came in to play carrom with her brothers. (TT 211)

CARROM

- The Bridge Federation was housed in the grandstand of the Colombo racecourse, along with a host of other sports bodies from carom to hockey. (FSD 278)

- Selvi found Carom boring and she excused herself and went to talk with one of her friends on the phone. (SMS 154)

- We were certainly not going to play carom. (M&P 271)

carter
bullock cart driver (rare in BSE)

- Viva rode the bullock-cart to show the carter the way … (JFT 62)

- The old carter told me that Missiya was in a bad way. (OM 48)

- When the buggy cart stopped at our gate, the carter tapped on the bell, tang! tang!! (CM 77)

- "I remember the carters' strike like it was yesterday," … (WMD 55)

- Even the way the carter shouts at the bulls is the same, only the carter has changed. (WMD 139)

- There are more carts than motor vehicles and the bulls amble along with the carters nodding under the awning, the ropes gone limp in their hands, … (BTH 17)

- … because a bullock had been knifed in a brawl between two carters twenty yards down the track. (HC 174)

- The cart was piled high with vegetables but the carter, another white haired man with betel stained teeth, made room for them to sit at the rear of the cart facing backwards. (FSD 96)

case
/kēs/ (= **one**) (coll.) person (after an adjective, often with a negative connotation) ° *a boru case* ° *a chronic case* ° *a crack case* ° *a useless case* ° *a mara case* ° *a pandan case* ° *a last-minute case* → In BSE, this use of 'case' is usually restricted to people with medical or mental problems (e.g. 'a mental case').

cassette
/kǽsət/ cassette recorder → Note on pronunciation: This word (like 'gazette') would be pronounced with the stress on the second syllable in BSE, whereas in SLE it tends to be pronounced with the stress on the first syllable.

cast: to cast remarks
(= **pass comments, pass hints**) to verbally abuse somebody, to make veiled comments or innuendos about somebody ° *After the announcement of the results, certain people cast remarks on the Basnayake Nilame.*

- "You're the one who will get it, wait and see, everyone casting remarks." (JFT 69)

caste immaterial
(a notice sometimes included in **marriage proposals** published in the newspaper, to show that the prospective partner's caste is not considered a significant factor)

catch up
pick up, improve ° *Chanaka's work has caught up this term.* → In BSE, to 'catch up

(with somebody)' means to reach the same point as somebody else, e.g. in a race or a piece of work: 'Chanaka has caught up with the rest of the class'.

catcher
acquaintance, contact, hanger-on (usually subordinate); **fellow**, guy (expressing slight disapproval) ° *I don't know who he is - must be one of my mother's catchers.*

♦ "I know she's beautiful, but that doesn't mean she's going to marry this catcher," ... (July 284)

♦ "Others in the know are all cops and political catchers." ... "Those who pay a fee to the Minister's catcher get their job done right away." (FSD 110)

cat snake
(= **mapila**) a mildly venomous snake which has an unjustified reputation of being highly venomous

cat wash
a quick wash

caught: to get caught to somebody/something
to get caught by somebody (e.g. the police), to get caught in something (e.g. the rain), to get caught out by somebody/something (e.g. a trick) ° *He's sure to get caught to the rain.* ° *We got caught to the traffic on the way home.* ° *Make sure you don't get caught to the police!* ° *Their vehicle got caught to a suspected LTTE landmine.* ° *Live happily ever after? Don't get caught to the fairy tale!*

♦ By asking for the diaries I feel that I have got caught to one of his tricks. (OD 84)

cease
/sīz/ stop ° *Luckily the rain had ceased when we left.* ° *Hope it ceases by tomorrow.*
→ In BSE, pronounced /sīs/, and restricted to more formal contexts.

♦ The sun was up, the rain had ceased, the road before him was streaked with watery light. (WMD 34)

♦ ... in about an hour's time the rain ceased altogether and there was absolute silence. (BTH 25)

♦ My mother came back and Sunil's visits to the house had to cease. (Z 3)

♦ Thankfully the rain had ceased when Ravi put the van in a slot ... (FSD 128)

♦ "If it is raining, we have to wait until the rain ceases." (KCS 152)

♦ ... but those phones had ceased to ring long ago. (CU 377)

♦ They ceased to fight and ruminated about the sexual antics of Mr. Karunaratne, ... (M&P 85)

celltel
mobile phone (brand name used as a generic term)

♦ ... a nonchalant young man sporting dark sunglasses and carrying his celltel. (Z 35)

cess
a type of tax levied for a particular purpose (also India, Scotland and Ireland; dated in BSE) ° *Cess on manufactured rubber: good or bad?*

Ceylon
the former name of Sri Lanka until 1972 (still used by a number of older English-speaking Sri Lankans; and still used officially in certain contexts); adjective: **Ceylonese** ° *Ceylon tea* ° *Bank of Ceylon* ° *Ceylon Daily News* ° *Ceylon Electricity Board* ° *Ceylon Workers' Congress* ° *'The Good Little Ceylonese Girl' by Ashok Ferrey*

♦ We were now the proud owners of Ceylon tea ... (M&P 194)

□ Ceylonisation

the process of replacing foreign staff with local staff before and after independence in 1948

♦ The Legislative Council had decreed that in the process of 'Ceylonization', Gonpala would be the country's choice as General Manager of Railways. (YY 186)

♦ While other British firms rubbished all talk of Ceylonization, Sanderson Bros. had cautiously welcomed the idea; ... (SG 14)

♦ He was promoted swiftly to fill the vacancies left by the more disillusioned British executives in the firm who could not understand the need for any form of Ceylonization. (SG 21)

□ Ceylonism

a derogatory term for a feature of **Sri Lankan English**

cha!

(Sinhala/Tamil exclamation expressing anger, disgust or disappointment)

♦ "Tchah! Feel like chasing both from here." (JFT 19)

♦ "Tchach! Useless bugger. Big bloody coward, that's what." (YY 168)

chain

/chēn/ necklace → In BSE, this might be called a 'gold chain', but not just a 'chain'.

♦ I donned several of her chains and bangles and studied the effect in the mirror. (FB 50)

chaitya

/chaityə/ (= **dagoba, stupa**) a dome-shaped Buddhist shrine (sometimes spelt **cetiya**; orig. Sanskrit, also Sinhala)

chalk

(nc) piece of chalk ° *Can I borrow a chalk for a minute?*

chance

(in a game) turn, go ° *It's your chance!*

chandiya

/chanɒiya/ (= **thug**) also (coll.) an aggressive or mischievous child (Sinhala) ° *Their small fellow is a real chandiya.*

♦ Everything about him suggested defiance. ... his sarong was hitched up a few inches to let him stride like a *chandiya*. (Reef 49)

♦ ... a savage brutalizing whereby our *chandiyas* - our braggarts - would become thugs, our dissolutes turn into mercenaries and our leaders excel as small-time megalomaniacs. (Reef 118)

♦ Every village had its Chandiya, or Big Cheese, who held sway because he was bigger, stronger, more murderously inclined, more brutal than the others. It was a pastime of up-and-coming young bucks to challenge this position or stage a palace revolution. This was usually done by making the Chandiya very drunk and then carving him up like a Christmas turkey. (YY 81)

♦ "No money, no *chandiyas*." ... No money, no hired killers. (FSD 227)

change money

(coll.) small change ° *Can you give me some change money?*

channel

(vt) make an appointment with (a specialist doctor) ° *Dr Perera can be channelled at the Asiri Hospital.* ° *He has a channel practice.* ° *e-channelling - the easy way to channel your doctor*

chappals

/chappals/ Indian style leather **slippers** (also India, orig. Hindi)

- Indian *chappals*, leather braids and solid plain slab-silver jewellery. (Reef 116)

- ... and he continued going round in his sarong and chappals, always smiling, always carefree. (CP 138)

chatti

/chaᴛᴛi/ (= **hatti**) a shallow earthenware pot used for cooking (Tamil) → In Anglo-Indian, a 'chatty' (from Hindi) is an earthenware water pot.

CHATTI

- "... cooking and pounding and grinding and washing *chatti*-pots (earthenware cooking vessel) and all, ..." (JFT 63)

- With yellow soap and a scrap of coconut husk, Soma scrubbed grease from the clay *chatties* in which the lunchtime curries had cooked. (HC 214)

chee!, chi!

/chī, chi/ (= **chickay!, ee!, eeya!**) ugh! yuk! (Sinhala/Tamil exclamation)

- "*Chee*! What are you doing!" (JFT 5)

- Not like the other ladies - the *nonas* - who screeched *chi, chi, chi* at their servants. (Reef 82)

- "*Chi*! This country will end up like a bloody banana republic." (Reef 145)

- "Chi, chi, chi! No politics." (FB 160)

- "Chee, men, don't sing that song. Take no notice, men. Buggers are all jealous." (YY 111)

- "Chi!" my father would say in an expression of disgust. (WMD 145)

- "Chee, child, can even see her bum and all!" (July 34)

- "Chee! Are you mad?" (GC 150)

- "Chee, ... why would you want to do something so ghastly as become a nun?" (SMS 33)

- "Chee, I don't want to have that ugly thing." (M&P 245)

cheesecake

a small round sweet pastry → In BSE, a 'cheesecake' is a rich dessert made with cream cheese on a biscuit base, and usually with a fruit topping.

- ... his swing was flatter than a Bambalapitiya cheesecake. (SG 16)

cheetu

/chīᴛᴛu/ (= **seetu**) a rotating loan scheme popular with working women (Tamil/Sinhala)

- Every month he sent Malli money as soon as he got his pay, but last month he had to give twenty rupees for the cheetu. (OD 13)

chena

/chēnə/ (= **hena**) an area cleared by 'slash and burn' for cultivation (Tamil) ° *They make their living from chena cultivation.*

- After the monsoon, chena cultivators clear areas of jungle and plant crops. (GC 88)

- "When the chena cultivator burns the forest, you think only ashes remain. Yet, with the first rain, the plants spring up again." (GC 345)

♦ What a remedy it is for their hunger and for their toil on the chenas, which lasted more than five months. (KCS 101)

Chetty, Colombo Chetty

/cheᴛᴛɪ/ a member of a minority Catholic community of South Indian descent (orig. Malayalam)

chickay!

/chikē/ (= chee!, chi!) ugh! yuk! (Sinhala exclamation)

♦ "*Chickay* (Sinhala expression conveying contempt or disgust), that's not enough," ... (JFT 16)

♦ "Chee, chee, cheekay ... I would never have guessed sister Beet! And that woman spoke such good English no?" (M&P 16)

♦ "Cheekay, you are not wearing an underskirt?" (M&P 32)

chicken parts

chicken breasts, thighs, drumsticks, etc.

chief guest

guest of honour

♦ Between episodes she urged me to serve more as though she were the hostess instead of the chief guest. (Reef 98)

♦ Once the chief guest arrived, the national anthem would be sung, followed by a presentation by the Sinhala Dramatic Society. (FB 279)

♦ The drill display is a great success, and Wije Sir, the principal, beams with pleasure when the chief guest congratulates him. (PMS 257)

chief incumbent

the head monk at a Buddhist temple ° *The chief incumbent has dedicated his life to develop the temple.*

Chief Minister

the elected head of a **Provincial Council**

child!

(a colloquial term of address, more often used by women, a more intimate variation of **men!**) ° *What are you telling, child!*

♦ "Never mind, child, you go and boil some water, will you." (JFT 41)

♦ "Yes, child," the old lady replied, laughing mischievously, "must keep up with the times, no?" (WMD 312)

♦ "What, child? What's the matter with you?" (SG 47)

♦ "See, child, can never tell looking at someone's face, no?" (July 68)

♦ "Come, child, let's go to my place and have a cup of tea." (July 328)

chilli pieces

(= **miris kaeli**) dried chilli flakes

chilli powder

(= **miris kudu**)

♦ "Maybe we can put some chilli powder in the water and throw it on the Beligas fellows, ... They won't be able to ride with chilli powder in the eyes." (PMS 186-7)

chimney

the cylindrical glass cover of a kerosene lamp or candle

♦ A table lamp with a smoke-blackened chimney was burning low ... (BTH 27)

Chinese roll

a savoury roll fried in breadcrumbs (like a spring roll) (> **short eats**)

♦ ... and went to the Pagoda for lunch, wincing at what a few Chinese rolls cost, ... (July 79)

- They had already been bribed for the day with a sumptuous breakfast of Chinese rolls, prawn pies and cutlets. (M&P 47)

- "... if you are my friend, I will give you a bite of my Chinese roll." And she pulled out the most scrumptious looking Chinese roll, crisp and golden, bathed in quality coconut oil. (M&P 81)

chinnamma; chittappa
/chinnamma, chittappa/ (= **punchi amma; baappa**) aunt (mother's younger sister) (also **chiththi**); uncle (father's younger brother) (also **chinniah**) (Tamil)

chips
(potato) crisps (also US)

chocolate biscuit pudding
a type of pudding made with layers of biscuits in a chocolate mixture

choli
/chōli/ (= **saree blouse**) (also India, orig. Hindi)

- The short, form-fitting Indian choli that exposed a good deal of midriff had not yet come into fashion. (CG 63)

choo
/chū/ (= **pippy**) pee (children's word) (Sinhala) ° *I think she's done a choo!*

Christian
a member of any Christian denomination other than Catholic (Anglican, Methodist, Baptist, Presbyterian, etc.) → In BSE, a 'Christian' could belong to any Christian denomination, including Roman Catholic.

Christmas flies
flying insects which come in swarms especially around the Christmas season

- A Christmas fly, seduced by the lamp at his elbow, was disintegrating in half an inch of brandy. (HC 240)

- Christmas flies, drawn to the lamp, left a litter of taffeta wings on his blotter. (HC 259)

Christmas weather
dry, windy weather associated with the Christmas season

chronic
(of people) weird, strange, mad ° *She's a chronic case!* ° *Compton was also a chronic case where his memory was concerned.* → In BSE, 'chronic' can mean 'serious' (e.g. of an illness) or colloquially, 'very bad' ('a chronic film').

chummery
/chaməri/ male boarding house (also India, from 'chum')

- Perhaps he should go and live with some of the Jaffna boys who had rented their own house in Kotahena near his uncle Segaram's place. They had their own cook too, a Tamil, and shared all the expenses. A 'chummery', yes, that was what they called it, a 'chummery'. (WMD 18)

- And they in turn brought to the chummery a gaiety that even Uncle Nayagam reluctantly gave in to. Two years later, the chummery broke up. (WMD 21)

chunam
/chunæm/ (= **hunu**) lime paste which is used in the preparation of **betel**; also used for whitewashing houses, etc. (Tamil chunnambu; also India, from Portuguese) (> betel, arecanut)

- I still remember the fascination with which I watched her digging into the folds of her cloth at the waist and coming up with a betel leaf crumpled and warm with the warmth of her young body, a chunam smeared piece of arecanut and popping the bundle into her mouth. (OM 45)

♦ He opened it slowly and extracted a betel leaf, a piece of areca nut and a daub of chunam. He popped the areca nut into his mouth and chewed it thoroughly, contemplatively. Then he placed the chunam and the betel leaf in his mouth and chewed those too, pausing every few seconds to roll the mixture together in his mouth. (July 117)

♦ The wall was soft brick covered with the cheapest local building material - a lime-based stucco called *chunam*, which had been used to front most of the other buildings. (MiP 404)

♦ Mrs. Sarath saw only the blued *chunam* walls, ... (CP 100)

♦ Sumanasiri took out a couple of *Bulath* leaves (betel leaves) and *Puwak* (arecanut) from his shirt pocket and began to chew. In order to increase the acidic taste, he added a lump of Chunam. (WCS 29)

chundu

/chunᴅu/ a quarter measure, i.e. half a pound (of rice) (Tamil; Sinhala hundu) (> **measure**) ° *3 chundus of rice*

♦ ... a *chundu* (a local measure, usually a quantity slightly less than what could be held in a cigarette tin) of salt. (TT 37)

♦ ... rations from the co-op store - the smelly yellowy big grained milchard; six chundus of it at two per coupon, ... (BTH 10)

♦ Two chundus (each a fraction bigger than a tea cup) of rice per person per week, ... (July 39)

♦ The price of a chundi of rice! (HC 252)

churuchurufy

/churuchurufai/ (coll.) drizzle (Sinhala); also whimper (of babies) (> -**fy**) ° *How to go out? It's still churuchurufying.* ° *She's been churuchurufying all day.*

circuit bungalow

a government **bungalow** run as a guest house (originally for government officials touring the country on duty)

♦ "The Minister takes over a circuit bungalow, even a resthouse sometimes, and the lady is brought over to spend the night." (FSD 111)

clamp

(v) clamp down, impose (e.g. a curfew) ° *An 18-hour curfew has been clamped in Trincomalee.*

classical

(of music) traditional → In BSE, 'classical music' refers to the Western classical tradition of Bach, Mozart, etc.; in SLE it can also refer to traditional Sri Lankan music.

♦ Then, the radio station ... began to play a classical song by Visharada Madduma Bandara. (WCS 9)

♦ In addition, he was a unique guy who loved classical music, especially Savan's father's music. (WCS 11)

clean

(v) wipe, dry (something, yourself, etc.) ° *Go and clean your head, you'll catch a cold!*

cleaner

a lorry driver's assistant, reponsible for loading, unloading and cleaning the lorry

♦ … the twosome, the driver and the cleaner of the lorry, vanish into the bushes by the road. (KCS 87)

♦ The cleaner of the truck must have put it there before the logs were loaded, … (PMS 227)

cleared areas
(in the North and East) areas controlled by the Sri Lankan Army, not by the LTTE (> **uncleared areas**)

close
/klōz/ (v) turn off (a tap) (> **open**) ° *Don't forget to close the tap.*

closer to
close to, near ° *My hometown is closer to Pinnawela.*

♦ … who lived in an old house … closer to where I was standing now, … (BTH 49)

♦ By then the party was closer to Raja's mansion, … (KCS 16)

cloth
(= **redda**) a length of material worn round the waist, esp. by women

♦ The bathing cloth kept slipping from her swollen belly and she found it hard to lift the bucket. (OM 30)

♦ "It seems that though he spent a number of years at Cambridge, he only speaks in Sinhala, dresses in a banian and cloth, does not wear slippers and carries a reed bag." (OD 108)

♦ She had finally trounced him in their fight by dropping her cloth and exposing her bearded self: the ultimate line-room insult. (CP 112)

♦ Her cloth had got caught on a nail and she was hanging like a flag at half-mast. (M&P 98)

□ cloth and jacket
(= **redda hatte**) an outfit worn by Sinhala women, esp. of lower social status (> **jacket**)

CLOTH AND JACKET

♦ The woman was in her twenties, swathed in a flowered cloth and with a tight jacket that accentuated her pointed breasts. (TT 65)

♦ At all other times when she went out into the village, she wore a pretty flowered cloth and an embroidered long sleeved jacket. (CM 86)

♦ "I have to get Bisso a cloth and jacket first, for the Sinhalese New Year." (WMD 144)

♦ … a woman dressed in cloth and jacket, … (WMD 167)

coat
/kōt/ jacket (e.g. of a man's suit) (also US) ° *You'll have to wear a coat and tie.*

♦ … and some with coats and sarongs and hair scraped back into topknots. (JFT 51)

♦ … he wore a white coat over a white shirt with a white cloth to match … (WMD 205)

♦ … it was obvious they were the drivers because they were wearing checked sarongs and coats and had walrus moustaches ... (BTH 26)

♦ Inside there were about four or five police officers and several others dressed formally in tie and coat. (OD 33)

♦ Without a "coat" (as a blazer is commonly known) Samare would look just like the clerk he was, she said. (WCS 58)

cocked, cockered

(coll.) drunk ° *Coming home cocked every night!* ° *Fellow was fully cockered.*

coconut arrack

(= **pol arrack**) arrack distilled from **coconut toddy**

♦ ... a small but troubled distillery that had a production plant for local gin and coconut arrack a few miles out of Colombo. (SG 109)

coconut estate

an estate where coconuts are produced

♦ On the coconut estates that had once belonged to the Obeysekeres, there were villagers who could remember the old days at the house. (HC 153)

♦ The paddy gave way to huge coconut estates in some areas, ... (CU 54)

coconut husk

the outer husk of a coconut, used to make **coir**

♦ Almost everyday in the dry season Loku Amma went to thresh coconut husk at a certain spot on the bank of the stream. (CM 22)

♦ The garbage was collecting outside the gate and mosquitoes were beginning to breed in the coconut husks that had fallen out of the bursting garbage sacks. (M&P 219)

coconut milk

(= **polkiri**) the milky juice squeezed from grated coconut mixed with water, and used in cooking → In BSE, 'coconut milk' usually refers to the liquid inside a coconut. In Sri Lanka this is called 'coconut water', and it is usually thrown away, unless it is **king coconut** (**thambili**) or **young coconut** (**kurumba**).

♦ I carried her bundle down to the gate. It smelled of boiled rice and coconut milk, just as she did. (Reef 35)

♦ She mechanically added more coconut milk and stirred the curry, but her mind was far away. (July 255-6)

coconut oil

(= **polthel**) oil used in cooking, and as fuel for **oil lamps**

♦ Romiel was the typical easygoing Sinhalese with no ambition other than to daub coconut oil on his head and strut around to be admired by assorted village girls. (YY 12)

♦ ... an enormous copper cauldron for making coconut oil ... (CM 15)

♦ Through his fancy blue bottle, if not through his dealings in coconut oil, ... (SG 145)

♦ The servants' room was pungent with coconut oil. (HC 164)

♦ Conscious of quiet mastery, he filled leaf-shaped lamps with coconut oil and arrayed them on the flat-topped verandah wall. (HC 208)

♦ A few barely evident strands of hair flattened with coconut oil made my head look like a butter nylon sari. (M&P 41)

♦ Aunty Magdalena had to buy extra coconut oil to remove the chewed gum from her servant's naked feet. (M&P 207)

coconut plucker

a person who climbs **coconut trees** to pick coconuts (> **pluck**)

- The audience, a motley crew of people from brewers of illicit liquor and coconut-pluckers to toddy-tappers and vegetable sellers ... (WCS 61)

- Only daytime's coconut pluckers who became night time's toddy tappers were able to climb coconut trees. (M&P 126)

coconut rock

a type of sweet made with coconut and cut into small squares

coconut sambol

(= **pol sambol**) a **sambol** made with grated coconut with **chilli powder**, lime, salt and onions (> **sambol**)

- Caroline and some of the women cut onions, scraped coconut, pounded chilli and maldive fish to make a good quantity of coconut sambol. (CM 81)

- Fried dry fish and coconut sambol were extra. (REP 318)

- Her mother was bending over his plate, serving him coconut sambol. (WE 24)

coconut scraper

(= **hiramane**) an implement used to grate coconuts; either a low stool with a round serrated blade attached, or a device which can be clamped to a table-top, with a handle which turns the blade (> **scrape**)

- She sat back on the coconut scraper and tied her hair high on her head, hitched her cloth more tightly at her waist and stood up. (OM 29)

- Then the women sat on several coconut scrapers around this huge basin, scraping coconut. (CM 60)

- "Lanterns, matches, candles, kerosene oil, a soiled-linen bag, a coconut scraper," ... (HC 178)

coconut scrapings

grated coconut

coconut toddy

toddy made from the flower of the **coconut tree**

- There was Wadduwa where the finest coconut toddy could be drunk. (YY 62)

- "Hmm, this is nice, refreshing, different from coconut toddy, ..." (WMD 216)

coconut tree

palm tree, coconut palm

COCONUT TREES

- Sat on the verandah looking out onto coconut trees, ... (RF 199)

- I remembered the coconut trees of my childhood, ... (Reef 43)

- ... urchins who would suddenly emerge from behind coconut trees to throw missiles at the train. (YY 83)

- I watched the sun come up above the coconut trees and knew it was time for the walk to the well ... (OM 20)

- A squirrel scampered up a coconut tree. (WMD 30)

- Niranjan looked at the coconut trees on his side of the road and wondered what Priyanthi was thinking. (July 87)

- The coconut trees against the wall swayed and ducked behind each other, ... (HC 233)

- "My, how Tammy has grown! Like a coconut tree, no?" (FSD 187)

- Distant coconut trees and rocks shimmered like a mirage. (SMS 174)

- ... and a half-wit called Thomas who had fallen from a coconut tree when he was young ... (CP 11)

- ... hair flattened with coconut oil; un-oiled section tied into a coconut tree with white ribbon at root and sent to school. (M&P 43)

coffee morning
a fund-raising event, often organised by and for women at a five-star hotel, and including fashion shows, etc. ° *"Lean On Me", a coffee morning organized by the Police Seva Vanitha Unit to raise funds for police personnel who are disabled and bedridden due to injuries in the line of duty, was held on March 4 at the Holiday Inn, Colombo.* → In BSE a 'coffee morning' is a much more modest affair, usually a social event held in a private house, often organised by and for women.

coil
(= **mosquito coil**) ° *Bring a coil will you.*

coir
/kwaiə/ coconut fibre, used to make ropes, brushes, mats, etc. (also India, from Malayalam/Tamil) ° *rubberised coir mattresses* → In BSE, coir mats (pron. /koiə/) are known as 'coconut matting'.

- ... his large, dreamily soft bed with its padding and coir and coiled springs. (Reef 23)

- ... as she stepped in through the rear door wiping the mud of the fields from her bare feet on the coir rug. (OM 19)

- During the day she worked, weaving coconut branches or making coir. (OM 48)

- Making coir string coils was done only once a week. (CM 23)

- Maidenhair spilt from coir-lined hanging baskets. (HC 162)

- Dried and varnished palmyrah fronds, imported from Jaffna, covered the walls, and coir rugs softened the floor. (CU 275)

□ coir rope
rope made of **coir**

- It had been placed in a seated posture and tied securely, the coir rope looped around a buffer as well. (YY 67)

- ... I had him on a thin coir rope with one end tied to my trouser buckle ... (BTH 12)

- At about two-foot intervals, strong coir rope made footholds right up to the top of the tree. (July 115)

- A rusty tin tied with a short length of coir rope had served to draw out the water. (REP 29)

- ... an improvised rope ladder made by tying knots at regular intervals on a thick coir rope. (FSD 225)

- We wind lengths of coir rope round our waists ... (GC 99)

- A ragged shirt covers the upper body and a sarong is tied at the waist with coir rope. (PMS 169)

COL

cost of living

Colombo Chetty

(= Chetty)

- ♦ "So you're Tamils, no?" the driver said, looking at them through the rear-view mirror. "Colombo Chetties," Violet said, squeezing Nirmala's hand. Colombo Chetties weren't Jaffna Tamils. (July 337)

Colombo 7

the smartest residential area of Colombo: stereotypical residents of Colombo 7 are rich, Westernised, English-speaking, etc. ° *Colombo 7 types*

- ♦ As the dinner progressed she felt that every trick in the Colombo Seven social book was being used against her. (AG 143)

- ♦ Here, down these quietly expensive Colombo 7 streets, everything was normal enough. (July 346)

- ♦ "Why Carmen, it's only a Colombo 7 Madame who would call bus travel fun ..." (Z 78)

- ♦ Bright red cars, fast clubs and Colombo 7 women, or do I mean fast cars, Colombo 7 clubs and bright red women? (CP 46)

- ♦ Savan was furious by the time he arrived at the posh Colombo 7 house, which served as his office. (WCS 10)

colour

(after red, blue, etc. where it would not be included in BSE) ° *blue colour* ° *a red colour dress*

- ♦ "That blue shirt. You know my blue shirt, where is it?" ... "Blue colour?" (Reef 84)

□ to see the colour of somebody

(coll.) to lay eyes on somebody ° *I haven't seen the colour of him.*

colour fish

tropical fish

colour lights

traffic lights ° *Turn left at the colour lights.*

colour pencil

crayon, coloured pencil

colour-wash

(v) paint (a house, etc.) with coloured distemper ° *We have to get the house colour-washed.* → In BSE, a house is usually either 'painted' or 'whitewashed'; in Sri Lanka it is common to use different coloured distempers.

comb

/kōm/ bunch, hand (of bananas)

COMB OF PLANTAINS

- ♦ So Tommyboy's bananas are carried to the Guards Inspector's Office where the bunch is cut into several combs and the driver gets a share, ... (JFT 198)

- ♦ "We might as well eat if the train is going to be stuck here," she said as she brought out a comb of bananas. (WE 84)

- ♦ Ravi bought a small comb of bananas and a packet of cream crackers for their breakfast. (FSD 69)

come

come back ° *At what time will you come?*

□ **come!**

(coll.) come in! come on! come here! come with me! (> **sit!**) → In BSE, 'Come!' is usually said only to a dog.

♦ Sir John says "come" and begins to stroll into the garden with the food under his arm. (RF 157)

♦ "Come, come and sit." (JFT 180)

♦ "Come, come, sit, sit." (FB 159)

♦ "Come, akka," ... (CG 223)

♦ "Come, let's go." (July 63)

♦ "Come-come, child, I have something I simply must tell you." (SMS 75)

□ **come go!**

(coll.) come on! let's go!

♦ "For goodness sake come go," ... (JFT 83)

♦ "Then come go home and you rest awhile." (JFT 152)

♦ "Come go inside and wait." (JFT 202)

♦ "Come go to that boutique for a little." (TT 83)

□ **come to show/give/tell you something**

(coll.) come here, I want to show/give/tell you something ° *Come to show you something!* ° *Come to give you a present.* ° *Come to tell you a secret.*

□ **to come to know**

to hear, find out, get to know (less common in BSE, where it suggests finding something out gradually) ° *I came to know about the class today only.* ° *The accused had first visited Sri Lanka in 2001 and had lived with a family he had come to know here.*

♦ And now everybody will come to know and snigger at her and point and whisper in church ... (JFT 107)

♦ "Only thing is if the papers come to know." (YY 108)

♦ "Yes, I went to their house in Kalutara just after I joined the post office and came to know Tissa." (WMD 76)

♦ The family was reunited at last, and I was coming to know my father and Leela and Ram and my mother and Ganesh and Premi all over again. Or, rather, it was another way of knowing them, my father in particular. I was coming to know him like a friend. (WMD 147)

♦ ... the four mango trees; only two were there when I came to know the place, ... (BTH 9)

♦ It had been three days - I came to know later of course - since I had got into that position. (BTH 21)

□ **come to think**

(coll.) come to think of it ° *I think I use it myself, come to think.*

□ **to come down** (1)

to come from abroad ° *They're living in Australia, but they came down for their daughter's wedding.*

□ **to come down** (2)

to fail (an exam) ° *She came down in maths.*

□ **to come off**

to leave ° *We came off early.*

□ **to come up**

to be built ° *Lot of new houses are coming up in our lane.* ° *The two-storey building coming up on a 240-perch land is expected to cost about Rs. 200 million.*

□ **to come of age**

(= **attain age, cross, grow up**) (of a girl) to reach puberty (> **big girl**) → In BSE, to 'come of age' is to reach adulthood, at the age of 18 or 21.

- ♦ It was like an initiation, like when Saraswathi came of age. (WMD 66)

- ♦ ...temple festivals and coming-of-age ceremonies ... (WMD 141)

- ♦ I spent ten days designing the kit I was going to wear for my coming of age party. (M&P 233)

☐ **come or go, Chicago!**
(coll.) come what may, whatever the consequences

coming
next ° *Then I'll see you coming Friday.* → In BSE, 'coming' is only used to mean 'next' together with an article: 'in the coming week', 'this coming Sunday'.

commence
begin, start (restricted to more formal contexts in BSE)

commerce subjects
a set of subjects studied for A levels (economics, accounts, commerce) (> **bio-science**)

committed to do something
committed to doing something ° *The President said the government was firmly committed to maintain law and order.*

- ♦ Today Jaffna was in flames and I was now committed to cross the entire length of the country, illegally too, with this strange and unpredictable woman. (REP 63)

commode
/kəmōd/ a toilet with a seat (also US but dated) → In BSE, a 'commode' is a portable toilet for the sick and the elderly.

- ♦ I could see him sitting on the commode every night with his head in his hands, ... (MM 72)

compound
garden, yard, the enclosure round a house (Anglo-Indian, from Malay 'kampong')
° *He sweeps the compound every morning.*
→ In BSE, a school or factory may have a compound, but a private house has a garden or a yard.

- ♦ And he had hardly recognized her when, returning from his bath at the well one morning, he saw her in the kitchen compound, pounding rice. (WMD 43)

- ♦ There was an old man with grey hair on his chest standing by the bamboo wicket in the compound right next to the Big House ... (BTH 51)

- ♦ After some time his father was well enough to hobble about the house and compound with the aid of a stick. (OD 6)

- ♦ He rose and went out into the compound, and hurled the pillow over the wall to rot in the jungle. (HC 271)

- ♦ For the first time since his cousin had come to stay, he was smoking within the compound of their home. (SMS 185)

con
(coll.) (n/vi) lie; **conner:** liar ° *I'm sure he was conning.* ° *It must have been a con.*
° *He's a real conner!* → In BSE, 'con' is more specific in meaning: a 'con' (n) is a confidence trick; to 'con' somebody (vt) is to trick somebody; and a 'con man' is a person who tricks others (esp. for money).

con chat
(coll.) small talk, a polite chat ° *Go and put a con chat with her mother.*

confab
(= **parley, pow-wow**) (in newspaper headlines) conference, meeting ° *an all-*

party confab → In BSE, 'confab' is a dated word for a private chat.

conjee

/kanji/ (= **kanji, kenda**) a rice broth (from Tamil)

- ♦ "Like to eat some rice *conjee* (thin rice porridge), ... With small piece of jaggery." ... Maudiegirl swallowed two spoons of the *conjee* and lay back. (JFT 72-3)

- ♦ ... and shouting instructions to the lone kitchen help that the cunji must be brought hot and the lunu miris must not be forgotten, ... (Z 177)

conk off

(coll.) conk out, break down, die ° *Must do it now before it conks off.* ° *Must have conked off last night.*

consult

see, go to (a doctor, etc.) (restricted to formal contexts in BSE) ° *You should consult a doctor immediately.*

convey

send (wishes, regards, etc.) (restricted to formal contexts in BSE) ° *Please convey my regards to your wife.*

cook appu

(dated) a male cook (> **appu**)

cook woman

(= **kussiamma**) a female cook

- ♦ Anna was filling in the family on her many clashes with the cookwoman ... (JFT 205)

- ♦ ... Lucy-*amma*, the very first person I had met in the house, Mister Salgado's cook-woman. (Reef 19)

- ♦ But the cookwoman had opened a tin and curried some mackerel for him. (HC 239)

cool drink

soft drink

- ♦ "Would you like a cool drink or tea?" (WMD 298)

- ♦ The other two hundred was spent on bus fares and cool drinks under hot umbrellas. (July 251)

- ♦ One of the shop assistants mistook him for a customer and tried to sell him a "cool drink". (WCS 29)

cool spot

a small bar/café selling soft drinks

coolie

(dated) unskilled labourer, esp. toilet cleaner or estate labourer (Anglo-Indian, from Tamil; archaic and derogatory in BSE) (> **latrine coolie**)

- ♦ ... and Viva felt that a coolie could be pressed into service to tend the yard and grow more vegetables. (JFT 131)

- ♦ Railway coolies stopped to listen to a shrieking Revathy ... (YY 49)

- ♦ ... he was a coolie Indian and entitled to nothing. (WMD 80)

- ♦ Just ahead of them were the coolie quarters, ... (WMD 101)

- ♦ "He is afraid of being called a coolie and tries to hide his pottu." (WMD 163)

- ♦ "No, no, ... we were coolies, high-class coolies, administrative coolies who kept the government services running. ... From south India they got the plantation coolies and from north Ceylon, the service coolies." (WMD 217)

- ♦ "You may be content to live in a servile fashion under the British, howling and bowing like coolies, but some of us are more manly than that." (CG 70)

♦ "Your coolies still swear they found the watch near the path where Hamilton was murdered." (HC 88)

♦ "The police didn't press too hard - you couldn't expect them to exert themselves over a dead coolie - ..." (HC 290)

□ coolie lines
(= line rooms) (dated) estate labourers' accommodation

♦ "I'll take you down to the coolie lines, ... and you can see for yourself." (WMD 100)

♦ Sanji was the son of an estate shopkeeper who ... had broken from the coolie lines to set himself up in business. (WMD 116)

♦ Suspicion fell on the coolies. ... The coolie lines were searched. (HC 96)

♦ "Have you forgotten that we went about those coolie lines together, you and I, enquiring into conditions on the estates?" (HC 287)

cooling
(of certain foods or combinations of foods) deemed to 'cool' the system according to **ayurvedic** medicine. Examples of **cooling** foods include: **thambili, curd**, yoghurt, sago, **mung ata, belimal drink**, etc. (> **heaty**)

cop (1)
(n) policeman ° *Cops held in drugs probe* ° *Torture cops reinstated* → In BSE, 'cop' is a colloquial word; in SLE it is also used in more formal contexts, e.g. newspaper headlines.

♦ The cops were questioning the passengers directly in front of them. (FSD 151)

♦ "Fortunately there was a cop at the boutique and I was able to recover it." (KCS 163)

cop (2)
(coll.) (v) catch (e.g. for a traffic offence) ° *I got copped for speeding.*

cope up
/kōp/ (= **bear up**) (vi) cope (with something), bear something, endure something ° *He's finding it hard to cope up on his own.*

copra
dried coconut kernel, used to make **coconut oil** (also India, from Malayalam via Portuguese)

♦ I took a deep breath, but the air had turned sour, blowing in over the copra pit at the edge of the compound. (Reef 120)

♦ He lived far away, in Galle, anyway, working in his father's copra business, ... (WMD 50)

♦ ... with the daughter of a copra millionaire on his arm, ... (HC 120)

copy book
(dated) exercise book

corner
edge, end ° *Don't leave the glass on the corner of the table!* → In BSE, 'corner' refers to the angled corner of a surface; in SLE it also refers to the edge or end of a table, wall, etc.

□ every nook and corner
every nook and cranny ° *The innovative cooling technology ensures that every nook and corner of your refrigerator gets cooled.*

♦ ... they were few and far between and every nook and corner was covered with ugly box-like structures - ... (BTH 48)

♦ Aunty Lydia's house had no balconies where ghosts copulated but every nook and corner of the house had a symbol of Jesus Christ. (M&P 100-1)

□ **to have a soft corner for somebody/something**
to have a soft spot for somebody/something ° *The youngster revealed the soft corner he has for Sachin Tendulkar.*

correct
right (restricted to more formal contexts in BSE)

corrupted
(adj.) corrupt, immoral ° *a corrupted girl* → In BSE, 'corrupted' is used as the past participle of the verb 'to corrupt', but not as an adjective.

cortege
funeral procession → Less common in BSE, and needs to be specified: 'a funeral cortege'.

could
can (> **can, would**) ° *Application forms could be obtained from the secretary.* ° *Cancer could be prevented.* ° *Daily Mirror: News you could trust* ° *Payment could be handed over in cash or forwarded in the form of a cash cheque.* → In BSE, 'could' suggests either a past tense, or a conditional, giving the examples an element of doubt which is not there in SLE.

country rice
(= **kekulu hal**) a popular variety of rice (red or white) (> **red rice**)

♦ Red, unpolished country rice with dry fish gravy and coconut sambol. (July 155)

countrywide
(= **islandwide**) nationwide, all over the country (rare in BSE) ° *Student Union threatens countrywide strikes*

couple
(coll.) a couple, a few ° *couple of years back*

course
an unspiced Western style dish (e.g. fried fish or meat with plain boiled vegetables) ° *fish course* ° *chicken course*

♦ At night, when alone, he usually liked to eat bread and western food: *courses*. (Reef 18)

cousin brother; cousin sister
male cousin; female cousin

♦ That is where my cousin-brother Kantha went, ... (WMD 128)

♦ "One of my cousin-sisters is at the Kelaniya Campus." (WE 74)

♦ "My brother and two of my cousin-brothers are here, and also Rani's people." (WE 91)

cover (1)
(n) top, lid (of a saucepan, etc.); envelope → In BSE, 'cover' is used to mean envelope only in formal contexts ('under separate cover').

cover (2)
(vt) (in carrom) to follow up (the red piece, by potting one of your own pieces) (> **carrom**) ° *Now you have to cover the red.*

covering sheet
top sheet (on a bed)

♦ ... the bed in the middle of the room, a pale covering sheet drawn up to the neck ... (GC 199)

cover up
cover (e.g. costs) ° *We managed to cover up our expenses.* → In BSE, to 'cover something up' means to keep it secret.

cowcatcher
(dated, humorous) protruding teeth

♦ Women ... with stained armpits and stained cowcatchers. (M&P 18)

♦ They had nothing in common except the cowcatcher, but even after Nenda's cowcatcher had been replaced by a perfect set of man made teeth they still fought. (M&P 57)

crack, cracked
(adj.) (coll.) crazy, eccentric ° *a crack case*

□ to crack
(coll.) in the extreme, a great deal ° *He was boasting to crack about his new job.* ° *My, that woman is so thin but she eats to crack.*

cracker
firecracker, banger

♦ "The government should ban those damn crackers." (FSD 123)

♦ The people are shouting, crackers are thrown to frighten the wild elephants. (KCS 103)

creeper
a trainee tea **planter**

♦ Many Burgher boys wanted to be 'creepers' - training on plantations and tea estates. (YY 52)

♦ Hamilton had run across Taylor in India when they were both young creepers, apprentice planters in the same company. (HC 94)

crock
a vintage or veteran car ° *driving an old crock* → In BSE, a 'crock' suggests an old vehicle which is worthless; in SLE it is something valuable because of its age.

cross
(= **attain age, come of age, grow up**) (of a girl) reach puberty (> **big girl**)

♦ I crossed sometime between night and day. Crossing did not mean that

I crossed the Red Sea like Moses. ... My crossing was into womanhood. A simple, uncomplicated, bloody process. (M&P 229)

♦ "When you have children don't ever forget that the black prince loves only two things. Newly crossed girls smelling of blood and fried foodstuff." (M&P 233)

c'ship
(in newspaper headlines) championship ° *an all-island carrom c'ship*

CTB
a state-owned bus belonging to the Ceylon Transport Board (later the Sri Lanka Transport Board, which was then privatised)

♦ "Educated people, university graduates, are driving CTB buses and working as labourers." (July 29)

cubby, cubby hole
(in a car) glove compartment → In BSE, a 'cubby-hole' is a small room or cupboard.

cueist
(in newspaper headlines) a billiards or snooker player; also **cue sports** (billiards and snooker) (> **cager**) ° *Ten cueists qualify for pre-quarter finals*

Cultural Triangle
the area of the ancient cities of Sri Lanka (including Anuradhapura, Polonnaruwa, Sigiriya, Dambulla and Kandy), which are being restored under a UNESCO-funded project

cumbly
/kambli/ (dated) a woollen blanket used as a head cover by **tea pluckers** (Sinhala/Tamil 'kambili'; also India)

♦ ... a swarm of *cumbly*-clad tea-pluckers. (WMD 257)

CUMBLY

curd

(= **buffalo curd**) a milk product similar to yoghurt, made with buffalo milk

♦ "Nuts? Honey and curd?" (Reef 170)

♦ … we were starving and, except for glances at each other, silently scooped the curd and treacle into our mouths. (Z 123-4)

□ curd and honey

curd and treacle, a popular dessert (> **honey**)

♦ … the best curd and honey at Aluthgama. (YY 102)

□ curd chillie

a red chillie soaked in **curd**, then dried and fried

□ curd pot

a shallow earthenware pot in which **curd** is sold; also refers to the full pot (BSE 'pot of curd')

CURD POTS

curly curly

(coll.) curly ° *She has curly curly hair.*

current

(coll.) electricity, power (less common in BSE) ° *We didn't have current for three hours.*

curry chicken

free range chicken (> **broiler**)

curry leaf

(= **karapincha**) a leaf used to flavour curries

♦ … and herbs - curry leaves, rampe, lemon grass. (CG 14)

curry stuffs

spices used to make curry powder

curse

(vi) curse somebody/something, get angry with somebody ° *They must be cursing!*
→ In BSE, to 'curse' (vi) means to swear, to use bad language.

cushion works

(= **hood works**) vehicle upholsterer's, a place where car seats, etc. are repaired

cussed

/kasəD/ mean, callous, nasty → Less common in BSE (pron. /kasiD/), and restricted to the sense of awkward or stubborn.

custard apple

(= **aatha, anoda**) a type of fruit the size of a large apple, with a green skin and white pulp → There are several varieties of **custard apple**, known by a number of different names. The most common are the **custard apple** itself (Sinhala: **veli aatha** or **veli anoda**) and the **soursop** (Sinhala: **katu aatha** or **katu anoda**).

♦ Mangoes, mangosteen, custard apple, avocado, woodapple, belli, soursup, durian, rambutan, guava, jumbu and grapes came into the house during the season. (Z 3)

CUSTARD APPLE

♦ … the warty skin of a custard-apple. (HC 180)

♦ … where rose apple and custard apple and pineapple vending women often walked … (KCS 145)

cut (1)
(n) route ° *We took a long cut to come.* → In BSE you can take a 'short cut', but not a 'long cut'.

cut (2)
(= **shot**) (n) slap, hit ° *I gave him a cut on his face.*

♦ "What is this? Again? In the morning I gave you six cuts. Now what?" Later he didn't even ask. But one day the wily man checked after the fourth cut and gave his victim a quizzical look. … The six cuts, vigorously applied on his thin underpants, smarted like the devil. (TT 177)

cut (3)
(vt) miss (school, etc.) (also US) ° *She cut school again today.*

♦ But curiously, it was during my 'good' periods that Kantha would take it into his head to 'cut' school (except when there was cricket practice) … (WMD 136)

♦ "You'll have to cut classes." (July 290)

♦ "But you can't be a pundit if you roam here and there and if you cut school." (KCS 169)

cut (4)
(= **give somebody tight**) (vt) to put somebody in their place, cut somebody down to size, give somebody a hard time ° *If he tells that again I'll cut him properly!*

cut (5)
(vi) turn (left or right, e.g. in a car) ° *Now cut hard to the left!*

cut (6)
(adj.) (of a phone) cut off ° *The line got cut.*

cut (7)
(adj.) drunk ° *He's fully cut!* → In BSE you can be 'half-cut', but not 'fully cut'.

cut (8)
(adj.) (in **carrom**) behind or touching the base line, and therefore unplayable ° *Is the red still cut?*

□ **to cut your ticket**
to be discharged from hospital

Cutex
nail polish (brand name)

♦ "I am not wasting your time, you are only putting Cutex on your toe nails." (M&P 88)

cutlet
a fish or meat ball fried in breadcrumbs (> **short eats**) → In BSE, a 'cutlet' is a piece of meat, like a 'chop'.

♦ Then she herself would turn out the mutton patties and fish cutlets for which she was renowned. (WMD 125)

♦ A ten-minute breakfast of fish cutlets in the lesser dark. (AG 229)

♦ "We'll have some coffee, some fresh bread and - what cutlets do you have?" (July 90)

♦ … with sandwiches and meat cutlets that Amily had left in the refrigerator. (MiP 400)

♦ Mrs. Dias walks in with a tray of food, sandwiches and cutlets. (GC 122)

♦ As we watched, he finished the last of the cutlets and threw the box away. (CP 55)

♦ I hung around near the tray of cutlets and kept popping them into my mouth. (M&P 184)

cutpieces
remnants, small pieces of left-over cloth

cutter
pencil sharpener

cynosure: the cynosure of all eyes
the centre of attention and admiration (an idiom favoured by Sri Lankan journalists, but rare in BSE) ° *The bride was the cynosure of all eyes.* ° *The two sisters were the cynosure of all eyes, winning as much as five gold medals between them.*

♦ In 34th Lane, however, the von Blosses home became the cynosure. (JFT 206)

D

Dada, Dadda
/ˈdædɑ/ Daddy, Dad (> **Mama**) ° *Dada and Mama*

♦ "Your dadda knows you came here?" … "You go and tell your dadda." (TT 185)

♦ "Oh! Dadda, it's a matter of perspective," … (Z 15)

dagoba
/ˈdɑːgəbə/ (= **chaitya, stupa**) Buddhist shrine, a dome-shaped structure containing Buddhist relics (Sinhala)

DAGOBA

♦ … the huge cupola of the Ruwanweliseya* … (* An ancient and one of the greatest Buddhist dagobas in the island. It was built by hero-king Dutugemunu.) (TT 121)

♦ We worshipped at the dagoba, shrine room and across the road at the old Bo tree. (CM 63)

♦ … the mighty *dagobas* he had built to the glory of the Sangha and the Sinhala nation. (WMD 199)

♦ I kept to the new road and passing the Bo tree on my right and a little temple with a small white dagoba down below on my left … (BTH 18)

♦ ... all the other kings who had come before and after him built boring Buddhist temples, Stupas and Dagobas but not castles. (M&P 193)

daham pasal

/daham pāsœl/ Buddhist Sunday school (Sinhala)

daily

/ɒēli/ (adv.) every day ° *We used to go there daily.* → In BSE, 'daily' either goes with a noun ('a daily occurrence'), or stands on its own in the sense of 'per day' ('Take one tablet three times daily'). In other cases, 'every day' would be more common in informal contexts.

♦ This rationing of purchases forces her to visit the market daily. (Z 4)

♦ Sharona visited me daily. (M&P 145)

daily needs

provisions, groceries

dallo

/dœllo/ squid, cuttlefish (Sinhala)

dam

/dām/ a game similar to draughts (Sinhala)

dambala

/dambələ/ (= winged bean) a type of vegetable (Sinhala)

DAMBALA

damn cheek!

(coll.) what a cheek!

♦ "And damn cheek, no? Telling will take Leah to big ship. And in front of me!" (JFT 19)

damn shame!

(coll.) what a shame! → In colloquial BSE, 'shame' and 'pity' are used interchangeably; in SLE, 'shame' suggests a feeling of guilt or humiliation, whereas 'pity' or 'sin' suggests a feeling of sympathy.

♦ "Damn shame if they get angry because of your nonsense." (JFT 13)

♦ "Here, here, see, men, all the other houses people coming to the gate. Damn shame, no?" (YY 209)

damn sin!

(coll.) what a pity! (> **sin!**)

♦ "Only yesterday my wife was saying damn sin to marry so young." (JFT 139)

♦ "My God, they have gone and shot Simon Navaratne. ... Aney! Damn sin, men! How can they do that, ah?" (WCS 46)

damn wild

(coll.) really angry

♦ "Same thing for me also. Edna is damn wild." (TT 111)

♦ "I must say I was damn wild, that pawnbroker bugger going straight to you." (HC 88)

damsel

young woman (archaic in BSE) ° *village damsels*

dance

(coll.) trouble (with somebody/something) ° *They're having a dance with that child.*

♦ "Every year this dance, no? And see the amount of work." (JFT 183)

♦ "... you must see the dance at home, men." (TT 53)

□ to dance the devil
(= **play socks, play pucks, play hell, play pandu**) (coll.) to mess around, make trouble, play the fool

♦ "I suppose your whole jing-bang family will come and drink and dance the devil and no sleep for the baby." (YY 2)

♦ "Not enough he's getting, still dancing the devil." (TT 200)

dandu lena
/dandu lēna/ a large species of squirrel (rock squirrel or giant squirrel) (Sinhala)

DANDU LENA

dane
/dāne/ (= **alms-giving**) a religious ceremony, involving giving alms to Buddhist monks, or as charity to poor people, for example at fixed periods after someone has died (Sinhala) ° *the three-month dane* ° *The monks had just had their dane of rice, pathola and karawila that had been brought by a villager.*

♦ The funeral festivities were endless: the seventh day dhana, the one month almsgiving, the memorial mass; ... (CP 204)

♦ "... but didn't the family do the proper death rituals, like *Danas* (inviting the Buddhist priests for lunch and preaching in order to ensure the deceased's direct flight to Nirvana) ..." (M&P 317)

♦ "... if I feel like giving a Dana, I give a Dana to the beggars or to the orphanage." (M&P 317)

dansala
/dansala/ a place where a **dane** is held; (at **Vesak**) a stall where free food and drinks are served (Sinhala) ° *A top Health Ministry official warned the public patronising dansalas to be alive to the dangers of consuming unsafe food and requested dansal organisers to prepare food in a hygienic manner.*

♦ ... decided to liven things up by tossing a white phosphorous grenade into a nearby *dansala*. The latter is a stall that provides free food - usually rice and curry - to the crowds touring the streets. ... being extremely lucky that no one in the *dansala* was killed or even seriously injured. (CU 86)

dara lipa
/dara lipa/ (= **hearth**) a traditional open stove for cooking with firewood (Sinhala)

DARA LIPA

darling!
(as an exclamation) sweet! cute! ° *Ane darling!*

dasasil
/dasasil/ the 10 Buddhist precepts which are supposed to be observed by all Buddhist monks (Sinhala) (> **sil**)

dash

slam (a door), slam down (the phone)
° *Please don't dash the door.* ° *As I said hallo he dashed the phone.* ° *And with that the guy at the other end dashed the phone.*

♦ He listened for a moment, juggled the cradle violently and dashed the receiver. (FSD 138)

davula

/daulə/ a traditional cylindrical drum which is hung from the waist (Sinhala)

day after; day before

the day after tomorrow; the day before yesterday ° *They're coming day after.* ° *I saw her day before.*

♦ "Mm, OK. But you'll come back day after, no?" (CU 46)

♦ "I checked one of these out day before," …(CU 234)

dayakaya

/dāyəkəya/ a patron or benefactor of a Buddhist temple (Sinhala)

day bed

an item of furniture, a rattan sofa without back or arms

dead rope: to give somebody a dead rope

to let somebody down (also **D-rope**) (derived from a Sinhala idiom) ° *You gave me a real dead rope yesterday!* ° *State radio's 'Prabha dead' story a dead rope*

death anniversary

the anniversary of somebody's death, when a **dane** is often held

♦ Amrith was furious at them for this delicacy around his mother's death anniversary. (SMS 32)

♦ … and SWRD was celebrating another death anniversary with all the Buddhist

priests in Sri Lanka wishing him eternal life in Nirvana. (M&P 206)

decoction

(= **kasaya**) an **ayurvedic** remedy (> **peyava**, **paspanguwa**)

♦ … from the day he brought some bottled decoction to school. (PMS 15)

♦ "That old rogue needs one of his own decoctions." (PMS 97)

deega

/dīgə/ (in **Kandyan** law) a marriage where the couple move to their own house, or the bride goes to live with the groom's family (opposite: **binna**) (Sinhala) ° *… and left her parental home in Kurunegala on a blissful "deega" (marriage in which the bride shifts to her bridegroom's house) …* ° *The Kandyan law stipulates that a "deega" daughter from a family in the Kandyan region is not entitled to inherit property from her father.*

Deepavali

/dīpāvəli/ Diwali, the Hindu festival of lights (also India)

♦ "… I was going to give her a new skirt and blouse for *Dheepavali* …" (WE 34)

deep South

the Southern Province (esp. beyond Matara) (also used in the US to refer to the Southern states)

♦ He would be gone for days, right down past Joseph's home town to where the deep south bottoms out and begins to curve up again … (Reef 61)

♦ … a Hindu shrine in the deep south … (YY 132)

♦ Mrs Ellapola herself came from the deep south, … (WMD 200)

dehusk
husk, remove the husk from (a coconut)
° *Can you find someone to dehusk these coconuts?*

del
/del/ (= breadfruit) (Sinhala)

♦ Even the sun seemed to rise out of the garage and sleep behind the *del* tree at night. (Reef 27)

♦ Everything was bubbling nicely in the kitchen, the beer was flowing, the cashew nuts and the *del* chips crunching. (Reef 92)

delist
leave, resign from (e.g. the army)
° *Hundreds of soldiers who had volunteered to de-list from the army, queued up yesterday at the Army HQ to fill up de-listing forms. On Monday alone more than 1500 soldiers had opted to de-list.*

delouse
defuse (a bomb) ° *The bomb was deloused early morning.* → In BSE, to 'delouse' is to remove the lice from somebody/something.

delum
/delum/ pomegranate (Sinhala)

demalichchas
/demalichchas/ (= babblers, seven sisters) (coll.) a small grey thrush-like bird which is often seen in noisy groups of around seven birds (Sinhala; but this term, being derived from a derogatory term for Tamil people, is considered offensive by many people)

♦ ... the demalichchas were keeping up a chorus ... (BTH 21)

demerge
separate (the Northern and Eastern provinces); noun: **demerger** (rare in BSE, and restricted to a business context) ° *plans to demerge the North-East province* ° *JHU calls for N-E demerger*

demerit
(nu) negative **merit** (> merit) → In BSE, a 'demerit' (nc) is a fault or defect in something: 'the merits and demerits of the system'.

deregistered
(of a vehicle) having had the registration withdrawn or cancelled

Deshabandu, Deshamanya
/dēshabandu, dēshamānya/ titles given by the President to honour individuals for their service to the country; others include **Vidya Jyothi, Kala Keerthi**, etc. (Sinhala)
° *Deshamanya Lalith Kotalawela*

destone
remove the stones from (rice) ° *destoned rice*

detenu
detainee (also India, orig. French)

detrain
alight, get out of a train (formal in BSE) (> entrain)

♦ ... as Sonnaboy said as they detrained at midnight and dragged themselves home, to bed. (YY 164)

devale
/dēvāle/ a shrine room devoted to a Hindu god, found in a Hindu or Buddhist temple (Sinhala) ° *Just last week we took him to the Kataragama devale to make an offering.* ° *the few acres of paddy belonging to the Kataragama devale*

♦ The drums were beating at the Devale ... (BTH 34)

♦ "We will smash coconuts in the *devale* (a place where gods are worshiped) and curse you" ... (WCS 50)

devil bird

(= **ulama**) a mysterious bird with a loud screeching cry (forest eagle owl)

- ♦ They were told that it was the devil bird or Ulama, as the Sinhalese called it. "That is devil bird. Very bad bird." (YY 172)

- ♦ "That's the mark of the devil-bird. It always leaves a dead lizard to show that it passed." (HC 171)

- ♦ Mr. Karl told me he had heard the call of the devil-bird once, while camping near Inginiyagala. It was a most dreadful noise heard only late at night, a combination of shrieks, wails and howls, very much like the sound of a woman being strangled. Many hunters and naturalists had heard, and written about, a devil-bird in our forests. Villagers living close to jungle areas also live in absolute dread of it, believing that, if one heard a devil-bird, someone in the village would die that very night. (REP 200)

devil dance

a traditional dance, part of a **thovil**, performed by masked **devil dancers**

DEVIL DANCER

- ♦ Ambalangoda was the centre for devil dances and exorcism rites, ... The

devil dances cured sickness, catarrh, deafness, aloneness. (RF 51-2)

- ♦ ... the enchanted region of exorcists, devil-dancers and wild elephants ... (Reef 61)

- ♦ He announced that an eighteen-masked devil dancing ceremony had to be performed in our home. (CM 43)

- ♦ ... and he couldn't talk until there was a devil dance to chase away the demon who had possessed him. (BTH 28)

devil drum

(= **yak bera**) a drum used in a **devil dance**

- ♦ ... and the low mysterious tone of the devil drum always gave me a creepy feeling. (BTH 34)

devilled

(of food) hot, spicy, fried with chilli (also US) ° *devilled beef* ° *devilled cadju*

- ♦ ... garnished with finely-minced devilled pork ... (JFT 61)

- ♦ ... and a dish of devilled venison ... (WMD 57)

- ♦ ... devilled prawns with a yoghurt dipping sauce, ... (CG 375)

- ♦ Right along the buffet table, Samare's blazer got the taste of almost every single dish, from Dhal to Deviled Potatoes. (WCS 59)

dhal

/ḍāl/ (= **parippu**) lentils (Anglo-Indian, orig. Hindi) ° *dhal curry*

- ♦ "I've made everything: chicken, rice, dhal ..." (MM 58)

- ♦ "Hors d'oeuvres: prawn cocktail; soup: dhall consomme" ... (CG 65)

- ♦ She went back into the kitchen, where her dhal curry had almost dried up on the stove. (July 255)

♦ The simple fare of rice, dhal &
fish looked poor but tasted fine, ...
(REP 89)

♦ He was balancing his tin plate with one
hand, eating the rice and dhal with the
other. (WE 24)

♦ The food, bread with dhal and fish
curry, would have been adequate if the
curries had any taste. (GC 14)

♦ ... paper cones of fried spiced dhal, ...
(SMS 153)

♦ First the stones had to be eliminated
from the rice and the dhal. (M&P 79)

♦ The rice and dhal queues in front of
the co-operative stores lengthened.
(M&P 185)

♦ He ... retails everything they need from
dhal and canned fish to kerosene and
soap. (PMS 31-2)

Dhamma
/damma/ Buddhist doctrine (= Dharma)
(Sinhala)

dharmachakraya
/darmachakraya/ Buddhist wheel symbol
(Sinhala; also India, from Sanskrit)

DHARMACHAKRAYA

dharmishta
/darmishta/ following the Buddhist dharma
(Sinhala, from Sanskrit)

♦ To the Buddhist Sangha, Saint
Dickie presented his programme as
the sublime expression of *dharmista*
government and himself as the

reincarnation of an ancient Buddhist
ruler, ... (WMD 274)

♦ JR was no ordinary president. He
was a 'Dharmishta' president. That
is, a president who follows the
teachings of the Buddha. Before JR
became president, he was not even
a dharmishta person, but now, he
straight away became a dharmishta
president. A new word entered our
vocabulary. 'Dharmishta': a person
who follows the dharma. (M&P 251)

dhatha
/dāta/ (= akka) elder sister (used by
Muslims) (> nana, kaka)

♦ "Why! Soraya Dhatha will be there ..."
(Z 132)

dhobi
/ɒōbi/ a person who washes clothes (Anglo-
Indian, orig. Hindi)

♦ ROLLO SYLVESTER who ran away
with the girl who came with the dhoby
woman. (JFT 121)

♦ "*Annai*, ... shouldn't we be sending
for the priest and the *dhobi*, ..."
(WMD 31)

♦ When the offer was rejected, Esra tried
subterfuge and sent a dhobi in disguise
to buy it on his behalf. (SG 30)

♦ He was more likely to work beside a
stonemason or listen to a *dhobi* woman
washing clothes at a newly discovered
rock pool ... (AG 82)

♦ She was in their bedroom, sorting
linen for the dhobi, when Hamilton
came in ... (HC 114)

♦ To the dhobi children who came
swarming around him, he replied
that he was looking for a gold chain.
(HC 220)

- On the trunk of the massive banyan that grew near the dhobi colony measurements were marked off in white paint. (HC 220)

- Samare had heard that *dhobis* (launderers) had a habit of lending their customers' clothes to family and friends. (WCS 62)

- So, as they continued to ruminate about why a burgher wife would run away with a dhobi, which was worse than being burgher, ... (M&P 86)

- "So it will begin like this: the dhobi will come at five-thirty am." (M&P 234)

Dick, Tom and Harry

(coll.) Tom, Dick and Harry

dicky

boot (of a car; US trunk) (also India) ° *They made me get down and open the dicky.* → In BSE, 'dicky' is an archaic word meaning an extra folding seat at the back of a two-seater car.

- The dickey boot sprang open, and I heard the thump of baggage. (MM 29)

- All the boarders came out to admire Kumar's shiny blue motor-car and I was much envied when I took my seat in the dickey. (HC 25)

- There were two suitcases and a steamer trunk on the back seat of his car and a second trunk in the dickey. (HC 145)

- Karunawathie, Magi and the driver caught the animal and pushed him into the dickey of the car. (M&P 316)

diet: a light diet

a small meal ° *Tonight we're having a light diet.* → In BSE, a 'diet' means the type of food a person normally eats ('a healthy diet'), or a special type of food someone

eats when they are ill or want to lose weight ('He's on a diet').

different different

various different ° *They're telling different different things.*

dig: to dig your nose

to pick your nose ° *Stop digging your nose!*

- ... my brother, Varuna, who, because of a prevailing habit, had been renamed Diggy-Nose and then simply Diggy. (FB 3)

- A woman in a beautiful crimson sari was surreptitiously digging her nose. (July 232)

- "... Miss Lily Marlene is digging her nose because she thinks no one is looking." (M&P 84)

- "Chee, don't dig your back!" (M&P 323)

DIG

Deputy Inspector General (of Police)

- "... we can take this matter up wth DIG Gunathillake, who is a *very* good friend of mine." (July 71)

dim

(vt) dip (headlights) (also US)

dimiya

/dimiya/ a large red ant (Sinhala)

- My pleasure was to follow the big red ants called the *dimiyas* as they went on their never ending trek along the fence. (CM 7)

diplomate

a person who has passed a diploma course (also US)

directress

female director → In BSE, female forms such as 'directress' and 'manageress' are no longer comonly used.

dirty

(coll.) (of a child) naughty ° *Dirty fellow!*

♦ "You are a dirty fellow, ... You went without saying a word." (M&P 332)

disave, disava

/disāvə/ (dated) a provincial governor in the **Kandyan** kingdom (Sinhala)

dispose

dispose of

♦ When aunty Lydia and her family reached England after disposing their last rupees on excess luggage, ... (M&P 117)

divul kiri

/divul kiri/ a drink made with **woodapple** and **coconut milk** (Sinhala)

diya hakuru

/diyə hakuru/ a preparation of dried fish blood (Sinhala)

♦ ... Maldivian preparations - (lots of Maldivian buggalows sail into Galle harbour) - like diya-hakuru - dried fish blood mixed with crushed spices ... (YY 92)

diya labu

/diyə labu/ (= **labu, bottle gourd**) a type of gourd used as a vegetable (Sinhala)

♦ "Have crab curry and pappadam and dhal and diya-labu (bottle gourd) with mustard." (YY 92)

DIYA LABU

diya redda

/diyə reddə/ a **cloth** worn by women for bathing (Sinhala) (> **redda**)

DIYA REDDA

♦ She undressed by the well, unstrapped her watch and got into the *diya reddha* cloth, and dropped the bucket into the depths. (AG 90)

♦ The older women all wear a *diya reddha* for bathing. This is a long strip of cotton fabric that is wrapped round the body to cover it from breast to knee. (GC 34)

Diyawadane Nilame

/diyəvadənə niləme/ the chief lay custodian of the Temple of the Tooth in Kandy (Sinhala) (> **nilame**)

DIYAWADANE NILAME

dodol

/dodol/ (= **kaludodol**) a dark brown, jelly-like sweet made with **rice flour, coconut milk** and **jaggery** (Sinhala, also Malay)

dog

(coll.) **carrom** piece (> **carrom**)

□ not a dog

(coll.) no-one, not a soul ° *Not a dog was on the street.*

dolphin

butterfly (swimming stroke)

domestic

(= **servant**) ° *Can't you help me find a good domestic?*

donkey

(= **goat**) (coll.) fool, idiot, ass

♦ "Will you two donkeys shut up," ... (GC 231)

♦ "That woman is a donkey," ... (M&P 25)

♦ "These donkeys will never pass the examination." (PMS 275)

donkey bed

(= **buru anda, camp bed**) a folding bed consisting of a piece of **gunny** on a simple wooden frame

♦ ... and it was known that the Trincomalee toddy tavern-keeper's wife rented sleazy cubicles with a 'donkey bed' - a length of gunny sacking slung on a cross-legged frame that could be folded and stowed away when not in use. (YY 37)

don't you know?

(coll., dated) you know

doo

/dū/ (= **duwa**) (coll.) daughter (a term of endearment) (Sinhala)

dorai

master (Tamil); commonly used to refer to an estate **superintendent** (> **periyadorai, sinnadorai**)

♦ ... they were roused by the apu; the *dorai's* horse had returned, riderless. (HC 95)

♦ The day after the White *dorai* left, Nadesan *dorai* moved in. (WE 23)

♦ It was then that the *dorai* gave her father the watch, ... (WE 24)

dosai

/dōse, tōse/ (= **thosai**) a type of pancake made with slightly fermented batter made of **rice flour** and **kurakkan** flour (also India, orig. Tamil) (> **paper thosai**)

♦ He went to a table at the back and ordered dosai. (FSD 106)

dosi

/dōsi/ a type of sweet made with preserved fruits, a Muslim speciality (Sinhala/Tamil) (> **puhul dosi**) ° *ala dosi* ° *pol dosi*

♦ "... to buy some ash pumpkin dosi - white as snow and sweet as nectar." (KCS 86)

dot-dot

(coll.) decorated with dots, polka dots ° *a dot-dot dress* ° *dot-dot-dot material*

double orphan

a child who has lost both parents; a child who has lost one parent is a **'single orphan'** → In BSE, an 'orphan' always refers to a child who has lost both parents.

doubt

query ° *Call me if you have any doubts.*

down

(adv.) below, downstairs (> **up**) ° *They're not here - they must be waiting down.* → In BSE, 'down' is normally used as a preposition ('down the drain'), or with a verb ('come down'), but not on its own as an adverb; you can 'go down', but you can't 'be down' unless you specify where: down in the basement, down by the river, etc.

down South
in or to the South of Sri Lanka ° *We went down South for the long weekend.*

♦ The report assumed he had drowned off the reef down south. (Reef 177)

♦ … when his father died and left him their ancestral walauwwa down south. (July 7)

♦ Every July, they went down south for a week, … (July 77)

♦ "We'd go upcountry or down south for the weekend …" (MiP 144)

down train
the train going down from the hills to Colombo (> **up train**)

♦ The station was deserted when he got there but a down train pulled in a few minutes later. (FSD 247)

drama
/brāma/ play → In BSE, a 'drama' suggests a serious theatrical performance; 'play' is more common, and more general in meaning.

drape
/brēp/ (vt) put on (a **saree**); (vi) (of a **saree**) hang

♦ The second was the pleasure of watching Amma drape her sari, watching her shake open the yards of material, … (FB 15)

♦ She would try the white khaddar; it didn't drape as well but it clung in the right places, and it was homely. (WMD 311)

♦ Yet her mouth felt dry and she had to concentrate while she draped her sari, nervousness making her fingers stiff. (CG 15)

drip ledge
a ledge carved above the entrance to a cave temple which stops rainwater from running into the cave ° *The forests abound with caves with drip ledges and ancient inscriptions.*

driver
chauffeur → In BSE, a 'driver' is any person who drives a vehicle; a person who is employed to drive a private car is called a 'chauffeur'; and a person employed to drive other types of vehicle is called a 'lorry driver', etc.

♦ They had reached the Mudaliyar's car now and the driver held the door open for them. (CG 135)

♦ … and such things were not permitted in the presence of the driver. (CG 208)

♦ "If he wants I'll get him a job as a driver." (AG 131)

♦ The driver wasn't happy when I told him to turn back. (REP 334)

♦ "I stay in the drivers' quarters at the hotel." (CU 55)

D-rope
(= **dead rope**) ° *Don't get caught to UNP's D-ropes, JVP tells Govt.*

drumsticks
(= **murunga**) a type of vegetable with long green pods

♦ "Have murunga* …" (* The long green pods of the horse-radish tree, eaten as a vegetable. The pods are commonly called drumsticks.) (TT 31)

♦ … and watched with sly amusement as her lunch guests attempted to tackle their curried drumsticks with spoons and forks. (CP 102)

dry fish

(= **karawala**) fish which has been salted and dried in the sun

- ♦ ... and sometimes he gave Upul a whole plate of rice, with a little grated coconut and a bit of fried dry fish. (OM 35)

- ♦ "Dry fish, is it? He has made his money on dry fish? And now he wants to make my son a dry fish merchant too?" (WMD 9)

- ♦ Rice to boil and then two vegetables, ... and a small piece of dry-fish for my uncle. (GC 33)

- ♦ If grandma cooks, those who walk along the road know that it is the dry fish dancing in the pot. (KCS 118)

- ♦ A burly woman in a printed housecoat gives them plates filled with boiled manioc and dry fish. (PMS 145)

- ♦ "The bag was stinking of dry fish but I hopped like the wind." (PMS 255)

dry rations

food supplies (rice, **dhal**, flour, sugar, milk powder, etc.)

- ♦ He writes letters asking for medicines, for clothes and dry rations during periods of drought, ... (GC 98)

dry zone

the northern, north-central, eastern and south-eastern parts of Sri Lanka, where the rainfall is lowest (> **wet zone**)

- ♦ Then a ruby-red Jaffna wine Miss Nili had winkled out of a dry-zone vicar, especially for Mister Salgado. (Reef 98)

- ♦ ... even of this person who had brought her into the dry zone. (AG 104)

- ♦ We were passing through the arid zone of the country, the driest part of the dry zone. (REP 43)

- ♦ "It's a British NGO involved in constructing wells and restoring village tanks in the dry zone." (GC 216)

- ♦ This was the Dry Zone and there was little other greenery. (SMS 188)

- ♦ He was attempting to improve and redesign some of the irrigation systems in the country's dry zone. (CU 229)

- ♦ "Aunty Magdalena's servant making delicious dry zone food." (M&P 206)

dumbara

/dumbərə/ a type of weaving used to make mats, wall hangings, cushion covers, etc. (Sinhala village name)

DUMBARA WALL HANGING

- ♦ ... she squinted past the dumbara wall hanging and plonked herself on the sofa. (Z 39)

- ♦ ... fingering a delicate black and white dumbara cushion, ... (Z 106)

durave, durawa

/durāve/ the '**toddy-tapper**' caste (Sinhala)
° *Buddhist Durawa/Karawa respectable retired parents from South now residing Battaramulla ...*

durian

/būriən/ a large green fruit with a hard prickly skin, famous for its pungent smell (orig. Malay)

DURIAN

- ♦ … where there are eighteen ways of describing the smell of a durian, … (RF 69)

- ♦ "Can you please tell Piyadasa not to bring durians home from the market? They stink like anything." (HC 182)

Dutch Burgher
a **Burgher** of Dutch origin

- ♦ They were Dutch burghers, the products of various intermarriages between the Ceylonese and the Dutch invaders, and had pale skin and blue eyes, unlike the Portuguese burghers, who were more swarthy and therefore looked-down-upon. (July 12)

- ♦ Miss Vanderstraaten was the first Dutch Burgher I knew. (HC 18)

- ♦ The majority of the residents were Dutch Burghers. (SMS 163)

duwa
/duwǝ/ daughter (also a familiar term of address, used by an older person to a girl or young woman) (Sinhala)

- ♦ "Now don't you keep whining for me all the time, *duva*," … (WE 46)

- ♦ "They need your help, duwa," … (GC 99)

- ♦ "Aney, *duwe*, open your eyes and look at me." (M&P 26)

E

each and every
each, every ° *The police are finding it difficult to remove each and every poster.* → Less common in BSE, and only used for special emphasis.

- ♦ Thereafter that week's ration of two pounds reduced itself to fourteen ounces and each and every one of us had to minimize our consumption. (M&P 79)

ear drops
hanging earrings

- ♦ Chains and bracelets, dangling ear drops, sarees and dresses. (OM 9)

earlier
before ° *The minister earlier told he will come.* → In BSE, 'earlier' is less common and more formal. It would also tend to come at the beginning of the sentence, and to be used with the past perfect tense ('Earlier, the minister had said he would come.')

earliest: at your earliest
as soon as possible, at your earliest convenience ° *Please reply at your earliest.*

early morning
early in the morning ° *I had to get up early morning.*

- ♦ "Can't, Uncle," he said, "I've got to get up early morning. The Chief wants me to go up-country with him to see Natesa Iyer." (WMD 73)

- ♦ "I washed my hair early morning and it still hasn't dried." (July 24)

- ♦ "Why don't you stay the night and leave early morning?" (GC 255)

♦ "It is easier to catch me after six in the evening, or else early morning before going to school." (M&P 63)

ear stud

a stud worn on the ear ('earring' is more common in BSE) (> **nose ring, nose stud**)

♦ ... watching the last rays of the sun fall across Lali's face and light up the ruby earstuds I had brought her from my mother that day. (WMD 209)

♦ No ring, bangles or chain, just tiny gold ear studs. (REP 10)

♦ She had seven ear studs in her lobes. (M&P 1)

earthslip

landslide, landslip

♦ "... they could shift the earth and start earth-slips and landslides, even wash away the railway lines, especially in the rainy season." (WMD 121)

Eastern food

Sri Lankan food (as opposed to Western food and Chinese food)

eat: to eat from

to eat at (a hotel, restaurant, etc.) ° *We ate lunch from a hotel.*

□ to eat (from) outside

to eat out or get a take-away meal ° *They never eat from outside.*

econ

economics

ee!, eeya!

/ī, īya/ (= **chee!, chi!**) ugh! yuk! (Sinhala/Tamil exclamation)

Eelam

/īləm/ the name given to the separate state claimed in the North and East of Sri Lanka by the LTTE and other separatist groups (Tamil)

egg boats

half hard-boiled eggs with the yolk mixed with butter, salt and pepper

egg hopper

a **hopper** cooked with an egg in the middle (> **plain hopper**)

♦ Sonnaboy also decided that he couldn't miss the early morning egg hoppers and curried sprats with lots of tomato that was a speciality of a small café in Colombo Fort. (YY 63)

♦ Drivers in the northern peninsula would rave about the egg hopper breakfasts in Kankesanturai. (YY 92)

♦ ... or devilled prawns or biriani or egghoppers, ... (HC 49)

♦ Marcus had the remains of an egg hopper in front of him and a dot of yolk on his chin. (HC 104)

egg roti

a **godamba roti** folded up with an egg inside (> **plain roti**)

egg ruloung

a dish made with spiced scrambled eggs (from Dutch)

♦ We are having a formal dinner. String hoppers, meat curry, egg rulang, papadams, potato curry. ... It is my favourite meal - anything that has string hoppers and egg rulang I eat with a lascivious hunger. ... I listen intently, making sure I get a good portion of the egg rulang. (RF 137)

♦ Her last conversation in Sinhala was the distressed chat she'd had with Lalitha that had ended with her crying about missing egg *rulang* and curd with jaggery. (AG 145)

ehela

/æhœlə/ a type of tree with hanging yellow flowers (Indian laburnum) Sinhala)

ekel

/īkəl/ the spine of a dried palm frond, used to make brooms, etc. (Tamil) ° ... *little squares of meat skewered on short lengths of ekel.*

♦ ... sweeping sand castles with long thin *ekels* - the dry spines of palm fronds; ... (MM 90)

♦ She coaxed the oil cake into a shapely mound twirling the ekel in one hand and basting the cake with the boiling oil with the other. (OM 32)

♦ Harry's mother had shown him how to feed these lizards, with grains of boiled rice impaled on the point of an *ekel*. (HC 226)

□ ekel broom

a broom made with **ekels** and used for sweeping leaves, etc.

EKEL BROOM

♦ ... a grinning porter who was loading bundles of eekel brooms into the brake. "And what the hell are all these eekel brooms for?" (YY 38)

♦ Poddi would give hers a toss and ply her eekel broom, ... (TT 2)

♦ When the servants went home to their villages for Sinhalese New Year, Thornton cooked and scrubbed and swept the leaves from the drive with an ekel broom. (HC 181)

♦ Sita swings the ekel broom in her fury. (PMS 176)

♦ "You'll get enough practice when she comes after you with an ekel broom." (PMS 250)

ela

/œlə/ a small stream or irrigation channel (Sinhala)

elabatu

/eləbaṭu/ a type of **brinjal** (Sinhala)

elbow bend

hairpin bend

♦ The cart track to Egodawatta at this elbow bend moved along one border of the Camp ... (BTH 8)

elder to

older than (> **younger to**) ° *She is three years elder to me.* → In BSE, 'elder' is only used before a noun ('my elder brother').

elders

elderly people ° *an elders' home* (BSE: an old people's home)

electorate

constituency → In BSE, the 'electorate' is the people qualified to vote in an election, and a 'constituency' is an electoral district.

♦ "We can show it is by Sinhagala and therefore near the Minister's electorate." (FSD 83)

electric bill

(= **light bill**) electricity bill

elephant orphanage
a place where abandoned elephants are raised in captivity, e.g. at Pinnawela

elle
/elle/ a popular game similar to rounders or baseball; the national sport of Sri Lanka (Sinhala)

ELLE

elocution class
a private English class focusing on pronunciation, reading aloud, etc.

♦ In less than twenty-four hours, TM Mozart began elocution classes with the first available teacher. (M&P 31)

emporium
a large shop (less common in BSE) ° *Sri Lanka Handicrafts Emporium*

♦ I went with Mister Salgado to the big emporium to choose the new cloth. (Reef 81)

enasal
/enəsal/ cardamom (Sinhala)

encash
cash (a cheque); noun: **encashment** (formal in BSE) ° *the encashment of dud cheques*

English knowledge
knowledge of English ° *I like to improve my English knowledge.*

enjoy
(vi) enjoy yourself ° *Thank you very much - we really enjoyed.* ° *A great opportunity to enjoy with your family.* → In BSE, 'enjoy' cannot stand on its own, but must be followed by an object, so you enjoy something, or you enjoy yourself: 'We really enjoyed the day', or 'We really enjoyed ourselves'.

enough
(coll.) more than enough (showing annoyance or exasperation) ° *Enough we walked!* ° *Enough I did for him!*

enough of
enough ° *Is there enough of salt?*

♦ Land needed to be cultivated and there had to be enough of food. (TT 136)

enter
go in, go to, get in (to something) (less common and more formal in BSE) ° *I couldn't enter the house.* ° *She's hoping to enter university next year.*

♦ Sumanasiri had bought it ... for his son ... when the boy had entered university ... (WCS 27)

entrain
board, get into a train (formal in BSE) (> **detrain**)

♦ It appeared that the M.P. for Vavuniya would entrain for Colombo ... (YY 204)

entry: to make an entry
to report something to the police (> **police entry**)

♦ It is true that he drinks and has this other woman and he hit me and we even had to go to the police station and make an entry. (OM 33)

EPF; ETF
Employees' Provident Fund; Employees' Trust Fund (workers' savings schemes which workers and employers contribute to every month: EPF is paid on retirement; ETF is paid on leaving a job)

Esala
/æsələ/ the July **poya day**, the start of the Kandy **perahera** (Sinhala)

♦ In the holy city of Benares in northern India, the Buddha held his first discourse on Esala full moon poya day. (M&P 341)

estate bungalow
the residence of the **superintendent** of an estate (> **bungalow**)

♦ In the planters' clubs and the estate bungalows, they would be saying that Nagel had bungled it. (HC 97)

♦ He was running along the road that led to the estate bungalow, in a panic. (SMS 73)

even
also, too ° *Tomorrow even we'll be open.* → In BSE, 'even' suggests something surprising or unexpected, while in SLE it is used in the simple sense of 'also'. Note also the word order: in SLE, 'even' follows the word it refers to, while in BSE it comes before the main verb ('We'll even be open tomorrow.')

♦ "We still haven't got money to do that even." (WCS 14)

evening
afternoon (> **night**) ° *today evening* ° *last evening* → In BSE, the 'evening' begins at around 5.00 or 6.00 pm; in SLE, it begins at around 2.00 or 3.00 pm, and goes on until it gets dark.

eversilver
stainless steel, a silver-coloured metal alloy, commonly used for plates, cups, etc. (also India) ° *Keep an eversilver pot filled with water and place a coconut on it.*

everyday
every day (two words) ° *They are open everyday.* → In BSE, 'everyday' is an adjective which goes before a noun ('an everyday event').

♦ "Not everyday, men. How to write everyday?" (JFT 90)

♦ "You can go and see everyday if you want." (YY 179)

♦ … shabby people who wore one suit of woollens everyday and lived on poor allowances of twenty shillings a week. (TT 20)

♦ "Going out everyday and boozing," … (WE 109)

♦ She just nodded her head as if that kind of thing happened everyday. (FSD 222)

♦ At precisely 8:12 am, a cyclist crossed through the intersection, as he did everyday at the same time, and turned down Ziegestrasse. (CU 268)

everytime
always, all the time ° *He is everytime telling me to get a new car.* → In BSE, 'every time' (two words) means each time, on every occasion. Note also the word order: in BSE, adverbial phrases like 'every time' usually come either at the beginning or end of the sentence; in SLE, they can come before the verb.

♦ "I know, no, everytime I'm the one he's caning." (TT 185)

ex.
e.g., for example

expect

wait for (somebody) ° *We were expecting you from morning.* → In BSE, to 'expect' something means to think it will happen.

expensive

(coll.) aloof, stand-offish ° *Come and sit without being so expensive!*

expire

(= **pass off**) die, pass away → In BSE, 'expire' is normally used in the sense of coming to an end or no longer being valid (e.g. of a lease or a driving licence, or in the sense of the 'expiry date' on food). As a euphemism for 'die' it is considered formal and dated.

F

face

/fēs/ (v) have (difficulties, etc.) ° *They are facing lot of difficulties.*

face cut

the shape of the face ° *They have the same face cut.*

♦ "… you have the look of a Manipay boy, I can tell the face-cut anywhere." (WE 93)

facilities

resources and opportunities for doing things ° *Colombo has lot of facilities.* → In BSE, 'facilities' is not such a common word; and it would usually be specified, e.g. 'sports facilities', 'educational facilities', etc.

factory girl

(= **Juki girl**) (coll.) a garment factory worker (> **girl**)

♦ "If poor Alfred had not clutched onto another passenger, a rather plump factory girl he would have positively been hurled out of the bus," … (Z 77)

faintish

/fēntish/ (coll.) faint ° *feeling faintish*

fair (1)

(= **pola**) (n) market ° *the Sunday fair*

fair (2)

(adj.) fair-skinned (opp. dark) → In BSE, 'fair' normally refers to hair colour rather than skin colour.

♦ "Nice fair fellow, no? And see the dimple in the cheek." (YY 48)

♦ "He wanted the fairer of the two." (WMD 98)

- The soldier who had brought my kit was chatting with a tall, fairer man who turned out to be the driver. (REP 333)

- Athma's eyes were focused like binoculars on the fair boy in glasses who tossed this question to his friends. (WCS 17)

- "For a girl, her chances are always better if she was fair." (M&P 21)

fall

(= **saree pota**) (n) the part of the **saree** which is draped over the shoulder (> **headpiece, pallu, palu**)

- ... a sari was sewn onto belting that hooked around the waist very much like a skirt, the only dressing required being the pleats and the fall draped once about the body and over the shoulder. (CG 7)

- In the style of many low-caste women, she did not wear a blouse, the fall wrapped tightly around her breasts for modesty. (CG 181)

- ... adjusting the emerald brooch which clasped the fall of her crimson sari. (July 56)

fall into/onto

(of two roads, etc.) join, come out on ° *This lane falls into/onto Galle Road.*

- Minutes later I fell into the Borella-Pannipitiya road at Polwatta ... (BTH 49)

- "You know how to get there? You go right from your place and fall into Buller's Road." (AG 152)

- It curved gently to the left and finally fell on to the main road that led from Paranthan to Pooneryn. (REP 32)

- "If we can head southwards, we should fall on to the road at some point." (REP 96)

- The river commenced near Kekirawa in the interior, first fell into the Rajangana reservoir, then continued westwards to form the southern boundary of the Wilpattu National Park. It fell into the sea at Dutch Bay near the mouth of the Puttalam lagoon. (REP 258)

- "The trouble is, there are other roads from Hambantota that fall on to the same road, here at Pelmadulla." (FSD 124)

- The corridor led past the staff meal room and fell into a small yard common to all the business houses in the block. The yard, in turn, fell into the driveway leading to the school. (FSD 210)

- ... through the side exit falling into Manning Place. (FSD 210)

faluda

/faluɒa/ a sweet drink made with milk and rosewater (also India)

- He nervously comes forth with the faloodas two at a time. The last falooda spills on Ravi as the boy stumbles against the chair. (Z 137)

- Here Niresh was introduced to the pleasure of faluda, a rose-flavoured milkshake, with bits of semolina floating in it, and crisply fried samosas. (SMS 138)

- ... a melted pink liquid, like a Faluda; ... (M&P 47)

- The Bombay sweet-mart where I always drank a Faluda on the way back from school was still emanating smoke. (M&P 352)

family bandyism
nepotism, esp. in a political context

family member
a member of somebody's family (more formal in BSE) (> **member**) ° *All their family members will be there.*

♦ Some shelters had been erected by the side of the lake to house the family members coming to HQ to ask for news of their soldier sons or husbands. (REP 342)

♦ Anxious family members milled around as the blood soaked victims of yet another motor mishap were rushed in for emergency treatment. (FSD 193)

♦ The fortunes of the family members were such that when we lived together as a family, the house number had to be divisible by two. (M&P 85)

♦ "Are family members all similar?" (PMS 159)

fancy goods
ornaments, gifts, accessories, etc. ° *a fancy goods shop*

fannings
(= **tea dust**) low grade tea

fare
do, get on (well/badly, e.g. in an exam) (more formal in BSE) ° *How did you fare?*

fast
(coll.) (of girls) loose, immoral (less common in BSE) ° *She's a bit of a fast case.*

♦ "They say she is fast." - "Our Annalukshmi *fast*? She has nothing to do with boys." (CG 85)

♦ Eurasian girls were known to be fast. (HC 102)

♦ But I knew, vaguely, that his people were grand. And rather fast. There was a whiff of scandal. (HC 277)

♦ "Not with a bunch of stupid girls who are constantly giggling and carrying on and acting like fast-pieces." (SMS 123)

♦ It was our first date, I did not want him to think I was fast. (M&P 293)

fast unto death
(n/v) hunger strike ° *Monks fast unto death demanding transfer of OIC*

fed up of
fed up with ° *I'm fed up of waiting.* → In BSE, usually 'fed up with something', occasionally 'fed up about' or 'fed up of'.

♦ "He must have got fed up of her after he came here." (OD 124)

felicitate
honour somebody with a formal ceremony or presentation; noun: **felicitation** (also India) ° *Royal College felicitates teachers* ° *Army Commander felicitated by alma mater* ° *a message of felicitation* ° *a felicitation ceremony*

fellow
/felō/ (coll.) man, boy, chap, bloke, guy; can also refer to animals, e.g. a pet (dated in BSE) ° *Our small fellow is sick.* ° *That carpenter fellow was good.* ° *Useless fellows they are!* ° *Better take the fellow to the vet.* ° *The fellow puts his beak into the flower.* ° *Rat traps have been placed every night. We caught two fellows up to now.*

♦ "It was a bad show killing the Prime Minister like that but you have to hand it to our fellows, they know how to do these things." (Reef 145)

♦ "Where will they get another fellow like MacArthur?" (TT 225)

♦ "You Jaffna fellows live a dreary bloody life, ... Especially that married fellow, Nayagam?" (WMD 20)

♦ "Fellow could have just shown that he recognized me!" (OD 10)

♦ These fellows, they are so loath to look one in the eye that they have a rather shifty look about them. (Z 10)

♦ "A fellow like that always knows how to get his hands on a gun." (HC 289)

♦ A young fellow at the back of the bus was carrying a camera. (FSD 152)

♦ "They'll force us to listen to the fellow." (GC 70)

♦ "Let's invite her to the little fellow's birthday party," ... (CP 13)

♦ "Mad fellows, ... Dunno who taught them to drive." (CU 57)

♦ "You want to sell the fellow? ... Who will have twenty rupees to buy a baby hare?" (PMS 104)

few
(coll.) a few ° *There are still few vacancies in following classes: ...* ° *Only few seats available for the March 2006 intake.* → In BSE, 'a few' means 'some', while 'few' emphasises the fact that there are 'not many', so omitting the article 'a' can lead to misunderstandings.

♦ "Only few people and no sermon or anything." (TT 149)

♦ "My sister died few years ago." (CG 131)

♦ They stepped back few paces, kicking some of the small chairs aside. (FSD 277)

♦ ... but after few minutes the man passed away. (KCS 129)

fight
(n) argument; (v) argue ° *They had a big fight.* ° *You should have seen them fighting in the meeting!* → In BSE, 'fight' is less commonly used to refer to a verbal confrontation, especially as a verb; it normally implies a physical confrontation.

file cover
a cardboard file or folder

♦ Floating stock such as pins, paper clips, file covers, pens and pencils, ... disappear. (YY 100)

♦ I was in civilian clothes and held a blue file cover in my hands. (REP 353)

fillip
boost, incentive (formal in BSE) ° *a fillip to farmers*

film hall
cinema

film roll
film (for a camera)

♦ He took out the two used film rolls from his pocket ... (FSD 133)

♦ I longed for a flood. Preferably before the film roll finished. (M&P 237)

film show
(= show) film, movie

filth: to abuse/curse/scold somebody in filth
to abuse somebody, to swear at somebody, to use bad language ° *The soldiers abused him in filth and demanded to know who he was.*

♦ A woman's high-pitched wail, a man's fierce curse in filth, a child's hopeless scream, ... (WCS 49)

find: to find for
(coll.) to look for ° *He's finding for a new job.*

□ to find out

(coll.) to find ° *Did you find out a new house yet?* → In BSE, to 'find out' means to discover some information.

fine

(= **mara**) (coll.) funny (often used ironically) ° *A fine thing happened to me yesterday.*

- ♦ "Fine thing, no? to come and tell all this to your grave." (JFT 10)

- ♦ "And fine one, you are. Don't know your children's handwriting even." (JFT 106)

- ♦ "Fine thing to give for his birthday, no?" (YY 189)

- ♦ "You're a fine one," ... (CG 346)

finger bowl

a bowl of water used to wash the fingers after eating (less common in BSE)

finished!

(coll.) forget it!, there'll be trouble! ° *If you don't go today, finished!*

finish up

(vt) finish, finish off ° *I'll just finish up my work and come.* → In BSE, 'finish up' (vi) doesn't take an object: 'You'd better finish up now.'

fire

heat (for cooking) ° *Put the dhal on the fire.*

fist

(dated) handwriting (rare in BSE) ° *You have a lovely fist.*

flick

(coll.) pinch, nick ° *I flicked this pen from the Oberoi.* ° *The JVP has this habit of flicking things from all over and patenting them in their names.*

flirt

(v) to make sexual advances; (n) a person who flirts ° *She's a real flirt!* → In BSE, 'flirting' is usually a playful act without serious sexual intentions.

floods

(coll.) trousers which are too short (also US) ° *teased in school for wearing floods*

floor case, floor patient

a hospital patient without a bed, who has to lie on the floor

- ♦ The wards were always in turmoil - outpatients in General Surgery, floor patients in the corridors, technicians arriving from a radio store to fix the electrocardiogram unit. (AG 239)

floor polisher

a machine like a vacuum cleaner for polishing floors (less common in BSE)

flower girl

(= **little maid**) a young child who accompanies the bride at a wedding (also US) → In BSE a 'flower girl' is a girl or young woman who sells flowers. A girl accompanying the bride at a wedding would be referred to as a bridesmaid; in SLE a 'bridesmaid' is older than a 'flower girl'.

- ♦ It was almost eleven when the newly-weds rolled up with Leah in tow and a sister of Colontota's and a sweet-faced flower girl who was Colontota's sister's daughter. (JFT 52)

- ♦ "And how many flower girls should I have?" (FB 51)

flower vase

vase ° *Add doses of salt to flower vases and ant traps.*

flowery pekoe

a high grade of tea (> **pekoe**)

foguete

/fugeti/ a sweet pastry made with **pumpkin preserve**, a **Burgher** speciality (Portuguese)

following

the following ° *I am resigning for following reasons:...* ° *Following is the interview in full:...*

food stamps

food vouchers issued by the government to poor families under the **Samurdhi** programme (also US)

footboard

the step at the door of a bus where passengers stand if the bus is full ° *footboard travellers* → In BSE, a 'footboard' is a board at the foot of a bed.

♦ ... and with a rear entrance with a two-step footboard on which the conductor usually rode. (BTH 8)

♦ The buses are packed with office workers, some of them hanging desperately to the edge of the footboard. (GC 60)

♦ ... as he watched one of the overloaded buses struggle past, heeling over on its suspension, passengers crammed in like sardines and jammed onto the footboard, clinging like monkeys to whatever was at hand. (CU 22)

♦ Paduma, followed by the other two, are the first to jump off the footboard. (PMS 109)

for (1)

because of, due to, as a result of ° *Can't do anything for the heat.* ° *They ripen quickly for the sun.* ° *The car got washed for the rain.* ° *They get angry for the slightest thing.* ° *This area is notorious for flooding even for the slightest rain.*

♦ Three deaths for one landmine. (OM 26)

♦ He closed his eyes, but couldn't sleep for the racket. (CU 456)

♦ Every night he cried in pain for the scars ... (M&P 132)

♦ More people did not use it for the simple fact that one had to walk more ... (M&P 273)

for (2)

per, in (a period of time) ° *over hundred visitors for a month* ° *six times for a year* (BSE: over a hundred visitors per month, six times a year)

♦ Fuel is severely restricted in these border areas with civilians owning motor bicycles being issued some 15 liters for the month. (REP 71)

♦ ... it was Tuesday and already her third bath for the week. (M&P 211)

♦ "We have twelve poyas for a year ..." (M&P 302)

for (3)

until ° *A/level exam put off for June 6*

forex

foreign exchange ° *today's forex rates*

forget: to forget to do something

to forget how to do something (> **know**)

♦ "What is the matter, woman, do you think your son has forgotten to eat off a plantain leaf?" (WMD 15)

fork and spoon; fork and knife

spoon and fork; knife and fork → In Britain, most main courses are eaten with a 'knife and fork'. In Sri Lanka, people either eat with their fingers, or with a 'fork and spoon'.

♦ There is no point in using a fork and spoon for this meal. (RF 26)

♦ I disdainfully put aside the fork and spoon provided by the waiter and used my fingers. (REP 318)

♦ When foreign visitors came one would expect them to eat with fork and knife, but they too would try to be like us and eat with their fingers. ... What we needed were not forks and knives, but finger bowls. (M&P 92)

formula film

a Hindi, Tamil or Sinhala film with a standard formula of songs, dances, fights and love scenes (> **bioscope**)

for my luck

(coll.) luckily, fortunately ° *For my luck he never called back.*

forthwith

immediately (more formal in BSE) ° *White Tiger go home forthwith!*

forward

cheeky (less common in BSE) ° *Forward case she is!*

♦ "They would have thought us too forward and done something to my girl." (WMD 374)

♦ Nali, ever the forward one, speaks to him while I hang back feeling awkward. (GC 35)

□ forward Peter

a cheeky person; female: **forward Peter's eldest daughter** ° *What a forward Peter!*

foster parents

a couple who sponsor a child → In BSE, 'fostering' means looking after a child in your own home for a period of time; 'sponsorship' means paying money to support a child from a poor family.

fourth

quarter (less common in BSE) ° *One fourth of the class are Muslims.*

♦ ... and it had risen and grown in the countryside because it was there that three-fourths of the population lived. (WMD 250)

frikkadel

/frikəɒel/ a small, deep-fried meatball, a **Burgher** speciality (Dutch) (> **lamprai**)

♦ Christmas lunch called for the Dutch *frikkadels* - the forcemeat balls which were deep-fried and delicious; ... (JFT 186)

frock

dress → In BSE, a 'frock' is usually a dress worn for a special occasion, e.g. a 'party frock'.

♦ She was fair and had blue eyes and wore frocks and spoke in English, of course. (OM 18)

♦ "My God, *men*, I have not seen you since you were a little pip-squeak hanging onto your sister's frock." (SG 211)

♦ The next day the nurses returned, not in uniforms but in frocks and slippers. (AG 127)

from

since ° *We're waiting from morning.* (BSE: We've been waiting since morning.)

♦ "And they were the ones who kept the Vice Chancellor and the others who were in his office and held them hostage from morning." (OD 28)

♦ I spent the whole day, from morning, my mind enthused by this idea ... (OD 137)

♦ "From this morning a man has been trying to find me," ... (KCS 135)

♦ "Gamini practised and practised from last year," ... (PMS 160)

from where

where … from (> **whom**) ° *From where did you get it?* ° *I don't know from where they came.* ° *From where to get the money?* (BSE: Where did you get it from? I don't know where they came from. Where can we get the money from?)

- "From where did you get the gunny?" (TT 165)

- We knew all about the shops in Colombo, … bookshops from where he brought us books and the clothes stores from where he bought sarees for my mother and big sister. (OM 21)

- … when I look back towards the east from where I came … (BTH 17)

- "From where did he appear?" (OD 111)

- "I don't know from where she will emerge and speak to me." (OD 131)

- "From where are you calling?" (GC 243)

front house

the house opposite ° *They stay in the front house.* ° *the front house neighbours*

- At the queen's command, Babun Appu Aiyya, our front house neighbour slowly and silently scaled a tall jak tree. (CM 19)

full-boiled

(of an egg) hard-boiled (> **half-boiled**)

full suit

formal suit with jacket and tie

- Instead I was shoved into a hotel ballroom with a multitude of other men dressed in full suits, … (Z 13-14)

- One only wore it once - on the wedding day - simply to please society, which dictated that a man should get married in "full suit" … (WCS 57)

- He never got invited to functions where the "full suit" was necessary. (WCS 58)

fully

really, completely, totally, absolutely (more formal in BSE) ° *He was fully drunk.* ° *I can't eat any more - I'm fully full!*

- … and I got back into the car fully wet once more … (RF 70)

- The stationmaster's shriek woke him fully. (YY 205)

- An hour later they were running through rain and were fully wet by the time they climbed into the car. (AG 28)

- Has Daddy lived these past years in this country with his eyes fully closed? (OD 142)

- "Let's get the tarp up before it's fully dark," … (REP 217)

funeral house

a house where a person has died and visitors come to pay their respects to the body

- Since Samare was at work, Mala went alone to the 'funeral house'. (WCS 63)

- The funeral house draws them like a magnet, for there isn't anything else going on in the village. (PMS 162)

funk-stick

(coll.) wimp, coward

further

(word order) ° *The minister further stated* … ° *Abdul Cader further remanded*

further studies

higher education

-fy

(ending used colloquially to make Sinhala words into English verbs, e.g.: **ambarenafy, churuchurufy, gnurugnurufy, kendirify, kichibichify, komalafy, kunukunufy, kusukusufy, mukulufy, pandanfy, pattafy, poojafy, pulfy, rasthiyadufy**; also used to make English adjectives into verbs which do not exist in BSE, e.g.: **giddify, stingify**)

G

G (1)

(= goday) ° *Their new house is a bit G, no?*

G (2)

(= govigama) ° *They must be G's.* (> **B/G, G/B, K**)

GA

(= Government Agent) (> **AGA**)

gadget

(coll.) thing ° *What's this gadget?* → In BSE, a 'gadget' is an electrical or mechanical device; in SLE it can refer to any object.

gajeying

(coll.) scrounging, living cheaply (university slang, from Sinhala 'gaja gahanava')

gal

/gal/ (coll.) stern, hostile, unfriendly (Sinhala) ° *He gave me a gal look.* ° *At first we didn't do much other than stare and give gal looks from the balcony.*

gal arrack

low grade **arrack**

- ♦ When Bala and Stanley did their arrack run, the boys went with them. And while Bala and Stanley were deciding on whether to buy gal or pol, the boys slipped away … (July 144)

- ♦ Two days later, he sat at the Perlyn with his junction friends, drinking gal arrack and cursing Kamini and Prakash. (July 168)

galkatas

/galkaτas/ a crude home-made shotgun (Sinhala)

Galle Face

/gōl fēs/ (slang) fly, zipper (Galle Face is the name of an open area by the sea in central Colombo) ° *Your Galle Face is open!*

- ... and went to sleep with his trouser buttons open. "Saw him opening his Galle Face. Shame, no, took out his thing in front of everyone." (JFT 58)

□ like Galle Face

(coll.) looking sad, having a long face

gallon

a plastic container for petrol, etc. → In BSE, 'gallon' refers only to the quantity (8 pints).

gama

/gamə/ (= **village**) native place, the place where a person originally comes from (Sinhala) ° *They must have gone back to their gama.*

gamarala, gamaya

/gamərālə, gaməya/ (= **godaya**) (coll.) peasant, yokel, country bumpkin (Sinhala)

- "She's always been a *gamarala* at heart." (HC 146)

- "Take that silly sarong off first. You look like a bloody gamarala." (FSD 117)

- "Burghers or the gamayas who wear sarongs and are scared of motorbikes?" (FSD 143)

- "His classmates mocked him, you know, called him names like 'gamaya' and 'godaya', ..." (GC 57)

game

/gamē/ (coll.) rural, from the village ° *real game rice and curry*

ganu denu

/ganu denu/ an exchange of money or gifts, a **New Year** tradition (Sinhala)

garandiya

/gœrənɒiya/ (= **rat snake**) a very large green snake which is common but harmless (Sinhala)

- "... and those awful pigtails hanging behind her head! Just like two *gärandiyas*." (GC 115)

- ... and we even have a pair of snakes, though I have only ever seen one: a six-foot-long *garandia*, a sort of harmless (*harmless?*) constrictor that swallows rats whole. (CP 109)

garden

estate, field, plantation ° *tea garden* ° *coconut garden*

- Magnificent tea gardens spread out on either side of the road following the contours of the hill, ... (FSD 133)

gas

/gæs/ (coll.) wind (in the stomach) (also US) ° *I'm having gas.*

gatha

/gāta/ Buddhist verse (Sinhala)

- ... and the driver was found at the wheel, reciting Buddhist gathas with his eyes firmly closed. (YY 79)

- I did learn to say most of the prayers which the Buddhist people call *gathas*. ... Buddhist *gathas* are recited in Pali which is not a spoken language. (CM 9)

- "Then ask him to recite a *gatha*," ... (WMD 234)

gazette

/gæzət/ (n) a weekly government publication containing official announcements, etc.; (v) publish (government announcements etc.) in the gazette ° *Vacancies for accounts clerks will be gazetted shortly.* ° *Graduates urge Govt.*

to revise gazette notification → Note on pronunciation: This word (like cassette) would be pronounced with the stress on the second syllable in BSE, whereas in SLE it tends to be pronounced with the stress on the first syllable.

G/B

(= B/G) (in **marriage proposals**) **Govigama** Buddhist (> **K/G/B**) ° *G/B Doctor seeks partner for sister …*

gear

(v) gear up ° *Govt gears for next round of talks*

gedige

/geᴅige/ a Buddhist temple building or ornamental entrance (Sinhala)

GEDIGE

gediya

/geᴅiyə/ (coll.) lump, bump, growth, swelling (Sinhala) ° *She got a huge gediya on her head.*

geetic

/jīrik/ (= **godayatic**) (coll.) flashy, gaudy, tasteless (British slang: naff) (from **goday**) ° *geetic earrings*

gejji

/gejji/ anklets (Sinhala)

gemming

gem-mining

ge name

/gē nēm/ a traditional Sinhala family name, consisting of one or two names ending with the suffix '-ge'; this name comes at the beginning of a person's name and is often replaced by initials (e.g. Ratnayake Mudiyanselage = R.M.) (Sinhala: ge = house) ° *To this day, many upcountry Moor families bear typical Kandyan patronymic ge-names.*

get: to get a smell

to smell something, to notice a smell ° *Don't you get a funny smell?*

- ♦ Suddenly he sniffed. He could almost get the smell of his mother from somewhere. (OM 38)

- ♦ If he had gone back there, he was sure to get my scent - … (BTH 34)

- ♦ "And my son do you get the smell of vomit?" (KCS 136)

- ♦ "When they get the smell of the festive food they will come to the table to eat, …" (M&P 177)

☐ to get away

to get away with something ° *I don't know how they get away.* (BSE: I don't know how they get away with it.)

☐ to get back

to go back ° *I think we'd better get back.* ° *It happened while we were getting back.* ° *I was scared to get back alone.* → In BSE, to 'get back' means to arrive: 'We got back at 6.00.'

- ♦ There were times when Ravi thought he'd have to chuck it in and get back. (FSD 5)

- ♦ "You can get back now. We'll look after our guests." (GC 328)

□ to get something/somebody down

(= **bring down**) (vt) to get/bring something/somebody from elsewhere (esp. abroad), import ° *I got it down from UK.* ° *The team has got down two players from Fiji to play for them.*

- ... he invited Vijay and Yogi to a pot or two of fresh palmyrah toddy which he had got down specially for them. (WMD 337)

- "We got down specialists from Colombo too," ... (OD 33)

- "It was a trick to get the police down." (OD 38)

- "What about your boyfriend? ... Will you get him down as well?" (REP 269)

- "Next year, if everything is going like this I'm going to get my parents down from Jaffna." (WE 91)

- "He had got down all his rich friends for the gambling party." (PMS 166)

□ to get down (from something)

(vi) to get off (a bus), get out (of a car) ° *He got down from the bus in Galle.* ° *They will have to get down and walk a further three kilometres.*

- Whereupon the officer got down and, signalling Vijay to remain in the jeep, went off with the sergeant. (WMD 409)

- ... no one got down and no one boarded ... (BTH 54)

- He got down at Bagatelle Road and made his way to Michael's. (MiP 426)

- "Was that you who got down from the car parked outside Cargill's? That fellow inside the car did not get down." (OD 111)

- They made you get down and sign the books. (Z 126)

- I was relieved to see them get down without their guns. (REP 124)

- Mithra brings the vehicle to a halt and gets down. (GC 265)

- ... Jackson the lorry driver carrying a white puppy and getting down from the police jeep. (KCS 153)

- "Son, are we close to Yakkala? We have to get down." (PMS 201)

□ to get off something

to get out (of a car, swimming pool, etc.) (> **off**) ° *I got off my vehicle and walked up to them.* ° *The officer got off the Pajero and entered the house.* ° *Get it hot off the oven!*

- I got off at the gate and crossed the road. (REP 342)

- Another three-wheeler took them to Cinnamon Gardens. They got off and walked towards the OIC's office. (FSD 27)

□ to get out from something

to get out of something ° *When did he get out from prison?*

□ to get round somebody to do something

to persuade somebody to do something → In BSE, to 'get round somebody' has the same meaning, but without the action being specified: 'She managed to get round her father.'

- ... he was trying to get round me to read them. (OD 76)

- Mahi Bada has got round his mother for the money. (PMS 193)

□ to get up

to wake up ° *I got up at 5.00, but I didn't get out of bed till later.* → In BSE, to 'get up' is to get out of bed.

geta bera

/gɶтɘ berɘ/ (= **magul bera**) a traditional drum held at the waist and played with both hands (Sinhala)

geuda

/geuɒɑ/ a stone with no intrinsic value, but which can be chemically treated to give it the qualities of a blue sapphire

giddy

(coll.) flirtatious ° *a giddy case* → In BSE, 'giddy' can mean frivolous or excitable.

□ giddify

(coll.) flirt (> -fy) ° *Stop giddifying will you!*

gift

(v) give, donate (formal in BSE) ° *He has gifted thousand rupees.* → In BSE, 'gift' is normally used only as a noun.

♦ Just before leaving father gifted some money wrapped up in a betel leaf to the chief member of the family. (CM 70)

♦ Could Daddy have gifted Marx's books to the Party office? (OD 138)

♦ … Carmen and Douglas had gifted their house to their four children in 1972 … (Z 90-1)

♦ Ravi's mother had gifted the house to him when he turned twenty-one. (FSD 40)

gingelly, gingili

/jinjɘli/ (= **thala**) sesame (also India, orig. Hindi) ° *gingelly seeds*

□ gingelly oil

sesame oil

♦ … and his brown pork-pie hat stained at the brim from the *gingili* oil that ran off his hair. (WMD 133-4)

♦ In the morning, after church, a woman would come to the house and give each girl a massage with gingelly oil. (CG 170)

♦ His wife cooked with *gingelly* oil, in the Tamil fashion. (HC 153)

♦ "Last night I covered my entire body from head to toe in *gingelly* oil and slept on newspapers." (CP 130)

giraya

/girɘyɘ/ an implement used to slice **arecanut** in the preparation of **betel** (Sinhala, from Malay)

GIRAYA

girl

young woman (> **factory girl, Juki girl**) → Although in BSE young women are also commonly referred to as 'girls', it is becoming politically less acceptable to do so; in SLE, men and women are often referred to as 'boys' and 'girls' until they are either married or reach middle age.

give

give something to somebody ° *Give!* → In BSE, 'give' normally takes both a direct object (it, them, the book) and an indirect object (to me, to him): 'Give it to me', 'Give me the book'. In colloquial SLE it can stand by itself: 'Give!'

□ to give somebody, to give it to somebody

(coll.) to hit somebody (> **one, properly**) ° *I'll give you!* ° *I'll give you one!*

♦ "Give you properly!" (TT 7)

♦ "Next time he comes I'll give him with the broomstick!" (TT 194)

♦ "… they must be giving it to Patholay." (PMS 136)

♦ "I'll give them two across the ear." (PMS 181)

□ **to give somebody to eat**
to give somebody a meal, give somebody something to eat, feed somebody ° *They gave us to eat before we left.* ° *Have you given the cats to eat?*

♦ "Don't I give him to eat, couldn't he ask me?" (WMD 129)

♦ … because he has got used to Proctor Gunawardana's place where they give him to eat … (BTH 35)

glassmaker's daughter
a person who sits or stands in front of you and blocks the view

glass pieces
pieces of glass

♦ The next day the wall between our house and the maternity hospital had jagged glass pieces on it. (M&P 147)

gnurugnurufy
/nyurunyurufai/ (= **kunukunufy**) (coll.) moan, whinge (from Sinhala) (> **-fy**) ° *Now stop gnurugnurufying and eat your rice!*

go
/gō/ go away ° *Go from here!*

□ **to go to do something**
to do something, to go and do something, to go to the effort of doing something ° *If you go to cook everyday, it's a lot of work.* ° *If you go to take a photograph it will disturb the children.* ° *She doesn't go to complain.* ° *When she goes to write she makes a lot of*

mistakes. ° *Don't go to open the door for unknown people.*

♦ "Why did you go to argue with him?" (JFT 87)

♦ "If police come and say anything happened in Wellawatte at five o'clock don't go to say anything." (TT 149)

□ **to go and come**
to come back, come again ° *I'll go and come!* (BSE: See you later!)

□ **to go as**
to be known as ° *Her first name is Priyadarshani but she goes as Kumari.*

□ **to go behind**
(= **run behind**) to go after somebody/ something, run after somebody/something, chase somebody up ° *You'll have to go behind him if you want him to help.*

♦ "If you ask me, going behind that girl." (TT 166)

□ **to go down**
to lose weight (> **put on**) ° *She's gone down since I last saw her.*

□ **to go for**
to go to (a party, film, class, etc.) ° *Did you go for the show last evening?*

♦ We are going for a party. (Z 125)

♦ "It will be very grand. … We must go for it." (GC 125)

♦ I had been going for Tower hall plays every weekend since the dawn of the JR era. (M&P 272)

□ **to go off**
to leave ° *I think they went off early.* → In BSE, to 'go off' suggests leaving home to go out somewhere; in SLE, it suggests leaving a party, etc. to go back home.

□ to go through

to read ° *I go through the newspaper everyday.* → In BSE, to 'go through' something suggests reading it in detail, or looking for particular information.

goat

/gōт/ (= **donkey**) (coll.) fool, idiot, ass ° *Don't be such a goat!*

gob, gobbaya

/gobbǝya/ (coll.) fool, idiot (Sinhala) ° *He's such a gob he failed his O levels also.* ° *Aiyo, he's a real gobbaya!*

gobbish, gobba

/gobbǝ/ (coll.) stupid, foolish, dim (Sinhala) ° *Gobba fellow, no?* ° *She's a bit gobbish, failed maths also.*

goblet

(= **gurulettuwa**) a long-necked earthenware pot used for storing drinking water (from Anglo-Indian 'goglet', from Portuguese) → In BSE a 'goblet' is a drinking cup shaped like a wine glass.

♦ … the earthenware goblet with a beaded lace cover in which boiled water was stored, … (HC 163)

♦ She picked up a goblet to pour herself a glass of water … (HC 225)

godamba roti

/gōdambǝ rōтi/ a large, thin **roti** used to make **kotturoti** (Sinhala; from Tamil kodumai = wheat)

♦ Ravi bought *godamba roti* to take home for their dinner. (FSD 179)

♦ "But what about godamba rotis? … I thought we were getting a godamba man to set his cart up in the courtyard." (SMS 62)

♦ … 200 eggs for the hoppers and godambas, … (SMS 137)

♦ "Sharona, see that man over there, he is the one who makes *Gothamba roti* near the rail tracks." (M&P 338)

goday

/goдē/ (= **G, geetic, godayatic**) (coll.) (of people) unrefined, unsophisticated, common, lower class; (of clothes, jewellery, etc.) flashy, gaudy, tasteless (British slang: naff) (from **godaya**) (> **nats**) ° *She's a bit goday, no?* ° *wearing a goday dress*

♦ "Aney those *goday* teachers from the village don't know how to talk proper English," … Nandamalini was a goday name, and even the acquisition of English would not remove the goday mantle from a person who possessed the unfortunate karma of being named Nandamalini. Once goday, always goday. Goday was the opposite of fashionable. (M&P 29)

godaya

/goдǝya/ (= **gamarala, gamaya**) (coll.) peasant, yokel, country bumpkin (Sinhala = villager)

♦ "OK, OK, … you can go back to your sightseeing, you *godaya*." (WMD 93)

♦ "Continue to call me a *godiya*." (MiP 369)

♦ "As if I'm a *godeya* who's never heard of weedkiller." (HC 79)

♦ Mithra grumbles about *godayas* not being able to appreciate modern conveniences. (GC 287)

□ godayata magic!

/goдǝyaтǝ mǣjik/ (Sinhala expression used when someone is impressed or baffled by something technical or sophisticated) ° *You should have seen his car - for me of course it was godayata magic!*

godayatic

/goɒəyæтik/ (= **geetic**) (coll.) flashy, gaudy, tasteless (British slang: naff) (from **goday**)
° *Godayatic clothes, no?*

godown

/gōɒaun/ (dated) shed, store, warehouse (Anglo-Indian, from Malay)

gokkola

/gokkolə/ young palm fronds used as decoration (Sinhala)

GOKKOLA

♦ Half a mile away a pyre was being built on the cinnamon land and people were constantly coming and going with white paper, streamers and string, gok kola decorations. (OM 22)

♦ They made ornamental decorations with tender yellow coconut fronds, called *'gokkola'*, to make the offering ceremony more pleasing to the devil. My father took some coconut fronds and taught us how to make *'gokkola'* snakes. (CM 43)

golaya

/gōləya/ assistant, apprentice (Sinhala)
° *The baas is here with a couple of golayas.*
° *He had been the Loku Hamuduruwo of a temple but as he grew old and feeble the golayas were not treating him well.*

golu lamp, goluwa lamp

/golu/ a traditional glass hanging lamp
° *The entrance is paved with granite tiles and supported by Dutch period pillars with overhung Goluwa lamps.*

GOLU LAMP

goma green

/gomə/ a dull brownish green colour (Sinhala: goma = cow dung) ° *a goma green bag*

gona, gonbaas

/gona, gonbās/ (coll.) fool, idiot (Sinhala: gona = bull)

♦ "After all those papers and all, and the letter you wrote that *gonbass* minister." (Reef 58)

♦ "Then some foolish *gona* like me will see all this *penuma* and want to come to America ..." (Z 70)

gon case, gon fellow

(coll.) useless person, no-hoper (from **gona**)

gonibilla

/gōnibillə/ an informer, e.g. during the JVP troubles, his head covered with a sack to protect his identity (Sinhala: goni = sack) (> **billa**)

♦ At night a light was left on in his room, wasting money, because he was afraid of *gonibillas*, the bogey-men with whom his ayah had once threatened him. (HC 215)

♦ His bus was stopped twice. ... On the second occasion, by army men and a hooded man who was kept chained inside a vehicle. This *gonibilla* was a captured rebel, the passengers later whispered. (WCS 29)

good

(coll.) I'm glad, it's lucky ° *Good we went.* ° *Good you came.*

□ to be good in something

to be good at something ° *She's very good in maths.*

♦ God, they were confident, was very good in saving the king. (TT 95)

♦ "Mummy said you're good in English," ... (TT 229)

♦ True, I was not particularly good in mathematics. (M&P 137)

□ to be good with somebody

to have a good relationship with somebody ° *He's good with the boss.* ° *Be good with your neighbours.*

good name

(dated) (also India) ° *And what is your good name?*

good time

an **auspicious** period according to astrology (> **bad time**)

goon, goonda

/gūn, gūnɒa/ (= **thug**) (also India, orig. Urdu; goon also US) ° *A tense atmosphere prevails in the Ampara district as several dozens of goons allegedly hired by UPFA strongmen in the district have started hanging around in the SLMC strongholds.*

♦ Thuggery, *goondas*, terrorism. (MM 98)

♦ The election had gone off too quietly for that, there were no government goondas about and he himself had gone around unmolested and unwatched. (WMD 363)

♦ "No wonder the goons today think they can get away with anything." (SG 141)

♦ These cops, all dressed in civvies, were very much beholden to the Minister, and often acted as a private goon squad. (FSD 19)

♦ "I am not going to be scared off by these goons," ... (FSD 23)

goraka

/gorəka/ gamboge, a dried fruit which is used in cooking, especially in the preparation of **ambul thiyal**; an orange fruit in its natural state, but sold as dried, black, kidney-shaped segments (Sinhala)

♦ ... she recalled how Bandu would tell her of ghosts under those huge goraka trees, ... (OM 2)

♦ It was a seasoned *goraka* tree with dark green leaves, widely spreading branches and a thick black trunk. ... *Goraka* is a golden orange coloured fig. The sweet and sour juicy kernel is delightfully edible. The ribbed outer sour rind is sundried and used as a seasoning for cooking fish. (CM 16)

♦ He learnt to pick out the drooping branches of the *goraka* tree, whose leaves and lobed fruit act as an aperient, ... (HC 228)

gori, goriya

/gōri, gōriyə/ (= **stir**) trouble (usually violent), fight (Sinhala)

♦ "Some *gori** there, ... everyday *gori* there, no?" (* Sinhalese: loosely a 'fight', a disturbance, a breach of the peace.) (TT 206)

gotukola

/goʈukolə/ a green leaf used to make **mallung** (Sinhala)

♦ It is from him that I got the taste for *gottukola* ... (WMD 123)

♦ As I serve my frugal meal of red rice, gotukola sambol and dhal ... (Z 11)

- Thereafter Padma had instructions to prepare *gotukola* leaves mixed with shredded coconut every day. (HC 208)

- Take gotukola - those leaves are as round as little cart wheels. (KCS 85)

government
the government ° *Government has announced new measures ...*

Government Agent
(= **GA**) the senior government administrative officer at district level

- It was he, after all, who had persuaded the government agent of Jaffna to run the main road from Manipay to Chunnakam through Sandipilay, ... (WMD 142)

government servant
civil servant

- Sinhalese parents had one aim: their sons must be doctors, or lawyers, or engineers or 'government servants'; and their daughters must be married to doctors, or lawyers, or engineers or 'government servants'. 'Government servant' was an appellation that could be construed in many ways. After all, even the office messenger in the Railway office in Maradana was a government servant. ... Eligible government servants had to belong to the upper rungs - men of the Ceylon Civil Service or the Ceylon Administrative Service. (YY 113)

- It was also the time of year when, as though by common consent, the government servants returned to Sandilipay on holiday from their various postings outstation. (WMD 140)

- Then there was the man who levied those killer taxes who certainly never paid taxes himself, proud government servant that he was, supported by an ever-grateful paying public. (CP 71)

- "... there is no one with vision to rule a country, and we government servants have to do what we are ordered to do." (M&P 175)

government service
civil service

- Perhaps the boy would enter government service, who knows, a government agent one day even, eh? (WMD 8)

- The impartial civil service metamorphosed into the partial government service. (M&P 192)

govi, govigama
/govi, govigamə, goigamə/ (= **G**) the 'farmer' caste, considered the highest caste (Sinhala) (> **B/G, G/B, K/G/B, vellalan**) ° *Govi Catholic respectable family from Kandana area ...*

- Mrs. Van Der Hoot, well tuned to the racial and caste sensitivities of Ceylon, was very careful to pair off like with like, Karava Sinhalese with Karava Sinhalese, Goyigamas with Goyigamas, Burghers with Burghers, Tamils with Tamils, and so on. (CG 144)

- "That may be okay for people from *some* communities, but not for Sinhalese Govigama people like us." (July 58)

- But she would probably carry on from there and bring shame to their Govigama name. (July 276)

- Siya's upper caste respectable Govigama father had gambled away ninety-nine percent of a part of Colombo he had inherited from his forefathers, ... Achi, being the second daughter of the second wife of a Govigama civil servant who already had three daughters from his first marriage, ... (M&P 8)

govt
(in newspaper headlines) government ° *JVP accuses govt of corruption*

grad
(coll.) graduate (also US, less common in BSE) (> **undergrad**) ° *Unemployed grads to discuss job issue with minister*

grade
/grēɒ/ class, form, level (in school) (also US) ° *He just started in grade seven.* (US: 'seventh grade')

♦ Miss Premini had been the class teacher in Grade Four. (PMS 7)

gram
/grǽm/ (= **kadala**) chick peas (Anglo-Indian, from Portuguese) (> **black gram, green gram**)

♦ ... I would smuggle home spicy sweet packets: mixes of cardamom, gram, almonds, saffron and silver coated sugar pearls. (MM 83)

♦ "Moreover, take this two-rupee coin to buy some gram. Fried gram mixed with chilli powder and lime juice like I munched during my school days." (KCS 136)

☐ **gram seller**
roadside vendor of **gram** and other fried pulses, etc. ° *It's a hot day's work for this gram seller, whose spicy nibbles are a hot favourite among customers.*

♦ Dias, ears flattened, bumped into a gram-seller's cart on the pavement and toppled a basin full of peanuts to the ground. (Reef 67)

♦ Gram-sellers lined the pavements and red banners hung from the trees. (WMD 61)

♦ The gram-seller looked at us standing side by side before him, his flickering oil lamp between us, and held out a packet of gram with both hands, gesturing us to accept it, together. (WMD 153)

♦ ... the one-eyed gram seller who squatted by a culvert in Sea Street behind her basins of devilled pulses. (HC 173)

grama sevaka
/grāmɒ sēvɒkɒ/ (= **GS**) an administrative official at village level (also **grama niladhari**; formerly **village headman**) (Sinhala)

♦ A Grama Sevaka was a sort of village headman and a prestigious title to hold. (July 247)

♦ "And we can get someone from the Grama Sevaka's office to be the second witness" (July 290)

grappler
(in newspaper headlines) wrestler (> **cager**) ° *He also requested the Minister to assist in providing more facilities to train the grapplers and gymnasts.*

gravy
/grēvi/ (= **hodi**) the spiced sauce in which a curry is cooked → In BSE, 'gravy' usually refers to the fatty juices from cooked meat.

♦ ... or cuttlefish in a thick black gravy of roasted spices, ... (YY 92)

♦ Normally there would be a crackling seeni-sambol and some gravy to go with them, ... (YY 102)

♦ "... so you can cook it, in one of your hot Jaffna gravies, eh?" (WMD 87)

green gram

(= **mung ata**) mung beans (> **gram**)

♦ ... but Carloboy found that he could drop a green gram pellet down the barrel, pull the clip spring, and fire. (YY 189)

♦ ... all except the last one containing boiled green-gram. (PMS 74)

green thumb

green fingers (an expression used to describe someone who is good at gardening)

♦ "She's so wonderful with plants ... real green thumb." (July 241-2)

GROBR

(coll.) "good riddance of bad rubbish" (BSE: 'good riddance to bad rubbish')

groomsman

a man accompanying the bridegroom at a wedding together with the **bestman** (also US)

ground

(= **playground**) sports ground, playing field ° *Turn left after passing the ground.*

grow up

/grō/ (= **attain age, come of age, cross**) (of a girl) reach puberty (> **big girl**) ° *She still hasn't grown up.*

♦ ... their little sister (who had grown up a year ago and had small rounded breasts) ... (TT 167)

♦ "She grew up only last year ..." (OM 28)

♦ Priyanthi, after months of secretly wondering if she would ever 'grow up', which was what menstruating was known as around here, ... (July 159)

♦ He knew that this 'growing-up' thing was like a formal introduction to womanhood, but suddenly, she felt different to him. (July 165)

♦ "When you grow up you have to. For the next few days, until the astrologer gives an auspicious time for your bath, you will be drinking a coffee every morning with two raw eggs." (M&P 231)

GS

(= **grama sevaka**)

guardstone

a carved stone flanking the entrance to a temple ° *fallen statues and beautifully carved guardstones*

GUARDSTONE

gudu

/guɒu/ a game played with sticks; also **chakgudu** (Sinhala)

♦ For days I would sit at the edge of the field by the bole of the jacaranda tree and watch them play *thaatchi* and *gudu* and, occasionally, when they could lay their hands on a ball, rounders. (WMD 115)

guli

/guli/ an **ayurvedic** pill or a small ball (e.g. of rice) (Sinhala)

♦ ... because his father had served in one of the dispensaries in Kegalle, dishing out *gulli beth* (a mixture of quinine and marmite rolled into a pill) to the villagers ... (WMD 183)

gully bowser

sewage **bowser**, a tanker for transporting sewage

gultik

/ɡalтik/ (n) a tough nut ° *It'll take more than that to offend a gultik like him!*

gum

(n/v) glue (less common in BSE, esp. as a verb) ° *a gum bottle* ° *You must gum the receipt to the back of the application.*

♦ Her lips were sealed as though a bottle of gum had fallen into her mouth. (M&P 122)

gunny

jute, a coarse material used to make sacks (also India, from Hindi)

♦ The metal bowl and Rex's platter were there on the gunny mat where Rex was chained … (KCS 150)

□ gunny bag, gunny sack

a sack made of **gunny**

♦ Covered it with a brown gunny sack to keep the cool in. (Reef 88)

♦ But she was intrigued to see her son, a large gunny sack of leaves slung over his shoulder, … (TT 165)

♦ Thousands and thousands of tea bushes climbing relentlessly up the mountainside, and women, shrouded in gunny sacks, bent double over their labour. (WMD 96)

♦ The gunny bag stiff and bulging with the provisions stood upright on the ground … (BTH 14)

♦ In the store rooms at the back, more unopened gunny bags waited. (July 186)

♦ "With that face you can go to a fashion show in a gunny sack." (MiP 150)

♦ … fifteen gunny sacks of rice, two sacks of orange lentils, … (HC 178)

♦ … gunnysacks that were brimming with cloves, cardamoms, dried chillies, and a dozen varieties of rice. (SMS 137)

♦ When I was small they would bring it in gunny sacks and throw it in the end room there, … (CP 64)

♦ … squatting on the ground under the jam fruit tree, on a carpet made by a folded gunny bag … (KCS 31)

♦ "You slept all these years between gunny bags?" (M&P 333)

gurulettuwa

/ɡurulēttuwə/ (= **goblet**) a long-necked earthenware pot used for storing drinking water (Sinhala)

GURULETTUWA

gutty

(coll.) gutsy ° *Gutty Sri Lankans hold favourite Turks* ° *Navy edge out gutty old Zahirians*

gypsy earrings, gypsies

hooped earrings

H

habalapeti

/habalapeti/ rice flakes (Sinhala; Tamil aval)

hack (1)

tease, bully ° *I got hacked at office today.*
° *They hacked me about my haircut.*

hack (2)

wear out (a machine, clothes, etc.) ° *Don't hack the car like that!* ° *He wears his clothes till they're fully hacked.*

□ hackable

hardy, sturdy, tough enough to be 'hacked'
° *hackable jeans*

hackery

(= thirikkale) (dated) a small **bullock cart** used for carrying people, smaller and lighter than a **buggy** (Anglo-Indian, from Hindi) (> **race cart**) ° *Police ban cruelty in hackery races*

HACKERY

♦ … and I still have a clear recollection of seeing the wounded pilot being taken on a hackery by carter John along the road in front of the house … (BTH 49)

♦ His book included etchings - a hackery travelling along canopied roads, … (AG 227)

had

(use of past perfect tense) ° *The robbers had escaped in a white van.* → In SLE, the past perfect tense ('had done') is frequently used to report something in the past which the speaker did not witness first hand. It is therefore common in story-telling and newspaper reporting, where the simple past tense would be used in BSE: 'The robbers escaped ...' The past perfect is only used in this way in BSE if it is an example of reported speech introduced by a past tense verb such as said/told/reported: 'The police said that the robbers had escaped…' or 'It was reported that the robbers had escaped …' The other context in which the past perfect would be used in BSE is to show that one event happened before another: 'When the police arrived, the robbers had already escaped.'

♦ She is the only child in the family and the father had died long ago leaving everything to her. (OM 19)

♦ "A bear had fed on termites here, … Not long ago, because sand in the hollow is still damp." (REP 197)

♦ "He'd been knocked down while crossing Galle Road," … (REP 273)

♦ Kurunegala is a large and prosperous town that had grown around the foot of an enormous rock outcropping called Athagala or Elephant Rock. (REP 318)

♦ "Colonel Srikantha and at least five other cadres had been killed in the attack." (REP 354-5)

♦ She tapped her bell, and a minute later Dilini had come out holding the hand of an older girl. (FSD 293)

♦ "In the beginning of this century a white man called Sir Samuel Baker had killed in Ceylon more than one

thousand five hundred elephants."
(KCS 107)

♦ "It is believed that the Lord Buddha had come to my country three times during his lifetime." (M&P 68)

ha-ho
/ha-ho/ hoo-ha ° *So he has created a big ha-ho about adult movies and cinema posters.* ° *Hell of a ha-ho, police cars everywhere ...*

hail from
/hēl/ come from (dated and formal in BSE) ° *He hails from a good family.* ° *hailing from a humble farming family*

♦ They hailed from Mutwal and Modera, Chilaw and Negombo, Galle and Batticaloa. (JFT 28)

Haj
/haj/ an annual Muslim festival (Id-Ul-Alha) marking the traditional pilgrimage to Mecca (Arabic)

♦ That they attend the Jumma prayers, observe the Ramadan fast, slaughter the Hajj goat and wear the wedding Fez. (Z 10)

hakuru
/hakuru/ (= **jaggery**) a coarse brown sugar made from the sap of the **coconut tree** or **kitul tree** (Sinhala)

halapa
/hælapa/ a sweet made with **rice flour** and **jaggery** and steamed in a folded 'kenda' leaf (Sinhala)

half: a half bottle
half a bottle

♦ Velaithan had used her water sparingly and had at least a half bottle left. (REP 173)

half-boiled
(of an egg) soft-boiled (> **full-boiled**)

half plate
side plate

half saree (1)
(= **lama saree**) an outfit like a white **cloth and jacket** worn by young girls (esp. Sinhala) on festive occasions

♦ "It is your father's wish that you wear half sari ..." (M&P 234)

half saree (2)
a garment worn by older girls (esp. Tamil) consisting of a half-length **saree** worn with a skirt and draped over the shoulder like a **saree**

half sheet
an A4 size sheet of paper

hall
living room, sitting room → In BSE, the 'hall' is the space inside the main entrance of a house; in SLE it is the main reception room, traditionally in the centre of the house, and sometimes distinguished from a more informal living area.

halmassas
/hālmæssas/ (= **sprats**) small fish (anchovies), usually dried and deep-fried (Sinhala) → The Sinhala plural is 'halmasso', but more often 'halmassas' in colloquial SLE.

♦ She had made *string-hoppers* and *pol-sambol* and some of Vijay's favourite *haal-massas* for lunch, ... (WMD 232)

halt
(= **bus halt**) (also a stop on the railway, smaller than a station) ° *Get down at the next halt.* ° *It was only two halts away so I walked.*

♦ ... now there was no station at Udahamulla like the one in Pannipitiya; there was no solid brick building but a wood cabin with just enough room for the booking clerk ... and the place was called a Halt, ... (BTH 41)

♦ The Maharagama Halt - once-upon-a-time a wood cabin on a long platform like Udahamulla - has become a Station with a two-storeyed main block and an overhead pedestrian walk ... (BTH 47)

♦ Ravi saw a bus going to Dehiwela slowing down as it approached the halt and leapt aboard, ... (FSD 107)

hamine

/hāmine/ a high caste lady (Sinhala)

♦ ... the beautiful white Taj Mahal looking like a white skinned Kandyan hamine. (M&P 160)

hammer

(coll.) hit, beat up (less common in BSE)
(> **paste**) ° *The villagers caught the thief and hammered him.*

♦ "I'll keep them together, even if I have to hammer them everyday." (JFT 72)

♦ "Mother gave her a good hammering." (TT 210)

♦ "Her boyfriend waiting to hammer you? Is that why?" (FSD 200)

♦ "Sit down, ...I'll hammer you if you move." (PMS 111)

♦ "They will know it is us. Catch and hammer for sure." (PMS 187)

hamuduruwo

/hāmuduruwo/ Buddhist monk (Sinhala); also used (dated) to mean **mahatteya**, sir, master ° *Humble home for hamuduruwos*

♦ On Christmas morning when the *hamuduruwo* and *nonamahatheya* returned from church, the gardener would be waiting on the back verandah, ... (HC 138)

♦ That they would contradict the *hamuduruwo* was unthinkable. (HC 141)

hand

arm → In Sinhala, there is one word for hand/arm, and one word for foot/leg. This is reflected in SLE, where 'hand' often refers to the whole arm, and 'leg' often refers to the foot.

handcart

a small cart pushed by hand (less common in BSE)

♦ ... a bewildered firewood man who was told to bring along his handcart. (JFT 67)

♦ ... while coolies push their hand carts heavy laden with goods, ... (KCS 133-4)

hand tractor

a small two-wheel tractor used for agricultural purposes and for transport in rural areas

HAND TRACTOR

♦ We travel through small villages and brown-dry patches of cultivation, passing an occasional hand tractor or bullock cart. (GC 300)

hang: to hang on the phone

to spend a long time on the phone

♦ "She must be hanging on the telephone as usual," ... (M&P 17)

♦ "Hangs on the phone and talks tons of gossip to every Tom, Dick and

Harry who has time to waste, ..."
(M&P 269)

hansiputuwa

/hānsipuтuwə/ (= armchair, planter's chair)
a large rattan armchair with folding leg-rests
(also called an **easy chair**) (Sinhala)

HANSIPUTUWA

♦ "Bring out the other *hansiputuwa*. It's
cooler here." (MiP 126)

♦ The next afternoon as Hortense took
her lie down on the hansi putuwa in
the verandah, ... (Z 85)

hartal

/hartāl/ an unofficial strike, organised
closing of shops, etc. as a mark of political
protest (also India, orig. Hindi) ° *Hartal in
North-East over killing of journalist*

♦ "What exactly is a *hartal*?" - "It's
when everybody stops work -
clerks, labourers, teachers, hawkers
- everybody. They are calling it for
August 12th, for one day, to protest
against the government cuts."
(WMD 166)

hat

(= **thoppi**) (coll., dated) problem, trouble,
disaster

♦ "Hell of a hat, no?" (JFT 54)

♦ "Don't laugh, men. If hear, hat for us."
(TT 99)

hate: to hate to do something

/hēт/ to hate doing something (> **like**) ° *I
hate to cook.*

♦ "I really felt as if I belonged. I hated to
come back." (CG 282)

♦ "About a year ago Carmen told me
that she hates to live in those Western
countries ..." (Z 91)

hatti

/haттi/ (= **chatti**) a shallow earthenware pot
used for cooking (Sinhala)

havadiya

/havəɒiyə/ a gold chain worn around
the waist, traditional **Kandyan** jewellery
(Sinhala)

♦ "I, Liyanage Sumanawathee, had to
pawn my expensive *havadiya*, the
gold chain wrapped around my waist,
in order to pay my creditors. ... The
Hawadiya is my insurance policy."
(KCS 93)

have: to be having something

to have something (> **know, must**) ° *I'm
having a fever.* → In BSE, 'have' is one
of several common verbs which are not
normally used in the continuous ('-ing')
form: 'I have a cold', 'She has a dog', etc.
However, there are exceptions, e.g. when
'have' is used in the sense of 'eat' or 'take'
(i.e. for something that takes a certain
length of time): 'He's having a bath', 'We're
having our lunch', etc.

♦ "Yes, he also must be having to go
along with these chaps ... I suppose he
too must be having to do things their
way ..." (OD 13)

♦ "We just want to get some money off
him. He seems to be having plenty."
(WCS 37)

♦ "Cecil has been having a bad heart for
years." (M&P 309)

♦ "You two look like you are having
an acute case of conjunctivitis, ..."
(M&P 342)

have; haven't

(coll.) yes (we have); no (we haven't), etc. (> **can**) ° *Do we have any rice? - Have!* ° *Haven't any petrol.* → In SLE, 'have' and 'haven't' commonly stand alone where BSE would require a full sentence with pronoun, etc. ('Yes we have', 'We don't have any petrol').

have got

have had ° *Have you got chickenpox?* ° *She hasn't got the injection yet.* → In BSE, 'have got' refers to the present, 'have had' refers to some time in the past.

♦ "Thanks to me, the police have still not got a chance of seeing Nimal's diaries and critically examining them." (OD 72)

♦ "That is the result of the education they have got from the beginning." (OD 112)

having

with

♦ Two men came the other way, riding ancient bicycles having little racks at the back for carrying goods. (REP 33)

♦ She had bought a sling bag of about the right size having two small carrying handles. (REP 73)

♦ Mr. Karl told me of a single Banyan he'd seen having over 300 major, and as many as 3000 minor, trunks. (REP 162)

head up

(vt) head, lead, run ° *She's heading up the whole department.*

head bath

washing your hair, getting your hair wet (> **bath**) ° *You should avoid having a head bath.*

headman

/heɒmən/ (= village headman) (dated)

♦ I was sent with some specific things to do: buy the weekly rations from the co-op store, collect the new ration books from the Headman's office, ... (BTH 9)

♦ Soma had been a servant since she was ten years old, had weeded the headman's paddy fields since she was seven. (HC 212)

head massage

(a service commonly offered in a **saloon**)

headpiece

(= **pallu, palu**) the decorated end piece of the **saree** (> **fall, saree pota**)

heart case, heart patient

a person with heart problems

hearth

(= **dara lipa**) a traditional open stove for cooking with firewood → In BSE, a 'hearth' is a fireplace.

heaty

(of certain foods or combinations of foods) deemed to 'heat' the system according to **ayurvedic** medicine. Examples of **heaty** foods include: **blood fish** (e.g. **balaya**), **breadfruit**, seafood, pork, tomatoes, etc. (> **cooling**)

♦ It was explained that the Bala or Balaya (bonito) is very heaty. It makes the blood sizzle.... Breadfruit and bonito is a combination of the heatiest foods, ... (YY 82)

♦ "Avoid eating heaty food and it will not get any worse." ... Goat meat was too heaty for Dagma's consumption. (M&P 200)

heelbath

/hīlbɑt/ leftover **rice and curry** eaten for breakfast (Sinhala) (> **bath**)

♦ Mother and Caroline relished eating the rice and curry of the night before - *heelbuth*. Most villagers preferred left-over dinner as breakfast the next morning. *Heelbuth* was an accepted breakfast. (CM 30)

♦ I have a special fondness for rice and curries left over from the previous night's meal. In the village we call it 'heel buth', meaning literally cold rice. My mother often saved it for me to eat before I went off to school. (REP 120)

help

(nc) a hand ° *Do you need a help?* ° *Shall I give you a help?* → In BSE, 'help' is uncountable: 'Do you need any help?', 'Do you need a hand?'

hena (1)

/hēnə/ (= **chena**) an area cleared by 'slash and burn' for cultivation (Sinhala)

♦ Some of the village folk took up temporary shelter on the hilly area above our house, in the *hena* under the *gan del* trees. (CM 81)

hena (2)

/henə/ (coll.) very good, great (Sinhala) ° *We had a hena time!*

hence

so (formal in BSE)

hereafter

after this, from now on (formal in BSE) (> **thereafter**) ° *I won't say anything hereafter.*

herewith

(formal in BSE) ° *Please find enclosed herewith ...*

hewisi

/hēvisi/ traditional Sri Lankan music played in a band, e.g. in a **perahera** (Sinhala) ° *hewisi band* ° *hewisi drummers*

hi-bye friend

casual acquaintance

hi-fi

(adj.) (coll.) posh, snobbish ° *hi-fi girls* ° *Don't be so hi-fi, men!* → In BSE, 'hi-fi' is a noun meaning a music system (cassette player, CD player, etc.): SLE **set-up**.

high

(coll.) drunk → In BSE, 'high' is used in the context of drugs, but not alcohol.

high-grown

(of tea) grown at a high elevation; also **low-grown, medium-grown**

highly

very, extremely (more formal in BSE) ° *highly worried* ° *highly taken up with his work*

hike

(n) rise (in prices, salaries, etc.) ° *a massive price hike* ° *parliamentarians' salary hike* → In BSE, 'hike' is used as a noun and a verb, but only in informal contexts.

hikmeeya

/hikmīyɑ/ (musk) shrew (earlier known as the muskrat), a small grey rat considered a household pest (Sinhala)

hill country

(= **up-country**) the central hills of Sri Lanka (> **low country**) ° *a hill country town*

♦ It was then that Amma decided to take me away to convalesce in the hill country. (FB 114)

♦ A few more refugees from the hill country straggled into the camp over the next two days, ... (WMD 384)

- Every month when Jason came back from touring the estates in the hill country he would find he had been given new responsibilities, and risen higher up the firm. (SG 21)

- As a boy I had loved the hill country. (HC 81)

- ... the road runs along the southern edge of the hill country, through Balangoda and Beragala, ... (GC 82)

- In April, the hottest month of the year, Amrith and the Manuel-Pillais, like almost everyone else in their social circle, escaped to the chalets and cottages of the cool hill country. (SMS 21)

- MD is a tall, fair man who attributes his complexion to hill country origins. (WCS 34)

- He had been told that it was always cool and comfortable in Canada, like the hill country. (CU 484)

- But my heart was beating like a double-decker bus on its way up the hill country, ... (M&P 290)

hill station

(dated) a town in the hills (also India)

- A deserted air hung over Cinnamon Gardens as most of its residents had fled to the cooler climate of the hill country, to the town of Nuwara Eliya, a hill station once the exclusive domain of the British but now increasingly populated by wealthy Ceylonese, many of whom owned cottages there. (CG 245-6)

- March nights in the hill station of Nuwara Eliya were bracing. (HC 81)

hipster saree

a **saree** worn low on the hips

- The other: fat, black, cut away blouse, hipster sari, ... (M&P 46)

hiramane

/hirəmənə/ (= coconut scraper) an implement used to grate coconuts (Sinhala) (> **scrape**)

HIRAMANE

hiring car

hired car

hodi

/hodi/ (= **gravy**) the spiced sauce in which a curry is cooked (Sinhala; Tamil sodi) (> **kirihodi**)

Holy Prophet's Birthday

an annual Muslim festival commemorating the Prophet Mohamed's birthday (Milad-Un-Nabi)

home: to come home

/hōm/ to come to my house ° *You must come home for a meal some time.* → In BSE, 'home' as in the example suggests that the person being spoken to lives in the same house as the speaker, or is a family member who has gone to live elsewhere.

- "Useless bugger, men. ... Came home last Christmas and my devils were lighting crackers." (YY 168)

- Uncle Gnanam was a frequent visitor to our house. He lived in a chummery in Borella and came home every Sunday to 'sample' my mother's cooking (as he put it) and to talk politics with my father. (WMD 149)

♦ "Why don't you come home, on
Sunday evening, we can talk then."
(WMD 166)

home and home
internal, domestic ° *Black Tiger day marked
by home and home shootouts*

homecoming
a ceremony a few days after a wedding,
when the bride and groom return home
from their honeymoon

♦ Ajith is about to host a few of his office
colleagues at a little home-coming
party. (WCS 32)

homeguard
a member of an armed village defence force
in the **border villages** ° *5,000 new home
guards to be recruited* → In the UK, the
'Home Guards' were a civil defence force
during the Second World War.

Homerun pas
pastel crayons (brand name)

♦ The blank paged drawing book and
the box of Homerun pas crayons.
(M&P 102-3)

honey
(= **pani**) treacle (> **kitul, curd and honey**)
° *a honey bottle* → In BSE, 'honey' means
bees' honey. In SLE it is treacle from the
coconut tree or **kitul tree**, commonly
served with **curd** as a dessert. Bees' honey is
less common and is sometimes referred to
as 'bee honey'.

□ honey hopper
(= **pani aappa**) a **hopper** made with **honey**
in the batter

hood
roof (of a car) → In the US, the 'hood' is
the bonnet of a car. In BSE, the roof would
only be called a 'hood' if it is a soft folding
top.

□ hood-rack
roof-rack

♦ The vehicle is loaded to the roof and
more things are tied to the hood rack
above. (GC 144-5)

♦ The conductor grumbles when Mänika
insists that her sack of vegetables is put
on the hood rack. (PMS 196)

□ hood works
(= **cushion works**)

hook
(coll.) run away, hook it ° *Soon as he saw us
the bugger hooked.* (BSE: … hooked it)

hooniyam, hooniyama
/hūniyam, hūniyəmə/ an evil spell or charm
(Sinhala; Tamil sooniyam) ° *There must be
a hooniyama on me!* ° *There's a hooniyam
place in Boralesgamuwa.*

hopper
(= **aappa**) a bowl-shaped **rice flour** pancake,
a popular morning or evening meal (from
Tamil/Sinhala) (> **egg hopper, plain
hopper, honey hopper, milk hopper**)
° *hopper mixture* ° *hopper pans*

HOPPERS

♦ Sir John's breakfasts are legendary,
always hoppers and fish curry, mangoes
and curd. A breeze blows magically
under the table, a precise luxury, and
I stretch my feet to its source as I tear
apart the first hopper. (RF 158)

♦ "Come and have some *hoppers*, hot." …
Prema put a plate of *hoppers* in front of
him. (WMD 34)

♦ He would tell the bungalow cook that there should be hoppers for breakfast. Hot hoppers, he thought, with crisp crust and each cradling a poached egg. (YY 102)

♦ I had to go out and buy a hopper for breakfast almost every morning. ... Hoppers are a kind of pancake with crisp edges, usually eaten at breakfast. ... Seedakka was an active young woman skilled in the art of hopper making. Wearing a short strapped jacket and a cloth, Seedakka sat at the hearth making hoppers from early dawn. The smell of the baking hoppers floating around aroused everyone's appetite. ... Those days the hoppers were as big as a dinner plate. We bought only one hopper, paying only one cent and that was for me. (CM 30)

♦ That night she lay in bed after a dinner of soup and hoppers, an odd combination admittedly but she bought the hoppers on impulse on her way home only to find that she had no curries. (Z 40)

♦ Her small round hopper pans lay like shiny silver moons on the floor next to her. A huge container of hopper mixture sat next to them. ... There was hardly anyone in Sri Lanka who didn't like crispy hoppers, with their soft, spongy centres, ... (July 210)

♦ I served myself a full plate of hoppers and curry but derived little enjoyment from it. (REP 333)

♦ She wanted to eat then and brought out their parcel of hoppers. (FSD 254)

♦ Curries and surprisingly crisp hoppers are still on offer at the buffet table. (GC 285)

♦ "Magi is making hoppers for dinner." I don't know whether my father

liked hoppers, but I would have woken up from the dead for hoppers. (M&P 167)

□ **hopper boutique**
(= **aappa kade**) a small **kade** serving **hoppers**

♦ Across the road was the wattle and daub hut with the thatched roof where Mary Akka had her little hopper boutique. (BTH 35)

□ **hopper boy**
(dated) a boy who sells **hoppers**

♦ "Come go, ... told, no, the *hopper* boy to come by seven." And sure enough the *hopper* boy would come with his basket and Maudiegirl would count a quantity of *hoppers* (a type of thin griddle cake made of flour and fermented coconut water) for breakfast and tip the packet of *sambol* into a tin plate and note the account in a little book. (JFT 6)

♦ "You remember when we were little and mother was ill, a boy would come with a steaming basket of hoppers?" ... He cast his mind back and remembered thinking that the boy was too neatly dressed for a hopper-boy and looked more like a proper schoolboy. (WMD 30)

□ **hopper woman**
a woman who makes **hoppers**

♦ The hopper woman would arrive later and start cooking when the guests were ready to eat. (July 206)

♦ The old hopper woman, who had been fetched from her shanty home, was busy setting up her portable stove on the floor. (July 210)

♦ "... she had the most wonderful hopper woman. I have never tasted hoppers like that, so light and crisp and delicious. We could hire her to do hoppers for your birthday." (SMS 62)

hora

/horə/ (coll.) sly, secretive, mischievous, illicit (Sinhala) ° *a hora look* ° *a hora smile* ° *a hora affair* ° *hora votes*

♦ "Puts *hora* score." (FSD 217)

♦ "What's it about? Some Minister caught with his hora woman?" (GC 227)

horanewa

/horənǣvə/ a pipe played in a **hewisi** band in **peraheras**, etc. (Sinhala)

HORANEWA

♦ The main musical theme played by the horanewa emerges on the sound track, ... (BTH 1)

hora police

/hora polis/ cops and robbers (children's game) (Sinhala: hora = thief)

♦ ... this paddy field ... where we would play Hora Polis in the evenings, ... (BTH 36-7)

hori

/hori/ (coll.) itch, sore, infection (Sinhala)

horn

(v) hoot, honk, sound/blow the horn ° *Stop horning!* → In BSE, 'horn' is only used as a noun.

♦ ... and Kumaradeven cut across to the right-hand lane, causing other vehicles

to brake and horn in protest as, without checking his speed, he curved into the exit. (CU 302)

♦ Sharona's father was horning like mad at the top of the lane, waiting to drive us to school. (M&P 212)

horoscope

an astrological chart drawn up at a person's birth, used to predict his/her future and consulted at important times such as weddings ° *Their parents didn't approve of the wedding because their horoscopes didn't match.* ° *Reply with horoscope. Dowry available.*

♦ All our neighbours will tell you he is a good man, a good astrologer. He casts horoscopes in double quick time. ... Remember the time he said Malini's horoscope was not a good match for Ranjith, ...? (OM 23)

♦ "He is a man I suppose, ... and the horoscopes match and they say he has a good job, ..." (WMD 196)

♦ "The most important thing is to see that the horoscopes agree." (PMS 264)

hot drinks

alcoholic drinks

hot hot

freshly made and/or steaming hot ° *hot hot hoppers* ° *delivered hot hot to your doorstep*

♦ I would bring the patties in four at a time ..., fried only after she arrived to ensure they came fresh and hot-hot, straight from the pan. (Reef 77)

♦ "Can eat some hot hot roti at Pallai. How about that?" (YY 164)

hotel

/hoʈel/ a small restaurant serving cheap meals (also India) ° *a Muslim hotel* → In BSE, 'hotel' is only used in its other sense, i.e. a place where people pay to stay in a room. Note on pronunciation: This is one of several words which tend to be pronounced with the stress on the first syllable in SLE, and the second syllable in BSE.

♦ ... and he would be going on from there to speak to the hotel and shop workers. (WMD 64)

hotu
/hoᴛu/ (coll.) snot (Sinhala)

houseboy
(= boy, servant boy) (dated) male servant (archaic in BSE)

♦ Balendran and Sonia had finished eating and the houseboy began to remove their plates. (CG 56)

♦ That Sunday, the grizzled house-boy relieved Sam of his hat and hymn book and informed him that Green Crescent *nonamahatheya* and Jayasinghe *mahatheya* were in the drawing room. (HC 117)

house full, houseful
fully booked, sold out ° *The receptionist told me they were house full.* ° *3rd houseful week!* → In BSE, a cinema or theatre can have a 'full house'.

♦ Perhaps Nirvana is 'house full' and karma keeps prolonging rebirth as a result. (M&P 163)

how?
(coll.) how are you? ° *So how?*

♦ "So, how *men*? Feeling good?" (Reef 154)

♦ "So how? Just dropped in, men." (YY 135)

♦ "How, how Richard?" (FSD 187)

♦ "How?" he said in greeting. "How was leave?" (CU 80)

□ how ...?
(coll.) how about ...? ° *How the weather!* ° *How the small fellow?*

♦ "How the money we're making?" (YY 223)

□ how if ...?
(coll.) what if ...? ° *How if nobody comes?*

♦ "How if they dive bomb or something?" (JFT 196)

♦ "How if somebody comes?" (YY 1)

♦ "How if we stay here and you go to Trincomalee and come and see us when you have the time?" (YY 30)

♦ "How if they come back? ... How if they come as bloody pythons or something?" (YY 180)

□ how much of
(coll.) how much (> so much of) ° *How much of money do you have?*

□ how to ...?
(coll.) how can I/we/you ...? (> what to do?) ° *How to go? We don't have the car.* ° *Hot no? How to eat?*

♦ "How to control, *anney*?" (JFT 10)

♦ "Sir, how to serve the turkey?" (Reef 96)

♦ "How to see anything in the dark?" (YY 76)

♦ "How to play cricket with cows all over the ground, men?" (YY 168)

♦ "Not ashamed! Chee! How to ask my friends to come here, I don't know!" (YY 210)

♦ "I've thought about it, but how to, child? He's my only boy, no?" (July 25)

♦ "Have another, have another!" ... - "How to? This imported whisky must have cost a bomb," ... (July 248)

♦ "But what about the gates? You're not going to lock them, are you?" - "No. How to, with people still here?" (July 340)

♦ "So how to stop once I started?" (CU 197)

♦ "How to leave these children?" (M&P 210)

♦ "How to find them in this crowd?" (PMS 122)

HQI

Headquarters Inspector, **OIC** of a 'headquarters' police station

♦ ... a third was the HQI of the nearby police station, ... (CU 487)

hump: to put a hump

(= **put a jump**) (coll.) to hump, screw (crude slang for having sex)

♦ "Dayan? It's me. ... Putting a hump, or what?" (CU 208)

huna

/hūna/ gecko, house lizard (Sinhala)

HUNA

hundred

a hundred, one hundred (> **thousand**) ° *I told you hundred and fifty times!*

♦ "Who knows. Hundred years maybe." (TT 117)

♦ ... thereby implying it to be well over hundred years old. (BTH 42)

♦ "Hundred and fifty rupees," the driver said. Violet stared at him. "You said hundred!" (July 338)

♦ They were about hundred yards upriver from us, yet clearly visible as they stood in the sunlight. (REP 264)

♦ He had hundred heads and two hundred arms. (M&P 69)

♦ I don't know how he continued to live when people less than hundred were dying. (M&P 141)

♦ I never got more than fifty out of hundred for them. (M&P 148)

hunu

/hunu/ (= **chunam**) lime, a white substance used for whitewashing houses, etc.; also used in the preparation of **betel** (Sinhala)

♦ The walls were coated with *hunu*, which gave them a rough texture and a bright white color. (WE 10)

hurulla

/hurulla/ a type of fish (trenched sardine) (Sinhala)

I

ice coffee
iced coffee

ice palam
/paləm/ ice lolly (from Tamil)

♦ ... and called out to an ice-cream vendor to bring an ice *palam* for his new paramour, ... (Reef 144)

♦ Radha Aunty bought me an ice palam and told me to sit in the arena and wait for her. (FB 83)

ice water
iced water (> **plain water**)

♦ Even my glass, which holds just ice water, ... (RF 79)

icy choc
choc ice

♦ People all around were screaming and there were ice *palams* and icy-chocs all over the place, melting in the sun. (Reef 144)

♦ Niresh bought a lot of things - icy chocs, packets of devilled cashews, banana chips, ... (SMS 153)

Id
/id/ one of two annual Muslim festivals: Id-Ul-Fitr, marking the end of **Ramazan**, the month of fasting; and Id-Ul-Alha, marking the end of the **Haj** pilgrimage (Arabic)

iddly, idli
/ibli/ a steamed **rice flour** cake (also India, orig. Tamil; OED 'idli')

♦ Vijay sat down at the table and pecked at the *iddlee* Chitra had placed before him. (WMD 323)

♦ Hooting men lobbed vadais and idlis out into the street ... (July 339)

♦ It was his dinner. Two iddli's, two thosai's and two vaddais. (Z 26)

if at all
if anything ° *If at all they'll come tomorrow.*

I F if
(humorous expression used to describe a couple with a large difference in height) ° *Look at them, like I F if!*

ifthar
/iftar/ the evening meal taken after sunset by Muslims during the month of **Ramazan**, which marks the end of the daily fast (Arabic) ° *Conducting Ifthar programme for Quran madrasa students during Ramazan*

IGP
Inspector General of Police (the highest ranking police officer)

♦ The officer at the head of the table must be the IGP or someone of similar status, ...(OD 33)

♦ "I shall write to the IGP and, if necessary, to the President." (FSD 19)

♦ The IGP, a non-smoker for years, was fumbling for one of Perera's cigarettes. (CU 437)

iguana
(= **land monitor, thalagoya**) (> **monitor lizard**) ° *A woman was taken into custody for possessing eight iguanas ready to be sold for meat.* → In BSE, an 'iguana' is a type of lizard found in South America.

♦ At Anuradhapura it was venison and iguana meat; ... (YY 92)

♦ They hunted the unwieldy iguana and went after crane and bronze pigeon or ash doves. (TT 116)

♦ An iguana slunk in the watergrass, its long tail twisting as it clumped in an ungainly fashion. (TT 169)

illicit liquor, illicit hooch

(= **kasippu**) illegally distilled alcohol (US hooch, moonshine)

♦ The quick tempers, coupled with a heavy use of illicit hooch in our villages, unfortunately led to countless violent conflicts. (REP 90)

♦ His frequent visits to the boutique at the end of the street, which sold illicit liquor, had become a fact of life for his colleagues. (WCS 66)

illuk

/iluk/ a type of long coarse grass (Sinhala)

in

(adv.) inside, indoors (> **out**) ° *They're not in the garden, so they must be in.* → In BSE, 'in' is a preposition and is usually followed by a noun: 'in the house', etc. However, it can also be used as an adverb in the specific sense of 'at home': 'Is your mother in?' It is used more often as an adverb in SLE.

inauspicious

unlucky, unfavourable (> **auspicious**)

♦ It was he who had to accompany her to the temple on his brother's birthday so she could offer a pooja; he who, after she had an inauspicious dream about Arul, had to instruct the priest to make an offering to Ganesh or go, himself, to St. Anthony's in Kochchikade. (CG 232)

incumbent

the resident monk in a Buddhist temple (> **chief incumbent**)

indent (for something)

put in an official order (for something) (more formal and less common in BSE)

indiappa

/indiāppə/ (= **string hoppers**) (Sinhala; Tamil idiappam)

innala

/innələ/ a variety of sweet potato (Sinhala)

innings

(coll.) serving, helping (of food) (cricket idiom) ° *He's gone for a second innings.*

innocent

(= **simple**) kind, good → In BSE, 'innocent' is often used in the negative sense of 'naïve'. In SLE it does not carry this negative implication.

Inquirer into Sudden Deaths

coroner

inspite of

in spite of (3 words)

instant, inst.

this month (dated and formal in BSE) ° *your letter of 4th instant*

intercity bus

express bus → In the UK, there are 'intercity trains', but not 'intercity buses'.

♦ "... next thing you know they will be traipsing all over the country by train or intercity bus." (Z 78)

♦ ... as he swerves to allow an inter-city bus to blast past. (GC 279)

interdict

(v) suspend somebody from work; noun: **interdiction** ° *A group of wildlife officers have been interdicted.* → In BSE (especially in Scotland) to 'interdict' somebody is to prohibit somebody from doing something.

♦ "Now you will get interdicted, sure. ... Lucky you made report, otherwise interdicted on the spot." (YY 25)

♦ He had recommended interdiction but instead, an immediate transfer order had arrived. (YY 196)

interior
(adv.) inland (only used as a noun in BSE) ° *The house is situated a few miles interior.*

intermediate zone
the areas between the **wet zone** and the **dry zone**

inter-monsoonal
between the two monsoons ° *inter-monsoonal rains*

international school
an English medium school (> **local school**) ° *inter international school swimming meet* → International schools have become increasingly popular in the past 20 years. They are generally run as private businesses, independent of the Education Ministry, and offering English-medium education leading to London O levels and A levels.

♦ "Not any more, she is now at the international school which is close to your house." (M&P 310)

into
(in maths) times, multiplied by; (in sports) by ° *Two into six is twelve.* ° *the four into 100 metres relay* → In BSE, 'two into six' means 'six divided by two' (=3).

ironwood
(= **na**) a type of tree (national tree of Sri Lanka)

♦ ... mahogany, bombu, ironwood and the Bo Tree ... (TT 114)

♦ I tried to find some landmark to identify the spot and noticed a tall tree that looked like Ironwood by the side of the road. (REP 281)

is it?, isn't it?
(= **no?**) (coll.) (question tags used irrespective of the subject and tense of the verb) ° *You'll be here tomorrow, is it?* ° *They went together, isn't it?* → In BSE, the question tag has to correspond with the subject and tense of the main verb of the sentence: do you? has he? will they? aren't you? didn't she? etc. In the examples above, the question tags would be 'will you?' and 'didn't they?' Like many other non-British variants of English, SLE does not make these distinctions. These tags are also used in short questions: ° *He passed his test. - Is it?*

♦ "You are forgetting the presumption of innocence, isn't it." (HC 110)

♦ "And your wife is very beautiful isn't it?" (KCS 168)

islandwide
(= **countrywide**) nationwide, all over the country ° *an islandwide curfew* ° *available islandwide* → 'Islandwide' is very common in SLE, both as an adjective and as an adverb. It is also used in other island contexts (Singapore, Jamaica, Hawaii, ...) but not in the UK, where 'nationwide' is used. The alternative 'countrywide' is also more common in SLE than in BSE.

♦ ... she had stood first islandwide in English literature, ... (CG 3)

♦ "Savan, this is for an island-wide music concert poster." (WCS 15)

♦ JR implemented island-wide curfew. (M&P 263)

istoppuwa
/istōppuwa/ (= **stoop**) verandah (Sinhala, from Dutch 'stoep')

ISTOPPUWA

♦ Then came the Dutch with their ... fondness for building houses with stoeps, which were open verandas and which the Sinhalese called isstoppuwas. (JFT 26)

itself
(used like Sinhala **thamai** to add emphasis) (> **only**) ° *We have to leave now itself.* ° *I need it today itself.* → In BSE, the word 'itself' is used with nouns ('the name itself'), with reflexive verbs ('raise itself up'), or in expressions like 'by itself', but not with adverbs like 'now'. The equivalent of the examples given would be to stress the word to be emphasised by saying it louder: 'We have to leave <u>now</u>!' 'I need it <u>today</u>!'

♦ "Lucky for you we are Catholics. Otherwise would have kicked you out that day itself!" (YY 216)

♦ And that day itself he had a letter from you with a money order. (OM 13)

♦ "Today itself I must get a money order and send the money to Malli." (OD 13)

♦ "Must issue a leaflet on this tomorrow itself!" (OD 135)

♦ "That is why I came today itself." (OD 140)

♦ "Don't wait till tomorrow, ... You go today itself to the American Centre and register yourself ..." (M&P 304)

♦ "Their kite will fall to the ground on the first day itself." (PMS 205)

J

jacket
a blouse worn by women, with or without a **saree** (> **cloth and jacket, saree jacket**) → In BSE, a 'jacket' is an outer garment usually worn by men.

♦ But the ruffles on her jacket were crisp and the pearls round her neck gleamed. (OM 22)

♦ After she wore the jacket and the heavily embroidered skirt, she tied a tape around her waist. (CM 86)

♦ She owned two spare jackets and a flowered cloth. (HC 217)

♦ Women in simple cotton saris and white lace jackets ... (M&P 18)

Jaffna mango
(= **karutha kolumban**) a large green variety of mango, considered one of the best varieties

♦ Baskets of Jaffna mangoes arrived daily at his chambers. (HC 108)

jaggery
/jæɡəri, jagri/ (= **hakuru**) a coarse brown sugar made from the sap of the **coconut tree** or **kitul tree** (Anglo-Indian, from Portuguese) ° *jaggery toffee* ° *jaggery pudding* ° *jaggery cake*

JAGGERY

♦ They brought him pineapple and *jak-fruit*, plantains, *jaggery* and curd while he sat on the veranda ... (MM 96)

♦ Some days I was given a piece of jaggery to eat with the hopper. (CM 30)

♦ On the days Matara Aththa made jaggery, the wind carried the sweet message to me. I was there to watch the process of jaggery making. ... In order to make jaggery the treacle had to be stirred, till it was thick. (CM 42)

♦ She had specifically asked for curd and jaggery. (AG 18)

♦ "Bread and butter and jaggery for tea." Jaggery was the soft dark palm sugar they loved. (MiP 35)

♦ ... and ate mock turtle soup, mutton cutlets with lime pickle, and jaggery pudding. (HC 142)

jak

/jæk/ a very large green fruit, eaten either unripe (like a vegetable) or ripe (like a fruit) (also India, from Malayalam via Portuguese) → The **jak fruit** is also known by the Sinhala words for the three stages in its development: **polos** (small, unripe, eaten as a rich brown curry), **kos** (large, unripe, eaten boiled or as a mild curry or **mallung**), and **waraka** (large, ripe, eaten as a fruit with a sweet yellow flesh)

♦ They ate hot boiled jak with shredded coconut. (CM 19)

♦ Tea bushes and rubber trees gave way to coconut, mango and jak. (WMD 122)

♦ We ate from dried jak leaves shaped into cups, chewing and spitting the bones on the ground for the dogs to clear up. (WMD 141)

♦ ... a reheated meal of rice, jak curry and dried fish, ... (July 270)

♦ She described a rich man who was so stingy that he sold all his rice and ate only boiled jack. (HC 213)

♦ The table itself was of polished jak set with bowls of frangipani and jasmine flowers ... (CU 570)

▢ jak fruit

(= jak) the fruit of the **jak tree**

JAK FRUIT

♦ ... where the jak fruit rolls across your feet in the back of the jeep, ... (RF 69)

♦ Up on the tree, he tied the stem of a jak fruit with the rope. (CM 19)

♦ ... where they were dissecting a big ripe jak fruit. (WMD 16)

♦ ... she must have had to scour the whole country to find young jak fruit at this time of year. (WMD 245)

♦ Iron-skinned jackfruit, heavy as lambs. (HC 286)

♦ My aunt Seela is cleaning a jak fruit, sitting on a little stool. (GC 89)

♦ Grandma comes out of the kitchen still holding a long black coconut shell spoon perfumed with yellow jak fruit curry. (KCS 118)

♦ "Without laughing like a Jak fruit which is about to split, you had better try to do something about this child ..." (M&P 33)

♦ Paduma enjoys the ripe jak fruit Podihamy serves them, ... (PMS 61)

□ jak seeds

the seeds of the **jakfruit**, eaten as a curry

♦ "*Kool*, with crabs, nice young ones, and beans and fish-heads and jak seeds and prawns and -" ... (WMD 16)

□ jak tree

the large tree on which **jakfruit** grows from the trunk and branches

♦ There was a large jak tree in the garden. (TT 189)

♦ The gnarled old jak tree whose trunk I had leaned against and wept with some adolescent despair was still the same. (OM 49)

♦ There were quite a few jak trees surrounding our home, with an abundance of seasoned and tender fruit all the year round. (CM 19)

♦ ... and the huge jak tree which rose above the tiled roof in those days was gone too ... (BTH 51)

♦ The gates opened into an extensive cobbled front courtyard, with a large jak tree growing in the centre. (SMS 20)

♦ If the Heraths ever got their hands on the property they would begin by cutting down all the jack trees for seed money. (CP 102)

♦ Paduma wanders about the temple compound till he spies something moving under a jak tree. (PMS 246)

□ jak wood

the hard wood of the **jak tree**, which is similar to mahogany

♦ I left a tray on the small jakwood table for him to take at his own speed. (Reef 170)

♦ As she looked at him, Annalukshmi thought what a beautiful colour

his skin was, brown with a saffron undertone, like seasoned jak wood, ... (CG 360)

♦ Chairs had to be wiped with old newspapers but the damp seeped into the cheap jak wood. (July 139)

♦ A small jackwood cabinet flashed past, ... (HC 220)

♦ It was to do with the fifty odd acres of Jackwood plantation that Mrs. Herath's father did not leave her in his will. (CP 94)

jam, jam fruit

/jæm/ a small green fruit ° *'The Jam Fruit Tree'* by Carl Muller

♦ But in truth, the jam fruit tree was so symbolic. The ever-bearing tree. And never-dying too ... fruitful, tough, always in bloom, earthy ... always sprouting, reaching out, spreading over the leaf-strewn earth with its umbrella branches. It was the jam fruit tree that first gave the young ones an awareness of each other. (JFT 20)

♦ The jam tree shed so much fruit that the pond was soon full of rotting berries and dead leaves. (Reef 44)

♦ ... where he had spent his days lying in a hammock strung between two jamfruit trees, ... (HC 109)

♦ ... who'd set up a table under a jam fruit tree on the pavement. (FSD 234)

♦ The jam fruit tree that bore tiny white flowers and berries. (KCS 30)

♦ ... the squirrel that was prancing about on the branches of the Jam tree outside. (M&P 49)

♦ "There, she was screaming at all the servants down the road for stealing jam fruits from the jam tree when I was leaving the house to come and see you." (M&P 311)

jambola

/jambōlə/ pomelo, a large green fruit like a grapefruit (Sinhala)

jambu

/jambu/ (= **rose apple**) a small pink pear-shaped fruit with crisp white flesh (Sinhala and Anglo-Indian, from Malay and Sanskrit)

JAMBU

♦ ... picking *jambu*, escaping to the tree house, ... (MM 69)

♦ There were rose coloured *jambus* in the season. (CM 5)

♦ It was some jumbu fruit. (CG 309)

♦ "We spoke under the old jambu tree which still stands by the small pond." (July 153)

♦ The nose! ... Like a Jambu fruit run over by a bullock cart. (M&P 41)

♦ "The real Saro will become red like a jambu when she hears." (PMS 103)

♦ "When he went to steal jambu fruits, he left the books in a fence," ... (PMS 273)

Janasaviya

/janəsaviyə/ a government poverty alleviation programme during the Premadasa regime (Sinhala)

janaza

/janāzə/ a Muslim funeral cortege (Arabic)

Japura

/japurə/ (coll.) Sri Jayewardenepura University (> **Pera**)

jardi

/jāɒi/ a salted fish preparation (Sinhala)

Jataka tales

/jātəkə/ stories about the Buddha's life (Sinhala)

♦ There were also elaborate puppet shows of popular *Jataka* tales. (CM 74)

♦ Kusumsiri spoke in the lofty manner of a benevolent king in the Buddhist Jataka tales. (WCS 27)

♦ "But you only talk about the Jataka tales and the Lord Buddha's life ..." (M&P 87)

jathiya

/jātiyə/ (= **nationality**) race, ethnic identity (Sinhala)

♦ ... because Buddhism was not a religion, had no God, was secular and, because of that, had made *jathiya*, the race, the nation (notice, he said, how the Sinhala language had only the one word for both) its surrogate for God. (WMD 311)

♦ "... soon the Sinhala *jathiya* will be history." (WE 75)

Jayamangala gatha

/jayəmangələ gātə/ Buddhist verses sung at weddings to bless the couple (Sinhala)

jeelava

/jīlāvə/ a type of fish (barracuda) (Sinhala)

jerkin

jacket, anorak → In BSE, 'jerkin' is a dated word for a short sleeveless jacket or waistcoat.

jobless

free, idle, having nothing to do ° *I'm jobless today.* → In BSE, 'jobless' means unemployed, not having a job.

♦ "By the way, ... that servant boy was a real jobless character." (FB 134)

johnny batta, johnny mine

(= batta) home-made landmine

join: to join to something

to join (a club, etc.) ° *You should join to the Otters.*

□ to join somebody to a place

to go somewhere with somebody ° *I agreed to join Mahinda to Singapore.*

□ to join with somebody

to join somebody, go with somebody (e.g. some friends) ° *Will you join with us to go to Kandy?*

journo

(in newspaper headlines) journalist (> scribe) ° *Regional journos urge peace talks*

JP (Justice of the Peace)

an honorary title for a person given official authority to witness documents, sign affidavits, give personal references, etc. → In the UK, a JP is a local magistrate.

jugglery

trickery ° *He's upto his jugglery again.*

♦ She abstained from spinach, kankun, mukunuwenna and all iron rich foods, but the bandicoot that bit her leg had done hieroglyphic jugglery with Seela's iron storage, which no doctor could correct. (M&P 230)

Juki girl

(= factory girl) (coll.) a garment factory worker (> girl)

Juki machine

/juki/ a sewing machine used in the garment industry (Japanese brand name) ° *46 stolen juki machines recovered*

jumma

/jumma/ Muslim Friday prayers (Arabic)

♦ I would see them wending their way towards the mosque for Jumma prayers, beggars and the rich alike. (Z 9)

jump: to put a jump

(= put a hump) (coll.) to hump, screw (crude slang for having sex)

♦ "You never heard of locking the door when putting a jump?" (CU 44)

jump in

(of thieves) break in ° *Rogues jumped into the house.*

jump seat

a folding seat in the aisle of a bus

junction, junc

town centre ° *I'll go to the junction and come.* ° *Bambalapitiya junc* → In BSE, a 'junction' is simply an intersection of two or more roads; in SLE it suggests the focal point of a town or village, with shops, market, **bus stand**, etc.

♦ "You look like one of those junction hooligans you love so much." (July 316)

jungi

/jangi/ (coll.) underwear, knickers, pants (used when addressing children) (Sinhala/ Tamil; also India) ° *Why aren't you wearing your jungi?*

jungle

any wild, uncultivated land (also India, from Hindi) → In BSE, 'jungle' suggests rich tropical vegetation; in SLE it can refer to any area of uncultivated land.

jungle fowl

a brightly coloured wild fowl, endemic to Sri Lanka

JUNGLE FOWL

♦ Now it is time to feed the sambhur deer and jungle fowl. (RF 157)

♦ A turkey is not like wild duck or *batagoya* or jungle fowl. (Reef 88)

♦ Sometimes we heard a jungle fowl cry, kwikkuk kwikkukkuk … (CM 18)

♦ Chinked light brushed the silky feathers of a jungle-fowl's neck and his arched green tail. (HC 226)

♦ Jungle Fowl was easy. The books described their call as sounding like 'George-Joyce' that was silly, because to me it sounded more like 'Chruk-Chrruk'. (REP 119)

♦ Bothalay and Mahi take off like startled jungle fowl. (PMS 117)

just

for no particular reason ° *Why are you standing there? - Just.*

♦ "Then what looking-looking and doing?" - "Just, sir." - "Just!" (TT 157)

♦ When she came back and demanded to know what they were laughing about, they both looked innocently at her and said, "Oh, just." (July 313)

just be!

(coll.) mind your own business!

♦ "She didn't make any fuss, you see. She was happy to jus' be." (SG 21)

JVPer

a member of the Janatha Vimukthi Peramuna (People's Revolutionary Party)

♦ Only when the begging and pleading got too noisy had the occasional boot lashed out at the JVPers. (CU 525)

K

K

(= **karave**) ° *They're K's it seems.* (> **G**)

kaba

/kabə/ (coll.) the secretion normally found in the eyes in the morning (UK 'sleepy-eyes') (Sinhala)

kabaddi

/kabaɒi/ a traditional team game in which players have to cross a line into opposition territory while holding their breath and chanting the word 'kabaddi-kabaddi-kabaddi' (Sinhala/Tamil, also India and Bangladesh)

KABADDI

kabal

/kabal/ (coll.) old, broken, crummy (Sinhala) ° *driving around in a kabal car*

kabaragoya

/kabərəgoya/ (= **water monitor**) (Sinhala) (> **monitor lizard, thalagoya**)

KABARAGOYA

♦ I realize it is a kabaragoya. In English a sub-aquatic monitor. … Kabaragoyas and thalagoyas are common in Ceylon and are seldom found anywhere else in the world. The kabaragoya is large, the size of an average crocodile, and the thalagoya smaller - a cross between an iguana and a giant lizard. … And Robert Knox says of the kabaragoya that "he hath a blew forked tongue like a string, which he puts forth and hisseth and gapeth." (RF 73)

kabook

/kabuk/ (= **cabook**) laterite, a reddish clay which becomes hard and is used as a building material (from Portuguese)

♦ At the centre was a well. A smallish round construction made of old bricks and kabuk. (Z 150)

kachcheri

/kachchēri/ office of local government administration (Tamil/Sinhala; OED Anglo-Indian 'cutcherry' from Hindi)

♦ Upali was a cadet in the Kachcheri at Kandy. … After he was employed at the Kachcheri he started visiting Daddy often. (OD 87)

♦ "The road goes to the Kachcheri up there and then swings round in a loop behind the resthouse." (FSD 113)

kadala, kadale

/kaɒələ, kaɒale/ (= **gram**) chick peas (Tamil/Sinhala; Hindi 'channa') ° *Many people from outstation areas stop by to get some kadala on their way home.* ° *There are so many kadala karayas who quit this job because of the high expenses.*

♦ The old woman who would come to the school each day to sell gram (kadalay) and peanuts, … (TT 221)

♦ ... kadalay fried with coconut, mustard seeds, and chilli, ... (CG 375)

♦ The kadala seller pushed past us again, he smelt of liquor. When he sold kadala on poya days in front of the temple, he did not smell of liquor, he smelt of Lifebuoy soap. (M&P 339)

kadavule!
/kaɒʌvule/ my God! (Tamil exclamation)

♦ Then she rose from her chair in astonishment. "Kadavale!" she cried. (CG 221)

kade
/kaɒe/ (= **boutique**) a small shop or eating place (Sinhala/Tamil) (> **aappa kade, bath kade, rae kade, thee kade, thosai kade**)

♦ At the kadé two men are in a pool of street-light with their sarongs half hitched up, the night air cooling their legs. (MM 115)

♦ "There is money in the biscuit tin to get something from the kadé," ... (Reef 35)

♦ I knew the kadé - the tea kiosk at the top of the road, ... (Reef 39)

♦ "I waited near the kaday and then again he went near the police station." (TT 55)

♦ "People hang around caddays to gossip." (MiP 133)

♦ The vibrant hum of life, the neon lights, the blaring kadé music cannot be found. (Z 141)

♦ The kadai-owner rested his elbows on the plank that served him as a counter. (HC 176)

♦ "... nothing like good kadé tea, no?" (CP 87)

♦ "I've bumped into them several times at the kadé close to my house." (CP 190)

♦ "I will go to the Kadé and buy a loaf of bread," ... (M&P 350)

kadiya
/kaɒiya/ a large black ant (Sinhala)

kaduwa
/kaɒuwə/ sword (used as a metaphor for the English language, a symbol of power which divides those who have it from those who don't) (Sinhala) ° *The English Department is known as the kadu faculty.*

kaffrinja
/kafrinnya/ a dance to a **baila** rhythm (orig. Portuguese) ° *Kaffiringna Nite at OTSC*

♦ ... and a rollicking kaffrinja set everybody in motion ... (JFT 58)

kaftan
/kafтān/ a long loose gown worn by women → Less common in BSE, usually spelt 'caftan', and pronounced /kæfтæn/.

♦ ... decided it was too hot for a sari, donned a kaftan, hopped into a radio taxi ... (Z 73)

kaha
/kaha/ (= **saffron**) turmeric (Sinhala)

□ kaha bath
/kaha bat/ (= **yellow rice**) (Sinhala)

kaka
/kāka/ (= **aiya, anna, nana**) elder brother (used by Muslims) (> **dhatha**) ° *Hussein kaka wants to go to Galle.*

kakka, kakki
/kakka, kakki/ poo (children's word) (Sinhala) ° *I need to do a kakki!*

♦ "In Ceylon we use the left hand to wash our backside after doing kakki." (M&P 51)

kalabala
/kaləbalə/ (coll.) gaudy, cluttered, over-decorated (Sinhala) ° *I don't like his pictures - they're too kalabala.*

kalaya, kalagediya
/kale, kaləgeᴅiyə/ an earthenware water pot with a narrow neck (Sinhala)

KALAYA

kaludodol
/kaludodol/ (= **dodol**) a dark brown, jelly-like sweet made with **rice flour, coconut milk** and **jaggery** (Sinhala)

♦ And kalu dodol - the sweetmeat, black as my complexion and sweet as my love towards Baba. (KCS 87)

kalu pol sambol
/kalu pol sæmbol/ a dark roasted **pol sambol** (Sinhala)

♦ ... and the pungent *kalu pol sambol* where coconut meat is roasted dark brown in the ashes of the fireplace and then ground with onions, lime, salt and Maldive fish. (JFT 186)

kalusuddha
/kalusuddə/ (coll.) a derogatory term for a Sri Lankan who is highly westernised (Sinhala: kalu = black, suddha = white person) (> **suddha**) ° *Call me a kalu sudda if you like ...*

♦ They called encouragement to Suraj, referring to Niresh as kalusuddah, black-foreigner. (SMS 164)

kaluwa
/kaluwa/ (coll.) a dark-skinned person (Sinhala)

kamaranka
/kāməranka/ star fruit, carambola, a yellow fruit with a star-shaped cross-section (Sinhala)

kamatha
/kamətə/ the threshing circle in a paddy field (Sinhala)

♦ They circled back to the clearing, a clearing like a *kamatha*, the threshing circle in a paddy field. (AG 189)

kambaya
/kambəyə/ a type of **cloth** worn by women (Sinhala)

♦ Quite often Loku Amma sat below the arched window in her verandah wrapped up in her red checked cloth the *kambaya.* (CM 21)

kameez
/kamīz/ the long shirt worn with a **shalwar** (> **shalwar kameez**)

♦ I wore my favourite kameez and seemed to lounge about ... (Z 97)

♦ I noticed that Velaithan was limping and the sleeve of her kameez was torn. (REP 68)

kanay
/kanē/ (coll.) a thick ear, a slap on the ear (Sinhala)

♦ "*Ammo*, if I go to say like that I'll get a *kanay**." (* *Kanay* - a clout on the ear. Kana is Sinhala for ear.) (TT 56)

♦ "Elsie gave you a kanay?" (TT 83)

Kandyan (1)

/ˈkænɒiən/ (adj.) from the town or kingdom of Kandy ° *Kandyan jewellery* ° *Kandyan law* ° *Kandyan chief*

KANDYAN CHIEF

♦ Mrs Ellapola herself came from the deep south, but, having married into the remnants of the Kandyan aristocracy, felt herself a cut above the natives. She was a dark, squat, ugly woman, weighed down by heavy Kandyan jewellery and thick embroidered petticoats that peered menacingly from beneath her gaudy saris, worn in Kandyan style. (WMD 200)

♦ ... her fair Kandyan complexion ... (WMD 298)

♦ … that he was the unacknowledged offspring of a Kandyan chief, … (SG 151)

♦ Enid was fair-skinned and pretty and came from good Kandyan stock. (July 11)

♦ ... the monsoon rain with the rhythm of Kandyan drums. (Z 99)

♦ The girl returned with a Kandyan silver bangle, ... (HC 182)

♦ She had a pretty, coppery, Kandyan face. (CP 66)

♦ To go round her neck she chose a heavy piece of Kandyan jewellery, ... (CP 103)

♦ Her belly is big as the belly of a Kandyan chieftain who walks before a regal elephant, ... (KCS 33)

♦ The North Koreans who had arrived and opened their embassies amidst Jasmine garlands and Kandyan drummers were asked to leave. (M&P 134)

Kandyan (2)

(noun) a person from Kandy, or with **Kandyan** family origins

♦ The Kandyans kept rolling rocks down on them ... (TT 13)

♦ "Between you lot and the damn Kandyans wanting their separate state, you will split this country into a thousand pieces." (CG 69)

♦ It might have been because he was a Kandyan and I was from the south. (REP 8)

♦ ... because he was a tough old Kandyan from the mountains. (CP 201)

♦ "They brought tons of Indian Tamils to work on the tea plantations because the Kandyans who lived in the tea areas were too lazy to work." (M&P 151)

□ Kandyan dance

a traditional style of dancing seen in **peraheras** and other religious and cultural events; also **Kandyan dancer, Kandyan dancing**

♦ Charlie Chaplin was in Ceylon. He avoided all publicity and was only to be seen photographing and studying Kandyan dance. (RF 38)

♦ A Kandyan dance ensemble was at its liveliest. (YY 142)

KANDYAN DANCER

♦ "Why not? It'll be nice. Kandyan dancing and all." (July 146)

♦ "Fire-eaters and Kandyan dancers contribute to the glamour of the pageant." (M&P 68)

□ Kandyan king
a former ruler of the **Kandyan** kingdom

♦ Only Robert Knox, held captive by a Kandyan king for twenty years, wrote of the island well, learning its traditions. (RF 82)

♦ Dorothy saw a drawing of a Kandian king holding Padmani's Blood and went to Ali to ask if it was a myth. (MiP 182)

♦ The Kandyan kingdom remained unconquered in the hills until 1815, ... (HC 6)

♦ It was furnished in heavy wood in the style of the Kandyan kingdom, ... (CU 59)

♦ ... costumes of Kandyan kings ... (M&P 136)

□ Kandyan saree
(= osari) a saree worn in the **Kandyan** style

♦ ... an elderly woman in a Kandyan sari ... (WMD 93)

♦ She could wear the sari Kandyan style, with a small frill around the waist. (WMD 311)

♦ ... followed closely by his wife, a sweet-faced lady in a Kandyan sari. (FSD 177)

KANDYAN SAREE

♦ Mrs Algama, or Madam, was a plump, short woman with a brisk manner who wore a Kandyan sari, the pallu wrapped around her waist in a no-nonsense style. (SMS 44)

♦ ... and Mrs. Bandaranayake removed her Kandyan sari and spent a few days being photographed in Indian sari. (M&P 222)

kaneru seeds
/kanēru/ poisonous seeds commonly used in suicide attempts (Sinhala)

♦ "A few weeks later he killed himself by eating Kaneru seed." (GC 259-60)

kangany
/kangāni/ supervisor, esp. the person in charge of a group of estate labourers (Tamil)

♦ ... he was of Indian stock, the grandson of a *kangany*, ... (WMD 191)

♦ "Then there's trouble at the estate. Your kangany is up to his old tricks." (CG 180)

♦ Balendran was usually very careful to placate and humour the kangany while, at the same time, ensuring the welfare of the workers. (CG 190)

♦ "But he thought that in Colombo there would be a chance of picking up work on the docks. No *kangany* would hire him up-country." (HC 287)

kanji

/kanji/ (= **conjee, kenda**) a rice broth (Tamil)

kap

/kap/ a tree-planting ceremony, part of the Kandy **perahera** (Sinhala)

kapati

/kapəti/ (= **shrewd**) (coll.) crafty, cunning, scheming (Sinhala) ° *Watch out for her - real kapati one she is.*

kapok

/kæpok/ (= **pulung**) raw cotton, used for stuffing pillows, etc. (Malay)

kapurala

/kapurālə/ (= **kapuwa, poosari**) the lay priest of a Hindu **devale** (Sinhala)

kapuru bola

/kapuru bōlə/ moth balls (Sinhala: kapuru = camphor; Tamil katpuram)

kapuwa

/kapuwa/ (1) (= **marriage broker**) (Sinhala) (2) (= **kapurala, poosari**) the lay priest of a Hindu **devale** (Sinhala)

♦ Situated along the Galle Road in Colombo, it was frequented by a motley crew of people - labourers and prostitutes, Kapuwas from the kovil next door, and of course, the IT students. (WCS 18-19)

karapincha

/karəpincha/ (= **curry leaf**) (Sinhala) ° *He mixes the gram, adds chillies, a pinch of salt and karapincha ...*

♦ "Go and get some karapincha from the garden," ... (July 19)

♦ The dog would be removed from the kennel and tied onto the Karapincha tree. (M&P 52)

♦ But, because of that precise indefinable taste the Karapincha leaf possessed, it was a requisite for that inexplicable element that differentiated Ceylonese curry to Indian curry. (M&P 52)

♦ Achi had her hands filled with karapincha leaves and limes. She was making a Karapincha sambol for lunch. (M&P 143)

karapotta

/kærəpotta/ cockroach; also a derogatory term for a low-class **Burgher** (Sinhala, from Portuguese)

♦ Ceylon always did have too many foreigners ... the 'Karapothas' as my niece calls them ... (RF 80)

♦ The karapothas crawled over them and admired their beauty. (RF 82)

♦ When it gets dark the *karapoththas* come out. (MM 120)

karave, karawa

/karāve/ (= K) the 'fisher' caste (Sinhala) ° *A doctor or engineer non-smoker teetotaller son is sought by Buddhist Karawa/Govi parents ...*

♦ "... Karava caste versus Goyigama caste, ..." (CG 68)

karawala (1)

/karavələ, karōlə/ (= **dry fish**) (Sinhala)

karawala (2)

/karəvœla/ (= **krait**) a poisonous snake (Sinhala)

karawila

/karəvilə/ (= **bitter gourd**) (Sinhala)

KARAWILA

karaya

/kārəya/ vendor, dealer, etc. (Sinhala) (plural **karayas**) (> **kudu karaya, kunu karaya, malu karaya, pang karaya**)

♦ "Are you planning to set him up on Galle Road as a brass karaya?" (FB 48)

karuppi

/karuppi/ (= **kaluwa**) (coll.) a dark-skinned person (Tamil)

♦ The first and biggest difference between the imagined Radha Aunty and the real one was the colour of her skin. She was a karapi, as dark as a labourer. (FB 46)

karutha kolumban

/kārətə koləmbān/ (= **Jaffna mango**) a large green variety of mango, usually considered the best type (Tamil; also pronounced /karətə koləmbə/ by Sinhala speakers)

kasa-kasa

/kasəkasə/ small seeds used to flavour **faluda** (Sinhala/Tamil)

kasaya

/kasāyə/ (= **decoction**) an **ayurvedic** remedy (Sinhala; Tamil kasayam) (> **peyava, paspanguwa**)

♦ In the days following, the pain in the stomach became more acute but, apart

from taking the *kasaya* she had herself concocted, she paid no mind to it. (WMD 58)

kasili

/kœsili/ (coll.) restless, frustrated, fidgety (Sinhala = itch) ° *a kasili case*

kasippu

/kasippu/ (= **illicit liquor**) (Sinhala) ° *Police raid kasippu dens*

♦ He had no idea about the *kasippu* stills - the moonshine - the ganja garden, the opium trade, the big black economy at the back of the house. (MM 96)

♦ He disappeared from time to time, but only to dive into the nearest *kasippu* tavern and drink with his harbour touts and junkies. (Reef 86)

♦ Now the last drops were being diluted with kasippu. (OM 6)

♦ "The illicit brew, kasippu, had rotted his liver." (REP 189)

♦ He would buy a bottle of *kasippu*, a potent local brew produced in the next village, ... (GC 88)

♦ The hut was virtually empty except for several bottles of *Kassippu* craftily put away in a clothes suitcase. (WCS 50)

kata vaha

/katə vahə/ the evil tongue (comp. evil eye) (Sinhala) (> **as vaha**)

katha

/katā/ (coll.) chat (Sinhala) ° *She put a long katha.*

katheeb

/katīb/ a Muslim leader (Arabic; in the Maldives, an island chief) ° *the only daughter of Katheeb Sheik Mohamed*

kathi

/katti/ knife (Tamil)

◆ The first shop selling hardware items had what I most needed, a kathi. This is a type of axe with a blade shaped like a slice of watermelon, fitted to a rough wooden handle about two and a half feet long and two inches in diameter. Our villagers, especially those who lived close to the forest, relied on the kathi for a multitude of uses including personal defense. ... The kathi I bought for 150/- was crudely made but the blade was sharp and fitted snugly on the handle. (REP 76)

◆ He used the kathi in his hand to ease his way slowly through the undergrowth. (FSD 93)

◆ I pick up the kathi from behind the front door and run my finger along the concave edge. (GC 99)

kaththam

/kattəm/ a Muslim religious ceremony performed to ask for blessings for a person who has died (Muslim Tamil, from Arabic)

◆ "We have Zulfikar's mother's *kaththam*." ... That evening, after an exhausting *kaththam* ... (CP 141)

kathurumurunga

/katurumurunga/ the leaf of the **kathurumurunga** tree, used to make **mallung** (Sinhala)

kattadiya

/kattaɒiya/ an exorcist who performs **thovil** ceremonies (Sinhala)

katta sambol

/kattə sæmbol/ a very hot **sambol** like a red chilli paste (Sinhala)

◆ "But you have some *katta sambol* or something?" (Reef 100)

Katu

/katu/ (coll.) Katunayake (international airport and Air Force base)

◆ Security at Katu was just too tight these days. (CU 413)

katu aatha, katu anoda

/katu āta, katu anōda/ (= **soursop**) a large fruit with thick green skin and soft sweet white flesh (Sinhala) (> **custard apple**)

kavadi dancers

/kāvaɒi/ traditional Hindu dancers carrying a decorated arch ('**kavadi**') on the shoulders (Tamil)

KAVADI DANCER

◆ We had a few Kandyan dancers and some Kavadi dancers. (M&P 140)

kavichchiya

/kavichchiyə/ a traditional couch usually with a decorated back and arms and rattan seat (Sinhala from Portuguese)

KAVICHCHIYA

◆ There was an upholstered antique couch called a kavichchiya in these parts, four large rattan chairs with white rope seats and a low antique table. (July 95)

♦ "To Ashoka my friend, I leave my *kavichiya*." I held my breath. The kavichiya was not his most valuable possession, but easily his most valued. It was an ebony couch, a severely elegant thing with Grecian lines on which the old man used to take his afternoon naps. (CP 204)

kavili

/kævili/ (= **Sinhala sweets**) traditional sweets prepared for festive occasions such as **Sinhala New Year**, e.g. **kavum, kokis**, etc. (Sinhala) ° *The kavili-makers are expecting poor sales this avurudu.*

kavum

/kævum, kævung/ (= **konde kavum, oil cake**) a small deep-fried **rice flour** cake served at **New Year** with other **Sinhala sweets** (Sinhala) (> **mung kavum**)

♦ I made everything: little coconut cakes - *kavum* - patties, egg sandwiches, ... (Reef 74)

♦ Mother was frying *kavun* - oil cakes - in the kitchen. (CM 62)

♦ My mother scooped out the fried *kevun* from the bubbling hot oil and placed it on the strainer ... (CM 63)

♦ Inside, Priyanthi was helping her mother to lay kavums and kokis on a paper-doily-covered platter. (July 54)

keep

put something somewhere, place, leave, park (a car); also to leave something somewhere by mistake (> **put**) ° *Keep it in the drawer.* ° *Keep it on the table.* ° *She kept the cat on the floor.* ° *I kept my keys at home.* → In BSE, to 'keep' something somewhere means to leave it permanently in the place where it belongs; in the examples above 'put' or 'leave' would be more common.

♦ The master ... would sit in the lab, keep his pipe on the desk, ... (TT 177)

♦ She kept the cup on Father's writing table ... (BTH 21)

♦ I took the first of the diaries several times into my hand and kept it aside cringing with distaste. (OD 90)

♦ He kept his bag on the large, solid wooden table in front of the class. (WE 11)

♦ "Now I will keep my pawn here. ..." ... She kept my bishop back on the board ... (M&P 284)

♦ I kept the cassette player on my mother's lap with the speakers turned to my brother. (M&P 288)

♦ "I remember when I was a child, your grandmother keeping me on her lap and telling me stories ..." (M&P 328)

♦ "I want my chair kept there," ... (PMS 241)

□ to keep (the phone)

(coll.) to hang up ° *He kept the phone before I could say goodbye.* ° *Then I'll keep. See you tomorrow.*

□ to keep quiet

(coll.) to shut up, be quiet, do nothing ° *Just keep quiet!* → In BSE, to 'keep quiet' about something means to keep it a secret.

keera

/kīrə/ green leaves used to make **mallung** etc. (Sinhala; Tamil keerai)

♦ My mother turned from her vegetable man from whom she was buying keera, brinjals, pathola and thalana batu, and came towards Sunil and me. (Z 2)

♦ Lahiru aiya, the one eyed man who sold bundles of green vegetables harvested from his *kira kotuwa* by the lake. (FSD 255)

kehel kole

/kehel kolē/ (= **plantain leaf**) banana leaf, often used to serve **rice and curry** and to wrap **lamprais**, etc. (Sinhala)

kehelmuwa

/kehelmuwə/ **plantain** flower, used as a vegetable (Sinhala)

KEHELMUWA

kekiri

/kækiri/ a type of vegetable similar to a cucumber (Sinhala)

kekulu hal

/kækulu hāl/ (= **country rice**) a popular variety of rice (red or white) (Sinhala) (> **red rice**)

kela

/kelə/ (coll.) spit, saliva (Sinhala)

kelavalla

/keləvalla/ a type of fish (yellowfin tuna) (Sinhala) (> **blood fish**)

♦ Spanish Mackerel and Tuna, called Thora and Kelawalla, are local favourites freely available in the south. (REP 59)

kenda

/kændə/ (= **conjee, kanji**) a rice broth (Sinhala) (> **kola kenda**)

kendirify

/kendirifai/ (coll.) complain, moan, grumble (from Sinhala) (> **-fy**) ° *Aiyo, they never stop kendirifying.*

kesari

/kesəri/ a Tamil sweet made with milk, semolina, cashew nuts and sultanas, and cut into square or diamond shapes (Tamil; also India)

key-tag

key-ring

K/G/B

(in **marriage proposals**) Kandyan Govigama Buddhist (also a humorous pun on the name of the former Soviet secret police) (> **B/G, G/B**)

kichibichify

/kichibichifai/ (coll.) chatter, natter (from Sinhala) (> **-fy**) ° *Always kichibichifying at the back of the class.*

kimbula bunis

/kimbula banis/ a long thin sugar bun (Sinhala: kimbula = crocodile)

KIMBULA BUNIS

♦ "Right. Bring us a plate. And some kimbula buns for the children." Priyanthi grimaced. She hated kimbula buns with their crocodile look and sugary surface which melted into a sticky mess in no time at all. ... Even the kimbula buns were fresh and still crunchy, not limp and soggy like the ones the roll man brought round in his bicycle box every evening. (July 90)

king coconut

(= **thambili**) an orange coconut containing water which can be drunk: a popular, healthy and refreshing drink

♦ Underneath he has fixed a shelf for his bottle of red king-coconut hair-oil and his two-edged razor. (MM 113)

- "… when coming out in the sun you must put some King coconut oil on your head." (YY 125)

- … and offered Hayakawa a large glass of king coconut water which was gulped down at incredible speed. (YY 223)

- … a man carrying a large bunch of king coconuts on his gunny sack draped shoulders. (TT 208)

- A tamarind tree, two king coconut trees, and a flamboyant tree spread their shade across the lawn. (CG 14)

- The price of king coconuts shot up, but Violet still kept a supply at home for Bala and the children to drink. (July 60)

- … gulping down the cold king coconut water and sighing with pleasure. (July 61)

- I carried him over to Achi who fed him the king coconut water. (M&P 311)

- He races off towards the entrance by the road where vendors are selling baskets of flowers, king coconuts and sugar cane. (PMS 246)

kiri ala

/kiri alə/ a small round yam (Sinhala)

kiriamma

/kiriammə/ grandmother (Sinhala) (> aachchi)

- "You know I was five years old, only five, when Kiriamma sent me to Colombo to study." (M&P 63)

kiribath

/kiribat/ (= milk rice) (Sinhala) ° *a kiribath function at Police Headquarters*

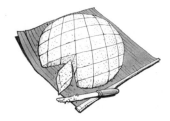

KIRIBATH

- A wicker box with pieces of kiributh, kavun and kokis stood near the front door and she was looking at it uncertainly. (OM 18)

- Mother and Caroline were in the kitchen with everything ready for the making of *kiribath*, waiting for the auspicious time to light the hearth. (CM 64)

- Finally the smell of *kiribath* came swirling out of every kitchen in the neighbourhood bringing with it the spirit of a happy New Year. (CM 65)

- "I was going to bring them here for some kiribath tomorrow morning, and now all we're going to give them is tea?" (July 151)

- "Amily is making you kiributh for breakfast." (MiP 117)

- Jane-Nona had made *kiri bath* for Niresh's last meal with them, … (SMS 197)

- It was not the first of the month. But Magi began to make kiribath to celebrate Podian's return. (M&P 332)

kirihodi

/kirihodi/ a mildly spiced **coconut milk gravy** (Sinhala) (> hodi, gravy)

- And the food, string hoppers, kiri hodhi and curried squid, kept him busy. (FSD 98)

♦ ... prompting Nelun to advise them that they had better eat their breakfast of string hoppers before the *kiri hodhi* got cold. (CU 558)

kirijje

/kirijjə/ a sweet made with coconut and honey (Sinhala)

♦ And what happened to the coconut refuse? Certainly it was not thrown away. Attamma knew just what the kids relished. So she put honey into the cauldron and mixed the left over contents well. ... The name for this sweet dish was *kirijje*. (CM 61)

kiri kos

/kiri kos/ a **jakfruit** dish prepared with **coconut milk** (Sinhala)

♦ Dierdre's servant Emmy cooked kiri kos for Violet so that her milk would come quickly, ... (July 30)

kiripani

/kiripœni/ (= **curd and honey**) (Sinhala)

kisses

meringues

kit

(coll.) clothes, outfit ° *Nice kit!* → In BSE, if it refers to clothing, 'kit' is usually qualified with another noun: 'PE kit', 'tennis kit', etc.

kitchen protest

a protest by women, armed with pots and pans, e.g. about the cost of living

kitul, kitul tree

/kitul/ **jaggery** palm, a type of palm tree used to make **honey**, **jaggery** and **toddy** (Sinhala; OED 'kittul, kitool')

♦ At the back, the kitul tree still leaned against the kitchen - tall, with tiny yellow berries which the polecat used to love. (RF 59)

KITUL TREE

♦ The giant cascading flower of the kitul palm became a gorgeous sight magnificently touched with gold. (CM 6)

♦ She beat the husk with a kitul wood pole about one foot long. (CM 22)

☐ **kitul honey, kitul pani**

honey produced from the **kitul tree**

♦ For dessert, there was buffalo curd and kitul honey. (July 18)

♦ The thick creamy buffalo milk combined with the kitul pani was sensuous and luscious without being cloying. (Z 124)

☐ **kitul jaggery, kitul hakuru**

jaggery produced from the **kitul tree**

☐ **kitul toddy**

toddy produced from the **kitul tree**

kiyala

/kiyəla/ (coll.) (Sinhala) ° *He called to tell he might be getting late kiyala.* ° *Customer is going abroad kiyala.* → 'Kiyala' is a Sinhala word which marks the end of a quotation, reported statement, indirect question, etc., and which is sometimes used in colloquial SLE in the same way.

knock

hit, knock down (e.g. in an accident) ° *He knocked a child on the Galle Road.*

139

♦ "You know how he got knocked by that lorry, no?" (TT 102)

□ to knock off

(coll.) to go to sleep ° *Haven't the kids knocked off yet?* → In BSE, to 'knock off' means to finish work.

□ to knock something on/off

(coll.) to switch something on/off ° *Who knocked off the light?*

♦ ... knowing very well that Stanley's small arracks were enough to knock off a horse. (July 21)

♦ Because between two and four we knock the phone off so we can get a decent after-lunch nap. (CP 107)

know: to be knowing

/nō/ to know (> **have, must**) ° *You must be knowing her.* → In BSE, 'know' is one of several common verbs which are not normally used in the continuous ('-ing') form.

♦ "Don't know. I'll ask and see. Must be knowing, no?" (JFT 89)

♦ "Somaweera, you must be knowing that at that difficult time, ... our very lives were protected by the three armed forces ..." (OD 18)

□ to know to do something

to know how to do something (> **forget**) ° *Do you know to swim?* ° *All we know to do is to fish.*

♦ "What, men, must know to pronounce English properly, no?" (YY 187)

♦ "Just dancing the devil. That's all he knows to do." (TT 148)

♦ Not that they knew to read, but solely as a souvenir for keeps. (CM 59)

♦ "I think even the government knows to select the right person ..." (OD 68)

♦ "As if you know to speak proper Sinhala, you haven't even been to school in your life!" (M&P 163)

□ a known person

somebody I/you know (> **unknown**) ° *Is he a known person?*

♦ She discovered many known people in the family circles. (M&P 296-7)

♦ "Don't be foolish, ... They're all known people. We can't accuse them of stealing ..." (PMS 86)

kochchi

/kochchi/ a small variety of green chilli with a strong flavour (Sinhala)

koha

/koha/ koel, a large black bird which looks like a crow and has a loud screeching cry and the habits of a cuckoo (Sinhala)

KOHA

♦ ... and the koha began to cry. (BTH 28)

♦ ... following the sound of koha birds busy with their claims and proclamations. (AG 14)

♦ A koha, red eyes gleaming, is huddled on a low branch: ...(PMS 216)

kohila

/kohilə/ a type of yam used in cooking (Sinhala)

kohomba

/kohombə/ margosa tree (the leaves are used in **ayurvedic** medicine and cosmetics) (Sinhala)

- ♦ The kohomba twigs she could break off and strip to clean her teeth, or burn to keep mosquitoes away. (AG 202)

- ♦ ... Maud learnt to rub the dogs with *kohamba* oil as a specific against fleas. (HC 179)

kohomba kankariya

/kohombə kankāriyə/ a ritual all-night **Kandyan dance** ceremony (Sinhala) ° *When a loved one is sick the family organise a kohomba kankariya.*

kohu

/kohu/ (adj.) (of mangoes, etc.) stringy (Sinhala = **coir**)

□ kohu amba

/kohu ambə/ a type of mango with a fibrous pulp (Sinhala)

kokis

/kokis/ a crisp **rice flour** snack deep-fried in a mould (usually in the shape of a wheel) and served at **New Year** with other **Sinhala sweets** (Sinhala, from Dutch) ° *a kokis mould*

KOKIS

- ♦ And it was only when she had finished lowering the last batch of *kokis* into the frying pan that she turned round and looked Sahadevan up and down. (WMD 24)

- ♦ ... crisp kokis in the shape of birds of paradise, ... (CG 375)

- ♦ "Elisabeth, why are you making so much *kokis*, is there going to be a party?" (M&P 175)

kola kenda

/kola kændə/ a thick, nutritious broth made with rice and **gotukola** and/or other green leaves (Sinhala) (> **kenda**)

kolam (1)

/kōlam/ a traditional masked folk dance (Sinhala)

kolam (2)

/kōləm/ floor designs (see quote) (Tamil)

KOLAM

- ♦ ... and could do nice kolam* ... (* The festive designs usually made on the floor and threshold of Tamil homes on Hindu holy days.) (YY 45)

kole, kola kaella

/kolē, kolə kællə/ (= **paper**) (coll.) piece of paper (Sinhala) ° *Can you give me a kole?*

kolikuttu

/kōlikuttu/ a large yellow variety of banana (Sinhala) (> **plantain**)

- ♦ "Here, I brought them some Kolikuttu from my own garden." (FSD 18)

kolla

/kollə/ (= **boy, houseboy, servant boy**); can also refer to any youthful-looking young man (Sinhala = boy) ° *Who was that kolla I saw you with?*

♦ "Yes, you will have to do the cooking. Wijetunga has only a small *kolla* there. (Reef 63)

♦ When I asked about the *kolla*, Wijetunga said he had sent him to school. (Reef 120)

♦ "What about you, baba? Have you found yourself a kolla?" - "No kollas for me, Nala." (GC 227)

kolu karaya

/kolʊ kārəyɑ/ (= **ponnaya**) (derogatory) homosexual (Sinhala) (> **karaya**)

♦ "MD is a "*kolukaraya*". You kn- know, he l-likes boys." (WCS 33)

komala

/komələ/ (coll.) shy, giggly, flirtatious (Sinhala) ° *She's a real komala case.*

□ komalafy

(= **mukulufy**) (coll.) get embarrassed, get the giggles, flirt (> **-fy**)

kondaya

/konɒəyɑ/ (= **bulbul**) a small black bird with a crest (**konde**) on its head (Sinhala)

KONDAYA

♦ Wood pigeon went flying up, also *shama, kondayas*, blackbirds, a shock of blossom-headed parakeets. (HC 188)

♦ One day I was seated near the front steps watching a pair of Kondayas building a nest, … (GC 50)

konde

/konɒe/ topknot, hair tied in a bun (Sinhala)

KONDE

♦ All with big breasts and black hair and some with *kondays** also. (* *Konday* - the bun of hair, twisted and knotted at the nape.) (TT 91)

♦ She undid her thin kondé and brushed out the knots … (Z 88)

♦ The happy moment was broken by a young woman with her hair in a konday and a green dress stretched tight across her pregnant stomach. (MiP 139)

konde kavum

/konɒə kævum/ (= **kavum, oil cake**) (Sinhala)

KONDE KAVUM

♦ "Sending me *aluwa* (halwa) and *konde kavun* (a small knobbed honey cake) …" (JFT 32)

konde koora

/konɒə kūrə/ a piece of ornate gold jewellery worn in the hair as part of a bridal costume (Sinhala)

♦ She wore gold bangles, ear studs and a gold filigree hair pin called the *koora* on her *konde* - hair knot. (CM 76)

kool

/kūl/ a rich seafood soup, a Jaffna speciality (Tamil) ° *Odiyal Kool is not merely dinner, it is a ritual feast. Its preparation is considered the epitome of culinary skill, which few can master. It's a rich broth of seafood, vegetables, yams and condiments.*

♦ I liked the *kool* parties most of all, … I don't know why Leela and I called them *kool* parties, because they were not parties as such; they just happened, people just came, when there was *kool* in the offing. But how they knew I couldn't say. I liked to think they got the smell of *kool* in the air, but Leela pointed out more prosaically that everyone knew who had been to market that morning to buy the '*kool* things' - the palmyrah flour out of which the 'soup' was made and the hundred and one other things that went into it like sprats and prawns and shrimps and fish-heads, *billing*, jak seed and coconut, long beans, and butter beans, *bandakka* and *brinjal*, tapioca, rice and tamarind. My aunts would start cooking the *kool* in the late afternoon, in a huge earthenware pot on an open fire in the middle of the kitchen compound. (WMD 141)

koonissas, kooni

/kūnissas, kūni/ a small variety of shrimp, usually dried and used in a **sambol** (Sinhala; Tamil kooni raal) ° *kooni sambol* → The Sinhala plural is 'koonisso', but more often 'koonissas' in colloquial SLE.

korale

/kōrəle/ (dated) an administrative district in the **Kandyan** kingdom (Sinhala)

kos

/kos/ (= jak fruit) (Sinhala)

kossa

/kossa/ (coll.) cop (Sinhala)

♦ "Then two police *kossas** came out …" (* *Kossa* - Sinhala derogative for constable.) (TT 57)

kottamalli

/kottəmalli/ coriander; also a herbal drink used as a medicine for fevers, etc. (Sinhala/Tamil)

♦ He ran for bread, for two limes, for ten cents worth kotthamalli (coriander), for a packet of pappadams, … (TT 37)

♦ The pungent smell of boiling koththamalli herbal tea drifted out of kitchen windows. (July 139)

♦ Jane-Nona rushed out of the pantry with a cup of hot kothamalli and a towel. (SMS 182)

kottan

/kotтan/ a type of tree with large leaves and edible seeds (Sinhala)

♦ … down the side roads there were bougainvillaea, araliya, mango and of course kottan trees, under which one always found a flat stone and a rock for cracking kottans open. (July 8)

♦ The garden was shaded by kottan and other shade trees and psychedelic red, pink and orange bougainvillea. (MiP 122)

♦ They had hurriedly climbed a Kottang tree by the side of the road near the gate of the Dias house. (FSD 11)

♦ But the boys know a way in, by jumping off an overhanging branch of a kottang tree by the fence … (PMS 177)

kottoruwa

/koʈʈōruwa/ (= **barbet**) a small green bird with a large beak (Sinhala)

kotturoti, kottu

/koʈʈuroʈi, koʈʈu/ a dish prepared with chopped **godamba roti** (Sinhala/Tamil) ° *chicken kotturoti* ° *fish kottu*

♦ ... and the women craved a kadé koththu after the dancing and Babycham. ... They sat outside in their cars, listened to pop music, and ate koththu roti with forks. (July 91)

♦ They parked across the road next to a stall selling hoppers and *kotthu roti*. ... The *kotthu* man made a loud drumming noise every time he pounded the skillet with two sharp-edged metal plates. (FSD 240)

kovil

/kōvil/ Hindu temple (Tamil)

KOVIL

♦ This time he was determined that the baby should be a boy and had even made a pilgrimage to a Hindu shrine in the deep south where he had stood sheepishly in the kovil and wondered whom to pray to. (YY 132)

♦ ... but had not gone to worship at the Sivan Kovil till he had a letter from his father saying that his mother had been taken ill again. (WMD 28)

♦ ... and so unlike the dark little Kali Kovil that stood some few hundred yards away like a crevice in the wall, ... (WMD 150)

♦ ... and the kovil floors were strewn in a cryptic maze with the offerings of smashed coconuts. (Z 23)

♦ Podian the driver had rushed out of the dusty shop, into the Pettah Kovil and dashed a coconut at Lord Kataragama's feet and begun to pray. (M&P 108)

♦ Achi sat in the back seat and they drove to the Kovil in the Morris Minor. (M&P 316)

kraal

/krāl/ (dated) a traditional method of catching elephants (Dutch, from Portuguese 'corral') ° *Tennent describes a kraal he personally witnessed in 1847.*

krait

/krēʈ/ (= **karawala**) a poisonous snake; two varieties are found in Sri Lanka: common krait and Sri Lankan krait (also India, orig. Hindi)

♦ He had them in cages, long green whip snakes, kraits and even a baby python. (REP 106)

kris knife

/kris/ a crude double-edged dagger (orig. Malay) ° *A gang of three armed with a revolver and two kris knives had snatched five necklaces from women commuters.*

KRIS KNIFE

♦ ... while the Kris knife looks sharp enough to penetrate the core of the pear with its glittering, silver blade. (KCS 157)

kudalla

/kūɒælla/ leech (Sinhala) ° *Watch out for kudallas if it's wet.*

kudu

/kuɒu/ (coll.) drugs (Sinhala) ° *100 kg of kudu at Govt Analyst's Department*

- ♦ Upul hated him. The man who provided the kudu to his crippled father. (OM 35)

□ kudu karaya

/kuɒukārəya/ (coll.) drug addict, drug dealer (Sinhala) (> **karaya**) ° *Lot of kudu karayas living around here.*

kukku

/kukku/ milk (children's word, also = breast) (Sinhala) ° *You want more kukku?*

kukula

/kukula/ (= **cad**) (coll.) a womaniser (Sinhala = cock) ° *He looks like a real kukula!*

kulam

/kuləm/ (= **tank, wewa**) (Tamil)

- ♦ A kulam, in Tamil, is a tank, and the northern tanks are fed by such rivers as … (YY 154)

kulambu

/kuləmbu/ a thick spicy **gravy** (Tamil)

kulla

/kullə/ (= **winnower, winnowing fan**) a shallow fan-shaped basket used to winnow rice (Sinhala) ° *the traditional kulla dance*

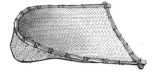

KULLA

- ♦ There was the winnower called the *kulla* to separate chaff from the rice. (CM 14)

kumbalava

/kumbəlāva/ a type of fish (Indian mackerel) (Sinhala)

kumbi

/kūmbi/ ants (Sinhala)

kumbuk

/kumbuk/ a type of tree valued for its timber (Sinhala)

- ♦ Huge, water loving, Kumbuk trees lined the sides of the stream and provided a shady canopy. (REP 82)

- ♦ The little ones and I would follow her to the old bund where kumbuk trees grow in a long row. (GC 34)

- ♦ They have a secret place; a boulder at the edge of the water shaded by an old kumbuk tree. (PMS 35)

kunju

/kuɲju/ (= **patiya**) (coll.) a term of endearment used e.g. by a parent to a child (Tamil = young bird)

- ♦ "Kunju, go and get your uncle some of your father's toddy, …" (WMD 15)

- ♦ "It's a possible meeting with a young man, kunju," … (CG 87)

kunu

/kunu/ (coll.) rubbish, garbage; (adj.) dirty (Sinhala) ° *Can't you put out the kunu?*

- ♦ Those of us who come from remote villages are referred to contemptuously as dirty, 'kunu' freshers. (GC 27)

□ kunu karaya

/kunukārəya/ (coll.) rubbish man, garbage collector (Sinhala) (> **karaya**)

kunukunufy

/kunukunufai/ (= **gnurugnurufy**) (coll.) moan, whinge (from Sinhala) (> **-fy**)

kuppi class

/kuppi/ (in universities) extra classes given by students for their peers (Sinhala)

kurakkan

/kurakkang/ finger millet, a type of grain commonly grown in the **dry zone** (Sinhala/Tamil) ° *kurakkan flour* ° *kurakkan pittu*

♦ There were still fields there in those years, emerald parcels of *kurakkan* and *keera*, and low, thatched huts set among thickets of plantain. (HC 133)

kurtha

/kurta/ a long loose shirt usually worn by men (also India, orig. Hindi)

♦ He was wearing a sarong and a white cotton kurtha shirt open at the neck. (CG 376)

♦ The speaker was an old and fragile man, at least seventy, dressed in a kurta over a sarong. (MiP 259)

♦ Ali, in a white knee-length kurta over loose white pants was also clean as a pin. (MiP 291)

♦ ... beautifully dressed in handloom cotton clothes - a bright blue kurtha top with a sarong of green, orange and gold squares. (WCS 36)

kurukkal

/kurukkəl/ (= **aiyar**) a Hindu priest (Tamil) (> **poosari**)

♦ The kurukkal who was conducting the funeral came towards them ... (CG 285)

kurumba

/kurumba/ (= **young coconut**) (Sinhala)

♦ ... stop for the cool *kurumba* ... (RF 90)

kussiamma

/kussiamma/ (= **cook woman**) (Sinhala)

kusukusufy

/kusukusufai/ (coll.) to whisper in a subversive way, e.g. spreading gossip, flirting, criticizing, etc. (from Sinhala) (> **-fy**)

L

labu
/labu/ (= **diya labu, bottle gourd**) a type of gourd used as a vegetable (Sinhala)

lacham
/lāchəm/ a measure of land (10 **perches**) (Tamil)

♦ His father was an inept farmer on whose *lacham* of land nothing seemed to grow but children, … (WMD 6)

laddu
/laᴅᴅu/ a type of sweet made with semolina, milk, cashews and raisins (Tamil; also India) ° *rava laddu* ° *boondi laddu*

♦ … ravva ladu spiced with cardamom in the way he liked them. (CG 209)

lady doctor
female doctor, woman doctor

lady's finger, ladies' fingers
(= **bandakka**) okra, a type of vegetable

lagna
/lagnə/ a sign of the zodiac (Sinhala) ° *What is your lagna?*

♦ "Of course she is Meena lagna, … What else could she be if not Meena lagna? Three astrologers assured us that she was a Meena lagna." (M&P 34)

lakh (1,00,000)
/læk/ one hundred thousand (100,000) (Anglo-Indian, orig. Hindi) ° *three lakhs of rupees* ° *Rs. 75 lakhs* ° *It should fetch a couple of lakhs.* ° *over one lakh of applicants* ° *The population is fifteen lakhs.* ° *Lakhs of tsunami victims still at sea*

♦ Six zeroes, ten lakhs, a million rupees, … (Reef 67)

♦ She has lakhs of rupees, they say, and houses in Colombo and estates and all sorts of things. (OM 19)

♦ … a lakh in cash … (OD 136)

♦ "… I was told that I had to pay five lakhs, up front, and they would get me to Europe." (Z 65)

♦ They had been designed by an upstart in dark glasses who passed himself off as an architect and was rumoured to have been paid a lakh for his vandalism. A *lakh*! (HC 253)

♦ "What are you expecting?" - "Seventeen lakhs, …" (FSD 238)

♦ "I now sell more than a lakh of eggs per day." (KCS 69)

lama saree
/lamā sāri/ (= **half saree**) an outfit like a white **cloth and jacket** worn by young girls on festive occasions (Sinhala)

LAMA SAREE

lamprai, lamprais
/lamprai/ a traditional **Dutch Burgher** rice dish baked in a **plantain** leaf (from Dutch 'lomprijst'); a traditional **lamprai** includes **lamprai curry, brinjal pahi, frikkadels, seeni sambol** and **prawn blachang** ° *a chicken lamprai* → The word may be spelt 'lamprai', 'lamprais' or 'lampries' in the singular, but the final s is not pronounced.

♦ ... she would produce such marvellous things as the true Dutch Lampries (from the Dutch word 'Lomprijst' - rice cooked in stock and baked in a wrapping of banana leaf); ... (JFT 186)

♦ "Then I shall wait till your lamprais comes," ... (FB 70)

♦ He unwrapped the leaf of another *lamprais* and ate with his fingers. (AG 132)

♦ "There are lamprais in the freezer." (FSD 181)

□ **lamprai curry**
a meat curry which is included in a traditional **lamprai**, made with chicken, mutton, beef and pork

land (1)
(nc) a piece of land (uncountable in BSE) ° *coconut lands* ° *I'm thinking of buying a small land and putting up a house.* ° *The SLFP headquarters is coming up on a government land which has been leased out from the UDA.*

♦ Father's younger sister who lived in the adjoining land was close to tears. (OM 18)

♦ We lived in splendid isolation in a large house built just on the eve of the war on a land which sloped down from a macadam road ... (BTH 3)

♦ Daddy had spent much of his income from his lands on Party activities. (OD 94)

land (2)
(vt) put something (into or onto something); (slang) screw ° *He lands something on my desk everyday.*

♦ "Land all of them, that's what I'll do!" (YY 210)

♦ "Half the buggers in the bloody Polytechnic must have landed her already." (TT 195)

♦ "Aha! You're thinking of landing a girl?" (TT 213)

landed with something
loaded with something ° *The curries are landed with chilli.*

land monitor
(= **thalagoya, iguana**) the smaller variety of **monitor lizard**, which lives on the land (> **monitor lizard**)

land side, landside
on the side away from the sea (esp. of the Galle Road) (> **sea side**) ° *We're staying in Wellawatte on the land side.*

♦ Elsie sent Ian and an odd-job man named Singho to wait on the land-side of the rail track. (YY 17)

♦ He would always walk on the land side track towards Bambalapitiya because he could see ahead and skip off the line when he saw a train in the distance. (YY 74)

♦ Galle Road ran parallel to the coast, about two hundred yards inland. The residents of Colombo thus identified buildings and other landmarks on Galle Road as being either on the "sea side" or the "land side" of Galle Road. (CG 18)

♦ On the other side of Galle Road, on what is called the land side, the network of large roads leading inland begins. (July 7)

♦ Priyanthi rushed over to the opposite window, the one on the land side. (July 263)

♦ The town was a dreary place with rows of small houses on the landside. (REP 76)

♦ The rock face sloped gently upwards from the landside but the angle was much sharper where it met the water. (REP 178)

♦ Ravi led the way across Galle Road and up a lane on the landside. (FSD 159)

♦ The bund is crowded with holidaymakers. Buses and vans are parked in a row on the landside. ... We keep to the landside and move through the mob. (GC 291)

♦ We lived on the landside, where people were serious and fine and upstanding, and infinitely dull. (CP 137)

lane
/lēn/ a small residential street ° *They live down our lane.* ° *5th Lane* → In BSE, a 'lane' is usually a small road in the country.

Lankan
(n/adj.) Sri Lankan

♦ The fact was, most Lankans had their war thrust on them, and fighting wars was not their style. (MiP 5)

♦ "I also didn't see how he could have done it without a Lankan accomplice." (MiP 451)

♦ I'm pleased when he gets down, Lankan style, for a final chat near the gate. (GC 232)

lass
(in newspapers) girl, young woman (dated and regional in BSE) ° *Lankan lasses retain netball title*

last minute case
a person who leaves everything till the last minute

last morning/afternoon/evening
yesterday morning/afternoon/evening, the previous morning/afternoon/evening ° *By last evening, there was no confirmation as to when she would speak.* ° *A major fire broke out in the area last evening.*

♦ "It seems that the taxi strike turned violent last evening." (CG 320)

♦ "He came home so late last evening and was so tired, I didn't have the heart to tell him." (July 25)

♦ "The ASP told me that from last afternoon the Vice Chancellor and everyone else in his office were being held hostage, ..." (OD 40)

♦ We set off then, going back towards Manikepola villu we had passed through last afternoon. (REP 155)

♦ "I want to use the same route we used last evening." ... There was no way we could retrace the precise route we had followed last evening, but we tried. (REP 301)

♦ ... so Kamala must have taken time to put everything in order before she left last morning. (REP 344)

♦ Construction work on the massive Maya City development project was launched at a lavish ceremony last morning. (GC 171)

♦ Entrepreneur Somasiri Jayakody and his son Sidath (18) were gunned down by unknown assailants while inspecting their project site last afternoon. (GC 194)

♦ Last evening, Mala and Niresh had played Carom again, ... (SMS 159)

♦ "In the meantime, as I said last evening, the Indians have already appointed a negotiator, ..." (CU 367)

♦ "I was on that bridge last evening." (M&P 273)

last price
final offer ° *What's your last price?*

lat

(coll.) latrine, toilet

♦ "An' we do have lats. Proper Army-issue squatting pans." (CU 483)

latapata

/lɑtəpɑtə/ clutter (Sinhala) ° *Can't you get rid of all this latapata?*

late: to get late (to do something)

/lēт/ to be late (for something), to do something late ° *I got late to go to office.* ° *We got late to come for class.* ° *Sorry for getting late!*

♦ "Son, what happened?" … "Bus got late," he muttered, … (July 223)

latrine coolie, lavatory coolie

(= **bucket man**) (dated) toilet cleaner

♦ … and to give the latrine coolie a snort when he came to the gate on New Year's Day to salaam and ask for baksheesh. Latrine coolie, you ask? Well, yes. In those days many homes had no drainage, sewerage or water service. Not even the best of them. So the lavatories had squatting plates and buckets - and each day around ten a.m. the coolies (also called bucket men) would come around with their carts (universally known as shitcarts for want of a simpler name) and carry away the nightsoil. (JFT 30)

♦ The lavatory coolies came in and asked for the wood. (YY 180)

♦ Lotus Cottage still used the bucket system, a latrine coolie coming by every morning to collect the night soil in his cart. (CG 14)

♦ … any time of day or night there were mango sellers, fish women and lavatory coolies knocking at their window, … (CP 161)

laundry soap

a bar of soap used for washing clothes

lavariya

/lævəriyə/ a sweet snack made with **string hoppers** and **pani pol** (Sinhala)

LAVARIYA

lazy: to be/feel lazy to do something

/lēzi/ not to feel like doing something ° *I feel lazy to go to school.*

L-board

L-plate (on a car)

LC-ite

a student or former student of Ladies' College in Colombo (also **Bishopian, Bridgetian, Vishakhian, Familian,** etc.) (> **Royalist**)

leading school

a popular or well-known school ° *attending a leading school in Colombo*

leaf tea

good quality tea (> **tea dust**)

leave

a holiday, a day off (more formal in BSE) (> **lieu leave, short leave**) ° *I took leave and came.*

leave: to leave to

to leave for (a place) ° *When are you leaving to England?*

leg

foot (> **hand**)

lemons

(in newspaper reports) half-time in a rugby or football match ° *At lemons the soldiers led 10-7.* → In the UK, players might eat oranges at half-time, but not lemons. 'At lemons' is a phrase often used in the sports pages of Sri Lankan newspapers; 'at the breather' and 'at the short whistle' are also used as alternatives.

lena

/lēna/ (coll.) squirrel (Sinhala)

less

a little, not much ° *I like less sugar in my tea.* → In BSE, 'less' is only used in comparatives: 'less than …'

level best: to try your level best

to try/do your (very) best (dated in BSE) ° *I'll try my level best to pass.*

lies: all lies!, don't tell lies!

(coll.) you're joking!, you're kidding! → In BSE, accusing someone of telling lies would be a serious accusation; in SLE (like the Sinhala word 'boru') the word is used much more lightly!

□ for lies

(coll.) as a joke, in vain, for no reason ° *He told you that for lies.* ° *We went all that way for lies.* ° *Don't cough for lies!*

♦ "What did I do? For lies they're shouting!" (TT 104)

lieu leave

a holiday taken in lieu of an extra working day (> leave) → In BSE, 'lieu' is only used in the rather formal expression 'in lieu of'. The expression 'lieu leave' can also cause confusion since the SLE pronunciation of the words 'lieu' and 'leave' is almost identical.

lifter

(in newspaper headlines) weight-lifter (> cager) ° *the best lifter in the 83.5 kilo category*

light

(of tea or coffee) weak

light bill

(= electric bill) electricity bill

light reader

clairvoyant, spiritualist, psychic (see quote)

♦ "Why not go to the light reader?" … Paduma has heard about light reading. By chanting and help from the spirit world, some fortunate holy men are able to dig out secrets not seen by ordinary people. (PMS 86)

like: do you like?

would you like? do you want? ° *Do you like some more rice?* → In BSE, 'do you like?' is used to ask about a person's general likes and dislikes; 'do you want?' or 'would you like?' are used in offers, i.e. to ask somebody if they want something.

♦ "What do you like to eat? Fish? Pork? String-hoppers?" (MM 128)

♦ "I'll tell Father Sebastian you like to be an altar boy. … You like?" (TT 149)

♦ "Do you think she'll like some coffee?" (FSD 181)

□ to like to do something

to like doing something ° *I like to play tennis.* → Verbs such as 'like/love/hate' can be followed either by the gerund ('playing') or by the infinitive ('to play'). In BSE the gerund is more common, while in SLE the infinitive is more common.

like that

and so on, etc.

♦ "First prize hundred rupees, then fifty
rupees, like that." (TT 172)

lime and spoon race
the Sri Lankan equivalent of the 'egg and
spoon race'

♦ "You want to enter the lime and spoon
race?" (PMS 252)

lime juice
a popular drink made with lime juice, water
and sugar (less common in BSE)

♦ He had sat by the pool, sipping a glass
of lime juice, willing himself to be
disciplined. (CU 187)

line: to put a line to somebody
(= **put a break, put a cap**) (coll., dated) to
chat somebody up, approach somebody
with romantic intentions ° *Can't put a line,
men. She already has a boyfriend.*

line rooms, lines
(= **coolie lines**) estate labourers'
accommodation

♦ "I am sorry I couldn't show you the
line rooms," ... (WMD 102)

♦ "They went to the government
sugarcane farm two nights ago and
drove the Tamil coolies out of the
line rooms into the cane-fields."
(WMD 226)

♦ When we used to come here for the
weekends Mummy used to take me on
walks through this vast estate, visit the
'lines' in which the labourers lived and
give them food, clothing and medicine.
... She used to come away from the
lines with the sick children and their
parents for Daddy to treat them.
(OD 93)

♦ On the estates, in the bungalows and
the lines alike, it was the only topic of
conversation. (HC 288)

♦ Agnes and her husband lived in a line-
room - a long narrow cabin partitioned
into sections for each worker. (CP 110)

lingus
/lingus/ a spicy sausage

link language
the term used for the official status of
English in Sri Lanka; also used in schools
to refer to Tamil when it is taught as a third
language

lion flag
the Sri Lankan national flag

LION FLAG

♦ All in white, walking in the same
direction with colourful lion flags
neatly folded in their pockets. They
were all Sinhala. Sharona and I were
Sinhala too, but we had not brought
the lion flag. (M&P 335)

little
(coll.) a little (> **lot of**) ° *Why don't you take
little more rice?*

Little Friends
Brownies, a branch of the Girl Guides for
younger girls (the equivalent of Cub Scouts
for boys)

little little
various little (with plural nouns) (> **small
small**) ° *I have lot of little little things to do.*

little maid
(= **flower girl**) a young child who
accompanies the bride at a wedding

living

alive ° *Are your parents still living?*

load shedding

controlled power cuts designed to conserve energy

loaf: to loaf (around), to go for a loaf

/lōf/ (vi) to go out, wander around, waste time ° *He's out loafing with his friends as usual.* ° *He must have gone for a loaf.* → In BSE, to 'loaf (around)' is to sit around doing nothing; in SLE it is to go out and have a good time. In both cases it suggests wasting time, not doing what you should be doing.

- ♦ "When he comes there can go fishing and loaf in the jungle and get some colour." (YY 152)

- ♦ "Whole day loafing with the catapult and annoying your sisters." (YY 153)

- ♦ "Must see him loafing all over." (TT 142)

- ♦ ... swimming in the sea or loafing in the countryside or just playing with the children. (WMD 21)

- ♦ Vijay spent the next few days lazing about the house, ... or loafing around and getting the feel of the place. (WMD 324)

- ♦ "... their parents sell their houses and land and send them to study and all they do is to loaf about the roads creating revolutions!" (OD 12)

- ♦ "... that is why she is loafing about with that Leslie." ... "I knew when you started loafing with that fellow, everything, all your pretensions will end like this." (OD 128)

- ♦ ... the market is the only place she can legitimately go to and not have anyone

complain that she is loafing around. (Z 4)

- ♦ When we had loafed around in a Land Rover, looking for something to take a pot shot at, it never mattered if we took a wrong turn. (REP 121)

- ♦ Janaki wanted to loaf around but Ravi, not trusting her to stay out of trouble, cowed her with a furious glare. (FSD 262)

- ♦ "He may loaf anywhere else, but the best taste remains with his wife." (KCS 133)

loafer

waster, useless person

- ♦ "I have told you girls a thousand times don't encourage every loafer on the road." (JFT 12)

- ♦ Once it was a loafer with a shifty, rolling gaze, who claimed to be Tissa's eldest son and tried to touch Sam for a loan. (HC 258)

- ♦ Getting off was another battle, pushing past women with shopping baskets, men with briefcases and loafers who wanted to rub themselves against Kamala. (REP 320)

- ♦ A bearded loafer told him they'd have to take a bus to Potupitiya, ... (FSD 70)

local

/lōkǝl/ Sri Lankan (opp. foreign or imported); (n) a Sri Lankan person ° *local and imported drinks* ° *the local newspapers* ° *the local languages* ° *hoping to attract locals as well as foreigners* ° *Pottu's LA adventure: How a local cat halted traffic at America's busiest airport* → In BSE, the 'local newspaper' would be the newspaper for a particular area, as opposed to a 'national newspaper'.

♦ … and these were the quarters for 'locals' and they were a mixture of Sinhalese, Tamils, Burghers and Malays, … (BTH 43)

♦ … or an orange - imported not local, as the local ones were prohibitively expensive … (Z 2)

♦ So, if we passed all our exams … and still did not manage to enter local university …, it was not a huge problem. (M&P 254)

□ localised
adapted to Sri Lanka ° *giving customers a taste of localised Chinese food*

□ local school
a government or private school which teaches mainly in Sinhala or Tamil **medium** (> **international school**)

♦ "Apo! Why did you put that child in the international school? All our children are going to local schools no?" (M&P 310)

loku amma; loku thaaththa
/loku amma, loku tātta/ aunt (mother's elder sister); uncle (father's elder brother) (Sinhala)

♦ On the opposite side was the room where my aunt, *Loku Amma* lived with her youngest son. (CM 15)

londe
/londə/ the soft flesh inside a **thambili** or **kurumba** (Sinhala)

longs
long trousers

♦ "All right, so I was sixteen and already in bloody college longs." (Reef 56)

♦ "Some in shorts and caps, some in longs." (FSD 192)

look
look like, look as if

♦ Then there were those who looked straight from the village. (Z 27)

♦ They looked a cross-section of Colombo's working and middle classes … (CU 371)

♦ Or would he look - like the embassy terrorist - just one more obscure Asian? (CU 410)

□ looks like
it looks like it ° *Are they winning? - Looks like.*

□ to look up and wait
to hang around, do nothing (> **wait**) ° *They're just looking up and waiting!*

loose
(coll.) crazy, mad ° *He's a real loose case.* ° *He's a bit screw loose.* (BSE: He's got a screw loose.)

loose-ending
(coll.) hanging around, doing nothing, at a loose end ° *The children are loose-ending here, what shall we do?* ° *If you're loose-ending on Sunday why don't you join us?*

loose motion
diarrhoea (also used euphemistically in BSE, but less frequently) ° *I had a loose motion this morning.*

lot of
(coll.) a lot of, lots of (> **little**) ° *He is having lot of friends.*

♦ "Said he's telling lot of lies in the class." (TT 49)

♦ "And lot of friends roundabout, no, near your old house." (TT 130)

♦ "Lot of things he can do if he likes," … (TT 148)

love: to love to do something

to love doing something (> **like**) ° *I love to go for films.*

love cake

a rich, sweet cake made with cashew nuts, **rulang** and **pumpkin preserve**

- ♦ Anna always made love cake for Christmas. (JFT 187)

- ♦ ... while huge chunks of the richest, juiciest love-cake disappeared into her as into a cavern. (Reef 74)

- ♦ ... the Christmas festivities, where Anna's love cake would have been called Bolo de Amor and nothing else! (TT 140)

- ♦ ... slices of moist love cake filled with cashew and pumpkin preserve, ... (CG 375)

- ♦ "Patties. Cucumber sandwiches. Love cake." - "No love cake today, sir." (MiP 55)

- ♦ ... Mrs Jansz, whose cardamom-scented love cake was greatly in demand at birthday parties. (HC 78)

love marriage

a marriage which is not arranged by the couple's parents (> **proposed marriage**) ° *Those were the days when love marriages were frowned upon.*

- ♦ Theirs had been a love marriage, quite rare in their society, but their parents couldn't have done better if they'd made the match themselves. (July 11)

lovi

/lovi/ lovi-lovi, a small, red, sour fruit (Sinhala, orig. Malay)

- ♦ I tell you, you haven't lived till you've tasted my wine-dark lovi jam, ... (CP 63)

low country, low-country

(n/adj.) the coastal region of Sri Lanka (> **hill country, up-country**) ° *low country dancing* ° *low-country vegetables* ° *the low-country Sinhalese*

- ♦ ... the *'parra Dhemmala'* (Tamil bastard) and his 'low-country Sinhalese whore'. (WMD 200)

- ♦ "Up-country Sinhalese versus low-country Sinhalese, ..." (CG 68)

- ♦ He decided to send a message to the local dance troupe and schedule a low-country dance performance for the evening. (July 136)

LTTEer

(= **Tiger**) a member of the Liberation Tigers of Tamil Eelam

- ♦ "The two on the right are known LTTEers, and are already wanted for murder in Sri Lanka." (CU 51)

lunch boy

(dated) a boy who delivers **lunch packets** to people in their offices

- ♦ She woke up before dawn to begin cooking, and by half past ten, two lunches were neatly served on enamel plates (to prevent breakage), covered with another enamel plate, tied up in a snowy napkin, tagged with name and office address and ready for the lunch boy. The lunches were placed in the wooden box on the back of his bicycle, and off he went to pick up more lunches for more people. When he finished his rounds, he joined the hundreds of other lunch boys at their rendezvous point near Thurston Road, where the lunches were separated according to office locations, loaded into the wooden boxes once more and delivered. (July 241)

lunch packet

(= rice packet, bath packet) a **rice and curry** meal wrapped up to be taken away (> packet, parcel)

- "I give lunch packet and ten cents every day, no?" (JFT 14)

- That bag in the hand must be the lunch packet. (OD 8)

- … or a special lunch packet from Mandarin Golden Apple Chinese restaurant, … (KCS 34)

- The younger officer … now brought in the tray with the lunch packet and the bottle of Elephant Ginger Beer himself. … "You ate already, Mayadunne?" he asked politely, opening the lunch packet's outer wrapping of newspaper and then the inner one of cling film. (CU 420)

- But first he had to wash his lunch packet rice off his right hand. (M&P 354)

lunch sheets

polythene sheets used to line **lunch packets**

lungi

/lungi/ a length of material worn round the waist, esp. by women; also used to refer to the outfit, a combination of **cloth** and blouse (also India, Burma, etc.; Urdu = loin-cloth) → In Indian English, a 'lungi' is normally worn by men.

lunu dehi

/lunu dehi/ lime pickle (Sinhala: lunu = salt, dehi = lime)

lunu miris

/lunu miris/ a **sambol** made with chopped onions, salt, lime juice and **chilli powder** (Sinhala: lunu = salt, miris = chilli) ° *Prince Philip enjoyed lunch at the hotel, but he complained that the lunumiris was too hot.*

- One could eat the *kiribath* with either the red chilli sambol called *lunu miris* that was there or with jaggery. (CM 66)

- As they both ate the bread, egg curry and lunu miris, Anura had arranged carefully on the table they continued their conversation of last night. (Z 69)

M

-ma

/-mə/ (Sinhala emphatic ending, also added to English words for emphasis and/or humorous effect) ° *sitting in the front-ma front seat* ° *You must-ma come!*

maaduru

/māduru/ sweet cumin (Sinhala) (> **suduru**)

maama

/māma/ uncle (mother's brother or father's sister's husband) (Sinhala/Tamil) ° *Mahinda maama*

- "Gnanamma," I whispered, mischievously, contracting Gnanam and *mama* (uncle) into a girl's name, as I used to when I was a boy. (WMD 208)
- "No, maama," ... (CG 122)
- How could a little girl play so much magic in the heart of her Maama, ... (KCS 42)

maami

/māmi/ (= **nenda**) aunt (father's sister or mother's brother's wife) (Tamil)

- "Yes, maamee." (CG 125)
- "Bala Maama, I came to see Sonia Maamee," ... (CG 333)
- "... and Niloufer Maami always asks after you." (Z 132)

machaan

/machān/ male cousin or brother-in-law (Tamil) (> **maini**)

- "Avoid Bullers Road Machaan. Too many check points and I don't have my ID." (Z 138)

machang

/machang/ (coll.) a familiar term of address between close male friends (Sinhala/Tamil; from **machaan**) ° *How machang?* ° *They're on machang terms.*

- You tell them *machang*, you tell them we must win. (MM 117)
- "Anil, machan, we will see you later." (FB 71)
- "*Machang**, Tony, your sister is looking nice these days." (* Sinhala 'brother-in-law' but universally used as a form of friendly address. A sort of acknowledgement that we are all brothers under the skin, perhaps.) (TT 195)
- "Why should we kill those innocent young fellows, machang, we are no different from them." (OD 11)
- Why does this fellow who greeted him and called him 'machang' a mere five years ago now behave like this? (OD 14)
- "Yes machang, ... You have my word." (REP 347)
- "I've been cutting back on my drinking, *machang*, can't put them back like in the old days." (WE 110)
- "Cool it machang," ... (FSD 3)
- "I'll take care of her, machang," ... (GC 307)
- "I say machang, give us a peep!" (CP 47)
- "I got very upset in the bus machang." (WCS 11)
- "Better strap in, *machang*," ... (CU 468)
- "Never mind *machang*," ... (M&P 296)

mad: are you mad?

(coll.) nonsense! rubbish! → Like 'lies', the word 'mad' is used in a more light-hearted way in SLE than in BSE.

madam

(term of respect, dated in BSE); also used (sometimes ironically) to refer to President Chandrika Kumaratunga (> **sir**) ° *Madam still hasn't turned up!* ° *Madam was very happy with the news.*

maddo

/mædɒ/ (coll.) a crazy person (usually female) ° *She's a real maddo.*

♦ "That old maddo will live more than all of us." (YY 19)

made-up saree

a **Kandyan saree** which is cut and tailored to make it easier to wear

madithi

/maditi/ a tree with small bright red seeds similar to **olinda** seeds (Sinhala)

♦ Claudia gathered up the crimson seedpods that had fallen from the *madhitchi* tree on the edge of the lawn and I threaded them onto cotton. (HC 83)

maduruwas

/maduruwas/ (coll.) mosquitoes (Sinhala 'maduruwa', plural 'maduruwo') ° *maduru coils*

maekaral

/mækaral/ a type of vegetable, a long green bean (Sinhala)

♦ ... slender green beans we called Maakaral, ... (REP 156)

magul bera

/magul berə/ (= **geta bera**) a traditional drum held at the waist and played with both hands (Sinhala)

MAGUL BERA

maha

/maha/ one of the two annual paddy harvests (Sinhala) (> **yala**)

maha gedera

/maha gedərə/ (= **ancestral home**) (Sinhala) (> **walauwa**) ° *All the family had gathered at the maha gedera for the event.*

mahal; mahan

/mahəl, mahən/ daughter; son (Tamil) (> **merlay; mernay**)

♦ "Meena, ... I am soaking wet, *mahal.*" (WMD 386)

mahanayake

/mahanāyəkə/ a senior Buddhist priest (Sinhala) ° *Malwatte Mahanayake's funeral today* ° *TNA delegation to meet Mahanayakes on Monday*

Mahapola

/mahapolə/ a scholarship scheme for university students (Sinhala)

mahappa

/mahappa/ (= **loku thaaththa**) father's elder brother (Sinhala)

mahar

/mahər/ a Muslim marriage payment made by the husband to the bride (Arabic)

Mahasangha

/mahasangə/ (= **Sangha**) the order of Buddhist monks (Sinhala, orig. Sanskrit)

♦ "The JVP and the Buddhist priests in the bloody *Mahasanga* are already screaming blue murder, accusing us of betraying the Sinhalese people." (CU 577)

Mahasivarathri
/mahasivarātri/ a Hindu festival (Tamil, also India)

mahatteya
/mahattəya/ master, boss, sir (Sinhala); (coll.) a self-important man (> **nona**) ° *He's acting like a real mahatteya.*

♦ I think they thought I was a real city *mahathaya* because when I got my money out, one of the men said he would clean the fish for me. (Reef 124)

♦ But then again, it's best that they think he is a pizza delivery boy, going to college at night and on his way to being a big mahattaya. (Z 61)

♦ Then she handed him the battered little cardboard rectangle the dhobi had returned with the *mahatheya's* shirts. (HC 158)

♦ The *mahattaya* walked slowly onto the verandah. (WE 41)

♦ Rani had always told him that the big *mahattayas* in companies were a funny lot. (WCS 22)

mahout
/mahūt/ a man whose job is to look after an elephant (also India, orig. Hindi)

♦ The tip of the pole had a metal hook like a mahout's stick used for tickling and tugging an elephant's ear. (Reef 163)

♦ A couple of elephants in scarlet livery carried their mahouts and a passenger each. (YY 142)

♦ Occasionally, to add to the confusion, there are even a few elephants on their way to some temple ceremony, and sometimes one of them runs amok and destroys a few cars and a mahout or two. (July 7-8)

♦ Rajah earned his keep by working at the timber yard, carrying heavy logs about, loading and unloading trucks. His mahout was Piyal, a thin wiry man, who became my friend. (REP 140-1)

♦ It backs up to the pile of logs and the mahout unties the elephant. ... Under the guidance of the mahout it loads the heavy logs first ... (PMS 227)

♦ The mahout, a grey haired man with a fierce moustache, waves his ankus to the beat of the drums. (PMS 245)

maini
/maini/ female cousin or sister-in-law (Muslim Tamil) (> **machaan**)

make
/mēk/ repair ° *Did you get the car made?*

□ **to make somebody to do something**
to make somebody do something ° *That really made me to think.* ° *On the whole there was a feeling of cordiality between teachers and students, which did not make the students to hate or dislike them.*

□ **to make a move**
to go, leave, be off ° *Then I'll make a move.*

□ **to make out**
to understand; to recognise ° *I can't make out what you're saying.* → In BSE, to 'make something out' means to see something clearly.

♦ Did he make him out, wondered Somaweera. Why shouldn't he have recognised him? (OD 14)

♦ I heard them shouting behind us but couldn't make out the words. (REP 210)

♦ There was some mumbled conversation we couldn't make out, ... (REP 241)

♦ "Shalindra Premasiri was in the lineup. I pointed him out. I couldn't make out any of the others." (FSD 28)

♦ With a sinking heart I make out what he is carrying. (GC 334)

♦ It took a minute or two, but he finally made out what she was screaming. (CU 581)

Malay
a member of a distinct Muslim community of S.E. Asian descent (> **Moor, Muslim**)

♦ ... he invited a huge Malay sergeant named Bongso to join him one evening. (YY 141)

♦ ... a determined few from the other ethnic groups - Sinhalese, Moors, Malays, and the fast-disappearing Burghers ... (CU 56)

Malay pickle
a mixed pickle traditionally served with **buriyani** (> **achcharu**)

Maldive fish, maldive fish
(= **umbalakada**) a type of **dry fish** commonly used for flavouring dishes ° *Maldive fish sambol*

♦ It was a small room, and it smelled of raw rice and Maldive fish and other dry provisions. (FB 296)

♦ A man came from the Maldive Islands carrying a series of cloth bags dangling from his shoulders. The bags contained maldive fish, fish oil and various other preparations, all made from fish. Maldive fish is sun dried fish used as a seasoning in cooking vegetable curries.

♦ The very best maldive fish still comes from the Maldive Islands. (CM 56)

♦ The whiff of Maldive fish depressed him every morning. (HC 206)

♦ The air was pungent with the odour of spices, curry powders, dried salty Maldive fish, ... (SMS 137)

♦ ... and he smells the frying fragrance of Maldive fish vadai. (KCS 137)

♦ Thathi returned from the Maldive islands with two suitcases. One full of dirty clothes and the other full of Maldive fish. Siya came out of his slumber and invited all his ten brothers for dinner and they played cards and drank arrack the whole night, eating Maldive fish. (M&P 194)

♦ Even Magi giggled like a young girl when she served the Maldive fish sambol. (M&P 202)

malefic
(according to astrology) **inauspicious** ° *a malefic period* ° *with a malefic in the 7th house* ° *marriage delayed due to malefic horoscope*

♦ A woman born with Mars in the Seventh House was *'malefic'*. (AG 138)

Maligawa
/māligāvə/ the Temple of the Tooth in Kandy (Sinhala = palace)

malla
/mallə/ (coll.) a woven reed bag (Sinhala) ° *Don't forget your malla.*

mal lella
/mal lællə/ a traditional carved wooden ventilation panel above a door or window (Sinhala)

MAL LELLA

♦ ... large and rambling with that stone floor polished like marble and the ornate carved wood frieze - the *mal lella* - under the roof, the Dutch tiles. (MM 68)

♦ It might have been spartan but for carved verandah pillars whose design of lotus flowers and vines was picked up on the fretwork mal lallis above the doors and windows and on the carved valance boards that ran along the bottom edges of the roof. (CG 13)

♦ What was unique and whimsical about the house was that the doors, the lattice-work windows, the fretwork mal lallis were all painted a sky blue, which contrasted sharply with the whitewashed walls. (CG 293)

♦ A carver from Galle who specialised in *mal lella* was hired to restore the damaged fretwork above doors and windows. (HC 150)

♦ Amrith pointed out how, above each window, there was a rectangle of intricately carved wood latticework, known as a *mal lallie*, which let in cool air even when the window was closed. (SMS 113)

malli

/malli/ younger brother; can also refer to a male cousin or any younger boy (Sinhala) ° *Tell malli to come for lunch.*

♦ Malli cried loud and long because his mother and sister were both crying. (OM 29)

♦ "Malli has no idea about money." (OD 13)

♦ "Sunil Malli, come, come. Have a cup of tea, come ..." (WCS 70)

♦ "Malli, do you know the story of the Ravayana?" (M&P 369)

mallung

/mællung/ a dish made with shredded green leaves (e.g. **gotukola, kathurumurunga, mukunuwenna**) and grated coconut; also used like **achcharu** in the sense of a mess, a mixture (Sinhala) ° *We always ate a balanced meal, and mallung was an essential part of it.*

♦ Alice's date chutney, seeni sambol, mallung and brinjals and iced water. (RF 137)

♦ She also made shredded green leaf mixed with grated coconut, which is called a *'mellun'*. (CM 21)

♦ The food was inedible - rice, mostly uncooked, and a dry *mallung* or a coconut *sambol* that had gone off, ... (WMD 365)

♦ "... the boys in the commune who loved the *mallung* and the condensed-milk desserts he was partial to." (AG 47)

♦ My own family is a mallung of Muslim misfits. (Z 18)

♦ She ate jack *mallung* heaped on cracker biscuits. (HC 161)

♦ How can they survive on cabbage curry and mallung? (GC 10)

♦ "... as a reward, we will be serving a special mallung only for them." (GC 29)

♦ I bit in to my tissue paper thin *Mallung* sandwich. (M&P 50)

malu karaya

/mālu kārəya/ fish man, fish seller (Sinhala)
(> karaya)

malu miris

/mālu mirîs/ capsicum, a large variety of
chilli used as a vegetable (Sinhala)

MALU MIRIS

malu pang

/mālu pāng/ fish bun (Sinhala: malu = fish,
pang = bread)

MALU PANG

Mama

/mama/ Mummy, mother (> Dada)

mammoty

/mæmərɪ/ an agricultural tool with a
wooden handle and metal blade, used for
digging and hoeing (also India, from Tamil:
OED mamoty, mamootie) ° *The farmer
will pull out a mammoty and symbolically
begin work at the auspicious hour.*

MAMMOTY

♦ Often it was the signal for the farmers
to shoulder their mammoties and walk
to the other side to their fields. (OM 1)

♦ Elsewhere, farmers tied their loin
cloths, hoisted mammoties on
sunburned shoulders and made their
way to the fields. (July 127)

♦ A few meters further, her Muslim
brother in law was hacked to bits with
a mamoty. (M&P 345)

manamalaya

/manəmāləya/ (coll.) flirt, ladies' man
(Sinhala = bridegroom) ° *That one looks a
real manamalaya.*

manavarai

/manəvərei/ the podium on which the
couple stand during a Hindu wedding
ceremony (Tamil) (> **poruwa**)

mangosteen

/mængustīn/ a small fruit with a thick
purple rind and juicy white flesh (orig.
Malay)

MANGOSTEEN

♦ Only the mangosteen tree, which I
practically lived in as a child during
its season of fruit, was full and strong.
(RF 59)

♦ They brought back mangosteens,
brooms, mats and sunburn. (July 77)

maniokka

/mannyokka/ manioc, cassava, a kind of yam
used as a vegetable (Sinhala)

mani pittu

/mani piᴛᴛu/ a type of **pittu** made without grated coconut (Sinhala)

manna

/mannə/ a large curved knife (Sinhala)
° *Murder suspect hacked with manna knife*

MANNA

♦ The cut on his chest where the *manna* had hit him was red and raw. (WE 45)

mapila

/māpila/ (= **cat snake**) a mildly venomous snake which has an unjustified reputation of being highly venomous (Sinhala)

mara (1)

/mārə/ (= **rain tree**) (n) a huge spreading tree, common on roadsides and at the edge of **tanks** (Sinhala)

MARA TREE

♦ The evening was closing in, the crows were cawing themselves noisily to bed on the lofty mara tree in the distance. (WMD 57)

♦ … and ahead of me it was already dark under the giant Mara trees, .. (BTH 1)

♦ I hear the crows squabbling for perches on the mara trees surrounding the union office as I climb the stairs. (GC 205)

♦ He settled for the nearest Mara tree. (WCS 62)

♦ "Has he got planted like the Mara tree and cannot remove the roots?" (M&P 347)

mara (2)

/mārə/ (= **fine**) (adj.) (coll.) fine, great, superb (often used ironically); strange, weird, unexpected (Sinhala) ° *A mara thing happened to me!* ° *He's a mara fellow!* ° *He hit a mara shot!* ° *Mara cool!* ° *It was a 'mara' problem when a huge tree on the Anuradhapura - Mihintale main road fell on a lorry loaded with gas cylinders.* → The last example is a play on the two meanings of 'mara'.

marketing

shopping (for food) ° *My husband does the marketing every Sunday.*

♦ This left Beryl time to wallop Carloboy, do all she had to do and also go marketing. (YY 3)

♦ "Must be going there quietly when going marketing." (TT 231)

♦ She goes to the newly bereaved stall, condoles and continues with her marketing. (Z 4)

♦ I fervently hoped the fat woman had planned to do her marketing today or maybe talk to the teacher about her children. (REP 307)

♦ "Anyway it's a good thing you came back because I want to do some marketing." (FSD 31)

♦ She had gone marketing and was returning with a heavy bag. (KCS 172)

♦ The last question was as innocuous as a wife asking her husband whether he'd finished the marketing. (CU 248)

□ marketing bag

shopping bag

♦ But he hadn't reckoned with the contents of the marketing bag. (YY 30)

♦ … and with a marketing bag that was sorry to behold. (TT 38)

marriage broker

(= **kapuwa**) professional matchmaker

♦ But none of the marriage brokers ever came to the house on the hill after that marriage! (OM 18)

♦ … the business would be done later, through a marriage-broker. (WMD 99)

♦ He received offers from twenty-seven marriage brokers. (HC 106)

marriage proposal

(= **proposal**) the offer by parents of their son or daughter in marriage (e.g. in a newspaper)

♦ … I gazed at Radha Aunty and Rajan Nagendra and thought of the first time I had heard about the marriage proposal, … (FB 99)

♦ After dinner, Maha filled in the details of the marriage proposal, stressing what a good family the boy was from. (WMD 98)

♦ In fact, he had been very attracted to the slight, fair girl whom he had gone to visit on a marriage proposal. (WCS 14)

♦ … because sometime back due to a marriage proposal, Anthoni had visited Princy with his mother and some friends. (KCS 74)

♦ The marriage proposal was an unattainable dream anyway, and this is the final blow to her hopes. (PMS 270)

married from

married to a person from (a particular place, e.g. a country) ° *Did you get married from Sri Lanka?*

maru (1)

/maru/ (coll.) great, superb (Sinhala)

♦ "*Maru* (expressive Sinhala word that could hazily mean 'tophole' or 'super') devils, these fellows." (JFT 181)

maru (2)

/māru/ (coll.) escape, getaway (Sinhala = change)

♦ "*Ado*, Sumith, our bugger's done a *maru*." (CU 207)

♦ "… and a car parked somewhere nearby for a quick *maru*." (CU 220)

mason baas

/mēsən bās/ builder, mason, bricklayer (> baas)

Masoor dhal

(= **Mysore dhal**) red split lentils, the most common variety of **dhal** (also India)

♦ Dhal: the variety referred to as 'Mysoor parippu', fine-grained and pink and mistakenly believed to be coming from Mysore in India and boycotted under the orders of the JVP when the Indian Peace Keeping Force was alleged to be raping girls in Jaffna in the late eighties until someone enlightened us that the dhal had nothing to do with India and was really 'Masoor Dhal' which came from Turkey, … (BTH 10)

♦ The others know what is Masoor dhal, which is yellow like a Buddhist monk's robe, … (KCS 18)

mas pang

/mas pāng/ meat bun (Sinhala: mas = meat, pang = bread)

♦ ... where a fellow with his head swathed in a gunny sack against the cold was doing a roaring trade in piping hot *mas paans*. (HC 81)

massas

/mæssas/ (coll.) flies (Sinhala 'massa', plural 'masso') ° *From where have all these massas come?*

master

male teacher (> **miss, tuition master**) ° *English master*

♦ Sumanasiri's best pupil, Kapila was embarrassed to see his Sinhala master. (WCS 28)

mat: on the mat

(in newspaper headlines) in trouble ° *Death of jumbo: Wildlife officials on the mat*

mati

/mæti/ clay; (coll.) stupid (Sinhala) ° *mati pots* ° *They're all made out of mati.* ° *Real mati case she is.*

mat slide

(children's) slide

mature

(adj.) ripe; (v) ripen ° *Are the mangoes mature?* → In BSE, 'mature' refers to people, but not to fruits.

matured

(adj.) mature ° *He's not matured enough to go alone.* → In BSE, 'matured' is used as the past participle of the verb 'to mature', but not as an adjective.

♦ "How come you are matured like this?" And Saroja is looking at the kapok tree and smiling like a matured kapok pod. (KCS 39)

♦ "It surprises me, ... A matured girl like you are ignorant of these matters." (KCS 40)

mawatha

/māvata/ (in addresses) road, street, avenue (Sinhala) ° *Bauddhaloka Mawatha*

may

(tenses) (> **might, must**) ° *You may be knowing her.*

MC

(coll.) Majestic City (a popular Colombo shopping centre)

meaning?

(coll.) what do you mean? what does that mean?

measure

2 pounds (of rice) (> **chundu**) ° *a quarter measure of rice*

♦ "It is impossible to get a decent measure of rice these days," ... (MM 92)

♦ As Tippy was coming, I made two extra measures of rice to make sure the dish was not cleaned out. (Reef 150)

meat

beef → While 'meat' can of course refer to any type of meat, it tends to refer specifically to beef in SLE.

meda midula

/mæda midula/ an internal courtyard or small garden (Sinhala)

♦ A corridor led to a meda midula, open to the sky, and beyond it there was another corridor that stretched far into the distance. (CG 293)

♦ ... and Amrith told him about the courtyards and *mada midulas*, which were interior gardens around which the houses were sometimes built. (SMS 81)

medium

language (as a medium of education) ° *She's studying in Sinhala medium.*

♦ ... he went to an English medium school; ... (BTH 28)

♦ This school had two mediums. The Sinhala medium and the Tamil medium. (M&P 43)

meet: to meet with an accident

to have an accident (less common and more formal in BSE) ° *Pradeep has met with an accident.*

♦ "If go loafing all over or meet with accident or something you'll come and scold." (TT 102)

meeya: to wait like a meeya

/mīya/ (coll.) to stay quiet, to keep a low profile (e.g. feeling guilty about something) (Sinhala: meeya = rat) ° *Look at him, waiting like a meeya as if nothing happened!*

melodica

/meloɒika/ a musical instrument, consisting of a keyboard like an accordion, with a tube for blowing air like a bagpipe

MELODICA

member

person (e.g. in a family) (> **family member**) ° *There are five members in my family.* → In BSE, 'member' is normally used to refer to a person who belongs to a club or other organization.

Memon

/memən/ a member of a small Muslim community of Indian origin ° *The first Memons arrived on the island as merchants and traders in 1870.*

men!

(a colloquial term of address generally used between close friends) ° *What men!* ° *Aiyo, sorry men!* ° *Sin men!* → Like the rather outdated 'man!' in BSE, 'men!' is a very common term of address, used irrespective of the number or gender of the person(s) being spoken to: i.e. it is just as common between female speakers as between male speakers.

♦ "You're a bloody fool, men." (JFT 18)

♦ "My God, men, what is that?" (JFT 79)

♦ "Why, men, I am Ivy's third cousin, no? Kelaniya Mullers, men." (JFT 119)

♦ "You owe it to the country, what *men*?" (Reef 58)

♦ "Come on, men!" (FB 27)

♦ "*Anney* just keep quiet men." (TT 94)

♦ "How about some golf, *men*?" (SG 171)

♦ "The way he was doing his hands, men ..." (WE 107)

♦ "What is this, men, embarrassing me." (SMS 108)

♦ "Mala, Mala, hurry, men, we're going to be late." ... "I'm coming, men," ... (SMS 110)

menu card

menu

mercantile holiday

a public holiday for private sector companies

merit

(in Buddhism) moral credit gained through **meritorious** acts such as charitable deeds, **alms-givings**, pilgrimages, etc. (> **demerit**) ° *a pooja to confer merit on the President*

♦ I thought we might get some merit from doing that. (Reef 171)

♦ In the Buddhist philosophy of sin and merit, sin had to be counterbalanced by acts of merit if one did not wish to be reincarnated as a cockroach or a dung beetle or something equally miserable. Therefore, the *dansala* was an act of merit by its owner. (CU 86)

♦ In order to gain additional merit, devout pilgrims bathe in the icy water of the stream before ascending the mountain. (PMS 113)

meritorious

bestowing **merit** ° *This period is set aside for meritorious deeds.*

♦ "You have done a meritorious act, ... by feeding a pregnant woman." (KCS 33)

merlay; mernay

/mālei, māĀei/ daughter; son (affectionate term of address) (Tamil) (> **mahal; mahan**)

♦ "Merlay, ... are you all right?" (CG 15)

♦ "What do you think, merlay?" (CG 88)

metal

small stones used for building roads etc. (less common in BSE)

might

(tenses) (> **may, must**) ° *They might be not wanting to come.*

migrate; migration

emigrate; emigration ° *They're hoping to migrate to Australia.* ° *migration to the US* → In BSE, 'migration' is used in the context of animals (birds, fish, etc.), or large numbers of people moving from one area to another (e.g. from the country to the city); individual people, when they move from one country to another, 'emigrate' and 'immigrate'.

♦ When they found the Sinhala-Buddhist nationalism beginning to get on their nerves they quit and migrated. (YY 114)

♦ The previous burgher owners had migrated to Australia ... (July 10)

miko

/miko/ (coll., dated) a derogatory term for a low-class **Burgher**

♦ What she needed, he told himself, was a 'good Burgher', not those *mikos* (a nondescript half-breed) who go about on bicycles and don't know to knot a tie. (JFT 100)

milchard

/milchāĐ/ a cheap variety of rice

♦ ... because I was carrying a bag full of smelly onions and milchard rice. (BTH 9)

♦ ... the smelly yellowy big grained milchard; ... (BTH 10)

milk hopper

(= **paal appam**) a **hopper** made with **coconut milk**

milk rice

(= **kiribath**) rice prepared with **coconut milk** and cut into diamond shapes, served on festive occasions (> **pongal**)

♦ Magi announced that the milk rice was ready. (M&P 334)

♦ He opens Saro's lunch box but is disappointed to find it filled with milk-rice; ... (PMS 75)

milk tea

white tea, tea with milk and sugar (> **tea**)

♦ She was beautiful, with almond-shaped eyes, long, glossy black hair, skin the colour of milk tea, and a shapely figure. (CG 233)

♦ He had already learnt from his mother that her friend was half-Dutch Burgher, half-Sinhalese, and so he was not surprised by her light complexion, like milk-tea. (SMS 16)

♦ She was more interested in Achi's milk toffee and the milk tea with King Parakramabahu the sixth's condensed milk. (M&P 152)

milk toffee

a type of sweet made with condensed milk

♦ Achi continued to make milk toffee … Milk toffees without cashew nuts were not the same as milk toffee with cashew nuts. (M&P 102)

miris

/miris/ chilli (Sinhala) (> **amu miris**)
° *Don't put too much miris.*

☐ miris gala

/miris galə/ grinding stone, a flat stone used for grinding chillies, spices, etc. (Sinhala)

MIRIS GALA

☐ miris kaeli

/miris kæli/ (= **chilli pieces**) dried chilli flakes (Sinhala)

☐ miris kudu

/miris kuɒu/ (= **chilli powder**) (Sinhala)

☐ miris malu

/miris mālu/ a hot fish curry made without **coconut milk** (Sinhala)

♦ "Everyday buying slice of seer and making nice *mirismalu* (fish cooked in condiments and water without a coconut milk base) …" (JFT 64)

Mirror Wall

a wall with a glazed surface at Sigiriya, famous for the ancient graffiti written on it

miss (1)

female teacher (> **master, sir**) ° *Miss didn't come to class today.*

miss (2)

(coll.) (of an engine) misfire ° *The engine is missing.*

miss: to miss not having/doing something

(coll.) to miss having/doing something ° *I really missed not seeing you.* (BSE: I really missed seeing you.)

missing

not here, not there, absent → In BSE, if someone is 'missing' it means no-one knows where they are and it is a cause of concern; in SLE, it can simply mean they are not around at the moment.

♦ My father was missing in the Veddha region, and my mother was about to go missing in the commonwealth. (M&P 204)

misunderstand

(vi) get upset with somebody ° *Don't misunderstand!* (BSE: Don't misunderstand me!)

mixture

a savoury mixture of nuts, pulses, **omapodi**, etc. (BSE: Bombay mix)

♦ ... then they went around the corner to Bombay Sweet Mart to buy bags of mixture filled with fried sticks of dough and cashews and chickpeas mixed with salt and chilli powder. (SMS 138)

MMV

(in the names of schools) Madya Maha Vidyalaya (Sinhala) (> **vidyalaya**) ° *Tissa MMV*

mobike

/mōbaik/ motorbike ° *The gunmen escaped on a mobike.*

mod

(coll.) trendy, fashionable ° *looking very mod*

modaya

/mōɒəya/ (coll.) fool, idiot (Sinhala) ° *We are a nation of modayas.*

moju

/mōju/ a preserved fish or meat dish (> **batu moju**) ° *prawn moju* ° *dry fish moju*

molgaha

/mōlgaha/ a large wooden pestle used with a **vangediya** for pounding rice to make **rice flour** (Sinhala) (> **vangediya**)

♦ "... I'll put a clout with the *molgaha* ..." (JFT 144)

♦ Inside the kitchen, Janaki was pounding something with the mol gaha.... I stayed like that for a long time, as the mol gaha pounded away monotonously in the kitchen. (FB 100)

moneys, monies

sums of money (formal in BSE) ° *The company has agreed to terminate the project and claim monies amounting to Rs 270 million for the work done.*

♦ Monies donated and allocated for deviation and development of the Mahaveli river basin stagnated in the minister's bank account, abroad. (M&P 267)

monitor lizard

a large lizard (also India, Africa, etc.) (> **land monitor, water monitor**) → There are two varieties of **monitor lizard**: the **land monitor** (Sinhala: **thalagoya**), which is smaller, and the **water monitor** (Sinhala: **kabaragoya**) which is larger. The **land monitor** is commonly referred to as an **iguana**.

♦ ... and the occasional mad scramble in the thicket which signalled the hurried departure of a monitor lizard. (YY 192)

♦ I spotted the monitor lizard when it moved again. (REP 204)

Montessori

any pre-school or nursery school → In BSE, a 'Montessori school' would be one specifically following the Montessori method of pre-school teaching.

moonamal

/mūnəmal/ a type of tree (Sinhala)

♦ She was in the garden alongside the moonamal tree and the kohomba tree. The flowers of the moonamal when shed always turned face up to the moon. (AG 202)

moonstone (1)

a semi-circular carved stone on the ground at the entrance to a temple

MOONSTONE

moonstone (2)
a semi-precious stone with a cloudy white colour

Moor
a Sri Lankan Muslim of Arab descent (from Portuguese) (> **Malay, Muslim**)

♦ "… Moors, Malays, Christian Tamils, Hindu Tamils, Buddhists, and so on and so on." (CG 68)

♦ When the Moor next appeared she asked to see the flat bales of cotton and muslin he kept in the bottom of his dented trunk. (HC 204)

moosala
/mūsələ/ (coll.) miserable, wretched, desolate, unfortunate, **inauspicious**; noun: **moosalaya** (Sinhala) (> **muspenthu**) ° *a moosala house* ° *a moosala face* ° *moosala weather* ° *a moosala beggar* ° *Don't say such moosala things!* ° *The husband is such a moosalaya!*

morala
/mōrələ/ (of vegetables) old, over-ripe, not fresh; (of **thambili** and **kurumba**) old and beginning to ferment (Sinhala)

more (1)
(word order) ° *10 days more* (BSE: 10 more days)

♦ Seven days more. … Six days more. … (M&P 92)

more (2)
(coll.) ° *It's much more healthier not to eat meat.* ° *Nothing could be more further from the truth.* ° *hoping to reach a more wider audience* → In colloquial SLE, 'more' is sometimes included with comparative adjectives where it would be superfluous (and incorrect) in BSE.

mosquito coil
(= **coil**) a coil-shaped device burnt to repel mosquitoes

MOSQUITO COIL

♦ Was there a mosquito net above them or a fan, or just a Lion brand mosquito coil? (AG 229)

♦ It was getting dark outside and the roomboy cum steward placed a mosquito coil under their table. (FSD 119)

♦ Once Jane-Nona had lit mosquito coils under the chairs and brought out a metal candelabra, … (SMS 37)

mosquito mat
an electric device used to repel mosquitoes

motor bus halting place
(= **bus halt**) (dated, on signs) bus stop

Mount
(coll.) Mount Lavinia; can also refer to the Mount Lavinia Hotel, or to St Thomas' College, Mount Lavinia

♦ "Well, I did book us a room at the Mount." (CU 231)

move: to move with somebody
to mix with somebody, associate with somebody, socialise with somebody
° *They're not used to moving with boys.*

♦ "You must move with people who have lost their homes, lost their families." (REP 329)

♦ He had moved easily with friends who came from genuinely wealthy families ... (FSD 5)

mudalali

/mudəlāli/ businessman, merchant, trader, shopkeeper; also used colloquially to refer to someone who is good with money, or to someone who is rather fat! (Sinhala/Tamil; also India, from Marathi/Malayalam)
° kasippu mudalalis ° He looks like a real mudalali!

♦ "He was a *mudalali* - a businessman." (MM 22)

♦ The only rich person in the town was the Banduratne Mudalali, who owned most of the hotels. (FB 170)

♦ First the old Mudalali, clearing his throat and walking to the junction to get his copy of the morning paper. (OM 49)

♦ ... to Jinasena *mudalali*, merchandising his loyalties on the political stock market. (WMD 274)

♦ "It's all right for you shop-keepers, *mudalali*," ... (WMD 372)

♦ "Gave those Colombo *mudalalis* and the police and the newspapers absolute hell - ..." (SG 213)

♦ Fish mudalalis, shop owners, restaurateurs and others swarmed down the beach to attend the early-morning fish auctions, ... (July 9)

♦ Hemantha wandered off and struck up a conversation with the mudalali, ... (July 90)

♦ By that time he had gone to Kurunegala and was engaged to be married to the daughter of a Mudalali dealing in coconuts. (OD 88)

♦ The mudalali only glanced at his driving license before returning it to him. (FSD 236)

♦ "Or maybe Miss Decima has found a mudalali's son for our gamey kella?" (GC 217)

♦ In the midst of all this chaos, the *mudalali*, who owned the store, sat cross-legged on a bench, ... The mudalali gestured for them to be seated ... (SMS 137)

♦ Kapila was not quite clear who he meant, and the Mudalali never brought up the subject again. (CP 190)

mudaliyar

/muɒliyə/ (dated) **headman**, chief (a traditional title); also a court official (from Tamil; OED modeliar)

MUDALIYAR

♦ Perhaps one of the grandest houses of Cinnamon Gardens was that of the Mudaliyar Navaratnam. (CG 12)

♦ In the days before European domination, a mudaliyar, in the domain in which he held sway, had served as a representative of the king. The British had continued the mudaliyarships, but now it was an appointment by the governor based on loyalty to the Empire. The mudaliyars served as interpreters to the British government agents in the different provinces of Ceylon, and they helped the agents execute colonial policy. They were also Legislative Council members. (CG 25)

♦ The Mudliyar realizing that something was amiss shushed the court sternly. (Z 8)

♦ My grandfather, Sir Stanley Obeysekere, was a *mudaliyar*, an office that placed a man at the pinnacle of our island's social system. A *mudaliyar* was a leader of men, with considerable influence in his ancestral district. By tradition he was a gifted soldier and a skilled diplomat, abilities he placed at the service of his sovereign. With the advent of the Europeans, however, the role of the *mudaliyar* evolved. ... The Europeans rewarded loyalty with land: whole villages were given in gift to the *mudaliyars*, vast tracts of jungle, tax-free estates. (HC 6)

♦ Upali's, the chocolate people, had recently been running an ad featuring a man in a *mudliyar* coat, a black coat with gold froggings that native officials used to wear in colonial times. (CP 115)

mudukku
/muɒukku/ (coll.) low, seedy, sleazy (Sinhala)
° *mudukku joints*

muffler
scarf (rare and dated in BSE)

♦ Harry produced a frightful checked muffler that he wound about his throat. (HC 250)

muhandiram
/muhəndirəm/ (dated) a senior official of the **Kandyan** kingdom

mukkuthi
/mūkkutti/ (= **nose ring, nose stud**) a stud worn on the nose (esp. worn by Tamil women) (Tamil)

♦ She smelled of stale coconut oil, and the diamond mukkuthi in her nose always pressed painfully against my cheek. (FB 2)

♦ The heavy gold mukkuthi in her nose enhanced the darkness of her skin. (CG 181)

♦ ... maybe she was the girl wearing a pink sari and a gold mukuthu on her nose, ... (Z 34)

mukulufy
/mukulufai/ (= **komalafy**) (coll.) get embarrassed, get the giggles, flirt (from Sinhala) (> -**fy**)

mukunuwenna
/mukunuwænnə/ a green leaf used to make **mallung** (Sinhala)

♦ And other greens, like mukunuwenna - those leaves are long and look like spikes. (KCS 85)

♦ I bit into my transparent *Mukunuwenna* sandwich. Two tissue paper thin slices of bread held together with a Mukunuwenna and green chilli mass, no butter, no margarine. (M&P 72)

♦ I got bread and Mukunuwenna mallung for dinner while the rest of the family ate hoppers. (M&P 147)

♦ She abstained from spinach, kankun, mukunuwenna and all iron rich foods, ... (M&P 230)

multiplug
(electrical) adaptor

mung ata

/mung œтə/ (= green gram) mung beans (Sinhala)

mung kavum, mung guli

/mung kœvum, mung guli/ a type of **Sinhala sweet** made with **rice flour** and **honey** and a little mung flour, and fried in batter; the **kavum** are diamond shaped, the **guli** are smaller and ball-shaped (Sinhala) (> **kavum**)

murder the King/Queen

(dated) speak incorrect English → The concept of 'murdering the King', which is completely outdated in BSE, survives in SLE, though it is probably restricted to the older generation.

murukku

/murukku/ a snack made with **rice flour** and spices fried into crispy spiral pieces (Sinhala) (> **omapodi**) ° *murukku mould*

♦ ... when they had sat down to the tea and *murukku* that Devi had set before them. (WMD 333)

♦ "Aney darling, can't you bring a bit more cake after you finish with the Murukku, ..." (M&P 238)

murunga

/murunga/ (= **drumsticks**) a type of vegetable, the long green pods of the 'horseradish tree' (Sinhala; OED moringa) ° *murunga leaves*

MURUNGA

♦ ... leaning his bicycle against the *murunga* tree. (WMD 338)

♦ "Superbly cooked, I must say," observed Vijay, working through his fourth crab-belly. "The *murunga* leaves make all the difference." (WMD 347)

♦ There were no onions or aubergines or *murunga* to give life to the land ... (WMD 390)

♦ It was legendary that every Tamil home on the Jaffna peninsula had three trees in the garden. A mango, a murunga, and the pomegranate. Murunga leaves were cooked in crab curries to neutralize poisons, ... (AG 240)

♦ She trained their lone domestic in the culinary art of making asparagus soup with murunga ... (Z 82)

♦ Jane-Nona made her famous crab curry in honour of Niresh's visit, with her own combination of roasted spices ground into a paste, coconut milk, murunga leaves, and tamarind to give it a nice tang. (SMS 113-4)

♦ Murunga flowers in scrambled egg, ... (CP 113)

muscat

/maskəт/ a jelly-like Indian sweet

♦ ... get her some real *muscat*, she'd like that, and some English marshmallows. (WMD 376)

♦ "Try a piece," urged Vijay trying to put a piece of *muscat* in her mouth. (WMD 378)

musical show

(= **beat show**) a live concert (> **show**)

Muslim

a member of one of several Muslim communities in Sri Lanka; refers to their ethnic group as well as to their religion (> **Moor, Malay, Borah, Memon**) ° *Sinhalese, Tamils, Muslims and Burghers* ° *Muslim law* ° *Muslim food*

♦ ... the Muslim's turn would come again, or the Burgher, or the Malay. (M&P 358)

♦ The young Muslim boy dressed in a faded sarong and torn Metallica T-shirt ... (Z 137)

□ Muslim hotel

a **hotel** run by Muslims and serving halal food

♦ Just to please her, Ravi thought to try another Moslem hotel on the main road. (FSD 265)

muspenthu

/muspēntu/ (coll.) miserable, morose; noun: **muspenthuwa** (Sinhala) (> **moosala**)
° *He has a muspenthu look.* ° *He's such a muspenthuwa.*

♦ The phenomenon was surely *moospainthu*, a bad omen. (HC 50-1)

♦ She knew the place was *moospainthu*. It blighted her cooking. (HC 164)

♦ Their presence in the house was *moospainthu*. (HC 169)

must, musth

/mast/ (n) an annual condition affecting male elephants, making them dangerous and unpredictable (also India, from Urdu)
° *When a tusker is in must, it has its legs tied with chains.* ° *Two young bull elephants in musth approached the camp.*

must

/mast/ (tenses) (> **know, have**) ° *You must be knowing them.* ° *You must be thinking I'm mad.* ° *She must be not liking to play.* ° *They must be not understanding you.*
→ In BSE, there are a number of verbs (know, think, understand, have, like, want, etc.) which are not normally used in the continuous ('-ing') form. In SLE, they are often used in this form, especially after 'must', 'may' or 'might' as in the examples.

♦ "He must be not knowing that my brother is about to sit for his Engineering finals ..." (OD 15)

♦ "They must be thinking we are all cattle!" (OD 37)

♦ He must be having the same feeling even about my reading the diaries. (OD 89)

♦ "So you must be having a lot of friends now?" (M&P 63)

muthusamba

/mutusamba/ a high quality variety of **samba** rice (Sinhala: muthù = pearl)

muttal

/muṭṭal/ (coll.) idiot, fool, mutt (Tamil)

♦ Muttiah as her husband. How preposterous. Muttal Muttiah. For he was a "muttal" chap, an oaf, an idiot. (CG 172)

mutti

/muṭṭi/ an earthenware pot (Sinhala)

♦ She thudded an earthenware mutti on the counter and grabbed at two plastic cups on the side. (Z 123)

mutton

goat's meat (also India) → In BSE, 'mutton' is always sheep's meat.

my!

(coll.) my God! my goodness! ° *My! How nice!*

♦ "My! He's absolutely charming," ... (FB 98)

♦ "My, child, that Beryl, real martyr, no?" (YY 72)

♦ "My, but what a commotion with that Mohan, no?" (SG 120)

♦ ... "myee, what a lovely dress" ... (July 54)

my dear

(a dated term of address used between males) → In modern BSE, 'my dear' is a more intimate term of address usually used with children or close acquaintances.

Mysore dhal

(= **Masoor dhal**) red split lentils, the most common variety of **dhal** (also India)

♦ "Only that vile stuff they call dhal. None of the red mysore." (July 63)

♦ Now rice, sugar, flour, onions and imported Mysore dhal sat outside shops in reassuringly huge gunny bags. (July 186)

N

na

/nā/ (= **ironwood**) a type of tree (the Sri Lankan national tree) (Sinhala) ° *the scent of a na tree in bloom*

♦ The old *na* tree that had shaded the shop front was scorched; ... (MM 21)

nab

catch, arrest ° *The police are hoping to nab the leader of the gang.* → In BSE, 'nab' is a colloquial word; in SLE it is also used in more formal contexts.

nadagam

/nāɒəgang/ a traditional musical drama (Sinhala/Tamil)

♦ Waving a silken scarf from one hand he sang a popular ditty, usually a nadagam melody. 'Nadagam' is a traditional ballad. (CM 58)

♦ "They are putting on a *nadagang*, with puppets. Let's go and see." (WMD 62)

nadun

/nadun/ a type of dark wood (Sinhala)

♦ ... and after great deliberation Sebastian had chosen to make the pews not of teak, as was customary, but of *nadoon*. Teak was easier to work on and light enough to be moved about, but *nadoon* had a grain and an incandescence which called to the light that broke in through the stained glass windows, ... (WMD 76)

naki visey

/nāki visē/ (coll.) an expression used to refer to an old man flirting with younger women (Sinhala)

nalal patiya

/nalal patiyə/ a gold chain worn on the forehead as part of a bridal costume (Sinhala)

nalava, nalavan

/nalavə, nalavən/ the 'toddy tapper' caste (Tamil)

♦ The Roman Catholic priests, he complained, had promised the *nalavans* that they did not have to be submissive and obedient to be born to a higher caste in their next birth. (WMD 10)

♦ ... before him lay the mud-houses of the *nalava* settlement. (WMD 44)

nambiliya

/næmbiliyə/ a bowl used for washing rice, with grooves to catch the sand, stones, etc. (Sinhala)

NAMBILIYA

name

/nēm/ the daily wage of an estate labourer

name board

(= **signboard**) sign, notice (e.g. on a shop or office)

♦ He followed, noted nameboard and number. (JFT 9)

♦ The Pannipitiya Railway Station ... remained unchanged right down to the name board where the English letters were still on top as it used to be; ... (BTH 53)

♦ She held out her hand, as if displaying a name board. "Mrs. A. Muttiah." (CG 172)

♦ He ... scanned the name board over the gate. (FSD 258)

♦ There had been a name board once but an elephant had knocked the post down and no one had bothered to replace it. (GC 86)

♦ As dawn breaks I see the name boards flashing past, Marawila, Madampe and Chilaw, ... (GC 145)

♦ "On your way back, Paduma only has to read the name board of the bus once." (PMS 194)

naminam, namnam

/naminam, namnam/ a type of fruit, brown in colour, which grows on the trunk of the tree (Sinhala)

♦ The fruit trees were the joy of the kids. ... Also *naminam*, *goraka* and *bakini*. (CM 5)

nana

/nāna/ (= **aiya, anna, kaka**) elder brother (used by Muslims) (> **dhatha**)

nangi

/nangi/ younger sister; can also refer to a female cousin or any younger girl; also **nanga** (Sinhala) ° *What's wrong with your nangi?*

♦ "You want to play with my nangi's dolls now?" (July 31)

♦ "I'm sorry, nanga," ... She sometimes calls me nanga, little sister, although we are nearly the same age. (GC 78)

♦ "What are you doing in Colombo, nangi?" (GC 243)

♦ "Putha, what is the meaning of Nangi's name?" (M&P 60)

♦ "Nangi, never in my life will I support such corruption, ..." (M&P 112)

natami, nattamy
/naʈāmi/ labourer (Tamil)

national dress
traditional male dress, a long-sleeved collarless white shirt and white **sarong**; also referred to as **national costume, national suit**, or simply '**national**'

NATIONAL DRESS

♦ ... neat and spruce and handsome in his national dress, all of silk - *verti*, shawl and *banian* - ... (WMD 134)

♦ He taught Buddhism and wore national dress (the umbrella was probably meant to go with it). (WMD 301)

♦ A distinguished-looking man in national costume stood next to a woman who was obviously his wife, ... (July 232)

♦ The teacher came in. Dressed in a white cloth and a long white shirt - what they called 'national' - he stood out brightly in front of the freshly cleaned blackboard. (WE 11)

♦ ... a small mob crowded through the entrance ushering a fat man in national dress. (FSD 197)

♦ A silver haired man in national dress is attempting a head count. (GC 291)

nationality
(= **jathiya**) race, ethnic identity → While 'nationality' can also be used to mean 'race' in BSE, a clear distinction tends to be made between the two: 'nationality' means Indian, Sri Lankan, etc.; 'race' means Sinhalese, Tamil, etc. This distinction is not necessarily made in SLE.

native doctor, native physician
(= **vedamahatteya, vedarala**) ayurvedic doctor

♦ The native doctor came on his rounds in his buggy cart riding leisurely into the village. (CM 76)

♦ The doctors couldn't do anything. Perhaps he should have listened to the native physician. (WMD 14)

native medicine
ayurvedic medicine

♦ But what do the doctors say, or are you still taking native medicine? (WMD 17)

nats
(= **goday**) (coll.) (of people) unrefined, unsophisticated, common, lower class; (of clothes, jewellery, etc.) flashy, gaudy, tasteless (used by Tamil speakers, from Tamil 'naatu puram')

needful: to do the needful
to do what's required, to take the necessary action (also India; rare and dated in BSE) ° *I'm sure Dr Perera will do the needful.*

nekatha
/nækəʈə/ an **auspicious** time according to astrology, the precise time at which something should be done (e.g. the start of a wedding ceremony, the lighting of the

hearth at **New Year**, starting to build a new house, etc.) (Sinhala)

nelli

/nelli/ a small green fruit with an acid taste (Indian gooseberry) (Sinhala/Tamil)

♦ There was a bowl of nellis by her and, not taking her eye off the page, she was dipping each fruit in a mixture of salt and chilli powder before popping it in her mouth, her lips puckering at its tartness. (SMS 44)

□ nelli crush
a drink made with **nelli**

Nelsonian eye

(in newspapers) a blind eye ° *The government have turned a Nelsonian eye on the problem.*

nelum

/nelum/ lotus flower, a type of water lily (Sinhala; OED nelumbo)

♦ "*Nelum* flowers and lilies, some goldfish to look at in the evening." (Reef 43)

♦ We chopped up the Nelum roots and made it into a curry of sorts ... (REP 129)

nelum ala

/nelum alə/ lotus root, used as a vegetable (Sinhala)

nenda

/nænda/ aunt (father's sister or mother's brother's wife) (Sinhala)

♦ "Nända, what is Palitha's condition?" (GC 187)

♦ I stopped crying and smiled at Nenda. She was my ally. (M&P 17)

net
mosquito net ° *Do you sleep under a net?*

nethali

/nettəli/ (= **sprats, halmassas**); also a humorous term for a skinny person (Tamil)

newly

recently ° *I bought it newly.* → In BSE, 'newly' is normally used with a past participle: newly arrived, newly discovered, newly-wed, etc.

♦ ... doubtless influenced by the new Reckard cabriolet newly in the market. (JFT 37)

new rich
nouveau riche

New Year

(= **Sinhala New Year, Sinhala and Tamil New Year, avurudu**) ° *New Year sweets* ° *New Year time the shops are packed.*

♦ From the time the swing went up on the mango tree, it was New Year celebrations for the kids, who more or less lived on the swing. (CM 60)

♦ "I have to go home for the Sinhalese New Year." - "What New Year for you?! ... You're a Catholic." (CP 107)

next day morning
the next morning ° *Next day morning we went back to the rock.*

nibbana
/nibbānə/ nirvana (Sinhala)

nicely

(coll.) thoroughly, properly, well (also used for ironic effect) ° *I of course ate nicely.* ° *She nicely told me to stop drinking.* ° *We're nicely eating all the nuts.*

♦ "See, will you, how nicely he walked in. As sweet as you please." (JFT 12)

♦ "What, men, delicate state your wife is in, no? I scolded Ivy nicely." (YY 137)

"When we were in 34th Lane nicely came to drink my father's arrack and eat and go!" (TT 173)

night

evening (after dark) (> **evening**)

nikah

/nikā/ Muslim wedding ceremony (Arabic)

nikang

/nikang/ (coll.) plain, normal (Sinhala)
° *nikang bread*

nikaya

/nikāyə/ one of three sects of the Buddhist **sangha** (Sinhala)

nilame

/niləme/ the secular head of a Buddhist temple (Sinhala) (> **Diyawadane Nilame**)
° *Incident mars Basnayake Nilame elections*

nivithi

/niviti/ spinach (Sinhala)

♦ *Nivithi sambol* too was prepared daily, as spinach develops a baby's brain. (HC 168)

no

(coll.) there isn't/aren't (any) ° *Big problem because no petrol.* ° *Won't eat if no sausages.* ° *Raining so no tennis.*

no?

(= is it?, isn't it?) (coll.) (a very common question tag used at the end of sentences, and often in the middle of sentences too) ° *He's a good player, no?* ° *You'll have to go, no? after lunch.*

♦ "Can buy eggs and meat and pay the baker and get kerosene oil, no? with that money." (JFT 14)

♦ "But better to wait, no, until the wedding." (JFT 18)

♦ "But you know, no, what I mean?" (Reef 72)

♦ "You go jogging with him, no?" (FB 182)

♦ "Last time saw, no, what happened." (TT 16)

♦ But they are from the South, no? (OM 19)

♦ "She went to America with him, no, on that scholarship of his." (WMD 314)

♦ "This is in the service of your country, no?" (CG 159)

♦ "You were born here, no?" (AG 9)

♦ "He should support her, no, without taking her money." (WE 116)

♦ "Useful to have a doctor in the family, no?" (FSD 200)

♦ "You saw him no, came in a beautiful vehicle." (WCS 15)

♦ "Now-a-days young girls are not wearing skirts no, they are wearing trousers like men." (M&P 237)

♦ "We are doing this to make Gamini win, no?" (PMS 188)

no more

no longer, not any more ° *They are no more living here.*

♦ He was no more a regular filmgoer. (KCS 42)

♦ The jackals are no more hooting. The elephants are no more running. (KCS 104)

nona

/nōna/ Madam, lady (Sinhala); (coll.) a self-important woman; also (dated) **nonamahatteya** (> **mahatteya**) ° *She thinks she's a real nona!*

♦ Miss Nili became the lady - our *nona* - of the house, ... (Reef 118)

♦ Each child received a coin, a soft drink, a paper cone of homemade toffees from the *nonamahatheya's* hand. (HC 138)

♦ She could see that the *nona* didn't believe her. (WE 42)

nonagathe

/nonəgəte/ the period of a few hours between the end of the old year and the beginning of the **New Year**, considered an **inauspicious** time (Sinhala) ° *Many will not eat, drink or even read during the nonagathe.*

♦ Until the dawn of the New Year it was *Nonagathe*, the time to devote to religious activities. During the *Nonagathe* no work should be done. The hearth should not be lit. ... Everyone went to the temple during *Nonagathe*. (CM 63)

no need of (doing) something

no need for something, no need to do something ° *No need of money.* ° *No need of crying!* (BSE: No need for money, No need to cry!)

♦ "No need of parents, ... We'll teach them a lesson." (PMS 114)

normalcy

normality (also US, less common in BSE) ° *East limps back to normalcy*

♦ It is their attempt to provide some normalcy to the day. (FB 287)

♦ He felt a flood of relief, and a return to normalcy, when he saw Tilak lying there. (FSD 8)

♦ ... she knew she wouldn't have been able to put up any semblance of normalcy. (CU 382)

nose ring, nose stud

(= **mukkuthi**) a stud worn on the nose (esp. by Tamil women) (> **ear stud**)

♦ What, wondered Vijay, would happen if Meena walked in now with her nose-ring and her *pottu*. (WMD 278)

♦ "It would have begun with tots of arrack for his cronies. A bottle of whisky for himself. Gold nose-studs for his mother." (HC 290)

no sooner

as soon as ° *I told him no sooner I got home.* ° *No sooner the fire was reported the Fire Brigade sent a fleet of fire engines.* ° *Please inform one of the undermentioned persons no sooner you receive this letter.* → In BSE there is a rather formal alternative with inverted word order: 'No sooner had I got home than I told him.'

♦ No sooner the swing came to a stand still Babun Appu Aiyya wrenched the screaming child off the swing. (CM 69)

♦ Velaithan jumped off no sooner I stopped. (REP 56)

♦ The workout and the Valium must have helped because I passed out no sooner my head hit the pillow. (REP 341)

♦ ... knowing full well that she'd call the company no sooner their office opened, ... (FSD 11)

♦ Ravi was on his feet and moving no sooner the disturbance started. (FSD 197)

note

(singular) notes (only used in the plural in BSE when referring to a student's notes)

♦ "Do you know that I cannot concentrate on a note for even five minutes? The moment I take a note into my hand, I tell myself what a useless thing it is!" (OD 104)

not enough
(coll.) as if it isn't enough

♦ "Wretches ... not enough that they are taught with the poor man's money!" (OD 12)

nothing to worry
(coll.) not to worry, no need to worry, there's nothing to worry about

♦ "It is all right. Nothing to worry, men." (TT 61)

♦ "But, nothing to worry, ... be patient." (M&P 97)

notify
announce, publish ° *Results will be notified later.* → In BSE, this use of 'notify' is rather formal; more commonly, to 'notify somebody of something' is to inform somebody about something: 'You will be notified of your results'.

not out
(coll.) still living, still going strong (cricket idiom) (> **bat**) ° *95 not out!*

not pot
/нот рот/ (dated) a derogatory or humorous reference to speaking English with a strong Sinhala accent, considered inferior (the English words 'not' and 'pot' pronounced with an exaggeratedly 'closed' vowel 'o') ° *talking with a real 'not pot' accent* ° *That 'not pot' minister can't teach me anything!*

♦ "Why didn't I realize all this time he was one of those 'not pot' English types?" (OD 113-4)

♦ "When the interview is over they will laugh at you; call you the not-pot fellows." (GC 74)

not the word
(coll.) (expression used ironically to add emphasis; less common in BSE) ° *Thorough is not the word!*

not to
(coll.) don't ° *Not to touch!*

♦ "Not to worry, dear. He'll be fine." (July 181)

nought
(in telephone numbers) O, zero

now
(coll.) soon ° *He'll come now.*

nuts
coconuts

♦ It takes time, and sweat, and his fingers are calloused and sore when the nuts are finally collected into several neat piles. (PMS 37)

O

observation car
first class railway carriage

OD
(= opening dose)

odd
(coll.) shy, embarrassed ° *I feel odd to ask.*

of course
(coll.) on the other hand ° *I of course don't like.* → In BSE, 'of course' is also used in the same sense, but only if it also includes the sense of 'naturally' (i.e. assuming that the listener already realises this is true); it is used much more often in SLE purely to express a contrast. Note also the word order: in SLE 'of course' comes between the subject and verb, while in BSE it usually comes before the subject: 'My wife doesn't eat sweets, but of course I've always liked them'.

off (1)
(prep.) from, out of; (of places) near, outside, away from (> **get off**) ° *three miles off Kandy* ° *800 kilometres off Brisbane* ° *a little village off Warakapola* ° *I haven't heard of mulligatawny being drunk off a glass.*

♦ ... a hill-station called Brookside, off Bandarawela ... (JFT 113)

♦ A man was seated on a crude bench outside, drinking something off a tumbler. (REP 56)

♦ They'd never taken alcohol before and took turns to sip off Tilak's cup. (FSD 6)

off (2)
(adj.) (coll.) crazy, mad ° *mentally off* ° *She's a bit off.* ° *He's really gone off recently.*

off (3)
(vt) (coll.) switch off, turn off, put off (> **on**) ° *Can you off the light?*

off-day; off-time
day off; time off → In BSE, an 'off-day' is a day when you don't feel well or things don't go right, and an 'off-time' is a period when business is slack.

♦ One day he would be an engine driver but in the meantime he would marry Elaine and spend all his off-time in bed with her. (JFT 7)

office
the office ° *He's gone to office.* ° *He's in office.* ° *He spends all day at office.* → In BSE, 'office' is used with the article 'the'; in SLE the article is often omitted, as with 'temple', 'campus', etc.

♦ All a husband could wish for was to come home from office, drink great quantities of tea, ... (JFT 3)

♦ He had just popped into office to 'show his face' ... (JFT 153)

♦ "I can't go to office," I said quickly. "It's Sunday." (FB 32)

♦ That afternoon he bustled out of office ... (TT 186)

♦ Back in office, Savan carefully avoided any discussion on Rap Music. (WCS 15)

♦ That evening Saman, the tea boy, who had struck up a friendship with Athma in office, came to see him ... (WCS 23)

♦ "I already took five days off from office," ... (CU 42)

OIC
officer-in-charge (e.g. of a police station)

♦ "God forbid," said the O.I.C. piously, ... (YY 208)

- The OIC swaggered over to meet them. (July 69)

- "Liyanage wasn't in but the OIC seemed to have lost interest in the case." (FSD 18)

- "This is the Cinnamon Gardens Police OIC." (CU 378)

- "I'll speak to the OIC." (PMS 154)

oil cake
(= kavum, konde kavum) a small deep-fried rice flour cake served at New Year with other Sinhala sweets

- The disfiguration made his face look like a crumpled oil cake ... (YY 82)

- She took the wicker basket with the fragrant oil cakes in one hand. (OM 33)

- It is a rare skill in this woodapple country, where oil cakes are fried according to the traditional methods. (KCS 100)

oil lamp
(= pahana, polthel pahana) a lamp with a cloth wick soaked in coconut oil: either a small clay lamp which is lit in temples etc.; or a large brass lamp which is lit on auspicious occasions (weddings, opening ceremonies, etc.) ° *The minister opened the ceremony by lighting the traditional oil lamp.*

OIL LAMP

- As we gathered in the shrine room to pray for my safe journey, my father lit the oil lamp and served up burning

camphor to the framed picture of Lord Siva. (WMD 120)

- Small notices with Srijan's latest epigrams had been dotted about, each with its own small oil lamp at the ready, ... (SG 155)

- The drummers returned from their performance sweating in the cold dark, their feet lit by the oil lamps as they came along the paths. (AG 304)

- Head of smoker shining like freshly polished brass oil lamp. (M&P 19)

oilman goods
(dated) different types of cooking oils, etc.

oilman store
(dated) a shop selling oilman goods

- The block held a sleazy eating house, an indistinguishable store, Danny's, a bicycle repair shop and a tumble-down oilman's store. (TT 28)

- ... but educated in Jaffna where his father, now dead, had kept a small oilman store. (WMD 191)

- It seemed inconceivable to me that anyone would want to attack the old man or burn down his oilman store. (WMD 209)

O/L
(= ordinary level) O level exam (> A/L)

ola leaf
/olə/ a palm leaf (usually palmyrah) used as paper in old manuscripts (Sinhala; OED olla, from Tamil/Malayalam via Portuguese)

OLA LEAF BOOK

- Here the Ola leaves which people wrote on were too brittle. (RF 83)

- How far do you get reading *ola*-leaf books by moonlight and slowly going blind? (Reef 68)

- ... for even the *slokas* on papyrus and bound *ola* leaves would be eaten by moths and silverfish, dissolved by rainstorms ... (AG 104)

- In the year 500 AD the great sage Adishanya had a series of visions that he inscribed on fifty ola leaves. (Z 135)

- The Mahavansa was a history of our people, covering a period of some two thousand five hundred years, inscribed on Ola leaf manuscript. (REP 130)

old arrack
high grade **arrack**

olinda keliya
/olində keliyə/ mancala, a traditional board game played with **olinda** seeds (small, bright red seeds with a black tip) (Sinhala) → Variations of mancala are played throughout Africa and Asia, usually with pebbles or cowrie shells.

olungai
/olungei/ a small lane (Tamil)

- ... the journey through the *olungais*, a tangle of sandy and bumpy lanes and by-lanes, ... (WMD 326)

omapodi
/ōməpoɒi/ a snack similar to **murukku**, an ingredient of **mixture** (Tamil)

on
(vt) (coll.) switch on, turn on, put on (> **off**) ° *Will you on the fan?*

once in a way
once in a while

- "Why don't you visit your parishioners once in a way?" (JFT 191)

- "Once in a way never mind." (YY 141)

- "Just because I once in a way go to see how she is." (YY 182)

- Once in a way, Loku Amma went to the reed field wearing her cloth short to make it easier to wade in the mud freely. (CM 24)

- ... Father's ancestral home at Havelock Town where he took me once-in-a-way to spend a few days ... (BTH 31)

- "Once in a way they will allow one person to succeed." (GC 74)

- But once in a way he has a need to get drunk! (GC 88)

one (1)
(= **shot**) (coll.) slap, hit (> **give**) ° *I'll give you one!* ° *You'll get one from me!*

- "Go away before I give you one across the ear." (PMS 99)

- "How did it feel when you got one with this?" ... "If I give you one, you'll really cry." (PMS 242)

one (2)
(= **case**) (coll.) person (after an adjective, often with a negative connotation) ° *a real one* ° *a funny one* ° *a forward one* ° *You're a fine one!*

one (3)
(with names) a certain (dated in BSE) ° *He is one Lionel Gunasekera.*

one thing ...
(coll.) one thing is ...

- "One thing, I don't know what's wrong with these men." (JFT 204)

- "One thing, that Viva won't touch, child." (JFT 205)

♦ "One thing, don't know how these Tamil buggers can live here," … (YY 163)

onion sambol
a **sambol** made with raw onions and green chillies

♦ She rushed into the kitchen, grabbed a heap of rotis from the plate where they sat, added a huge dollop of onion sambol on top of the pile, shoved it into a plastic bag and put it under her jacket. (July 148)

♦ At the other end of the gleaming rosewood his wife was smearing onion *sambol* on buttered toast. (HC 206)

only
(word order; also used like Sinhala **thamai** to add emphasis) (> **itself**) ° *Now only I came to know.* ° *Then only I saw her.* ° *Today only I heard the news.* ° *His sister only is married to Mahesh.* ° *Rs 70 only!* → In BSE, 'only' usually comes before the thing it refers to; in SLE it usually follows it. Note also the inverted word order in the BSE equivalents of the examples given: 'Only now did I come to know'. 'Only then did I see her'.

♦ "Last week only she said maybe you are not coming any more because you have somebody else …" (JFT 102)

♦ "Once you realise the reality of sorrow then only does one want the Noble Eightfold Path. (OD 32)

♦ "Now when I step out of the house at night I always look at the sky, and then only I go where I have to go." (M&P 311)

only thing …
(coll.) the only thing is …

♦ "Only thing, I don't know what I can do in this new system." (Reef 173)

♦ "Only thing is that girl is so highly strung, she sometimes says the most … odd things, no?" (SG 121)

onwards
upwards ° *Rs. 4000 onwards*

open
(v) turn on (a tap) (> **close**) ° *I can't open the tap.*

opened
open ° *Are the shops still opened?* → In BSE, 'opened' is used only as a past participle, e.g. in the passive: 'The building will be opened by the Prime Minister'.

opening dose (OD)
laxative (dated in BSE)

♦ "Give all the buggers an opening dose for the New Year." (JFT 187)

operate
(vt) operate on somebody (vi) ° *He was operated this morning.*

opposite (to somebody/ something)
opposite somebody/something ° *Their house is opposite to the temple.* ° *They live in the opposite house.* (BSE: … opposite the temple, … in the house opposite)

♦ She was seated at this very table, right there, opposite to where he sat now, … (WMD 246)

♦ "They did it, you know, the Boys. They did it," the man opposite to him suddenly leant forward and confided to Vijay. (WMD 340)

or?
(coll.) (a question tag used as a less common alternative to **is it?**, **isn't it?** and **no?**) ° *Your wife is sick or?*

orange pekoe
a high grade of tea (> **pekoe**)

ordinary level
(= O/L) O level exam (> **advanced level**)

orphanage
children's home (where the children are not necessarily orphans)

osari, osariya
/osəri, osəriyə/ (= **Kandyan saree**)

otherwise?
(= **why not?**) of course! (as the answer to a question) ° *Is this your car? - Otherwise?*

♦ "D'you really wan' to go tomorrow?" he asked finally. "Otherwise?" she snapped. (CU 46)

our friend
(coll.) an expression used to refer to another person, e.g. a child who is also present, in an indirect way ° *Our friend of course might have a different idea.*

our people
Sri Lankans (often used in a self-deprecating way); also used to refer to separate ethnic groups (Sinhalese, Tamil, etc.) ° *Our people of course, don't you know* ...

♦ "I'll never emigrate. I've seen the way our people live in foreign countries." (FB 195)

♦ "You can't put them with our people, can you? Never know what will happen." (WMD 367)

♦ He wanted our people to have some pride in what they produced ... (SG 99)

♦ "What is there for our people to realize? They have now got used to it." (OD 141)

♦ "Our people have occupied these regions from antiquity." (REP 130)

♦ "But our people didn't start this. The Sinhala attacked us first. We were reacting to atrocities committed on our people." (REP 270)

♦ "Whatever it is I'm glad one of our people is getting it." (WE 94)

♦ "I never thought that our people could ever sink so low." (M&P 356)

out (1)
(adj.) (of a phone) out of order ° *The phones are out.*

out (2)
(adv.) outside, outdoors, away (> **in**) ° *I can't see them - they must be playing out.* ° *Meet me out in 10 minutes.* ° *He's gone out - he'll be back next week.* ° *More and more people are buying their food from out.* → In BSE, 'out' is normally used as a preposition followed by a noun: 'out of the house', 'out of the country', etc. It can also be used as an adverb in the specific sense of 'out of the house' or 'out of the office', but not normally in the sense of 'outdoors'. In SLE, it can also mean either **outstation** (out of Colombo) or abroad (out of the country).

outdoor catering
outside catering

outrage: to outrage somebody's modesty
(a dated euphemism for sexual harassment)

outstation
(n/adj./adv.) out of Colombo ° *He's gone outstation.* ° *the outstation schools* ° *an outstation cheque* ° *in the outstations*

♦ They served in the outstations without their families, which was cheaper, too. (YY 44)

♦ Mahadev had sworn, then, that he would never leave his family in

Jaffna while he worked outstation. (WMD 97)

♦ Besides, he cared about the village - not like some of those other 'outstation' people, they said, for whom the village was just a dumping ground for their wives and children. (WMD 142)

♦ "... I even arranged for all the children to go to my outstation aunty." (SG 160)

♦ ... male missionaries who had come into Colombo from outstation on some business, ... (CG 97)

♦ ... four properties in Colombo, six or seven outstation bungalows, a cottage in the hills, ... (HC 6)

♦ ... or a minor official he had come across outstation and could no longer remember. (HC 257)

♦ "There've been a spate of unsolved bank and payroll robberies in the outstations, ..." (GC 312)

♦ "We are going outstation in a few days ..." (SMS 60)

♦ "They're all from out-station," ... (CU 41)

over
about (less common in BSE) ° *He's absolutely crazy over cricket.* ° *mad over girls*

oya
/oyə/ a small river or stream (Sinhala) ° *Fourteen bodies were recovered from the oya.* ° *Police said the water level of the oya had risen due to recent rains.* ° *The oya supplies water to several irrigation schemes in the Moneragala district.*

P

paal appam
/pāl appəm/ (= milk hopper) a hopper made with coconut milk (Tamil)

paatta; paatti
/pāтта, pāтti/ grandfather; grandmother (Tamil)

♦ "Is *patta* going to be all right, *appa*?" (WMD 127)

♦ "Hmm, the little fellows are all grown up now. Can't remember their *patta*, eh?" (WMD 140)

pachadi
/pachchəɒi/ a type of chutney made with coconut (Tamil) ° *prawn pachadi*

packet
(= parcel) a portion of cooked food (usually rice and curry) wrapped up to be taken away (> lunch packet, rice packet, bath packet)

♦ Joseph threw a ready-made packet of rice and curry on to the chair next to me. (Reef 37)

♦ "I eat packets from the caddays." (MiP 141)

♦ Marasinghe distributes the packets of rice and we sit in a circle to eat. (GC 320)

♦ ... he dispatched an orderly to the Officers' Mess to bring him a packet of rice and curry ... (CU 418)

padakkama
/padakkəmə/ a large pendant, an item of Kandyan jewellery (Sinhala; Tamil padakkam)

pada yathra

/pādə yatrə/ a pilgrimage or protest march, esp. the annual pilgrimage on foot from Jaffna to Kataragama (Sinhala; Tamil pada yathrai) ° *PC assaults pada yathra devotees*

padda boat

/pæɒa bōɪ/ (dated) a flat-bottomed boat or barge used for transporting goods

♦ *Padda* boats with thatched roofs slipped along the river. (HC 180)

paddler

(in newspaper headlines) table tennis player (> **cager**) ° *Veteran paddlers win trophy*

padikkama

/paɒikkəmə/ a traditional spitoon (Sinhala; Tamil padikkam)

PADIKKAMA

pahana

/pahanə/ (= **oil lamp, polthel pahana**) a lamp with a cloth wick soaked in **coconut oil**: either a small clay lamp which is lit in temples etc.; or a large brass lamp which is lit on **auspicious** occasions (weddings, opening ceremonies, etc.) (Sinhala)

PAHANA

♦ Strings of coloured lights lined the roof and clusters of tiny pahan flickered at the doorway. (July 228)

pahi

/pæhi/ a type of vegetable pickle (Sinhala) (> **batu pahi, brinjal pahi, polos pahi**)

pahila

/pæhila/ (of fruit) ready to be picked: not ripe, but mature enough to ripen off the tree; (coll.) (of children) precocious (Sinhala) ° *Don't buy unless they're pahila.* ° *Now she's going to school she's become really pahila.*

pain

/pēn/ (v) hurt ° *My leg is paining.* → In BSE, 'pain' is normally used only as a noun; the verb is 'hurt': 'My leg hurts' or 'I've got a pain in my leg'. As a verb, 'pain' normally means to cause distress: 'It pains me to have to tell you.'

♦ "Must be paining like hell." (JFT 69)

♦ "It's paining, *anney*," … (JFT 114)

♦ "Said his stomach was paining and went." (YY 64)

♦ … and I kept moving in a daze with hands straining feet paining knees hurting … (BTH 13)

pakis pettiya

/pakis peɪɪiyə/ packing case (Sinhala)

pakora

/pakōrə/ a deep fried savoury snack (also India, orig. Hindi)

♦ She had finished frying the *pakora* and was arranging them in a tin. (WMD 195)

palaharam

/paləhārəm/ traditional Tamil sweets prepared for festive occasions (Tamil) (> **kavili, Sinhala sweets**)

♦ I saw it all in my mind: the buying of the sari, the making of the confetti, the wrapping of the cake, the delicious pala harams, the jasmine garlands, the bridesmaids. (FB 42)

♦ My mother, however, went on tchik-tchiking in the kitchen over the *palaharams* she was making for the occasion. (WMD 195)

palandi

/palanɒi/ a meat curry made with **curd** (named after the owner of the restaurant which created the dish) ° *mutton palandi*

pallu

/pallu/ (= **palu, headpiece**) the decorated end piece of the **saree** (Sinhala) (> **fall, saree pota**) ° *a cream silk sari with sequins and stones on maroon border and pallu*

♦ ... the women pressing their handkerchiefs or sari pallus to their mouths in a pretense of modesty, but really to hide their titters. (SMS 139-40)

palmyrah, palmyrah tree

/pælmaira/ a type of palm tree which is common in the **dry zone**, especially associated with Jaffna and the North (also India, from Portuguese)

PALMYRAH TREE

♦ ... tall palmyra trees like long-handled bottle brushes, ... (YY 164)

♦ By noon we would sight the first palmyrah trees, still and solitary, sometimes a cluster but scarcely a grove, and know we were nearing our journey's end. (WMD 137)

♦ ...the palmyrah flour out of which the 'soup' was made ... (WMD 141)

♦ ... and the fences were still of woven palmyrah leaves. (WMD 213)

♦ ... the heavily thatched palmyrah fences hid everything else from view. (WMD 337)

♦ ... the huge prawns from the Jaffna lagoon, the barren landscape with its palmyra trees, even the saline water of Jaffna. (CG 305)

♦ The groves of coconut gave way to palmyrah palms and then scrub as we neared the lagoon. (REP 14)

♦ The fences of dry palmyrah fronds made a distinctive rustling noise in the wind. (REP 22)

♦ The palmyrah palm had a green, leathery leaf with a serrated edge. The leaves were about two feet in diameter, and fanned out around the crest of the palm, like a crown. (REP 218)

♦ I climbed up the next tree and had a close look at the palmyrah fruit, fibrous nuts like miniature coconuts, about the size of my fist. (REP 257)

♦ They stood with their arms around each other, against a stark sandy background with palmyra trees in the distance. (SMS 30-31)

♦ ... Devini longed for the open sandiness of the Jaffna Peninsula, its low scrub jungle and tall palmyrah trees; ... (CU 331)

□ palmyrah toddy

toddy made from the flower of the **palmyrah tree**

♦ From ten until noon we sit talking and drinking ice-cold palmyrah toddy from a bottle we have filled in the village. (RF 26)

♦ ... and joined his father on the verandah over a pot of palmyrah toddy. (WMD 15)

palu (1)

/palu/ (= **pallu, headpiece**) the decorated end piece of the **saree** (Tamil) (> **fall, saree pota**)

♦ Amma's tardiness and her insistence on getting her palu to fall to exactly above her knees drove us all to distraction ... (FB 6)

♦ ... and finally watching her drape the palu across her breasts and pin it into place with a brooch. When Amma was finished, she would check to make sure that the back of the sari had not risen up with the pinning of the palu, ... (FB 16)

♦ ... then she twitched to palu of her sari around her waist and returned to the kitchen. (FB 111)

♦ ... where he was sure to find his mother in the kitchen, her palu wound tightly around her waist as she worked alongside the servants. (CG 25)

♦ Wiping her face with the edge of her sari palu, she tucked it back into her waist. (CG 236)

palu (2)

/palu/ a type of tree which is common in the **dry zone** jungles (Sinhala)

♦ The rough-barked palu tree stands tall in the centre of the clearing. Fallen palu fruit cover the forest floor immediately under the tree. (GC 102)

pambaya

/pambaya/ a dummy used as a scarecrow and on construction sites to ward off the evil eye (Sinhala)

♦ Some said it was a 'pambaya' - a dummy, tied to the buffer. (YY 68)

pandal

/pænɒol/ (= **thorana**) a temporary structure (usually decorated with Buddhist scenes and flashing lights) erected for religious festivals (esp. **Vesak**) (OED: Anglo-Indian = shed or booth for temporary use; orig. Tamil = shed)

PANDAL

♦ Vesak was a simpler affair then, for there were no jet bulb studded massive pandals. (CM 73)

♦ The crowd thickened wherever a festive *pandal* arched over the road, its bamboo struts and crosspiece festooned with flowers and strings of coloured bulbs. (HC 238)

♦ The celebrations normally went on for several days, and were generally carried out by hanging colourful paper lanterns on everything in sight, and building huge 'pandols'. A pandol was more or less a large comic strip depicting the life of the Buddha, and was as tall as a five-storey building and festooned with lights that whirled and flashed in mesmerising patterns. (CU 85)

pandan

/pandang/ obsequious, grovelling, subservient (OED: Anglo-Indian = betel box, a small metal box for holding betel; orig. Urdu) ° *He's a real pandan case.*

□ to hold pandan to somebody

(= to pay pooja to somebody) to grovel, lick somebody's boots, suck up to somebody; coll.: **pandanfy** (> -fy)

pandu: to play pandu

/pandu/ (= **play socks, play pucks, play hell, dance the devil**) (coll.) to mess around, make trouble, play the fool (Sinhala/Tamil: pandu = ball)

♦ "Went to Ladies College and Bishops College and playing *pandu** in all the girls schools ..." (* *Pandu* - ball. In this sense, however, it could be interpreted as playing socks, merry hell, the dickens, the devil, etc. etc.) (TT 224)

pang

/pāng/ (coll.) bread (Sinhala) (> **roast pang**)

□ pang karaya

/pāng kārəya/ bread man, bread seller (Sinhala) (> **karaya**)

pani

/pæni/ (= **honey**) (Sinhala/Tamil) (> **kiripani, kitul, polpani**)

□ pani aappa

/pæni āppə/ (= **honey hopper**) (Sinhala)

□ pani pol

/pæni pol/ a mixture of grated coconut and **honey**, used as a filling in sweets such as **lavariya** (Sinhala)

pansala

/pansələ/ (= **vihara**) Buddhist temple (Sinhala)

♦ It has, after all, Hindu kovils, Buddhist pansalas, Catholic churches and Muslim mosques - all of great antiquity. (MiP 1)

pansil

/pansil/ the 5 Buddhist precepts which are supposed to be observed by all lay Buddhists (Sinhala) (> **sil**)

♦ Pansil-white egrets, openbills and spoonbills are patrolling the shallows. (GC 100)

pantry

/pæntri/ a kitchen with fitted cupboards, electrical appliances, etc. (as opposed to a traditional kitchen with a wood-burning hearth) → In BSE, a 'pantry' is a larder, a small room for storing food. The pronunciation is also slightly different: SLE /pæntri/, BSE /pæntri/.

♦ From the dining room, swinging doors provided an entrance to the pantry and kitchen. (SMS 20)

♦ Nenda shouted from the pantry and Magi from the kitchen while the dog barked in-between. (M&P 58)

□ pantry cupboards

kitchen cupboards

♦ Kandapola siya's new driver removed the pantry cupboards and we learned to call the pantry 'the television room'. (M&P 256)

papadam

/papəɒam/ a crisp deep-fried wheat flour bread which accompanies **rice and curry** or **thali** meals (UK poppadom; also India, orig. Tamil)

♦ ... pappadams in lined wire baskets ... (JFT 60)

♦ ... and the outer edges curled in like the edge of a puppadum when it hits hot oil. (Reef 99)

♦ Emma was eating papadams, mindlessly putting one after the other into her mouth ... (MiP 381)

papara band

/papərə/ an informal band consisting of trumpet and percussion, e.g. at cricket matches, etc. (from Sinhala)

PAPARA BAND

papaw

/pæpō/ pawpaw, papaya (an oval-shaped fruit with green skin and orange flesh) (from Portuguese) → Pronunciation: There are three different words for this fruit in BSE, none of which are pronounced the same as in SLE: pawpaw /pōpō/, papaya /papaya/, papaw /pəpō/.

PAPAW TREE

- ♦ The back garden was extensive and contained a variety of fruit trees - jak, banana, papaw, breadfruit, mango; ... (CG 13)

- ♦ "I'll have a slice of papaw - that big one." (MiP 190)

- ♦ The papaw was put in the bag. (Z 2)

- ♦ She studied the small jewelled flies that settled on the slice of papaw before her and made no motion to disturb their feeding. (HC 166)

- ♦ The moment he put the papaw down on a ledge, Kuveni flew to it and began to devour the pulp. (SMS 4)

paper

/pēpə/ (= kola kaella, kole) (nc) piece of paper ° *Do you have a paper?* → In BSE, 'paper' is uncountable; as a countable noun it means 'newspaper'.

paper thosai

/pēpə tōse/ a thin crispy thosai rolled into a long cylindrical shape (also India, orig. Tamil)

para

/pæra/ paragraph

paramour

/pærəmə/ (in newspaper reports) illicit lover (orig. French) (archaic in BSE) ° *Paramour remanded for bolting with minor*

parangi, parangiya

/parangi, parangiya/ (coll., dated) a foreigner or Burgher; historically, a derogatory term for the Portuguese; also used to refer to a type of venereal disease (Sinhala/Tamil, from Portuguese)

- ♦ And no story of the country - or, if of the country, not our story but theirs, the *parangis'.* (WMD 5)

- ♦ ...that he was barely considered part of the community by both men and women, that he was derogatorily referred to as *parangi maama*, ... (Z 8)

parapet wall

(= boundary wall) garden wall → In SLE, a 'parapet wall' is often a high wall built for security; in BSE, it is a low wall around the edge of a platform, balcony, roof, bridge, pier, quay, etc.

◆ The breeze blew over the low parapet walls and under the greenish tubes of the tats. (Reef 42)

◆ ... a middle-class residential area of neat houses with glass paned windows and parapet walls and well kept little gardens ... (BTH 8)

◆ The compound in which the Manuel-Pillai home stood had a tall parapet wall all around it. (SMS 20)

parata
/parāṭa, parāṭa/ a type of bread similar to a **roti** (also India, orig. Hindi)

paraw
/parau/ a type of fish (trevally or jacks)

◆ "Look," he said as he drew closer, holding up a large fish, "fresh *parau.*" (WMD 87)

parcel
(= **packet**) a portion of cooked food (usually **rice and curry**) wrapped up to be taken away (> **lunch packet, rice packet, bath packet**) → In BSE, a 'parcel' is a package for posting.

◆ My father packed my bag, while my mother and Bisso, the cook, made up food parcels for the journey. (WMD 119)

◆ Velaithan placed the parcels of food and the bottle of water between us. (REP 59)

◆ When they were done, Ravi asked for two parcels of food to take with them. (FSD 77)

◆ We open two of the parcels I had made that morning and share them, ... (GC 162)

◆ ... while giving her a parcel of string hoppers as her breakfast by her bed in the ward. (KCS 165)

◆ The banana-leaf parcels, when opened, reveal mounds of boiled sweet potato, grated coconut and ground chilli. (PMS 124)

pariah, paraya
/paraya/ (adj.) (of people) low, dirty (Sinhala/Tamil = low caste; also India) ° *He's a pariah fellow.* ° *He did a pariah thing.* → In BSE, 'pariah' (pron. /pə'raiə/) is used as a noun to refer to a social outcast, or in an Indian context, to a person of very low caste.

◆ "You good fellow, ... Not like other pariahs here." ... "Pariah? ... Who the pariah you're saying?" (JFT 31)

◆ "You pariah, wait and see what'll happen to you," ... (FB 168)

◆ "Any bloody pariah's car you get in?" (YY 136)

◆ He had probably been a Burgher, one of those half-caste pariahs who sold their souls to the Sinhalese just for the joy of the kill. (CU 101)

□ pariah dog
/paraya/ a stray mongrel dog living on the street (also India)

◆ ... a pariah dog with a magpie in its mouth ... (RF 76)

◆ An old pariah dog ... came out to meet them. (WMD 97)

◆ "There were even pariah dogs in there." (CG 310)

◆ ... and a brief skirmish with her pariah dog ... (Z 49)

◆ "Do you want to come to my house again like a pariah dog, with your tail between your legs?" (SMS 170)

parippu

/parippu/ (= **dhal**) lentils; (coll.) a mild term of abuse meaning 'useless' (Sinhala; Tamil paruppu) ° *parippu curry* ° *parippu school!*

♦ "At a "bring and come", if you wait till the end you only get parippu and rice." (FSD 189)

♦ ... the curried cubes of Spam for lunch, the *parippu* soup taken with thin slices of toast for dinner. (CU 73)

□ parippu vadai

/parippu vaᴅe/ a crisp **vadai** made with **dhal** (Tamil) (> **ulundu vadai**)

PARIPPU VADAI

parley

(= **confab, pow-wow**) (in newspaper headlines) conference, meeting (dated in BSE)

Parsee

a member of a small Zoroastrian community of Indian origin (orig. Persian)

part: to put a part, to put parts

(coll.) to be proud, arrogant, haughty, snobbish (> **boru part**) ° *That one is always putting parts, doesn't even smile, no?* ° *Now don't put a part, just get dressed and come!*

♦ "So what for you putting parts, woman." (JFT 17)

♦ "How the parts she's putting when going on the road?" (TT 196)

paspanguwa

/paspanguwə/ (= **peyava**) an **ayurvedic decoction** with 5 ingredients, given to treat coughs and colds (Sinhala) (> **kasaya**)

pass: to pass off

(= **expire**) to die, pass away, pass on ° *She passed off last night.* → In BSE, to 'pass off' means to take place, or to gradually disappear; the normal euphemism for 'die' is 'pass away' or 'pass on'.

□ to pass out

to graduate, leave (university) ° *What are you going to do when you pass out?* ° *He passed out as a doctor from Peradeniya.* → In BSE, to 'pass out' normally means to faint or to lose consciousness. In the alternative sense of completing a course of training, it is normally only used in a military context.

♦ "... the moment you pass out from here everything will be all right." (OD 103)

□ to pass comments, pass hints

(= **cast remarks**) to make veiled comments or innuendos about somebody ° *Sunethra said that some trishaw drivers pass comments at her.*

passing

(coll.) past ° *on the left side passing the bridge*

♦ "I lose time but that is no matter because once passing Wadduwa I can catch up." (YY 70)

♦ I was now moving away from the setting sun, along Bauddhaloka Mawatha, passing the BMICH and towards the General Cemetery, ... (BTH 1)

passiona

/pœshōnɑ/ passion fruit juice

paste (1)

/pēsᴛ/ stick, stick up (e.g. posters) ° *He was arrested for pasting posters.* ° *Though the police removed posters every morning the supporters of candidates repasted the posters in the evening.*

♦ ... to find a man pasting a large poster on our wall that had a picture of a lamp on it. (FB 167)

♦ "This morning Hameed came and pasted a large poster on it." (KCS 79)

♦ "Are you sure you did the job properly? ... Did you paste all the posters?" (PMS 171)

paste (2)
(coll.) hit, beat up (less common in BSE)
(> **hammer**) ° *They gave him a good pasting.*

♦ "Tell Sonnaboy. Catch and give a good pasting." (JFT 22)

pastol
/pasтol/ a meat pastry, a **Malay** speciality (orig. Malay) ° *You can have a bowl of soup for Rs 30 and a pastol for even less.*

pastry
/pēsтri/ a small savoury pie (> **short eats**) → In BSE a 'pastry' is more likely to be sweet than savoury.

patas!
/paтas/ (coll.) hey presto!, in no time (Sinhala) ° *She spoke to the minister and patas! the job was done.*

♦ "Patas! Before you know it, you'll be in Malaya." (CG 172)

♦ "I saw his shadow in the garden, ... and then *patas*! He jumped right over the house." (CP 115)

♦ "Anyone caught playing cards ... *patas* ... into jail." (PMS 163)

patchwork
patching up ° *It needs some patchwork.* ° *They're doing a patchwork job on the house.*

pater; mater
(dated) father; mother (archaic in BSE)

pathola
/paтōlə/ (= **snake gourd**) (Sinhala)

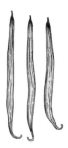

PATHOLA

♦ ... and a lone woman under a petromax lamp brandished a *pathola karala* at us in a threatening manner as we shot past. (CP 146)

♦ "I wonder if mother has cooked patholay for lunch today," ... (PMS 26)

patient
a person who is sick ° *a heart patient* → In BSE, the word 'patient' normally refers to a person who is in hospital; in SLE it can refer to anyone who is sick and needs nursing or medical care.

patiya
/pǽтiya/ (= **kunju**) (coll.) a term of endearment used e.g. by a parent to a small child (Sinhala = young animal)

♦ She was still a child. Her little *patiya* (Sinhala for 'tiny tot' or smallest child). (JFT 11)

♦ "Come Chooti *Petiya*, smile, smile with your Aunty Seela." (M&P 27)

pattafy
/paттəfai/ (= **hack**) (coll.) ruin, wear out (clothes, etc.) (from Sinhala) (> **-fy**)

patty
a small savoury pasty (> **short eats**)

♦ *Amma* has made sandwiches and *patties* and roasted cashew nuts spiced with red chilli ... (MM 108)

♦ She finished all the patties! (Reef 74)

♦ So Beryl rolled out the dough and cut circles in it with an upturned cigarette tin and beat up egg whites for stiffening and checked on the patti-curry which was the filling for the patties. (YY 3)

♦ ... as she went off to fetch the patties. (WMD 273)

♦ CV smiled at the waiter and took a patty from a proffered dish. (MiP 57)

♦ "Now shall we ask Sumana to bring us some patties as well? ... I haven't had patties with my tea for ages." (Z 86)

♦ There were mornings when the *nonamahatheya* devoured four pots of chocolate custard or a platter of fish patties. (HC 161)

♦ Amrith was left to his work with fish patties and a glass of mixed-fruit cordial. (SMS 200)

♦ ... pick up the birthday cakes and patties from Perera and Sons, ... (SMS 207)

♦ I set to work on the little bits of smoked salmon and caviar, a welcome change from the patties and cutlets I am more used to. (CP 115)

payasam
/pāyəsəm/ a Tamil dessert made with milk, semolina, cashew nuts and sultanas (Tamil; also India)

♦ "I am going to cook something really Tamil for after dinner, ... *Payasam.* You like it?" (WMD 323)

PC
(= Provincial Council)

PD
(= periyadorai)

♦ ... and the PD had received instructions from above to throw Perumal back on a daily wage. (WMD 267)

pedestal fan
a fan which stands on the floor (as opposed to a table fan or ceiling fan)

pedura
/pœdurə/ floor mat (Sinhala) ° *sleeping on a pedura*

□ **peduru party**
/pœduru/ an informal party usually with live traditional eastern music (Sinhala: peduru = mats)

pekoe
/pīkō/ a high grade of tea (> **flowery pekoe, orange pekoe, broken orange pekoe**)

♦ Fine plucking produces pekoes, while older leaves yield souchongs and congous. Pekoes consisting only of the buds or tips are known as flowery; those containing also the first young leaf are orange pekoes. (HC 83)

penda
/penɒa/ (= **sottaya**) (coll.) wimp (Sinhala)

pen off
(dated) (in a letter) sign off ° *I'll pen off now.*

peon
/piən/ (coll., dated as an official job title) office aide, office assistant, messenger (also India; from Portuguese = foot-soldier)

♦ He was a *peon.* He had a khaki uniform and spent the whole day ferrying messages between two old men in two grey rooms ... (Reef 157)

♦ Sonali left her cooking and came up the steps with the cringing attitude of the peons at my father's bank. (FB 32)

♦ The office peon had delivered a parcel to the wrong address ... (FB 189)

♦ "From the south they got the peons," he chortled. "All Tamils were clerks and all Sinhalese were peons. And today the peons are fighting to become clerks." (WMD 217)

♦ The doorman, the peons, the secretaries and the office workers passing by them bowed to the old man ... (SG 203)

♦ "I suppose she thinks she looks like a European now. More like a peon to me." (CG 20)

♦ "... he was too grand to talk to a peon." (MiP 332)

♦ The previous uniform of shorts and the tunic worn by porters, the hat worn by postal peons ... (OD 7)

♦ One afternoon ... a peon in a white sarong and khaki jacket slashed with the black-and-red government sash handed me a message. (HC 76)

♦ David came downstairs followed by two peons carrying cardboard boxes filled with papers. (FSD 39)

♦ Peons hurried about, carrying large manila envelopes, files, tiffin carriers; ... (SMS 64)

♦ ... the market research company, where Jeevan had been working as a peon for the past 10 years, ... (WCS 66)

peoplisation

privatisation (esp. during the late 1980s and early 1990s); adj.: **peoplised** ° *peoplised buses* ° *the government's peoplisation programme*

pera

/pērə/ guava (Sinhala)

Pera

/pēra/ (coll.) Peradeniya University (> **Japura, Sabara**)

perahera

/perəhœrə/ a procession of elephants, dancers, drummers, etc., usually held on a **poya day** to celebrate a Buddhist festival; the most famous is the Kandy **Esala Perahera** in July/August (Sinhala)

♦ He was wonderful at planning these things - picnics, trips to the Perahera. He loved the Perahera and always got into trouble during them. (RF 197)

♦ "What is that?" asked one. "*Perahera* (a religious procession)," said another. (JFT 150)

♦ There was a *perahera* passing by. ... "Come on! Let's go! The *perahera's* almost over!" (WMD 181)

♦ "What's this *perahera* thing then?" ... "Never heard of the Kandy *perahera*, sir? *Aiyo*, famous touris' attraction, no?" (CU 55)

♦ Once a year there is a perehara (pageant), where the temple's tusker carries the tooth relic and shows it to the world outside the temple. (M&P 68)

perch

a measure of land (5.5 x 5.5 yards = 30.25 square yards) ° *40 perches land for sale* ° *They're asking 8 lakhs a perch.*

♦ A new bungalow was being built on the fifteen perches of wasteland next to number ten, ... (Reef 62)

periamma; periappa

/periamma, periappa/ (= **loku amma; loku thaaththa**) aunt (mother's elder sister); uncle (father's elder brother) (Tamil)

♦ "You see, Peri-Appa's already there." (CG 347)

periyadorai

/periyadore/ (= **PD, superintendent**) the manager of an estate (Tamil) (> **sinnadorai**)

♦ And it was she who had got the *Peria-Dorai* interested in the child's future. (WMD 265)

♦ ... and dragged Vijay off to a garden party at the *Peria-Dorai's*. ... Vijay had not been to the PD's house before ... (WMD 273)

♦ "The *periya dorai* himself went down to the police station to put in a good word for him." (HC 289)

♦ She talked to the man about his family and the "*Periya Dorais*" he had worked under. (FSD 137)

persons

people (formal in BSE) ° *Several persons have been arrested.*

peruse

read; noun: **perusal** (formal in BSE) ° *attached for your kind perusal*

pet

(v) spoil, pamper, mollycoddle ° *She's petted by her family.* → In BSE, 'pet' is used in this sense as a noun ('teacher's pet'), but as a verb it normally means to stroke (e.g. an animal).

petition

a letter of complaint, often anonymous and usually targeted against an individual → In BSE, a 'petition' is usually a more public protest, often signed by a large number of people.

♦ Supposing someone sends a petition against him in their jealousy? (OD 24)

petrol shed

(= **shed**) petrol station, filling station (US gas station)

♦ ... facing the main road, the petrol shed with the Caltex star ... (BTH 17)

♦ It was directed at any business that supported the taxi company and, as a result, a chain of petrol sheds found themselves blacklisted. (CG 318)

♦ When they turned into the petrol shed and rest area, the Ford Focus was sitting exactly where Bandara had described it. (CU 264)

♦ He had explained to Dhampahana about his illegal entry into Europe, his first jobs as a janitor, waiter, petrol shed attendant. (CU 314)

♦ Mrs. Bandaranayake nationalized all the petrol sheds and raised the price of petrol. (M&P 182)

petromax lamp

a type of kerosene lamp

♦ ... with the man at the boutique trying to light his old petromax lamp ... (BTH 7)

♦ A Petromax lantern hanging from a rafter threw a pool of light on the road. (REP 56)

pettagama

/peттəgamə/ a large wooden chest (from Dutch)

PETTAGAMA

♦ Walls adorned with paintings, unfamiliar masks, an ancient *Pettagama* in a corner and a mirror with carvings on the door. (WCS 21)

petti kade
/peᴛᴛɪ kaᴅe/ a small shop made of wooden boards (Sinhala)

♦ A few yards away from Samare's small house was what people usually called a "petti kade" (a little corner shop or 'boutique' made from panels of wood). … only the poor people in the area patronised the petti kade. (WCS 60)

peyava
/pēyāvə/ (= **paspanguwa**) an **ayurvedic decoction** with 5 ingredients, given to treat coughs and colds (Sinhala) (> **kasaya**)

pharmacy
chemist's shop (US drugstore)

phlegm
(in **ayurvedic** medicine) a tendency to ill-health caused by a build-up of phlegm ° *Don't give thambili, she's having phlegm.*

pic, pix
picture(s) (abbreviation used in newspapers) ° *Pic by Kithsiri de Mel* ° *Student with nude pix commits suicide*

pichcha mal
/pichchə mal/ jasmine flowers (Sinhala)

♦ He tidied up the house, put temple flowers and *pichcha-mal* in the vases, … (WMD 387)

pick
pick somebody/something up, collect somebody (from a place) ° *Can you come and pick me from the airport?* ° *I seem to spend all day picking and dropping the kids.* → In BSE, to 'pick' something is to choose something.

♦ Often she balanced a full pot of water on her hip and used her other hand to pick a jak fruit or a branch to use for firewood. (OM 44-5)

♦ "I think I picked the habit from Mr. Karl." (REP 188)

♦ I was glad to pick my stuff and follow her. (REP 261)

♦ The driver stopped every fifty yards and they just kept picking more passengers. (REP 320)

♦ He had started life as a 'Ball Boy', picking balls at the driving range ... (FSD 17)

♦ ... so the driver went by himself to pick the little girl from St. Bridget's nursery on Maitland Crescent. (FSD 246)

♦ Premasiri picked the phone on the first ring. (FSD 285)

picnic
a day out (e.g. at a hotel) → In BSE, a 'picnic' is a meal eaten outdoors.

picturise
film (v) ° *His new teledrama is being picturised in the Kurunegala area.*

piggish
(coll.) fussy, finicky ° *I felt piggish seeing the dirty bathroom.* ° *If you're still piggish to eat fish, ...*

pimple
spot (also US, less common in BSE)

pinda patha
/pinᴅə pātə/ ritual begging for alms by Buddhist monks (Sinhala) ° *Buddhist monks going for Pindapatha at Temple Trees on an invitation from President Mahinda Rajapaksa*

♦ … knew how to go down on one knee and bow her head as she offered up *pinna-patha* to the mendicant monks of the Buddha ... (WMD 223)

pindrop silence

absolute silence (also India) (BSE: 'You could hear a pin drop.') ° *There was pin-drop silence when Lobo returned to the stage.* ° *Trading is done in virtual pin-drop silence.*

♦ There was pin drop silence in the room, ... (CU 28)

pine

(coll.) pineapple ° *a piece of pine*

pingo

(dated) a yoke carried on the shoulder by a street vendor, consisting of a long pole with two shallow dishes or baskets suspended from both ends for carrying goods (e.g. fish) (from Portuguese)

PINGO

pini jambu

/pini jɑmbu/ a large white variety of **jambu** (Sinhala)

♦ There were still signs here of where the wild fruit grew: the wood-apple, the *massang* and the *pinni-jumboo.* (WMD 150)

pinkama

/pinkəmə/ a Buddhist religious ceremony (Sinhala)

pin kate

/pin kæтe/ a box placed outside a temple for collecting alms (Sinhala)

♦ They reached Kalutara and stopped at the Kalutara Temple to put a few coins into the pin katé, the alms box, which apparently would ensure that the rest of their journey continued safely. (July 91)

pins: to be on pins

to be on tenterhooks, to be very nervous ° *The organisers were on pins because of the weather.* ° *I was on pins wondering what she would say.*

pinwheel sandwiches

party sandwiches rolled into a circular shape

♦ There were beef cutlets, pinwheel sandwiches swirled with orange, green, and dark-red filling, fish patties, ... (CG 375)

pippy

/pippi/ (= **choo**) (dated) pee (children's word)

♦ ... and Leah would sigh softly and go to the chamberpot to raise her nightdress and squat and do pippy. (JFT 5)

♦ "I want to pippie" ... (YY 163)

♦ "Again doing pippie all over me!" (TT 3)

pirith

/pirit/ Buddhist verses chanted during a religious ceremony (Sinhala) ° *The monks were chanting pirith.* ° *an all-night pirith ceremony*

♦ They had to perform an exorcism and do penance all night; afterwards go to temple for a formal *pirith* blessing. (MM 115)

♦ ... during a friend's *pirith* ceremony ... (AG 19)

♦ ... Joseph had returned to his upcountry family village to attend a pirith, a ceremony of mourning, for a nephew killed in the war. Two weeks later he would have to attend another pirith for a different nephew. (MiP 78)

♦ "We're holding a *pirith* ceremony this afternoon." Of *pirith* Sam knew only that it involved chanting. That was quite enough. (HC 121)

♦ ... his parents were active Buddhists, who always financed the annual *pirith* festival at school, ... (WE 12)

♦ "They say that the government will ask the monks to chant *pirith* at the Temple of the Tooth." (WE 75)

♦ "It is further advisable to tie on the child's hand a blessed Pirith thread which should be worn until the fifth year." (M&P 315)

□ **pirith noola**
/pirit nūlə/ a white thread blessed at a **pirith** ceremony and tied around the right wrist (Sinhala) ° *A bhikku ties a pirith noola on Mr Rajapakse.*

PIRITH NOOLA

pirivena
/pirivenə/ a Buddhist seminary (Sinhala)

pittu
/piᴛᴛu/ a dish made with **rice flour** and grated coconut and steamed in a **pittu bambuwa** (Sinhala; Tamil puttu, from Malay)

♦ That night by the ocean I made a *pol-kiri-badun* curry, a steamed *pittu* and my most special dish of brinjals, ... (Reef 122)

♦ She reached out and helped herself to some pittu. (FB 76)

♦ With the unhurried sound of the bullock carts came an appetising smell of either hoppers, honeyed hoppers, pancakes or *pittu* that was being prepared for breakfast in our kitchen by my aunt. (CM 90)

♦ The meal of lumpy white tubes of pittu with coconut milk and dry fish curry is surprisingly palatable. (GC 24)

♦ After a dutiful dinner of pittu and fish curry ... (CP 29)

♦ Peter was fat and spoke as if his mouth was full of *pittu*. (CP 39)

□ **pittu bambuwa**
/piᴛᴛu bambuwə/ a cylindrical steamer used to make **pittu** (traditionally a section of bamboo) (Sinhala)

PITTU BAMBUWA

plain hopper
/plēn/ a **hopper** without an egg (> **egg hopper**)

plain roti
a **godamba roti** without an egg (> **egg roti**)

plain tea
black tea, tea without milk (but normally with sugar) (> **tea**)

♦ Kanniah came back with a glass of plain tea. (WMD 166)

♦ Bus drivers let their engines warm while they sipped plain tea. (July 127)

♦ His mother had made the 'roti' for him and placed against the plate was a cup of plain tea. (OD 61)

♦ ... and a small extension was added on one side for plain tea and cool drinks ... (WCS 60)

♦ Nenda was in the kitchen drinking her afternoon plain tea. (M&P 169)

♦ Paduma ... has to be satisfied with a bun and a cup of plain tea. (PMS 201)

plain water
water which has not been iced (> **ice water**)

plantain
banana (also India) (> **ash plantain, sour plantain, sugar plantain**) ° *plantain flower*
→ In BSE, as in the West Indies, Africa, etc., 'banana' is the general term, while 'plantain' refers specifically to the cooking variety. In India, Sri Lanka, etc., 'plantain' is the general term, although 'banana' is also used. There are many varieties of **plantain** in Sri Lanka. The cooking variety is called **ash plantain** (Sinhala: **alu kehel**). The most common eating varieties are: **sour plantain** (Sinhala: **ambul**), **sugar plantain** (Sinhala: **seeni kehel**), **anamalu, kolikuttu, puvalu**, etc.

♦ A path about twelve feet wide bordered by plantain trees. (RF 65)

♦ I brought him his plantain, his soft-boiled egg, his toast and butter and pineapple jam, in real trepidation. (Reef 34)

♦ ... and the three brothers ... would teach me how to make a boat with plantain-tree trunks fixed together with thick pieces of bamboo ... (BTH 49)

♦ "He sat there eating my plantains and thinking of something clever to say." (SG 156-7)

♦ ... the waving leaves of plantain trees. (CG 10)

♦ After he had eaten, drunk his water and had his plantain, she spoke. (July 162)

♦ There was a scuttling among the white-haired mango stones and blackened plantain skins in the ditch; ... (HC 267)

plantain leaf
(= **kehel kole**) banana leaf, often used to serve **rice and curry** and to wrap **lamprais**, etc.

♦ On the other side huge plantain leaves like tattered temple flags hung over the road, browning at the edges. (MM 89)

♦ The menfolk were already seated cross-legged on the floor of the kitchen with their plantain leaves before them, waiting to be served, when Sahadevan came in behind his father. ... Sahadevan sat down, to find that his mother had taken his plantain leaf and replaced it with a plate resting on a stool. (WMD 15)

♦ At meal times he would make a table out of the suitcases and treat us to the *string-hoppers* and chicken curry that my mother had cooked and packed in plantain leaves, ... (WMD 137)

planter
the owner or manager of an estate (esp. tea or rubber) (also India)

♦ But soon I was hob-nobbing with the lawyers and civil servants and planters and the local bigwigs generally, ... (WMD 192)

♦ The man he was here to meet, was a rugby fanatic, having played it both as a schoolboy and during his time as a tea planter in the hill country. (CU 574)

□ planter's chair
(= **hansiputuwa**, **armchair**) (dated) a large rattan armchair with folding leg-rests (also called an **easy chair**) (also India)

♦ It contained a rattan-seat planter's chair piled with kapok cushions, ... (HC 162)

♦ Uncle Lucky was seated in a Planter's chair having a drink ... (SMS 108)

platinums
points (in the engine of a car, etc.)

play: to play somebody out
/plē/ to rip somebody off, cheat, trick, fool somebody (esp. for money) ° *He gets played out every time.*

♦ "Both getting together to play me out." (JFT 108)

♦ "He tried to play me out of my dowry, that's what, and then he tried to buy my land." (WMD 9)

♦ "But we played them out, you see," ... (WMD 216)

□ to play hell
(= **play pucks**, **play socks**, **play pandu**, **dance the devil**) (coll.) to mess around, make trouble, play the fool (less common in BSE)

♦ "Buggers are playing hell." (Reef 189)

♦ "Yesterday, one of these gays came to our office, and played hell." (WE 106)

playful
(of children) naughty, troublesome, disruptive; (of adults) flirtatious ° *He's a very playful child.* → In BSE, 'playful'

is normally used in a more positive way, meaning fun/not serious: 'in a playful mood'.

playground
(= **ground**) sports ground, playing field → In BSE, a 'playground' is a play area for small children with swings, slides, etc.

♦ An open pavilion stood to the left of it facing the playground. (FSD 280)

♦ The meeting has been arranged in the upper playground and a really large crowd has turned up to listen to the man. (GC 71)

pluck
pick (tea, flowers, fruits, coconuts, etc.) → In contemporary BSE, you 'pluck' a chicken, a guitar, or your eyebrows, but you 'pick' flowers, fruits, etc.

♦ "Asking for our Denver to pluck leaves and feed the rabbits." (YY 163)

♦ "Must be plucking mangoes in the back." (TT 146)

♦ To pluck a coconut, jak or a breadfruit from the trees, Attamma's permission was needed. (CM 19)

♦ "Two leaves and a bud, that is what they have to pluck, two leaves and a bud." (WMD 96)

♦ People only saw the plucking of the tea, he complained, as they climbed the mountain road that ran through the estate, because that was what the pictures showed: women plucking tea. (WMD 99-100)

♦ The tiny white flowers looked like little stars in the dark. Violet plucked a few every morning, ... (July 28)

♦ From him I learnt that plucking is called fine when a bud at the tip of a shoot and the two young leaves just below it are taken. (HC 83)

♦ Ravi saw women plucking tea on the hillside below him ... (FSD 135)

♦ "... while he was plucking wattu-sudda flowers to make religious offerings." (WCS 46)

♦ He plucked a pink honeysuckle and placed it on the carved star. (KCS 59)

♦ She plucked limes and Karapincha from the garden. (M&P 143)

♦ Podian's mother, his grandmother and her grandmother had plucked the tea that was captured in the picture postcards of Ceylon and the new Socialist Republic. (M&P 161)

plucker

(= **tea plucker**) tea picker

♦ ... and we walked under the thunder clouds that made the dark tea bushes brighter, through the lines of pluckers, ... (RF 166)

♦ ... between fields where the small hands of Tamil pluckers darted along the surface of the tea. Each woman carried a rod with which she checked that the top of every bush had been plucked level: not easy to determine on the steep hillsides, and a point of pride with the pluckers. (HC 82)

♦ No one sought the opinion of the pluckers or the factory-workers. (HC 93)

plug base

power point, socket (for a plug)

♦ "Two wires connected to the device are inside the wall; they lead to a plug base in an office on another floor." (GC 343)

plums

raisins and sultanas → In BSE, 'plum' is used in this meaning only in the context of a 'plum pudding'.

♦ ... Maudiegirl's famous home-made ginger beer ... The plums had grown fat and sleek in the effervescent mixture and they now floated in each glass like round, smooth dog-ticks, ready to burst tangily between the teeth. (JFT 54)

plus

(talking about somebody's age) ° *thirteen plus* (BSE: thirteen years old)

ply

(vi/vt) (of buses) run, operate (on a certain road or route) ° *There are no buses plying today.* ° *private buses plying the Galle Road* ° *We were told a bus plies every two hours.* → Much less common in BSE, and usually restricted to boats and ships.

♦ One rattled up eventually, a far cry from the fairly new and comfortable vehicle that plied the main route to Colombo. (REP 315)

♦ ... most middle-class parents hired privately owned vans and minibuses to ply the daily routes to Colombo's schools. (CU 296)

podian

/poɒiən/ (coll.) small fry, insignificant person; (dated) **servant boy** (Tamil = boy)

poffertje

/pofəchi/ a small round fritter made with batter and raisins, a **Burgher** speciality (Dutch)

pokuna

/pokunə/ pond (Sinhala)

♦ The four of them walked to the *pokuna* and stood by the dark water. (AG 97)

◆ "Somewhere in here is a swamp or small lake, a *pokuna* in the forest," ... (AG 153)

pol

/pol/ coconut (Sinhala)

□ pol arrack

/pol æræk/ (= coconut arrack) arrack distilled from **coconut toddy**

◆ In his younger days Tivoli Vatunas, like most of his social contemporaries, scorned the local *pol* arrack. (SG 198)

□ polkatu

/polkaTu/ coconut shell (Sinhala); (adj.) (coll.) phoney, fake (of a person's accent when speaking English) ° *polkatu spoons* ° *She's come back from England with a polkatu accent.*

POLKATU SPOONS

□ polkiri

/polkiri/ (= coconut milk) (Sinhala)

◆ ... from the Ponniahs' parcel of dosai to someone else's pittu and pol kiri. (FSD 189)

□ polkudu

/polkuDu/ grated coconut after the milk has been extracted (Sinhala)

□ pol mallung

/pol mællung/ coconut **mallung** (Sinhala)

◆ "A real *pol-mallum*." (SG 125)

□ a pol mess

(coll.) a complete mess

□ polmudda

/polmuDDə/ the tuft of fibre at the top of a coconut, used for cleaning plates, etc. (Sinhala)

◆ Trouble is Poddi's washing plates and scouring the cooking pots with a *polmudda* (the pointed tuft of husk that covers the eyes of the coconut - makes an ideal scrubbing brush) ... (TT 4)

□ polpani

/polpæni/ **honey** made from the sap of the coconut flower (Sinhala) (> **pani**)

□ pol roti

/pol roTi/ a small round **roti** made with wheat flour and grated coconut (Sinhala)

◆ "Rosa has made your favourite. Pol roti." (CG 94)

□ pol sambol

/pol sæmbol/ (= coconut sambol) a **sambol** made with grated coconut with **chilli powder**, lime, salt and onions (Sinhala) (> **sambol**)

◆ ... and you could not make a *pol-sambol* without breaking it. (Reef 25)

◆ Lunch on these days consisted of boiled yams, jak or breadfruit with shredded coconut or *pol sambal*. *Pol sambal* is shredded coconut mixed with chilli, onions and maldive fish. The mixture is flavoured with salt and lime. (CM 23)

◆ Three hours later Vijay was sitting down to a simple and tasty meal of *string-hoppers, pol-sambol* and fish curry, ... (WMD 298)

◆ ... or put a bit of *pol-sambol* in the freezer for another meal. (SG 236)

◆ String hoppers, *pol sambol*, chicken curry. (AG 216)

♦ True it wasn't string hoppers and pol sambol but it was good enough. (Z 69)

♦ After a dinner of string hoppers, beef curry and *pol sambol* everyone got ready to crash. (CU 42)

♦ Rice and dhal were a part of the meagre lunchtime buffet of three dishes. The third was pol sambol. Grated coconut mixed in chilli and seasoned with limejuice and Maldive fish. (M&P 79)

□ polthel

/poltel/ (= **coconut oil**) (Sinhala)

♦ "Someone," Baptiss grated, "has put pol thel!" (TT 99)

□ polthel pahana

/poltel pahanə/ (= **oil lamp, pahana**) a lamp with a cloth wick soaked in **coconut oil**: either a small clay lamp which is lit in temples etc.; or a large brass lamp which is lit on **auspicious** occasions (weddings, opening ceremonies, etc.) (Sinhala)

pola

/polə/ (= **fair**) market, often a weekly event (Sinhala) (> **avurudu pola**)

♦ Occasionally a master or mistress would stray into the bazaar or the Sunday *pola*, … (WMD 192)

♦ They drove past a pola where vegetable and fruit vendors, people selling clay cooking pots and coconut shell spoons, peanut and sweet vendors, shoe-makers, knife sharpeners and self-proclaimed spiritual healers fought a vocal battle to drown each other out. (July 87)

♦ "It was a pola day, when the villagers brought their produce to town." (REP 166)

polecat

/pōlkæт/ (= **uguduwa**) a large black nocturnal wild animal, which is rarely seen but often lives in the roofs of houses → In BSE, a 'polecat' is a European animal like a weasel; the Sri Lankan 'polecat' is more accurately called the 'palm cat'.

POLECAT

♦ "Women fought each other like polecats over certain men." (RF 47)

♦ He emerged out of his bedroom to damn whoever it was that was playing the piano - to find the house empty - … and the polecat walking up and down over the keys breaking the silence of the house, oblivious to his human audience; … (RF 60)

♦ There had to be some animal on the roof. A pole cat? Or a rat snake on safari? (YY 54)

♦ … sewn up an RIR's belly where it had been ripped open by a polecat. (WMD 369)

♦ … the little patch of wood … from which place would emerge rabbits, polecats, and even mouse deer … (BTH 52)

♦ But on the third morning of the trial there was a polecat, its throat cut, left at his door. (HC 108)

♦ It was true that there had been heavy rain the previous week, enough to have driven polecats indoors to nest in the roof. But she knew it was not a polecat she had heard. (HC 194)

- Damp and the urine of polecats had drawn a brown map of Africa on the ceiling. (HC 230-1)

- There was a narrow fanlight for ventilation that could have accommodated a polecat. (FSD 139)

- ... there are rats and polecats, and we even have a pair of snakes, ... (CP 109)

police entry

a complaint or report to the police (> **entry**) ° *You better make a police entry.*

- "Don't you have to make a police entry, at least?" (GC 296)

police post

a place where police are on duty, smaller than a police station and/or not manned permanently

- An opening in the fence near the barrier led to a lime washed building with a narrow verandah. It looked, and smelt, like a police post anywhere. (REP 44)

- The police came soon afterwards, a sergeant from the Cinnamon Gardens police station, accompanied by a constable from the police post at the hospital. (FSD 14)

polish

(of rice) remove the husk (> **unpolished**) ° *polished rice*

politico

(in newspaper headlines) politician (less common in BSE) ° *Politico's brother mining sand illegally, claim residents*

polkichcha

/polkichcha/ a common black and white bird (oriental magpie robin) (Sinhala)

POLKICHCHA

polonga

/polaŋga/ viper, a highly venomous snake (Sinhala) → There are several varieties of **polonga**. The best known (and the most poisonous) are the 'thith-polonga' (**Russell's viper**) and the 'pala-polonga' (green pit viper). The former is also known as the 'tic-polonga' in English.

- ... *the green pit viper pala-polonga,* ... (AG 39)

- "You are too kind to him. The guy has the morals of a *polanga*," ... (MiP 390)

- She told him the story of the age-old enmity between the cobra and the *polonga,* ... (HC 213)

polos

/polos/ unripe **jak fruit** (Sinhala) ° *polos curry* ° *polos cutlets*

- ... and hadn't she got a lovely slice of *pollos* 'from somewhere' which would make a nice *mallung* 'for someone'? (WMD 245)

- My aunt has prepared country rice with 'polos' curry and a 'mallung' of leaves from our garden. (GC 93)

▢ polos pahi

/polos pæhi/ a pickle made with **polos** (Sinhala) (> **pahi**)

pongal

/pongal/ sweet **milk rice** served on Tamil festive occasions; a ritual offering of food

(Tamil) ° *Next we prepare the pongal, go to the kovil and later visit our relatives.*

ponnaya

/ponnəya/ (= **kolu karaya**) (derogatory) homosexual (Sinhala)

- ... how boys in his school had referred to the old man as a 'ponnaya'. (SMS 204)

- In his society homosexuality is despised. Gay people are derogatorily called "*Ponnaya*". ... Beating up a "*Ponnaya*" was considered an assertion of manhood. (WCS 34)

- "Machang, your MD is a real bloody *ponnaya*." (WCS 37)

pooja, puja

/pūja/ a Hindu or Buddhist ritual offering (Sinhala/Tamil, also India; OED poojah, from Sanskrit)

- These araliya flowers would probably be offered to some god as a pooja by the very people who had plucked them, in order to increase their chances of a better life in the next birth. (FB 311)

- They never consulted horoscopes or made poojas or offerings to particular gods for good partners for their children. (YY 155)

- "Rama went to temple to do a *pooja* for Mother." (WMD 31)

- Thus, she had no compunction about appealing to a Catholic saint or making an offering at a Buddhist shrine, along with her daily pooja to Ganesh. (CG 35)

- "Now she'll spend her time offering poojas for his restless spirit." (GC 201)

□ **to pay pooja to somebody**
(= **to hold pandan to somebody**) to grovel, lick somebody's boots, suck up to somebody; coll.: **poojafy** (> -**fy**) ° *As long as we go on paying pooja to the politicians ...*

- Sri Lanka has always been quick to recognize and pay pooja to her most scoundrelly sons. (YY 101)

poonac

/pūnæk/ coconut waste used as cattle food and fertilizer (from Tamil punnakku)

- "... and then go and say cake is hopeless and must have put *poonac* (cattle cake mixture)." (JFT 183)

poori

/pūri/ a small round bread like a deep-fried **roti** (also India, orig. Tamil/Hindi)

- As they ate a vegetarian dinner of *poori* and curried potatoes, ... (CU 111)

poosari

/pūsāri/ (= **kapurala, kapuwa**) the lay priest of a Hindu **devale** (Tamil; OED pujari) (> **aiyar, kurukkal**)

- He had been to the Hindu kovil that morning and had offered a basket of hibiscus flowers and bananas to god Murugan and been marked with favour by the poosari. (YY 26)

porch

car-port, a covered area outside a house for parking a car → In BSE, a 'porch' is usually a small covered area outside the front door, which serves as an entrance but is not used to park a car.

Portello

/pōṭelo/ a popular sweet drink (brand name)

poruwa

/pōruwə/ the decorated podium on which the couple stand during a Buddhist wedding ceremony (Sinhala) (> **manavarai**) ° *a poruwa ceremony*

POORUWA

♦ "It's the poruwa, modified into a throne." (Z 15)

pose off

pose, pass (oneself) off ° *a man who had been posing off as a Major in the Sri Lankan Army* ° *The alleged child trafficker had posed off as an aid worker.* ° *The IGP said they had received information that LTTE cadres would pose off as beggars, to carry out assassinations against VIPs.*

♦ "Indira, he poses off to you as if he is well versed in Sinhala literature." (OD 114)

Poson

/poson/ the June **poya day**, commemorating the arrival of Buddhism in Sri Lanka (Sinhala)

♦ It was difficult enough trying to tear him away from his unending work on the farm to go to temple even on *Poson* or *Wesak* days, ... (WMD 251)

♦ "Mänika is a good woman and I mustn't prevent her from going to the temple on Poson day," ... (PMS 239)

pottu

/poṭṭu/ a mark or dot in the centre of the forehead (esp. worn by Tamil women) (Sinhala/Tamil; India 'bindi')

♦ A glass jar contained a selection of shiny stars and circles. I leaned over to examine them more closely. "They're pottus," Radha Aunty said. She picked one up and stuck it in the middle of her forehead to demonstrate what it looked like. I gazed at her forehead, enchanted by the pottu, so different from the coloured pencils Amma used. (FB 49)

♦ I ridiculed her wearing of the *pottu* and accused her of trying to be more Tamil than the Tamils. And on the train going back to Anuradhapura, I suddenly leant across her and wiped the *pottu* off her forehead ... (WMD 223)

POTTU

♦ Annalukshmi could tell that one of them was Tamil. Like her, she wore a pottu on her forehead and draped her sari in the Tamil style, the palu wound around the hips and tucked in at the back. (CG 196)

♦ On an impulse, she drew a small black dot in the centre of her forehead, slightly above her eyebrows. A pottu, which was traditionally the sign of a married woman. (July 225)

♦ Her black pottu had been carefully placed and her eyes lined with kohl stared big and hungering. (Z 31)

♦ On her forehead was a black *pottu* mark; Mrs. Nadesan wore a red one since she was married. (WE 27)

♦ He wore a white sarong, and there was a red pottu and ash on his forehead. (SMS 137)

- Nenda waddled behind him on her bowlegs trying to increase the size of my Pottu. I screamed again. ... I didn't want the Pottu; ... (M&P 26)

pound: a pound of bread
a loaf of bread

- "I could have bought a pound of bread on my way." (KCS 102)

pour
make (tea or coffee) ° *Have you poured the tea?* → In BSE, to 'pour the tea' means to pour it from the pot into a cup.

pow-wow
(= **confab, parley**) (in newspaper headlines) conference, meeting (dated in BSE) ° *Batti Tiger chief dodges pow-wow*

poya, poya day ╲
/pōyə/ the full-moon day, a Buddhist holiday and a monthly public holiday in Sri Lanka (Sinhala) (> **Esala, Poson, Vesak**) ° *No meat or liquor is sold on poya days.*

- "No flesh, no? I told you, it's the wrong time of the month - *poya*. Temple day." (MM 138)

- She came again the following *poya*-day - the lunar weekend as decreed by our leaders who thought the four phases of the moon should be used to eclipse the hegemony of the Judaeo-Christian imperial sabbath - ... (Reef 76)

- ... and by the end of the week - *poya* or no *poya* - they would invade in shoals. (Reef 143)

- It was Poya day, I remembered, and she would be taking her mother to temple, which of course was why she was dressed in white. (WMD 180)

- A *Poya* moon lit up the trees and the shrubs and the dry, parched land before him. (WMD 280)

- "Thank God it's not a full moon. *Poya* days are the worst." (AG 132)

- "My friend has a bicycle shop. It is Poya, so his shop will be closed, but he lives there." (MiP 374)

- In the courtyard of the Buddhist temple nearby they are drumming, because it is Poya day today. (CP 67)

- "January is the month where the *Duruthu* full moon Poya comes." (M&P 281)

- I wondered if they all had observed poya and closed the shops, ... (M&P 338)

pradeshiya sabha (PS)
/prādēshiyə sabā/ town council (Sinhala) ° *Elections to 320 municipal and urban councils and pradeshiya sabhas are to be held before the end of March.*

prefer
(vi) prefer something/it (vt) ° *I prefer if you don't do that.* (BSE: I would prefer it if you didn't do that.)

prelate
a senior Buddhist monk → In BSE, a 'prelate' is a bishop or archbishop.

pressure
(coll.) high blood pressure ° *Indranee's having pressure.*

previous; previously
last; before (more formal in BSE) ° *our previous residence* ° *We have been here three times previously.*

price: to put your price up
(coll.) to be standoffish or reluctant to do something, to refuse to do something for a particular purpose ° *Ah, come for the trip men. Don't put your price up so much.*

priest

Buddhist monk → In BSE, a 'priest' normally refers to a Catholic priest.

- Amongst these angry people were Buddhist priests who were angrier than the lay people. (M&P 335)

- Suddenly I saw the main priest of the Cemetery Road temple addressing the mourners and the government. (M&P 339)

private bus

a privately owned vehicle (often a van) operating as a bus

- Although traffic going out of Colombo at that time was relatively light, private buses coming in to the city often swung over to their side of the road to overtake, ... (FSD 55)

- The private bus moved slowly in the rush-hour traffic at Eye Hospital Junction in Colombo. (WCS 9)

- My father returned from the dry zone in a private bus. (M&P 253)

probation officer

a government officer working in probation and child care (> **social worker**) → In Sri Lanka, a 'probation officer' (employed by the Dept. of Probation and Child Care) is a social worker who works with children. In the UK, a 'probation officer' works only with offenders.

proceed

go, continue, carry on, go on (more formal in BSE) ° *Shall we proceed?* ° *Thereafter Jayawardene had proceeded to his residence in Ward Place.*

proctor

(dated) lawyer → In the US, a 'proctor' is an exam invigilator.

- I saw her one more time, when I was a proctor practising up-country. (HC 278)

produce: to be produced (in court)

(of a suspect) to appear in court; (of an object) to be produced as evidence; noun: **production** ° *The suspects were produced before the magistrate and remanded.* ° *The police station doesn't even have a place to keep court productions.*

prof

professor, lecturer → In BSE, the abbreviation 'Prof.' would only be used as a title e.g.: 'Prof. Hutchinson'.

properly

(coll.) thoroughly (> **give**) ° *She scolded him properly.*

- "Pukka bugger that MacArthur, no? ... whacked the Japanese properly." (YY 135)

- "Russians are giving the Germans properly also." (TT 84)

- "Catch you with a catapult again I'll hammer you properly!" (TT 116)

- He's sure to be caught and Patholay will give it to him properly. (PMS 27)

proposal

(= **marriage proposal**) the offer by parents of their son or daughter in marriage (e.g. in a newspaper) → In BSE, a 'proposal' is a request or offer of marriage, traditionally made by the man to the woman he wants to marry. In SLE, 'proposals' are traditionally made by the parents.

- A proposal arrived for Radha Aunty even before she returned from America. (FB 41)

- Saha's worry now was his sisters, Saraswathi especially. Every proposal for her had fallen through. Lakshmi, curiously enough, had received only one proposal, but that looked as though it might be successful. (WMD 90)

- ♦ "You know how I feel about proposals." (CG 87)

- ♦ "What happened with the proposal? The guy your grandmother brought over?" (July 290)

- ♦ "Amma had written last week about a proposal from the adjoining village, a girl who had studied in a Colombo school - ..." (OD 136)

- ♦ "Last time that girl who came for that proposal also changed her mind when she saw the house, I think." (WCS 13)

- ♦ "I have brought a proposal." (PMS 263)

propose
to offer somebody in marriage ° *She was proposed to my cousin but it didn't work out.*
→ In BSE, to 'propose' to somebody (active voice) is to ask somebody to marry you. In SLE it is often used in the passive voice as in the examples.

- ♦ "Jeya, the fellow who's been proposed to Saraswathi." (WMD 97)

□ **proposed marriage**
arranged marriage (> **love marriage**)

Provincial Council (PC)
government administration at provincial level

PS
(= **pradeshiya sabha**)

pucks: to play pucks
(= **play hell, play socks, play pandu, dance the devil**) (coll.) to mess around, make trouble, play the fool

pug
(n/v) (coll.) snub ° *I gave her a good pug.* ° *She pugged him in style!*

pugilist
(in newspaper headlines) boxer (formal in BSE) (> **cager**) ° *Sri Lanka pugilists off to Indonesia*

puhul
/puhul/ (= **ash pumpkin, alu puhul**) a type of gourd (Sinhala)

□ **puhul dosi**
/puhul dōsi/ (= **pumpkin preserve**) (Sinhala) (> **dosi**)

pukka
/pakā/ (coll., dated) great, superb (Anglo-Indian, orig. Hindi) ° *He's a pukka fellow!* ° *We had a pukka time!*

- ♦ "Pukka fellow, no?" (JFT 19)

- ♦ "I say, men, pukka plantains." (JFT 198)

- ♦ "Must have been a pukka match." (YY 168)

- ♦ "One thing, whatever anybody says that Hitler is a pukka bugger." (TT 53)

- ♦ "Pukka driver your daddy," ... (TT 161)

- ♦ "A pukka blend, I have to say." (SG 112)

pul
/pal/ (coll.) useless, rotten (Sinhala) ° *The film was pul!* ° *Pul fellow!*

- ♦ "I suppose she watched the *pul* parts of my life and decided entanglements only brought confusion and misery." (SG 90)

□ **pulfy**
(coll.) tease, bully (> **-fy**) ° *I got pulfied at school about my new haircut.*

pull: to pull somebody up
(= scold) to tell somebody off, tick somebody off, reprimand somebody, punish somebody (less common in BSE) ° *They ought to be pulled up for that!* ° *Ministry pulls up school heads*

♦ Over the next few months, he was constantly being pulled up by the form-master for being slack in his work, untidy and generally indifferent. (WMD 117)

♦ He felt worse now than he had felt when he had got pulled up this morning. (WCS 70)

pulung
/pulung/ (= **kapok**) raw cotton, used for stuffing pillows, etc. (Sinhala)

♦ Through the years, Beryl made a lot of pillows. The *pulun** (* kapok) man would come to the door carrying his large gunny sack of 'tree cotton' … (TT 6)

pump
put, fill with (petrol, etc.) ° *Don't forget to pump petrol!*

□ to put a pump
(coll.) (of men) to have a pee

♦ "Wait a bit. I'll put a pump and come," … (TT 211)

♦ "I'll jus' put a pump against that tree and come." (CU 196)

pumpkin preserve
(= **puhul dosi**) a sweet preserve made from **ash pumpkin** (**alu puhul**) and used in the preparation of **love cake** and **foguete**

♦ She kept a jar of pumpkin preserve to hand. (HC 161)

♦ Achi escorted them to buy dates and pumpkin preserve required for the Christmas cake. (M&P 108)

punchi amma
/punchi amma/ aunt (mother's younger sister); also abbreviated to **punchi** (Sinhala) ° *My punchi is teaching at the campus.*

♦ "But tell me. How are nända and Punchi?" (GC 244)

Punjabi kit, Punjabi suit
/panjābi/ (= **shalwar kameez**)

♦ A fair, small nosed, dainty teacher in a Punjabi suit, with a thick, black plait hanging down to her waist. (M&P 46)

punya kalaya
/punya kāle/ period of religious observances during the **New Year** (Sinhala) ° *Punya Kalaya from 6.05 am to 6.53 pm*

purchase
buy (more formal in BSE) ° *From where did you purchase it?*

purge
(vi) have diarrhoea ° *I was purging all night.* → In BSE, 'purging' normally refers to cleansing the system as part of a 'detox' treatment. It is dated in the sense of 'emptying the bowels'.

♦ Drivers came in on time and suddenly developed this urge to purge. (YY 63)

purse
wallet → In BSE there is a distinction between a man's 'wallet', which holds banknotes, credit cards, etc.; and a woman's 'purse', which also holds coins. In SLE 'purse' is commonly used for both.

pus
/pus/ (coll.) grumpy (Sinhala = mouldy) ° *Why are you sitting with a pus face?*

□ pus case
/pus kēs/ (coll.) spoilsport, killjoy, wet blanket ° *Don't be such a pus case!*

push cycle, push bicycle

bicycle (UK also 'push-bike')

put (1)

put something somewhere (> **keep**) ° *Put it soon and come!* → In BSE it is necessary to specify the place where something is put (on the table, in the drawer, etc.), which can be omitted in SLE.

put (2)

put something on (light, clothes, shoes, etc.)

♦ "Put the lamp and read the Bible. I'll go and come soon." (JFT 70)

♦ "So come will you. Put a shirt and slippers." (JFT 178)

♦ "I'll put a shirt and come," ... (TT 164)

♦ "Put the TV, *putha*," ... (SG 197)

♦ She put the kettle to boil. (FSD 181)

♦ "Put the radio men, quickly." (WCS 46)

put (3)

(in set expressions) have, give, make (> **put a bolt, put a break, put a cap, put a hump, put a jump, put a line, put a part/parts, put a pump, put a round, put a shot**) ° *put a chat* ° *put a fight* ° *put a nap* ° *put a rest* ° *put leave* ° *Shall we put a walk and come?* ° *I'll put a quick wash and come.* → In BSE, you 'have a chat/a drink/a fight/a party/a nap/a rest/a try/a walk/a wash/a word/etc.'; you 'give a clout/a shout/a whistle/etc.'; and you 'make a complaint/etc.'

♦ "... he says one for the road and puts two more drinks ..." (JFT 101)

♦ They were at home, and where else could they 'put a party' and enjoy life as much as at home? (JFT 137)

♦ "When I put a clout you must turn the face and ask for another clout, no?" (YY 95)

♦ "I want to put a complaint," ... (TT 185)

♦ "So just put a word, will you." (TT 195)

♦ "One day I put a whistle and should have seen the face." ... "Must put a hoot and say how the tuition!" (TT 196)

♦ "You like to put a try?" ... "And if put a shout or something ..." (TT 213)

♦ "Oh good. Can put a drink then." (FSD 96)

♦ "Put a look in the checkpoint while I check the Honda." (CU 18)

♦ "Saw him going in to put a piss," ... (CU 196)

□ to put something to something

to put something in(to)/on(to) something ° *Don't forget to put petrol to the car.* ° *Can you put some water to the flowers?* (BSE: ... put petrol in the car, ... put water on the flowers)

□ to put something to wash

to put something to be washed (also with other verbs) ° *Did you put your shirt to wash?*

□ to put on

to put on weight (> **go down**) ° *You've put on since I last saw you.*

♦ "She has put on since you got her, no, Kamalakka?" (WE 30)

□ to put up something

to build (a house, etc.) ° *We want to put up a house before the wedding.*

□ to put somebody up

to wake somebody up ° *They put us up early morning.* → In BSE, to 'put somebody up' is to give them a bed for the night.

putha

/pʊta/ son; also a familiar term of address, used by a parent to a son or daughter, or by an older person to a younger person (Sinhala)

- ◆ "*Aney putha*, you are too young to talk like that." (MM 118)

- ◆ "You keep out of their way, Putha." (OM 36)

- ◆ "Come on, *putha*, just two mouthfuls more, one for *amma* and one for *appa*, all right?" (WMD 209)

- ◆ "None of them ever understood, *putha*, what it was really like." (SG 242)

- ◆ "Putha! Come here!" (July 43)

- ◆ He had three names, ... but his mother always said *putha*, naming the relationship that bound him to her. ... "*Putha*! Where are you hiding, *putha*?" (HC 212)

- ◆ "That's right *putha* you tell her." (WE 44)

- ◆ "That's marvelous, putha, ... I'm sure you'll be very successful." (FSD 24)

- ◆ "Let's go inside putha, then we can talk." (WCS 13)

- ◆ "Putha should have had her ears and she should have had putha's ears." (M&P 21)

- ◆ "Putha you can talk to Thathi when he comes for the weekend," ... (M&P 59)

put-put

/pʊtpʊt/ (= trishaw, three-wheeler) (coll.)

putt!

/pat/ (coll.) quickly, soon ° *Do it putt putt!*

putt shot

/pat shot/ shot put, putting the shot → BSE pronunciation: /shot pʊt/

puvalu

/puvālu/ a large yellow variety of banana (Sinhala) (> **plantain**)

puwak

/puwak/ (= **arecanut**) (Sinhala; Tamil paakku)

- ◆ ... and a busload of "*puwakmal*" pilgrims. Puwakmal, arecanut flowers were traditionally tied at the front of a vehicle carrying villagers going on a pilgrimage. (FSD 114)

pvt.

(in company names) private ° *John Keells (Pvt.) Limited*

Q

quarter mile
quarter of a mile

♦ My plan called for a straight stretch of
road, perhaps a quarter mile in length,
… (REP 65)

quazi
/kāsi/ an Islamic judge (Arabic) ° *the
quazi courts* ° *the Board of Quazis office in
Hulftsdorp*

queen
the red piece in **carrom**

quietly
(= **slowly**) later, in your own time, at your
leisure; tactfully, discreetly, unobtrusively
° *I'll see you quietly.* ° *You go, I'll quietly tell
him.*

♦ "Don't rush it now, …Let things
develop quietly." (FSD 25)

♦ "Have some lunch and come there
quietly. Don't worry." (FSD 26)

quip
(v) joke ° *… the President quipped.*
→ Commonly used in this sense in
newspaper reports; less frequent in BSE,
and more likely to be used as a noun than
a verb.

R

rabana
/rabānə/ a shallow drum which comes in
different sizes; the large one is traditionally
played by a group of women at **New Year**
(Sinhala, from Malay)

RABANA

♦ There were voices chanting, *raban*
drums. (MM 39)

♦ Attamma had brought out her big
rabana, the large tambourine, propped
up on three wooden legs. Before
beating a tune with her fingers on
the *rabana*, Attamma heated it over
burning coals to make the tune clearer
when playing on it. … From far and
near came the rhythmic beat of the
rabana playing. (CM 64)

♦ At Wellawatte a thin little beggar
boy boarded the bus. He had a little
rabana, a drum, which he started
playing with his knuckles while singing
a sad song about his father … (July 80)

rabu
/rābu/ a type of radish used as a vegetable
(Sinhala) ° *rabu curry*

race cart
a **hackery** adapted for racing, for example as
part of **New Year** festivities

RACE CART

race paper
a newspaper with details of horse races for betting

♦ … and although he sometimes forgot and carried the race paper home … (JFT 14)

racer
/rēsə/ (ball-)bearing

radala
/radələ/ a derogatory term for people who feel socially superior (Sinhala = an aristocratic caste) ° *putting on radala airs*

rae kade
/ræ kaɒe/ a **kade** which stays open all night (Sinhala)

♦ Ravi spotted a *Rä kadè*, an all-night restaurant, near the bus stand and told Piyal to pull over. (FSD 124)

rag
(n/v) the practice of **ragging**

♦ "Wickka must have been scared to rag her because he would have heard what big shots her Mummy and Daddy are; …" (OD 131)

♦ I had been warned that the rag would be severe and had tried to prepare myself for it. There is no way to avoid being ragged; it is something to be endured and then forgotten; … (GC 3)

□ ragger
a senior student who **rags** the juniors

♦ He is dressed in neatly pressed clothes and shiny brown shoes, very different from the sandals and rubber slippers worn by the raggers. (GC 11)

♦ The raggers had kept Mithra kneeling on the rocks till he had fainted and fallen down. (GC 37)

□ ragging
bullying of first-year students at universities, schools, etc. (US hazing) → In Sri Lankan universities 'ragging' is a common and often very serious problem, but it suggests something more light-hearted in BSE.

♦ "It seems they are getting together to form an organisation to stop the ragging of freshers." (OD 131)

♦ After all, they said, while it will be unpleasant, thousands of other students have endured ragging and survived. (GC 8)

♦ "We are opposed to the ragging of freshers." (GC 11)

rainbow sandwiches
party sandwiches with alternate layers of beetroot, carrot and cucumber grated and mixed with butter

rain tree
(= **mara**) a huge spreading tree, common on roadsides and at the edge of **tanks**

♦ He sat under the rain tree and blinked. (YY 145)

♦ Outside, over the rain tree cathedrals, a full moon was doing business. (YY 171)

♦ The old rain trees on either side of the road gave welcome shade in the day, but at night the thick canopy screened the streetlights and forced them to watch their step. (FSD 7)

Ramazan

/ramazān/ Ramadan, the Muslim month of fasting; also the annual Muslim festival (Id-Ul-Fitr) marking the end of that month (Arabic) (> **Id**)

◆ Christmas, Vesak, Thai Pongal and Ramazan are national holidays. (M&P 70)

rambutan

/ramburan/ a small red fruit with a thick hairy rind and sweet white flesh (orig. Malay)

RAMBUTAN

◆ ... a sleepy hollow in the hinterland where the best rambuttans are grown. (TT 9)

◆ Para stopped by a *rambutan* seller. He had never seen the fruit before. (WMD 61)

◆ Malwana, a predominantly Muslim town, was known for its abundance of rambutans, a sweet, lychee-like fruit which grew everywhere. ... Ordinarily, Priyanthi, who loved rambutans, would have wanted to stop and buy some from the road-side vendors who held out bunches of fruit to passing motorists. (July 295)

◆ "I have been gorging myself on rambutans. Such fruit! Spiked scarlet globes the size of a hen's egg, split open with a thumbnail to yield segments of delectable white flesh." (HC 155-6)

◆ The *mahatturu* in the cars lowered their windows to look at the bunches of *rambuttans* the men held up. (WE 35)

◆ He had told her about his fall from the rambuttan tree on his father's Malwana estate. (CU 298)

◆ After that, Mrs. Bandaranayake chased the governor general to his Rambutan estate and lived happily ever after. (M&P 151)

rampe

/rampe/ pandanus, a leaf used in cooking to flavour curries (Sinhala)

◆ ... and herbs - curry leaves, rampe, lemon grass. (CG 14)

ranawara

/ranavara/ a shrub with yellow flowers, used to make a herbal tea (Sinhala)

◆ She picked the yellow flowers of the *ranawara* bush, dried them in the sun and brewed them into a tea that she drank twice a day. "*Cassia auriculata*. Excellent for purifying the blood." (HC 180)

range

/rēnj/ an administrative district in the police (also India) ° *the Southern Range*

rasam

/rasam/ a spicy soup eaten with a **thali** meal (Tamil)

◆ The meal was tasty but spare: rice, *rasam, dhal* tempered in ghee with hot red chillies and onion, ... (WMD 331)

◆ ... as she poured the rasam out into cups, ... (CG 148)

rasthiyadu

/rastiyādu/ (coll.) a hassle, a waste of time (Sinhala) ° *Today was a real rasthiyadu.*

° *Does finding what you need leave you in a real rasthiyadu?*

□ a rasthiyadu case

(coll.) a useless person, a waster, a **loafer**

□ rasthiyadufy, rastify

(coll.) go to a lot of trouble and achieve nothing; noun: **rastification** (> -fy) ° *We had to rasthiyadufy all morning in the visa office.*

ratemahatteya

/raTēmahattəya/ (dated) a district chief in the **Kandyan** kingdom (Sinhala)

rat snake

(= **garandiya**) a very large green snake which is common but harmless

- ♦ They did not notice the large rat snake that slunk past them, ... (YY 145)

- ♦ How the rat snake came to the balcony is anybody's guess. (YY 177)

- ♦ On examination it turned out to be a rat snake, harmless to men. (HC 220)

- ♦ The only snake I saw was a harmless olive green and yellow Ratsnake, crossing the path in a flash, like a drop of mercury skidding across a plate. (REP 285-6)

rattaning

weaving with rattan (from Malay, not used as a verb in BSE) ° *We need to get some rattaning work done.*

raw

(of fruits) unripe; (of rice) **unpolished**, wholegrain ° *raw mangoes* → In BSE 'raw' means 'uncooked'. It is less common in the sense of 'wholegrain', and never used in the sense of 'unripe'.

- ♦ It was a small room, and it smelled of raw rice and Maldive fish and other dry provisions. (FB 296)

- ♦ The man who took Dasa away gave us two sack loads of pineapples. One sack with raw pineapples, the other ripe. (M&P 208)

readymades

readymade clothes

real

(adj.) (depending on context) crazy, cheeky, flirtatious, etc.; (adv.) really, completely ° *She's a real one!* ° *a real case* ° *a real forward case* → In both senses, 'real' is very common in colloquial SLE.

reawakened village

a village developed by the government under the Gam Udawa programme

record bar

(dated) record shop

redda

/reddə/ (= **cloth**) a length of material worn round the waist, esp. by women (Sinhala) (> **diya redda**)

- ♦ People hurried about their Saturday business wearing colourful reddhas and harried expressions. (July 86)

- ♦ Out of the darkness appeared a tall, slim woman carrying another bottle lamp, with two small round-eyed children clinging to her reddha. ... but her reddha was torn and her blouse was threadbare ... (July 150)

□ redda hatte

/reddə hœTTe/ (= **cloth and jacket**) an outfit worn by women, esp. of lower social status (Sinhala)

- ♦ The folds of flesh between her tight hette and firmly tied redda shivered with every laugh ... (Z 123)

red onions

small onions (> **Bombay onions**)

- Underneath I found a small basket of red onions. (Reef 36)

- "But with an omelette. Red onions and green chillies." (M&P 231)

red rice

red wholegrain **country rice** (the equivalent in the UK is 'brown rice')

- When times were hard at home we had eaten red rice, grated coconut and a single green chilli. (GC 14-15)

- Red rice with gem-sized kernels of sand, ... (M&P 79)

- ... I wished this sweet Lord would put on our tables something other than red rice and dhal boiled in water, with neither coconut milk nor salt. (M&P 113)

reeper

/rīpə/ a small piece of wood which supports the tiles on a roof (Sinhala, also Anglo-Indian, from Portuguese)

refer

(vt) refer to something (vi) ° *You better refer your dictionary.* ° *Please refer the prospectus for details.*

refrigerator

fridge (formal in BSE)

regarding

about (formal in BSE) ° *What is it regarding?*

remain

(vt/vi) leave (the rest of your food or drink) ° *Don't remain on your plate!* ° *He's always remaining food.* → In BSE, to 'remain' (vi) means to be left over: 'There's a lot of food remaining'.

remand

(v) remand in custody ° *The suspects were produced before the Gangodawila magistrate and remanded.*

remnants

leftovers ° *We can keep the remnants for breakfast.* → In BSE, the 'remnants' of a meal are scraps which would not be worth keeping, while 'leftovers' might be kept for another meal.

- There is no talking till a bloated Paduma pushes the remnants away, unable to swallow another grain. (PMS 149)

remove

take off (e.g. clothes) ° *Shall I remove my slippers?* → In BSE, to 'remove' means to take away or take out, and is not normally used in the sense of taking off clothes, except in rather formal contexts.

- "Sidath, remove your shoes and give them to Suji," ... (GC 157)

reply

(vt) answer, reply to something (e.g. a letter) ° *Did you reply their letter?*

- Jayantha didn't reply that letter. (Z 67)

- Kumar Arasaratnam was already at his desk, checking his email, and replying the more urgent ones. (CU 285)

report card

school report

- His report cards from school always said the same thing. (July 31)

- Her children's report cards, vaccination cards, identity cards, ... (M&P 244)

request: to request for something

to request something ° *She has requested for an appointment.* ° *Bayliss requests for more time* → In BSE, 'request' is only used with 'for' when it is a noun: 'a request for an appointment'.

reside
live (in a place) (formal in BSE) ° *He is currently residing in Moratuwa.*

residence
house, home (formal in BSE) ° *Where is your residence?*

restaurant
/rɛsтoroнт/ bar ° *Bambalapitiya Restaurant*
→ In BSE, a 'restaurant' is a place that serves food; in SLE, it can be just a drinking place.

resthouse, rest house
a government-run hotel/guest house (also India, Malaysia, Africa, etc.)

♦ Resthouses are an old tradition in Ceylon. (RF 150)

♦ He had wriggled his way into a job in a government Rest House ... (Reef 19)

♦ Sonnaboy lazed in the Kitulgala rest-house and drank a lot of beer. (YY 221)

♦ "Next day we gave up the wild-goose chase and went for lunch at the Rest House." (SG 230)

♦ Gamini and the driver walked into the dark, sunless lobby of the old Negombo rest house. (AG 217)

♦ "Breakfast at a resthouse." (MiP 179)

♦ When they reached the main road, Ravi asked for directions and found the resthouse soon afterwards. (FSD 56)

♦ The rest house has been built on a bluff overlooking the bay. (GC 280)

♦ "I will be staying at the local rest house and I will wait for you to telephone me before I visit." (SMS 13)

♦ Owners of rest-houses, motels and hotels. (M&P 98)

□ resthouse keeper
the manager of a **resthouse**

♦ ... the resthouse keeper, a gang of carters and all manner of citizens ... (JFT 148)

♦ The resthouse keeper was an immensely fat man with a round hairless head, ... (FSD 56)

retrench
make redundant, lay off (workers); noun: **retrenchment** ° *The sacking comes hot on the heels of Bata retrenching 146 workers through a voluntary retirement scheme.*
→ To 'retrench' is rare in BSE, where it means to cut costs, but doesn't necessarily imply making people redundant.

returned
(adj. referring to a person who has returned from a particular place, esp. abroad)
° *England-returned* ° *foreign-returned*

returnee
a person who has returned from abroad
° *Middle East returnees*

♦ Really, the shamelessness of these Returnees! (CP 91)

♦ ... condemned to wander the streets of Colombo in their weird returnee clothes, ... (CP 174)

♦ They mingled with quiet, tired European tourists, standing in irritated discipline as the returnees argued and pushed and jumped the queue. (CU 229)

Rexene
the waterproof material used to make **trishaw** hoods, etc. (brand name)

♦ Ravi rolled down the Rexene rain covers at the back of the trishaw ... (FSD 279)

ribbon cake
a cake with layers of different colours

rice, rice and curry
(= **bath, bath curry**) the staple Sri Lankan diet, esp. at lunch-time, consisting of a large plate of rice and a variety of curries → The whole meal can also be referred to simply as 'rice'; in BSE, the nearest equivalent might be called 'a curry'.

♦ "Always there is a *kadé* nearby where you can get rice and curry for a few rupees." (MM 82)

♦ In those fine old days a meal of rice and curry, a cup of tea and a cigarette cost a mere nine cents ... (JFT 3)

♦ By noon we reached Hatton and a little later we ate the rice and curry my mother had packed for us. (WMD 122)

♦ Clutched in his hand was a letter, which he later told Anura over a dinner of rice and curry, was written by his fiancée. (Z 64)

♦ I was feeling hungry now and yearning for a good Sinhala midday meal. ... We ordered rice & curry. (REP 318)

♦ They had sat at the edge of the rear verandah and eaten the packets of rice and curry the girl had bought with her stolen money. (FSD 226)

♦ Most of the passengers order rice and curry but I ... ask for a bun and a banana. (GC 82)

♦ ... Amrith was delighted that, instead of boring rice and curry, they were having boiled eggs, ham sandwiches, lemonade, ... (SMS 15)

♦ It was the only way to enjoy good rice and curry, and Army mess cooks served up the best. (CU 420)

♦ And this sweet lord of aunty Lydia's served rice and curry that tasted like toilet paper. (M&P 114)

rice belly
(coll., humorous) a pot belly caused by eating lots of rice (the UK equivalent is a 'beer belly')

rice cooker
an automatic machine for cooking rice (less common in BSE)

rice flour
the flour used to make **hoppers, stringhoppers, pittu**, etc.

rice mill
a place where rice is **polished** and prepared for sale

rice packet
(= **lunch packet, bath packet**) a **rice and curry** meal wrapped up to be taken away (> **packet, parcel**)

♦ The first thing I did was tuck into my rice-packet; ... (Reef 37)

♦ "... Jeffrey, who complains when he finds a hair in his rice packet." (MiP 216)

rice puller
a strongly flavoured food or dish which 'pulls the rice' (i.e. makes you eat more); e.g. a **sambol**, chutney, pickle, raw onion, **curd chilli**, piece of **karawala**, etc.

♦ "And here some lime pickle also. Real rice puller. Give you appetite." (JFT 99)

♦ "I say, *machang*, pukka rice-puller no? Have you had?" (Reef 160)

rich cake

a rich, dark fruit cake ° *Include our famous rich cakes and breudhers when you make your exclusive Christmas hampers.*

♦ So it was wine and rich cake and Peak Freans crackers and cheese ... (JFT 179)

ridged gourd

(= **vatakolu**) a type of gourd used as a vegetable

right right

(coll.) all right, OK

rigifoam

/rijifōm/ polystyrene ° *a rigifoam cake structure*

♦ ... orange crush and beers in rigifoam boxes, ... (July 33)

♦ Once inside the toilet, Balachandran split open the heat-contoured rigifoam box and stuffed the pieces into the waste disposal. He then tore open the sealed plastic packet that had been inside the rigifoam. (CU 337)

river bath

a **bath** in a river (> **bath**)

♦ We have to get to Kokmotai campsite ... in time to have a river bath before lunch. (GC 145)

rix dollar

a silver coin from the colonial period (from Dutch 'rijks')

roast pang

/rōst pāng/ a thin, crisp, roasted loaf of bread (Sinhala) (> **pang**)

♦ Or two loaves and a roast paang, the small flat bread that children loved ... (July 39)

rob

steal ° *All my jewellery has been robbed.* → In BSE, you 'steal something from a person or place', or 'rob a person or place of something'.

♦ Then, four young men robbed a Morris Minor, strolled into a bank and stole twenty-six thousand rupees. (M&P 264)

Rodi, Rodiya

/roⅮī, roⅮiya/ a member of a low-caste community of South Indian origin (Sinhala) ° *a portrait of a Rodi girl*

♦ The next day Tissa sent his boy to the kitchen door to say there were two Rodi women at the gate. Buddhists shunned contact with the Rodiya, considering them unclean; yet they made their living by begging and were rarely turned away from a house. They were believed to possess second sight and the evil eye, and it was judged unwise to cross them. (HC 169)

rogue

/rōg/ thief, crook, devil ° *He's a real rogue!* ° *They caught the rogue and hammered him properly.* → In BSE, 'rogue' is rather dated; it may still be used jokingly in the sense of a crook or devil ('a likable rogue'), but never in the sense of a thief or robber.

♦ "See, men, if rogues are trying to get inside." (JFT 169)

♦ "A rogue on the roof, ... catch the bugger if he tries to jump down." (YY 55)

♦ "... and all the bloody rogues and pickpockets doing business." (YY 141)

♦ "But baby, they're thieves," ... "Nonsense. How can you call them rogues?" (PMS 144)

♦ "These conductors are big rogues, … Count the balance carefully and give it to me." (PMS 196)

Roman-Dutch law

the principal legal system in Sri Lanka, one of several systems still in operation; others include **Thesavalamai**, **Kandyan** law, Muslim law, etc. ° *The general law is a mixture of English and Roman-Dutch law.*

rose apple

(= **jambu**) a small pink pear-shaped fruit with crisp white flesh

♦ Two little children, chubby as rose apples, … (KCS 102)

roti

/roti/ a type of bread made with wheat flour and water (Sinhala/Tamil; also India) (> **pol roti, godamba roti, egg roti, plain roti, kotturoti**)

♦ "Here, take this and go and eat rotti." (TT 139)

♦ "Ah, *rotti* and *sambol*. I'm hungry." (WMD 26)

♦ … bought some tea and a potato roti at the street canteen and consumed them there, … (AG 211)

♦ There she stood, silently cooking rotis on a flat griddle over the roaring fire, while Siri shaped balls of dough into flat circles. (July 144-5)

♦ Was she going to make him a 'roti' for his breakfast? (OD 59)

♦ The boy stands on a side watching us as we wolf the roti. (Z 137)

♦ Not having plates, we just opened the roti, scooped a bit of curry inside and folded it over like a stuffed bun. (REP 59)

♦ Janaki asked for some money and bought stuffed rotis. (FSD 240)

♦ … Mithra mumbles, his mouth full of roti. (GC 276)

♦ "Jus' make some *rotti* or something." (CU 41)

□ roti thatiya

/roti tætiyə/ a flat round griddle for making **rotis** (Sinhala)

ROTI THATIYA

round

(n) a short outing or trip ° *Shall we go for a round?* ° *We'll put a small round and come.*

Royalist

a student or former student of Royal College, Colombo (also **Thomian, Josephian, Peterite, Anandian, Nalandian, Trinitian**, etc.) (> **LC-ite**)

♦ He was, thus, a Josephian turned Peterite. Soon, the schools developed a rivalry (as most schools do) and met in an annual cricket encounter (also as most schools do) and hordes of Peterites to this day carry blue, white and gold flags and jeer the Josephians who brandish their colours of blue, white and blue … (TT 17)

♦ "What? That rascal was a Royalist?" … "So he wants his revenge on all Royalists?" (GC 57)

Royal-Thomian

the annual cricket match between Royal College and St Thomas' College (> **big match**)

♦ The kabaragoya laid its eggs in the hollows of trees between the months of January and April. As this coincided with the Royal-Thomian cricket match, we would collect them and throw them into the stands full of Royal students. (RF 74)

♦ ... if you were a well-known cricketer you could breeze into a career in business on the strength of your spin bowling or one famous inning at the Royal-Thomian match. (AG 10)

♦ The Royal-Thomian cricket match souvenir had come out ... (M&P 266)

Rs.
(= rupees) ° *Rs 35/-*

rub
(coll.) rub on, rub in (e.g. an ointment) (> **apply**) ° *Rub some of this cream.*

rubber estate
an estate where rubber trees are grown

rubber slippers
(= bathroom slippers) flip-flops (> **slippers**)

♦ Far down the river two pairs of rubber slippers floated merrily away. (TT 168)

♦ ... Sam noticed two black-strapped rubber slippers arrayed side by side under the bed. (HC 144)

♦ Velaithan was finding it difficult with her rubber slippers, slipping and stumbling from time to time. (REP 123)

♦ Rubber slippers are the only permitted footwear, no shoes or sandals. (GC 9)

♦ Niresh threw his shoes into a corner and put on his rubbers slippers. (SMS 144)

♦ The astro looked critically at Frankie's shorts and skinny tee shirt and rubber slippers. (CP 168)

♦ ... chasing Magi out of the room with Thathi's rubber slipper. (M&P 174)

rubber tapper
a person who **taps** rubber trees

ruggerite
rugger player (> **cager**) ° *Schoolboy ruggerite of the year*

rulang
/rulang/ semolina (Sinhala) ° *rulang biscuits*

rum
(= **thraada**) (coll.) rough, unsophisticated ° *He's a rum fellow.* → In BSE, 'rum' means strange, weird, odd.

run: to run behind
(= **go behind**) to go after somebody/something, run after somebody/something, chase somebody up

♦ My father on hearing the name Cleopatra had raised his head from the pothole and begun to run behind the dog. My father does not usually run behind dogs. (M&P 121)

running bungalow
(dated) temporary quarters for train drivers (> **bungalow**)

♦ ... the Railway Running Bungalow where tired drivers ... are provided with a sort of hostelry ... There is also a cook and kitchen helper and running bungalow meals are hot and wholesome. (YY 92)

rupee
/rupi/ the currency of Sri Lanka (also India, from Urdu/Sanskrit) → Note on pronunciation: This is one of several words which tend to be pronounced with the stress on the first syllable in SLE, and the second syllable in BSE.

♦ Members had to pay Rupees 150/- to the starter before each round, and came through with a tip of another

Rupees 100/- most of the time.
(FSD 17)

♦ Rani paid him with a crisp hundred-rupee note, proudly drawn out of her black handbag. (WCS 24)

♦ He looks at her hopelessly as he picks up the ten-rupee note. (PMS 31)

♦ ... but only on condition that Paduma collects the balance forty rupees by himself. (PMS 97)

Russell's viper

a highly venomous snake (the most common, and the most dangerous, of several species of viper found in Sri Lanka) (> **polonga**)

♦ He learnt to avoid the marsh grass at dusk because the vipers would be hunting but had the confidence to raise the sluggish Russel's viper with a bent stick at midday because, as everyone knew, the viper would lie in a daze of sleep when the sun was hottest. (TT 117)

♦ "Russell's viper. We call it tith polonga in the village." (GC 157)

S

S.

St (Saint) ° *S. Thomas' Prep School, Kollupitiya*

saacha, chaacha

/sācha, chācha/ (= **chittappa, baappa**) uncle (father's younger brother) (Muslim Tamil, from Hindi)

saachi, chaachi

/sāchi, chāchi/ (= **chinnamma, punchi amma**) aunt (mother's younger sister) (Muslim Tamil, from Hindi)

Sabara

/sabəra/ (coll.) Sabaragamuwa University (> **Pera**)

sadhu

/sādu/ monk, priest, holy man (Sinhala; also India, from Sanskrit)

♦ "All he does is smoke and loaf and pretend he is some sort of *sadhu*, above work." (WMD 145)

♦ An ash-smeared sadhu. (HC 294)

safari suit

a lightweight suit worn by men, consisting of short-sleeved cotton jacket and trousers

♦ He was bent over with age, and wore thick glasses and a polyester safari suit. (SMS 141)

♦ My father got safari suits and bush shirts in all shades of khaki, beige and brown. (M&P 324)

saffron

(= **kaha**) turmeric → Saffron and turmeric are different spices, but the word 'saffron' is commonly used in SLE to refer to turmeric.

sahan

/sahən/ a large serving dish serving 6 people (Muslim Tamil, from Arabic) ° *We're having 5 sahans for dinner tonight.*

sahar

/sahər/ the pre-dawn meal eaten during the **Ramazan** fast (Arabic)

saivar kade

/saivər kaɖe/ a South Indian-style vegetarian **kade** (Tamil)

♦ It got so bad that the proprietor of the Saivar Kadé, the caff across the road, sent us a stern message: … (CP 108)

♦ To cheer him up, Rani had taken Athma out to lunch at this *saivar kade.* (WCS 18)

salad leaf

lettuce

salagama

/salāgamə/ the 'cinnamon peeler' caste (Sinhala) ° *Salagama Buddhist mother seeks educated partner for graduate daughter …*

salaya

/sāləya/ a type of fish (goldstrip sardinella) (Sinhala)

salmon

(= **tin fish**) tinned fish → In BSE, 'salmon' is an expensive variety of fish; in SLE, it refers to any canned fish, usually tuna or mackerel.

♦ … a creative genius who could build … a motor-bike with a rusted kitchen knife and a salmon tin, … (M&P 37)

♦ … eating salmon cutlets and drinking 'Sharona' … (M&P 183)

saloon

barber's shop, hairdresser → In BSE, a 'salon' or 'hairdressing salon' is a hairdresser's shop, while a 'saloon' is a large hall or public room, or (esp. in the US) a public bar (also 'saloon bar'). To add to the confusion, Sri Lankan 'saloons' often have the same double swing doors which are also associated with traditional 'saloon bars' in the US.

SALOON

♦ "Is Gabriel's Saloon still there for head massages?" (AG 9)

samanera

/samənērə/ a young boy apprentice Buddhist monk (Sinhala)

samba

/samba/ a popular, small-grained variety of white rice, usually sold parboiled (Sinhala) (> **country rice, red rice, muthusamba**)

♦ … and the best samba rice with beef, two vegetables, … (JFT 3)

♦ There was hot boiled samba rice mixed with honey. (CM 17)

♦ … using the fingers of his right hand to pick strips of curried chicken off the drumstick before mixing it in with the *samba* rice, dhal, beetroot, and *seeni sambol.* (CU 420)

sambar

/sambər/ a spicy gravy or soup made with **dhal** and vegetables (Tamil)

♦ … asked them to pass the thosai and sambar with a politeness that made her eyes narrow in suspicion. (CG 15)

sambhur

/sāmbə/ a large species of deer (also India, orig. Hindi; OED sambur)

SAMBHUR

- The sambhur has eaten all the bananas, … (RF 158)

- Sambhur drank at that sluggish stream, high-antlered deer bulky as elks. (HC 189)

- A glimpse between the trees revealed a sambhur stag, with a magnificent set of antlers, in headlong flight. (REP 176)

- They heard a Sambhur bell in the valley below, … (FSD 88)

- Animals are scarce but we see herds of deer and then a solitary sambhur stag. (GC 148)

sambol

/sœmbōl/ a spicy dish containing chilli and onions (usually uncooked) (Sinhala/Tamil; OED sambal, orig. Malay) (> **coconut sambol, katta sambol, onion sambol, pol sambol, seeni sambol**) ° *mint sambol*

- … *sambol* (a relish made of ground coconut, chillie, lime, salt, chopped onions, tomato and peppercorns, eaten with meals), … (JFT 3)

- I had to conjure up some chilli *sambol* … (Reef 126)

- "Nearly died, no? Spleen ruptured. Whole stomach like a sambol inside." (YY 208)

- … and straightaway set herself down to 'perform' her *sambol*. (WMD 212)

- Rice, beef or fish curry, deliciously prepared vegetables and sambols, and often a banana for dessert. (July 241)

- … ensuring that the governess's favourite curries and *sambols* succeeded each other at mealtimes. (HC 183)

- "Boiled pumpkins with red chillie sambol." (KCS 101)

- "Out, out, out of this room before I make sambol out of you," … (M&P 174)

same

/sēm/ (dated and formal in BSE) ° *Please acknowledge receipt of same.*

same (like)

(coll.) the same (as) ° *He is same like his brother.*

- In my own way I am a rationalist, same as Mister Salgado, but perhaps less of a gambler; … (Reef 65)

Samurdhi

/samurdi/ a government programme of issuing **food stamps** to poor families (Sinhala, orig. Sanskrit)

sandesha poem

/sandēshə/ a type of traditional Sinhala poem (Sinhala = message)

- They could replace sonnets with *sandesha* poems in every classroom if they liked; … (HC 267-8)

sandwich bread

a rectangular-shaped loaf of bread for making sandwiches (not necessarily sliced) → In BSE, 'sandwich bread' is always sliced.

Sangha

/saŋgə/ (= **Mahasangha**) the order of Buddhist monks (Sinhala, orig. Sanskrit)

♦ He built monasteries for the Sangha and tanks and temples for the people, ... (WMD 199)

□ Sangha sabha

/saŋgə sabā/ an organization of Buddhist monks (Sinhala)

sans

/sānz/ without (orig. French) ° *Kurunegala bus stand sans toilets* ° *A World Cup sans public interest* → This is a word favoured by Sri Lankan journalists, esp. in newspaper headlines; it is considered archaic in BSE, or else it is used in a humorous way.

♦ Eventually Mountbatten stalked away with his party to climb into his Riley staff car and drive to his command post in the Botanical Gardens sans eggs. (JFT 199)

♦ They couldn't think what a diesel was doing sans driver but it was a gift. (YY 67)

♦ He slipped to the cooler cement floor and lay there, sans shirt, waiting for his eyelids to shut out the world. (TT 162)

saree, sari

/sāri/ a garment worn by women, consisting of a length of material wrapped around the body (also India, orig. Hindi) ° *a going-away saree*

♦ She wore a dark green Manipuri sari with a gold border. (FB 98)

♦ ... and that night she was decked out in a crimson Manipuri sari, with a royal-blue blouse that left a scandalous quantity of midriff on display. (HC 58)

♦ The Kanjipuram sari he tried to sell me looked strangely familiar ... (M&P 352)

♦ "Huh, just because someone has worn a sari, ... she thinks she's a princess." (PMS 268)

□ saree blouse, saree jacket

(= **choli**) the tight-fitting blouse worn with a **saree**

SAREE BLOUSE

♦ Her black lace sari blouse was of the latest fashion, with a mere frill for a sleeve. (CG 62)

♦ She took out a handkerchief that was tucked in her sari blouse and blew her nose. (SMS 210)

♦ I don't know if Achi sent the postcard, but I saw her take something white out of her sari jacket and throw it into the kitchen fire. (M&P 221)

□ saree pota

/sāri poʈə/ (= **fall**) the part of the **saree** which is draped over the shoulder (Sinhala) (> **headpiece, pallu, palu**)

♦ The jacket was tight across her breasts and there was a tear under one arm. That didn't matter she said, the saree pota will cover it. (OM 33)

♦ Motorcycle riders weave crazily through the stationary cars, their sari-clad pillion riders sitting side-saddle and hanging on to handbags and sari potas. (July 8)

♦ ... shooting venomous looks at her daughter, who was inelegantly wiping her eyes with her sari pota. (July 301)

SAREE POTA

♦ Her sari-pota is counter-weighted perfectly on her head. (Z 13)

♦ She would wrap her sari potta around her and shift her buttocks so that she was comfortably placed. (Z 177-8)

♦ Ammi returned with a stack of horoscopes. The rolled palm leaves, unrolling themselves and following her like a curled sari pota. (M&P 318)

□ to hang on (to) somebody's saree pota

to be tied to somebody's apron strings, to be controlled by a woman (usually one's mother) ° *Anura was always hanging on Mrs B's saree pota.*

♦ "If you can't hold her hand then hold onto her *sari pota*!" (M&P 191)

sarong

/sǽrong, sarong/ a garment worn by men, consisting of a length of material tied around the waist (orig. Malay) → In BSE, 'sarong' is pronounced with a weak first syllable: /sə'rong/

♦ Quite easily and simply Sahadevan slipped into Tissa's way of life, got to wearing a *sarong*, which he found

less inhibiting than the *verti*, ... (WMD 20)

♦ The boutique-keeper wore his striped sarong low on his waist to accommodate his soft round belly. (HC 196)

♦ She had worn the sarong as a gown, tied in a firm knot over her breasts. (REP 148)

SARONG

♦ ... an egg bald man dressed in a spotless white shirt and sarong, ... (FSD 246)

♦ She hitched up her sarong to her knees and kicked off her slippers. (SMS 18)

♦ MD lifts his colourful sarong up a little and bends his head slightly in mock-humble acknowledgement. (WCS 36)

♦ Bald head, luxuriant moustache, expensive blue-checked sarong topped by a cream bush shirt: he looks an important person. (PMS 262)

□ sarong Johnny

(dated) a derogatory or humorous term for a person wearing a **sarong**, implying that they are socially inferior

sarpina

/sarpina/ harmonium (also India, orig. Hindi)

♦ From the house she heard a man singing in Sinhalese, accompanied by a sarpina and tablas. (CG 375)

satyagraha

/satyagraha/ a non-violent protest or demonstration (also India, orig. Sanskrit)

sau

/sau/ sago (Sinhala)

scale

/skēl/ (a pair of) scales

scavenger

street cleaner and rubbish collector; also **scavenging**

schol

scholarship ° *She's going there on a schol.*

school

(v) go to school ° *My brother is still schooling.* → In BSE 'schooling' is possible as a noun, but not as a verb as in the example; to be 'schooled' in something means to be trained in something.

♦ Sonnaboy was an 'old Joe' - having schooled, albeit sketchily, at St Joseph's College ... (TT 17)

♦ People schooling in Colombo had fat chances of entering university with standardization. (M&P 304)

school van

a private van transporting children to and from school (the UK equivalent is a 'school bus')

scissor

(a pair of) scissors ° *Can you lend me your scissor?* ° *testing the edge of the knife or scissor with his fingers*

scissor man

a man who sharpens knives, etc.

scold

/skōlɒ/ tell somebody off, tick somebody off, shout at somebody, blast somebody, be angry with somebody ° *I got scolded for getting late.* ° *He scolded me like a pickpocket!* (> **filth**) → In SLE 'scold' is a very common word, but it is much less frequent in BSE, where it is generally restricted to the meaning of scolding a child for doing something wrong. Even in this case, it is more often replaced by 'tell off' or 'tick off'. In the case of 'scolding' adults, the idea is more likely to be expressed in a different way: 'shout at somebody', 'blast somebody', 'be angry with somebody' or (colloquially) 'get pissed off with somebody'. SLE also has several other words and expressions with the same meaning, none of which are common in BSE: **blackguard, give somebody beans, give somebody tight, shell, give somebody a shelling.**

♦ She had hidden the two families upstairs and scolded the louts who came after them. (Reef 189)

♦ At this, the anger of the crowd seemed to die down as suddenly as it had erupted, and they fell to scolding the driver. (WMD 186)

♦ I wanted to write a letter scolding Amma. (OD 136)

♦ Nenda took me out of the room. Scolding him for being a civilized Colombo child who attended a respectable Buddhist school but did not have a molecule of compassion towards his sibling. (M&P 61)

scrabbler

(in newspaper headlines) scrabble player (> **cager**)

scrape

/skrēp/ grate (a coconut) (> **coconut scraper, hiramane**)

SCRAPING COCONUT

♦ Carolis was in the backyard scraping half a coconut for breakfast. The pure white grated coconut had fallen in a perfect cone-shaped mound on the plate under the scraper. (MM 99)

♦ No pounding of flour, no coconut-scraping, no onion-chopping. (Reef 40)

♦ She served him a big plate of rice and dry fish with a little coconut she scraped sitting astride the dilapidated scraper. (OM 31)

♦ ... when he heard sounds from the rear of the house, sounds of a coconut being scraped. Was it his mother scraping coconut? (OD 59)

♦ Padma scraped the flesh from coconuts and ignored him. (HC 207)

♦ Boiled pumpkins with white scraped coconut is the answer. (KCS 101)

scraps, scrap sheets
sheets of printed pictures used by children for school projects, scrapbooks, etc. (each sheet covers one topic, e.g. transport, musical instruments, etc.)

scratch
(vi) itch ° *My eye is scratching.* → In BSE, to 'scratch' (vt) is what you do to something (e.g. a mosquito bite) which is itching.

♦ "I remember my Uncle Rubin saying that if you crush kitul seed in water and pour it on someone, the whole body starts scratching." (PMS 187)

screen
clothes-horse, a wooden frame for drying clothes, etc.

scribe
(= **journo**) journalist ° *Scribe's father dies*

SD
(= **sinnadorai**)

sea bath
(n) a swim in the sea (> **bath**) ° *Let's go for a sea bath.*

♦ When we went for a sea bath that evening, I could hardly contain my excitement. (FB 63)

♦ "Why don't we go for a sea bath after breakfast," Chithra Aunty suggested. (FB 202)

♦ "Can do a seabath at KKS before we eat." (TT 139)

♦ Their bungalow had become her second home, and she spent most of her spare time with them, going for sea baths and occasionally taking holidays in the hill country. (CG 5)

♦ Balendran knew of it, for his family had often come to this very spot for picnics and sea baths. (CG 186)

♦ When they got back to the house, they used a shower in the side garden that had been built for rinsing off after sea-baths. (SMS 127)

sea bathing
(v) swimming/bathing in the sea ° *Couple drowns while sea bathing* ° *Many believe that sea-bathing here is safe.*

♦ People would go there on a Sunday to sea bathe, before the troubles started. (REP 218)

sea beach; sea coast
beach; coast

♦ There were pictures of them at the sea beach, making sand castles or swimming in the blue sea with sea gulls flying about. (CM 36)

search
(coll.) (vt) look for, search for ° *I've been searching this book all over.* → In BSE, you 'search' a place, but you 'search for' something you've lost, a new job, etc.

sea side, seaside
on the same side as the sea (esp. of the Galle Road) (> **land side**) ° *It's a small lane on the sea side.* → In BSE, the 'seaside' is a place by the sea where people go on holiday.

♦ The school was two streets away from St. Gabriel's, on the sea side of Galle Road. (FB 212)

♦ He then crossed to the sea side track for the walk back. (YY 74)

♦ The Colpetty Mission School, where Annalukshmi taught, was on the "sea side" of Galle Road, in the suburb of Colpetty. (CG 18)

♦ Further down these sea-side roads, you could hear the dull booming of the sea over the other sounds. (July 8)

♦ The traffic police did not permit parking on the seaside of Galle Road till after 12.00 noon. (FSD 101)

♦ ... an almost empty train ... rattled past on the seaside track leading to Fort station. (FSD 220)

♦ Seaside people seemed to spend their whole life going from christening to wedding to dhana, and work was the

last thing on their minds. Ayoub lived on the Seaside, and my father never quite approved. (CP 137-8)

seated
sitting ° *He's seated over there.* → In BSE 'seated' is more formal, e.g.: 'Please remain seated'.

♦ She was seated in front of her mirror while Kanthi Aunty arranged jasmines in her hair. (FB 98)

♦ It was late evening, and we were seated on the steps of the back porch, watching Vijay play with a stray kitten. (WMD 208)

♦ Balendran and Sonia were seated in the drawing room, listening to the gramophone when he walked in. (CG 363)

♦ Kamala was seated on a sofa. (REP 353)

♦ They were seated in the open rear verandah of their home at Clifford Place. (FSD 23)

♦ Kumudu is seated in his cubicle studying a sheet of paper. (GC 132)

♦ I had been seated next to her for the last twenty minutes. (M&P 240)

♦ The truck is packed with pilgrims seated on the mats. (PMS 242)

Sea Tigers
the naval wing of the LTTE

see
look, watch, look at ° *See this!*

♦ "Boy for sure. See, will you, how the stomach is so low." (JFT 152)

♦ "Janakiii! See what that boy did," ... (FB 36)

♦ "See the sacrifices we are making for you." (YY 112)

♦ "Entrance fee is ten rupees and see the prizes." (TT 172)

♦ "Look, child, ... Went away looking like two sprats and now see - proper young men." (July 47)

□ **to see ...**
(only) to find/discover that ... ° *We arrived by 9.00 - to see the meeting had already finished!* ° *I came home to see the driver had taken off!* ° *One time there was a bit of a hullabaloo outside. To see, thaththi was having an argument with the old lady next door.*

seem: it seems
apparently, they say, he said, I heard, etc. (a common way of passing on reported information) ° *It seems he won't be playing after all.* ° *They've already eaten it seems.* ° *Aruni called today. Can't come to the party it seems.* ° *Doesn't want to go to school it seems.* → In BSE, 'it seems' is normally restricted to more formal contexts, and/or used to suggest something in an indirect way. In SLE it is very common in colloquial contexts, is often used to quote direct speech, and commonly comes at the end of the sentence.

♦ "Japanese going to bomb Colombo, it seems ..." (JFT 193)

♦ "Some friend of Bunty, it seems." (YY 209)

♦ "She cried, it seems ..." (TT 230)

♦ "It seems they are now going down streets into Tamil houses, killing people and burning cars!" (July 344)

♦ "They have assaulted and broken the limbs of some of our fellows, about twenty-five in Peradeniya are in hospital, it seems." (OD 25)

♦ "What to do? A job has been brought forward, it seems." (CU 47)

seeni kehel
/sīni kehel/ (= **sugar plantain**) a small yellow variety of banana (Sinhala) (> **plantain**)

seeni sambol
/sīni sæmbol/ a **sambol** made with onions fried with **chilli powder** and other spices, and a little sugar (Sinhala/Tamil: seeni = sugar) (> **sambol, lamprai**)

♦ ... a bottle of *seeni-sambol* (a hot relish of onions, Maldive fish, chillie, garlic and tamarind, fried and sweetened to taste), ... (JFT 136)

♦ He ate it with a *seeni-sambol* that burned the roof of your mouth. (Reef 18)

♦ ... a crackling seeni-sambol ... (YY 102)

♦ His wife slipped in a minute later with a parcel of *string-hoppers* and *seeni-sambol* she had made for 'the boy's journey'. (WMD 241)

♦ In the kitchen, the huge pans of seeni sambol, chicken curry and devilled beef sat on the stove. (July 210)

♦ Within minutes we were seated comfortably in a circle eating seeni sambol sandwiches and boiled eggs. (GC 145)

seer, seerfish
(= **thora**) a popular type of fish with white flesh (Spanish mackerel)

♦ The head and shoulders of seer arrived in Italian sauce, ... (JFT 61)

♦ "... fish: grilled seer in a white sauce; ..." (CG 65)

♦ ... a seer fish curry of which he might eat his fill. (HC 139)

♦ "Evidently, he's only eating fish these days. Seer fish, at that." (SMS 141)

seetu

/sīttu/ (= cheetu) a rotating loan scheme popular with low-income women (Tamil/Sinhala)

seeya, siya

/sīya/ grandfather (Sinhala) (> aachchi)

- "You can't do that, *seeya*, ... Go on, *seeya*, keep it please." (WMD 241)

- "Are you also happy, *Siya*?" (SG 205)

- ... for Siya and Achi lived in the upstairs part of our house while we were in the downstairs part. (M&P 36)

select: to be selected

to pass the selection procedure, e.g. for university admission ° *She was selected to the Colombo campus.*

sema

/semə/ (coll.) phlegm (Sinhala)

sepalika

/sēpālika/ a type of tree with fragrant white flowers (Sinhala)

- "Do you know what sepalika is? ... It's the name of a flower. A small white flower like a star, with a bright orange stem. Some people call it Queen of the Night. It has the most beautiful smell at night. People say that if you have a sepalika tree in your garden, you are fortunate, blessed by the gods." (July 152)

sera

/sērə/ lemon grass (Sinhala/Tamil)

serpent

snake (less common in BSE)

servant

(= domestic) (less common in BSE)
→ 'Servant' is a very common word in SLE, without the taboo of political incorrectness which it carries in modern BSE.

- From the time I was small Sinhala was spoken in our home only with the servants. (OD 107)

- The servants' laughter echoed across the house. (M&P 203)

□ **servant boy**

(= boy, houseboy, kolla) a young male servant

- The servant boy seemed to recognize Amma's voice, for he opened the gate promptly. (FB 123)

- ... and I would sit perched on the embankment by the cactus bushes with Guneris the servant boy and watch the trains come and go in the station down below, ... (BTH 33)

- Then he gave notice to the lot of them and employed a cook servant-boy, a round-chinned youth named Ranil from a village near Lokugama. (HC 252)

□ **servant girl**

a young female servant

- ... that her aunt had been safely deposited in the verandah with a newspaper and the servant girl, ... (WMD 156)

- ... and I was wondering why Prema the servant girl was not sweeping the room ... (BTH 51)

- Mr and Mrs Perera couldn't come because they had just fired their servant girl ... (July 21)

- I remember the commotion when a servant-girl threw herself down the kitchen well; ... (HC 16)

- Karunawathie the servant girl came in with smoking incense in an iron pan ... (M&P 24)

□ servants' quarters

a room or rooms in a private house where **servants** are provided accommodation

♦ Beyond the servants' quarters, on the far side of the wall that marked the rear boundary of the compound, loomed the jungle. (HC 14)

♦ … and the door between the servants' quarters and the masters' quarters was padlocked … (M&P 203)

□ servant woman

an older female **servant**

♦ There was no answer but Chandrani the servant woman heard me and came to the stairs. (MM 131)

♦ The bearer, Somawathi, has been in my employment as a servant woman for sixteen years. (HC 218)

♦ … she probably had a good laugh behind my back with the other servant-women of the seaside. (CP 149)

♦ "Princes don't creep under tables to sleep with servant women." (M&P 214)

serve

take, help yourself (to something) ° *Serve some more rice!* → In BSE, you 'serve' someone else, or you 'serve yourself'.

♦ "Ah, really?" said Thathi serving rice onto his plate, … (M&P 320)

settee back

the flower arrangement which forms the backdrop at the back of the settee where the bridal couple sit during a wedding

settle down

settle ° *They've settled down in Sydney.* → In BSE, to 'settle down' means to become calm, or to adopt a quieter way of life, e.g.

by getting married; to 'settle' somewhere is to make your home in a new place.

set-up

music system, hi-fi ° *I just got a new set-up.*

sevala

/sevələ/ (coll.) (of men) seedy, slimy, sleazy; noun: **sevalaya** (Sinhala) ° *a sevala fellow* ° *Watch out for that sevalaya!*

seven sisters

(= **babblers**) small grey thrush-like birds which are often seen in noisy groups of around seven birds (> **demalichchas**)

SEVEN SISTERS

sha!

/sha, shā/ wow! (Sinhala exclamation)

♦ "How the cake? Sha! Looks good, no?" (JFT 185)

♦ "*Sha*! Excellent packing. How you got it all in, *men*!" (Reef 64)

♦ "Sha! Must have another drink." (YY 182)

♦ "Sha, must be pukka, no?" (TT 83)

♦ … "sha! nice slacks", … (July 54)

♦ "Shah! Living so close by - to think we didn't know." (WE 93)

shall I ...?

can I ...? may I ...? ° *Shall I use your phone?* → In BSE, 'Shall I ...?' is used to offer to do something for someone else, while in SLE it is also used to ask permission to do something.

shall we?

shall we go? let's go!

shalwar kameez

/shalvar kamīz/ (= **Punjabi kit**) an outfit
worn by women (esp. Muslims) consisting
of loose trousers (**shalwar**), a long shirt
(**kameez**), and a shawl; the whole outfit is
also called '**shalwar**' or '**salvar**' (also India,
Pakistan, orig. Urdu) ° *Sale of sarees and
shalwars*

SHALWAR KAMEEZ

♦ He saw that she was wearing her
   dangly pearl earrings and her neatly
   pressed red shalwar kameez. (Z 31)

♦ She looked calm and collected and was
   wearing her red shalwar once again.
   (Z 37)

♦ She would fantasize outfits, dresses,
   saris, blouses and shalwar kameezes.
   (Z 131)

♦ I noticed she had found a shalwar
   kameez for herself. (REP 58)

♦ Her flimsy shalwar, now ripped in
   several places, and wet to the bargain,
   was too revealing for her to be
   comfortable in the light of the fire.
   (REP 147)

♦ ... "keep the *salwars* at your mothers!"
   (WE 103)

♦ Fazlia wears shalwars to work and
   covers her head with a scarf; ...
   (GC 239)

shape

/shēp/ (coll.) (vt) arrange something,
organize something, sort something out,
settle something, smooth things over,
butter somebody up, win somebody over,
get out of an awkward situation (from the
colloquial Sinhala use of the English word
'shape') ° *Don't worry, I'll speak to his father
and shape it.* ° *Did you manage to shape
the boss?* ° *Referee blamed for 'shaping' All
Blacks rugby captain*

shed (1)

a temporary corrugated iron shelter erected
for parties, etc. → In BSE a 'shed' is a small
but permanent wooden structure, often
used for storage space in a garden.

♦ Ajith dashes to the living room
   and tells his colleagues about what
   is happening in the shed outside.
   (WCS 36)

♦ No sooner is a death reported, than
   these lads come to the house of the
   bereaved and offer their services to put
   up sheds, arrange chairs, hang white
   flags and plaster every fence post and
   wall with printed posters. (PMS 157-8)

shed (2)

(= **petrol shed**) ° *Around 30 shell casings
were found strewn about the shed.*
° *Petroleum Resources Minister A.H.M.
Fowzie confirmed that 100 sheds owned by
the government would be transferred to the
private company.*

♦ Sumith topped off the Passat's tank at
   the shed while he waited for Bandara.
   (CU 196)

shell: to shell somebody, to give somebody a shelling

(= **scold**) ° *She gave me a good shelling.*

♦ She started her chores and gave Banda a shelling because he had not washed the grinding stone the previous night. (July 334)

sherbet

a sweet drink made with rosewater (also India, orig. Arabic) → In BSE, 'sherbet' is a type of powder used in sweets or (dated) to make a sweet fizzy drink.

♦ Ten days earlier he had drunk a glass of sherbert and contracted typhoid. (HC 198)

♦ ... the sherbet cart with four wobbling wheels and an array of red and green and yellow and pink bottles around the crest of the cart. (KCS 32)

sherwani

/shɑrvāni/ a formal knee-length tunic worn by men (also India, orig. Hindi)

♦ He was an imposing and handsome figure in his cream cotton sherwani and matching turban, with the holy ash and the sandalwood potu on his brow. (CG 28)

shift

(vi) move house ° *When are you shifting?* ° *They're shifting house next week.*

♦ "Get two bullock carts and shift in no time." (JFT 194)

♦ ... and Mahadangahawatte Lane was turned on its side by the shifting of the von Blosses. (YY 132)

♦ "We will be shifting to Wellawatte, right?" (TT 33)

♦ ... the paddy field bordering the land where we lived after shifting from the big house. (BTH 19)

♦ It was planned that Ammi, Achi, Nenda and the servants were going to tell Thathi that the lorry drivers shifting our belongings had stolen the newspapers. (M&P 94)

♦ Three days before shifting houses no one comes on a social visit, since all the teacups are packed. (M&P 96)

shit!

(a common expletive in SLE, used in the same way as **chi!**, but considered stronger in BSE)

shitcart

(coll., dated) a cart used by **latrine coolies**

♦ Violently separated from his bicycle, he found himself astride the shitcart, which sobered him up in a trice. (JFT 30)

shock

(n/v) surprise ° *I got a shock when I saw her!* → In BSE, a 'shock' suggests a stronger sense of astonishment or disgust.

shoe cut

a cut or blister on the foot caused by a shoe

shoe flower

hibiscus

♦ ... or the hum of a hummingbird sucking nectar from a pink shoe-flower? (Reef 106)

♦ "You have to give me tips because poor Emma hasn't had as much as a shoe flower from me." (MiP 426-7)

♦ For days it flew back and forth from the shoeflower tree that grew by the verandah, ... (HC 162)

♦ To my left was a garden of Shoe-flowers and Crotons. (M&P 44)

Shona Tamil

the Tamil dialect spoken by the Muslim community

shopping bag

(= **sili sili bag, siri siri bag**) → In BSE, a 'shopping bag' is usually a more substantial bag which is reused many times; in SLE it is a lightweight disposable polythene bag.

short eats

savoury snacks, e.g. buns, **patties, pastries, vadais, cutlets, Chinese rolls**, etc.

- ... it was full of people bunched around tables crowded with glasses and bottles and short-eats, talking and drinking like a convention of alcoholics. (WMD 260-1)

- Amrith and the girls usually ordered a selection of cakes and short-eats, which were brought to them on tiered serving plates. (SMS 103)

short leave

a few hours of leave taken on a working day for a specific purpose

- "How did you get out of the office at this time?" ... "I got short leave," ... (July 289)

shot

(= **cut**) slap, hit ° *He gave me a shot on the face.*

- "What you did was fine, Ralahamy ... you should have given him a couple of shots too," ... (OD 12)

□ to put a shot

(coll.) to have a shot (e.g. of **arrack**) (> **put**)

- By evening he would decide that it would be nice to 'put a small shot' and in order to do so, needed company. (JFT 178)

- "What, men, both of us put a shot just now, no?" (YY 32)

- "Put two shots at that Vihara Lane joint." (TT 211)

- So they 'put a few shots', as Ed called it, and talked about everything from politics to parenting. (July 45)

- "Couldn't you wait until after the job to put a shot?" (CU 155)

show

/shō/ (= **film show; musical show**) film, movie; live concert → In BSE a 'show' usually refers to a play (esp. a musical) or a TV programme.

showcase

a glass-fronted cabinet, used for displaying crockery, ornaments, knick-knacks, etc. → In BSE a 'showcase' is found in a shop or museum; in SLE the same word is used to describe a cabinet in a private house.

showman

(= **zipper man**) (coll.) flasher, exhibitionist, a man who exposes himself in public → In BSE a 'showman' is a performer or entertainer.

shramadana

/shrəmədānə/ a voluntary community activity where a group of people get together to do a piece of work without being paid (e.g. clearing a piece of land, painting a school, etc.) (Sinhala)

- ... they were making plans for a shramadana at an old folks' home, which would involve cleaning, gardening, painting, and entertaining the residents. (SMS 35)

shrewd

(= **kapati**) crafty, cunning, scheming ° *He's a shrewd fellow!* → In BSE, 'shrewd' is less common, and with a more positive connotation ('a shrewd investment').

- "The mother and the daughter, they were shrewd creatures. They fed some charmed food to old Mrs. Wijedasa

and got her last will changed."
(M&P 15)

shroff
cashier (Anglo-Indian, from Persian 'saraf'
= banker, money-changer)

shutter
car window ° *Close the shutters and I'll put
on the a/c.*

♦ The man in the passenger seat rolled
down his shutter and looked at me
carefully. (REP 353)

♦ Dr. Gunapala has rolled down a
shutter and is speaking with one of the
security officers. ... I see the shutter
roll up and the car begin to move
towards us. (GC 136)

shuttler
(in newspaper headlines) badminton player;
also **shuttle** (badminton) (> **cager**) ° *UK
shuttlers arrive in Colombo* ° *a shuttle
tourney* ° *under-12 shuttle champs*

shy (1)
(n) try, attempt, shot (rare in BSE) ° *Have
another shy!* ° *She passed all the papers on
the first shy.*

shy (2)
(adj.) embarrassed ° *I feel shy to come.* → In
BSE, 'shy' is a permanent characteristic of
certain people, while 'embarrassed' is the
way people feel in certain situations.

Siddhalepa
/siddālēpə/ a popular **ayurvedic** ointment
used for muscular pains, etc. (Sinhala brand
name)

♦ He added two little vials of Siddhalepa,
a herbal balm and a box of mosquito
coils. (FSD 74)

side
area ° *They're from Negombo side.*

♦ "Why doesn't he come this side so
much now?" (Reef 120)

sight
(v) see (a person) ° *He hasn't been sighted
recently.* → In BSE, 'sight' is less common
as a verb, and normally restricted to the
sense of 'catching sight of something', e.g.
to 'sight land' from a boat.

signboard
(= **nameboard**) sign, notice, signpost (e.g.
on a shop or office) (less common in BSE)

♦ ... a Proctor S.C. & Notary Public (as
his signboard proudly proclaimed).
(WMD 123)

♦ A prominent new signboard carried
the Tiger emblem and some Tamil
lettering. (REP 43)

♦ The signboard pointed right for
Gampola and left for Nawalapitiya.
(FSD 144)

♦ The signboard sits by the street and the
chicken stall. (KCS 67)

sil
/sil/ the Buddhist precepts; a religious vow
taken as a form of self-discipline (Sinhala)
(> **pansil, atasil, dasasil**)

□ to observe sil
to follow the Buddhist precepts, e.g. as a
form of religious vow on **poya days** ° *We
had to observe sil every poya day.*

♦ Then I thought I would rest a few days,
even visiting the temple to observe sil,
... (KCS 93)

♦ ... we paid respect to our great teacher
on Poya days and observed Sil. During
Sil, one wore white and ate a vegetarian
meal before noon. Sat on the ground
and meditated ... No dinner was
permitted. This was classical Sil. I never
observed Sil. (M&P 83)

silent

quiet ° *a silent person* → Describing someone as 'silent' is more positive in SLE than in BSE.

sili sili bag, siri siri bag

/silisili, sirisiri/ (= **shopping bag**) a lightweight disposable polythene bag (from Sinhala) ° *Health group urges ban on sili sili bags*

- She has filled a siri-siri bag full of temple flowers and there is a faint flush to her cheeks. (CP 67)

- My father was laden with plastic 'siri siri' bags full of imported apples, imported grapes, imported carrots and even imported onions. ... Achi folded the siri siri bags and preserved them under her mattress. (M&P 253)

- The cyclist took a revolver from a 'siri siri' bag and shot the policeman. (M&P 260)

- "... the roadside is full of siri-siri bags and plastic bottles, ..." (M&P 275)

simple (1)

(= **innocent**) good, modest, unassuming → In BSE, 'simple' suggests naïve, unsophisticated, unintelligent; in SLE it does not carry this negative implication.

simple (2)

(of letters) small, lower case (opp. capital)

simple pass

(in an exam) an ordinary pass (not a credit or distinction)

sin!

(often used as an exclamation) what a pity! what a shame! poor thing! (> **ane!**) ° *Damn sin!* ° *Sin for him!* ° *Sin anney!*

- "Sin, no, to marry a girl this age." (JFT 11)

- "Look, will you, ... sleeping like a baby. And hardly touched any food. Sin, men." (JFT 190)

- "Sin, *anney*, looking like a scared black rabbit." (YY 45)

- "Sin for her." (YY 179)

- "And next door also they're coming to the fence and saying sin for your father and shame for the children ..." (TT 230)

- "*Aney*, it is a sin - his back is bleeding," ... (WE 80)

- "Sin, men, ... leave Amrith alone." (SMS 32)

Sindhi

/sindi/ a member of a small Hindu community from the Province of Sindh in Pakistan

- "The green stripe to the left represents the Muslims and other minorities such as Burghers, Malays, Chinese, Boras and Sindhis, the orange stripe, the Tamils." (M&P 105)

Singlish

a derogatory or humorous term for the mixing of Sinhala and English which is a common feature of **Sri Lankan English** → 'Singlish' is also used in Singapore to refer to Singaporean English.

Sinhala, Sinhalese

/singhala, singhaliz/ (n/adj.) the people and language of the majority community in Sri Lanka, of Aryan/North Indian origin (mainly Buddhist) ° *the Sinhala kings* ° *SWRD Bandaranaike's 'Sinhala only' policy* ° *a Sinhala-speaking family* ° *He's trying to learn Sinhala.* ° *She's a Sinhalese.* → 'Sinhala' is the Sinhala word for the English 'Sinhalese' (formerly 'Singhalese'). Recently it has become common practice to use the word 'Sinhala' even in English, especially to refer to the language, but also as an adjective referring to the people and their culture, while 'Sinhalese' is often used as a noun to refer to a person.

♦ I was in a Sinhala class at school and my friends were Sinhalese. (FB 59)

♦ "Would you allow your child to marry a Sinhalese?" (FB 68)

♦ Grumpy was an extremely fussy Sinhalese, tall and white-haired. (YY 74)

♦ "Now they have made Sinhala the official language ... Children must do all the subjects in Sinhala. Hell of a joke, no? ... Who is talking Sinhala in our homes? ... Good for the Sinhalese only. Their children go home and talk in Sinhala. What about our children? Not right, no? ... These buggers are bloody hypocrites, men. Saying Sinhala only and getting our children to study in Sinhala but they are sending their children to England and America to study!" (YY 228)

♦ At that time many Sinhalese were members of this Circle. (OD 93)

♦ That was why I started getting interested in Sinhala literature and Sinhala novels. (OD 101)

♦ The Tamils will learn their Tamil, the Sinhalese their Sinhala; ... (HC 32)

♦ "You must put away anything that can identify you as an army officer or even as a Sinhalese," ... (REP 23)

♦ "You say the Sinhala attacked your family, ... But it wasn't the Sinhala nation was it?" (REP 270)

♦ JR's new prime minister was on a fanatical quest to resurrect Sinhala theatre and Sinhala culture. (M&P 272)

♦ "Those days we said that it was the 'Sinhala only' call that had agitated the masses." (M&P 345)

☐ **Sinhala beheth**
/singhələ behet/ **ayurvedic** medicine (opp. Western medicine) (Sinhala)

☐ **Sinhala New Year, Sinhala and Tamil New Year**
(= **New Year, avurudu**) the Sri Lankan **New Year** festival in mid-April ° *April 13th (Day Prior to Sinhala and Tamil New Year)*

♦ Preparations for the celebrations of the Sinhala New Year in April began months ahead. (CM 60)

♦ They had gone to their villages for the Sinhala and Tamil New Year. (CG 246)

♦ "I don't think that he stays at home more than a day or two even when he comes home for the Sinhala New Year." (OD 54)

♦ Today was the last day of school for Daniel, the end of term before the long April holidays and the Sinhala and Tamil New Year. (CU 298)

☐ **Sinhala sweets**
(= **kavili**) traditional sweets prepared for festive occasions such as **Sinhala New Year**, e.g. **kavum, kokis**, etc.

☐ **Sinhala ulu**
/singhələ ulu/ traditional style roof tiles (Sinhala)

SINHALA ULU

♦ ... Errol was thankful that the tiles underfoot were of the flat European style; the traditional *Sinhala ulu,*

242

shaped like half-cylinders, would have been impossible to move across silently. (CU 477)

sinnadorai

/sinnədore/ (= SD) assistant **superintendent** of an estate (Tamil) (> **periyadorai**)

♦ They fancied the idea of being *Sinna-dorais* - little masters - with the British estate superintendent as the *Periya-dorai*, or the Big Master. (YY 52)

sir

male teacher (term of respect, dated in BSE) (> **madam, miss**) ° *Sir scolded us today!*

sirra

(coll.) serious; cool

♦ "Something sirra is up, ... The OC is here." (CU 80)

sit!

(coll.) sit down! take a seat! (> **come!**) → In BSE, 'Sit!' is usually said only to a dog!

♦ "Mister Colontota? Sit, men, sit. So you got my letter, no?" (JFT 34)

♦ "Sit, sit. Triton will bring some tea." (Reef 138)

♦ "Come, come, sit, sit." (FB 107)

situ

(coll.) situation

♦ "I better get over to HQ and see what we can find out about the situ." (CU 379)

siura

/siurə/ the saffron-coloured robe of a Buddhist monk (Sinhala) ° *respect for the siura*

six: to go for a six

(coll.) to go for six ° *All our plans went for a six.*

sixer

(in cricket) a six, six runs (rare in BSE)

♦ ... the element of tragedy that emanated from his soul when the batsman scored a 'sixer'. (M&P 280)

six-footer

a person who is six feet tall (less common in BSE)

siyambala

/siyəmbələ/ tamarind (Sinhala)

skinny

(n) a sleeveless T-shirt or vest ° *Members are requested to refrain from wearing rubber slippers, shorts and skinnies in the clubhouse after 7 pm.*

♦ Blue denim bell bottoms. A red skinny, blue denim platform shoes. (M&P 233)

skyrocket

(v) (of prices, etc.) rocket, increase rapidly (less common in BSE) ° *the skyrocketing COL*

♦ ... the supposed population of fifteen million people that had sky rocketed to perhaps seventeen million ... (M&P 184)

SLFPer

a member of the Sri Lanka Freedom Party

slicer

(in newspaper headlines) **carrom** player (> **cager**) ° *Lankan slicers to tour India*

slippers

sandals, flip-flops (> **rubber slippers, Bata slippers, bathroom slippers**) → In BSE, 'slippers' (or 'bedroom slippers') are loose shoes which are only worn inside the house; they are often made of a material designed to keep the feet warm. In SLE, 'slippers' are common everyday footwear; they are either made of leather (BSE 'sandals') or rubber (BSE 'flip-flops').

♦ Soon the heat of the rocks became unbearable and I stood up, removed my slippers, and went down the beach to the edge of the water. (FB 38)

♦ He dragged cracked leather slippers on his feet ... (TT 139)

♦ That Saturday morning I saw the umbrellas leaning tiredly against the front door and the fat clumsy slippers on the door mat as I went in. (OM 23)

♦ On her feet were a pair of men's slippers. (CG 293)

♦ She had an attitude about her and one of her slippers dangled from her feet in a don't-care manner. (Z 27)

♦ His eyes alighted on his mother's slippers, the indent of her heel and the ball of her foot plainly visible in the worn rubber. (HC 239)

♦ I saw it then, a black slipper with a loose rubber strap. (REP 136)

♦ They also make us reverse the slippers on our feet. (GC 26)

♦ The Kumarihamy gave up and led them into the house, leaving her slippers ostentatiously on the verandah and walking in barefoot. (CP 100)

♦ Even the man who used to look after the slippers at the temple on poya days was there. (M&P 337)

slowly
/slōli/ (= quietly) later, in your own time, at your leisure; tactfully, discreetly, unobtrusively ° *Finish it slowly.* ° *Tell it to him slowly or he'll get upset.*

♦ "Apo, ... saying he does not eat, he must be slowly buying chocolates and eating, ..." (M&P 261)

slowly slowly
gradually

♦ "It's not as if we are lucky enough to have brothers and might be introduced to a friend of theirs and then slowly-slowly fall in love." (CG 88)

♦ At first they hid in the jungle and then slowly, slowly made their way towards Colombo. (Z 34)

small finger, small toe
little finger, little toe

small made
lightly built (> **big made**) ° *a small made fellow*

small small
(coll.) small (usually with plural nouns) (> **big big**) ° *I am having lot of small small problems.* ° *living in small small houses*

smart (1)
(adj.) (of men) attractive, handsome, good-looking ° *He's a smart boy.* → In BSE, 'smart' means either well-dressed, or intelligent.

smart (2)
(v) burn, sting (less common in BSE) ° *My eyes are smarting.*

smash
crush, squash, mash ° *The bus was packed and I got completely smashed.* ° *Smash the ingredients with the back of a spoon.* → In BSE, to 'smash' something is to break it into pieces.

smile: to smile with somebody
to smile at somebody ° *She was so proud she didn't even smile with me.*

♦ Somaweera couldn't understand whether the girl tried to smile with him. (OD 34)

♦ And he frequently smiled with the young nurses. (KCS 167)

♦ A few girls tried to make an odd attempt to smile with me, but I pretended to be otherwise engaged. (M&P 44)

snake gourd
(= **pathola**) a long, thin, green variety of vegetable

♦ Patholay means snake-gourd. Sunil, with his long, hunched body and tiny head does look like that common vegetable. (PMS 16)

snap
photo ° *wedding snaps* → In BSE, 'snap' is a colloquial word suggesting a photo taken casually (e.g. 'holiday snaps'); in SLE it is also used in more formal contexts.

so (1)
(coll.) well, then, well then (a common way of starting a conversation) (> **so so**) ° *So how?* ° *So? Tell will you!*

so (2)
(coll.) (word order) (> **but**) ° *Are you coming so?* → In colloquial SLE, 'but' and 'so' can sometimes come at the end of the sentence; this will never happen in BSE.

soccerite
(in newspaper headlines) football player, soccer player (> **cager**)

social worker
any person who does charitable work (> **probation officer**) ° *She was a prominent social worker in the area.* → In BSE, a 'social worker' is a qualified professional working for the government or for a private organisation. The nearest Sri Lankan equivalent is a 'probation officer'.

socks : to play socks
(= **play hell, play pucks, play pandu, dance the devil**) (coll.) to mess around, make trouble, play the fool

♦ ... playing socks, merry hell, the dickens, the devil, etc. etc. (TT 224 footnote)

soft opening
the initial, informal opening (e.g. of a hotel), prior to the official 'grand opening' ° *... relaunched yesterday at a soft opening.*

sokkottan
/sokkoʈʈan/ a game played with dice (Tamil)

♦ There were times when the old lady would let me throw dice for her at *sokkottan* and then reward me with part of her winnings. (WMD 126)

so many
(coll.) lots of, a lot of ° *We're having so many problems.*

sometimes
(coll.) maybe, perhaps ° *He said he can't come to the party, but sometimes he'll come if he can get a lift.* → This use of 'sometimes' is a common source of misunderstanding; 'sometimes' is the usual word for 'perhaps' in SLE, but it is never used in this sense in BSE.

so much of
(coll.) so much (> **how much of**) ° *They must be having so much of money.* ° *Don't know when we had so much of rain.*

♦ They had so much of money, whereas he had none. (Z 66-7)

soon
(coll.) quickly, immediately; (as an exclamation) hurry up! ° *Come soon!* → In BSE 'soon' means 'in a short time from

now', but it doesn't necessarily suggest 'quickly'.

♦ "Menik! Come here. Soon!" (FB 66)

♦ "Get down soon." (M&P 147)

soon as
as soon as ° *Soon as I saw her I knew something was wrong.*

sore eyes
/sō aiz/ conjunctivitis → Pronunciation: In BSE 'sore eyes' would be pronounced with a 'linking r' and the stress on the second word: /sōr'aiz/. In SLE it tends to be pronounced without the 'linking r', and with the stress on the first word: /'sō aiz/.

so so
/so so/ (coll.) well, then, well then (> **so**)

♦ "So, so, what happened?" (CG 288)

♦ "So? So? What's our clever reporter up to these days?" (GC 227)

♦ "So-so, Selvi, have you heard of Mala's latest ambition?" (SMS 32)

♦ "So, so tell …" (M&P 237)

sottaya
/sottaya/ (= **penda**) (coll.) wimp (Sinhala)

sour plantain
(= **ambul**) a small yellow variety of banana (the most common and most popular variety) (> **plantain**)

soursop
(= **katu aatha, katu anoda**) a large fruit with thick green skin and soft sweet white flesh (> **custard apple**)

SOURSOP

SP
Superintendent of Police

♦ The SP and Somaweera travelled in silence and spoke only when they got down from the vehicle. (OD 51)

specko
(coll.) a person who wears glasses

specs
glasses → A common abbreviation in SLE, but restricted to informal, colloquial contexts in BSE.

♦ "So let me wear my specs and take a look at the child." (M&P 21)

spend: to spend for something
to pay for something, to spend on something ° *How much did you spend for your car?*

♦ "If I keep it I am sure it will be spent for something else, …" (OD 13)

♦ "He is the one who has spent for Nimal's education." (OD 141)

spend-the-day
(n) a day out at a friend or relation's house ° *Please come and join us for a spend the day.*

♦ Besides Christmas and other festive occasions, spend-the-days were the days most looked forward to by all of us, cousins, aunts, and uncles. For the adults a spend-the-day was the one Sunday of the month they were free of their progeny. (FB 1)

♦ "Get up, it's spend-the-day," … (FB 17)

♦ She had no children and welcomed the opportunity to 'spend the day', as she called it. (YY 3)

♦ Selvi, it seemed, had all sorts of plans for her holiday - various spend-the-days at friends' houses, day trips to a hotel that was owned by a friend's father, a carnival they wanted to attend. (SMS 38)

♦ "I've called your cousin and invited him to spend the day." (SMS 106)

♦ "Why don't you invite your friends to spend the day and we can go in the motor boat in the canal I just dredged." (M&P 272)

spiker
(in newspaper headlines) volleyball player (> cager)

sprats
(= halmassas) small fish (anchovies), usually dried and deep-fried → In BSE, a 'sprat' is a small fish like a herring.

♦ ... on Wednesday the fishmonger came balancing sprats and prawns in two baskets on a pole ... (Reef 27)

♦ ... and the hundred and one other things that went into it like sprats and prawns and shrimps and fish-heads, ... (WMD 141)

Sri Lankan English
the variety of English used in Sri Lanka; (coll., dated) a humorous term for broken English spoken by Sri Lankan learners of English (> Singlish, Ceylonism)

Sri Lankan omelette
an omelette with onions, chillies and karapincha

Sri Lankan time
(a humorous expression referring to the lack of punctuality seen as a national habit)

sri number
/shrī/ the number on a vehicle number plate, followed by the Sinhala letter 'sri', which shows the age of the vehicle (later replaced by a 'dash') ° *a one sri Morris Minor*

SRI NUMBER

♦ Somaweera peeped at the shining orange coloured car to see what Sri series it was. (OD 14)

SSP
Senior Superintendent of Police

staff
(with singular verb) ° *Staff is upset about the decision.* → In BSE, there are a number of singular collective nouns which tend to be used with plural verbs (e.g. police); these can also be used with singular verbs in SLE.

star class hotel
a hotel with several stars, e.g. a five-star hotel

♦ His immediate boss invited Samare for his home-coming at a star class hotel. (WCS 61)

stay (at)
/stē/ live (in) ° *Where do you stay?* ° *They're staying at Wellawatte.* → In BSE, to 'stay' somewhere - especially in the continuous (-ing) form - suggests being there temporarily, usually as a visitor or guest, while to 'live' somewhere - especially in the simple form - suggests having your permanent home there: 'Where do you live? - I live in Colombo'. 'Where are they staying? - They're staying with friends in Dublin'. However, in Scottish English, 'stay' can be used in the same way as in SLE.

♦ Now where the hell did he stay? Moratuwa - that's it. (FSD 221)

□ to stay without (doing) something

not to do something, not to have something, to go without something ° *He stayed without his lunch.*

- ♦ She stayed without speaking for a while, thinking it over. (FSD 282)
- ♦ "So during the evenings, never stay without mosquito coils, ..." (M&P 278)

sticker

(in newspaper headlines) hockey player (> **cager**) ° *UAE stickers on tour* ° *25 stickers picked for SA pool*

still

(word order) ° *Still we felt uneasy.* (BSE: We still felt uneasy.)

- ♦ I hadn't still finished my sugared bun and tea. (CM 36)

stilt fisherman

a fisherman who fishes close to the shore perched on a wooden 'stilt'

STILT FISHERMAN

stingify

(coll.) to be stingy (> **-fy**)

stir

(= **gori**) (n) trouble (usually violent), fight ° *There was a big stir at campus.*

□ stir case

a person who stirs up trouble

stiver

a coin from the colonial period (from Dutch)

stoop

(= **istoppuwa**) (dated) a small verandah at the front of a house (also US, from Dutch 'stoep')

- ♦ Uncle Para stopped pacing and sat on the cool of the cement stoop, leaning back against a pillar. (WMD 330)

strap-hanging

standing in a crowded bus and holding the straps hanging from the ceiling

- ♦ They pushed their way through the jam of passengers and strap-hung until Bambalapitiya, when two seats became vacant at the very front of the bus. (July 77-8)

stream

(in schools) a course of education in a particular language ° *He's studying in the Sinhala stream.*

- ♦ ... but, with the separation of the schools into Tamil and Sinhala streams, they had drifted away from her life and from Kurunegala. (WMD 306)

striker

(in **carrom**) the counter which is used to strike the other pieces (> **carrom**)

string hoppers, stringhoppers

(= **indiappa**) steamed **rice flour** noodles, a popular morning or evening meal; also referred to as **strings** ° *stringhopper buriyani* ° *stringhopper pilau*

STRINGHOPPERS

♦ ... judging the right temperature for a perfect string-hopper dough. (Reef 59)

♦ He saw my small pagoda of wicker steamers on the side counter ready for the strings. (Reef 60)

♦ I ignored him and began to help myself to some stringhoppers and curry. (FB 254)

♦ ... and a stringhopper* dinner. (* Steamed circlets of flour. The flour after steaming is pressed through a mould to drop in wriggly strands on the little basket-weave trays which are then re-steamed in batches until done. A favourite anytime meal in Sri Lanka.) (TT 101)

♦ After having his regular breakfast of reddish stringhoppers and fish curry on the terrace, ... (SG 106)

♦ I had promised myself a feast of crab claws that night; or stringhoppers and chicken curry; ... (HC 49)

♦ "We survived on garden produce ... and the few rupees my mother made, by getting up at four each morning, to make hoppers and string hoppers to sell to the eating-houses." (REP 103)

♦ "Stay and share our meal. We're having string hoppers." (FSD 97)

♦ We eat string hoppers with curried squid, sitting out there in the garden. (GC 231)

♦ The man behind the counter didn't look up, merely slapping down a newspaper and a breakfast packet of string hoppers before scooping up the proffered money. (CU 268-9)

♦ ... a creative genius who could build a radio with a string hopper mould and two hair pins ... (M&P 37)

studio
photographic shop → In BSE, a 'studio' is a place where a photographer works; in SLE it can be any place where photographs are developed, etc.

stupa
/stūpə/ (= dagoba, chaitya) a dome-shaped Buddhist shrine (Sinhala, also India, orig. Sanskrit)

♦ ... there is a buddha sitting lotus-position and a small white bell of a *stupa* with a brass spire. (MM 114)

♦ ... the 'sacred area' that bristled with ancient temples and stupas ... (YY 131)

♦ ... or the plain Buddhist temple down the road, its *stupa* a shrunken dome. (WMD 150)

sub-post office
a small post office

♦ ... and urged the villagers to petition the government for a sub-post office, though as yet to no avail. (WMD 142)

subsequently
then, next, after that (more formal in BSE) ° *Subsequently she was searched by the security guard.* → In BSE, 'subsequently' is rather formal in the sense of 'after that', and is more commonly used in the sense of 'consequently' or 'as a result': 'Subsequently, I have decided to resign'.

suddha
/sudda/ (coll.) a white man; female: **suddhi**, plural: **suddhas** (Sinhala) (> **kalusuddha**)

♦ "Not like our people, these *sudda** drivers." (* Sinhalese colloquialism for whiteskin or European. Comes from the word *sudu* - white.) (YY 97)

◆ ... his own reference to the Commissioners as *para suddhas* (bastard whites) ... (WMD 21-2)

◆ "And see what the *suddhas* have gone and done to the land." (WMD 38)

◆ The *suddas* came, they slummed, comfortable in their knowledge that they had an elsewhere to go to, and then they left. ... He liked this *suddi* it is true and would even have liked to marry her ... (Z 55)

◆ "And he takes children to the suddhas where?" (FSD 256)

◆ Agnes was very happy cooking for a *suddha*, a white man, and her cooking turned positively Michelin. (CP 113)

◆ "Easier for us Sri Lankans to work together than with these *suddha* buggers, no?" (CU 161)

◆ It had been bad enough several years ago, enduring the contemptuous stares of the haughty Sri Lankan lady sitting next to him on the flight to Saudi, but this *suddha* would be much worse. (CU 320)

suduru
/sūduru/ cumin (Sinhala) (> **maaduru**)

sugar
(coll.) high blood sugar, diabetes ° *He's having sugar.*

◆ Uncle Buddhi was diagnosed as having sugar. (M&P 261)

sugar plantain
(= **seeni kehel**) a small yellow variety of banana (with a sweet taste and a sticky texture) (> **plantain**)

suggest: to suggest somebody to do something
to suggest that somebody does something, to advise somebody to do something ° *I suggest you to come back tomorrow.*

sunbird
a small bird like a humming-bird

SUNBIRD

◆ He saw a beautiful sunbird drop ... (TT 114)

◆ I saw Sunbirds, Ioras and Bulbuls flitting from tree to tree. (REP 33)

◆ Tailor Birds, Drongos, Babblers, Bulbuls and my favourites, the lovely Sunbirds. (GC 51)

◆ "Our teacher is very pretty, isn't she? ... She looks like a sunbird." (PMS 50)

superintendent (supdt.)
(= **periyadorai, PD**) the manager of an estate

◆ My father was superintendent of a tea and rubber plantation ... (RF 144)

◆ "That was great, man, that was great. Can you imagine that white bugger's face, the superintendent's, when he was told he could not move hand or foot without consulting his coolie council?" (WMD 184)

◆ It centred on a bored Englishwoman named Cynthia Wilmot, who was married to the superintendent of a rubber plantation. (HC 264)

◆ Devendra didn't say anything
till he came to a board that read
"Superintendent's Bungalow".
(FSD 136)

supermarket
an indoor market with shops and stalls
° *Colpetty supermarket*

suraya
/surē/ a small cylindrical pendant
containing a lucky charm (Sinhala)

suriya
/sūriyə/ a type of tree with yellow flowers
(tulip tree); the flower was adopted as the
symbol of a protest campaign in the 1930s
(Sinhala)

◆ As a young man he had taken part in
the *suriya mal* campaign of the early
thirties and in the relief work the *suriya
mal* group had carried out in the rural
areas during the malaria epidemic.
(WMD 183)

◆ The most common of these was the
suriya tree, whose profuse blossoms
often formed a carpet of primrose
yellow on the pavements. (CG 10)

◆ The *suriya* trees had dropped yellow
blossoms on the pavements. (HC 211)

suruttu
/suruʈʈu/ cheroot, a cheap cigar (Tamil)

◆ "So that is why your women pluck tea
and work like dogs, while your men
smoke *suruttu* and waste away the
time?" (M&P 156)

swabasha
/swabāshə/ an indigenous language (Sinhala
or Tamil as opposed to English) (also India,
from Sanskrit) ° *Swabasha schools*

◆ It's just too complicated there - you
have caste, class, family, social status,
education, English speaking, Swabasha,

all these sticky tag markers that just
come and land on your head and won't
go away. (Z 69)

sweetmeats
traditional sweets prepared for festive
occasions (> **kavili, Sinhala sweets,
palaharam**) (archaic in BSE)

◆ The various types of sweetmeats were
arranged around the tray of *kiribath*.
There were *kevun, asme, athirasa, kokis*
and *aluwa* and also a luscious comb of
golden yellow bananas. (CM 65)

◆ Elisabeth came from the village and
made sweetmeats the whole night.
(M&P 175)

◆ The sweet smell of incense and sweetmeats offered to the gods circulated
in the air and entered my nostrils.
(M&P 362)

sworn translator
a translator with official government
authorisation

T

tabla

/tabla/ a pair of drums used in Indian and Sri Lankan music; a **tabla** player is called a **tablist** (also India, orig. Hindi/Urdu)

TABLA

- A tabla player began to beat a rhythm … the increasingly fast beat of the tabla, … The tabla reached a deafening climax … (FB 279-80)

- "Her mother plays the violin, and her brother the tabla." (CP 188)

tailorbird

a small bird which sews leaves together to make its nest

- … two azure flycatchers, a flowerpecker and a small, drab tailorbird. (TT 114)

- A tailor bird took hold of two leaves at the extremity of a slender twig and sewed them together at their edges, using a thread made of vegetable fibre and its bill for a needle. (HC 162)

- "Have you seen a Tailor-bird's nest?" (REP 271)

takaran

/takərang/ corrugated iron sheets (Sinhala) ° *a takaran roof*

- The *takarang* tank collapsed, the driveway flooded. (Reef 175)

- The high spiked gates were covered with sheets of takaran so no one could look in or out. (FB 55)

- His friends from the neighbourhood are to eat and drink separately in a "*takarang*" hut in the back garden made specially for the purpose. (WCS 32)

take: to take a call

/tēk/ to make a call ° *Do you mind if I take a call?*

□ to take a decision

to make a decision

□ to take something and go

to take something (away), take something with you (> **bring and come**) ° *Take the book and go.*

- "… now that it is finished I'll take and go but how to wear when it is not done properly …" (JFT 182)

□ to take up

to take, sit (for) (an exam) ° *She's taking up her A/L this year.*

□ to take something up (well/badly)

to take something (well/badly) ° *She took it up very well.*

□ taken up with/by something

interested in something, impressed by something, taken with something ° *I am highly taken up with his work.* → In BSE, to be 'taken with something' means to find it attractive or interesting, while to be 'taken up with something' means to be spending a lot of time on it.

- … and young ladies were quite taken up by his performances. (JFT 29)

♦ ... but he seemed to be quite taken up with the show. (TT 46)

♦ Carloboy was greatly taken up with this oddball uncle ... (TT 63)

♦ He had been very taken up with the way Marlene sat. (TT 170)

talk: what are you talking?

what are you talking about?

♦ "Not ruffians, *men*. What are you talking." (Reef 161)

♦ "What are you talking? Of course she was much, much fairer." (M&P 26)

tamasha

/tamāsha/ a public function or show; the word suggests unnecessary expense and ostentation (Anglo-Indian; Urdu = entertainment) ° *Mr Wijetunga did not want any birthday tamashas, but spent the day engrossed in his usual work.* ° *A tamasha to celebrate the military victory in Thoppigala tomorrow is the talk of the town.*

♦ "... the Muslims get married in this particular way not for love of multiculturalism but for love of expenditure, tamasha and pomp and ceremony." (Z 14)

♦ "Why· can't they elope? ... and save all of us the bother of attending these tamashas." (Z 16)

Tamil

/tæmil/ (n/adj.) the people and language of the largest minority community in Sri Lanka, of Dravidian/South Indian origin (mainly Hindu) ° *Jaffna Tamils* ° *upcountry Tamils* ° *studying in Tamil medium*

♦ He took his friends home to the chummery to give them 'a taste of good Tamil cooking' or a lesson in vegetable gardening. (WMD 21)

♦ "... they thought Lali was a Tamil because she had put a *pottu* on her forehead." (WMD 221)

♦ "Miss is from Jaffna?" he asked, indicating the potu on her forehead and the way she wore her sari, in the Tamil style with the palu wrapped around her· waist. (CG 100)

♦ "Seelan," he said in Tamil. "This is your parti." He turned back to his mother. "Amma, this is Arul's son." (CG 342)

♦ Some Tamils migrated too, but most stayed on. (July 40)

♦ It's true that if Velu had been arrested for the murder, the official line on up-country Tamils would have hardened. (HC 292)

♦ The heart of the Tamil homeland in the North remained a Palmyrah tree bearing barren land. (M&P 307)

♦ "Read the newspaper everyday, study well and don't forget the Tamil classes." (M&P 327)

tammattama

/tammætTama/ a traditional drum, a double kettledrum played with two sticks (Sinhala; Tamil thambattam)

TAMMATTAMA

tank

(= **kulam, wewa**) an artificial lake or reservoir (Anglo-Indian, from Portuguese; also used in Australia)

- "The kings who built the great tanks maybe were remembering that cleansing flood, just as we do." - "The tanks?" - "You know our tanks? The great reservoirs? Inland seas, really. That is why we say *muhuda*." (Reef 94)

- Since rice had to be grown in the hot scrub land, huge artificial reservoirs (called tanks) were also built. (YY 129)

- ... the tank country where the large man-made irrigation reservoirs (tanks) lay breathless in the sun, and the marsh country. (TT 113)

- There was only a parched land before us, stretching towards the ruins of tanks and temples in the distance. (WMD 137)

- ... the boys were going to show me the Boralesgamuwa Tank, and that was going to be the first time I would see a tank. (BTH 37)

- It was my King that built a tank that is like the sea, which contains a perpetual supply of water to nourish the fields. (Z 157)

- The frogs were in mid season form, croaking in chorus from all parts of the tank. (REP 189)

- Why should the government in Colombo care about what happens to an obscure village tank? (GC 93)

- "Though not as spectacular as the tanks built by the ancient Sinhalese kings to irrigate the dry zone." (CU 73)

- Recent rains have filled the tank and most of the weeds are submerged. (PMS 57)

tank fish

fish caught in a **tank** (i.e. fresh-water fish, opp. sea-fish)

- Velaithan had saved the balance of our dinner but I could not face another meal of rubbery roti and tank fish. (REP 66)

tap

(v) extract rubber, **toddy**, etc. from a tree

- ... two men with villainous faces and wicked toddy tapping knives ... (YY 66)

- ... crippled by a fall from a palmyrah tree (the story was that he drank the toddy even as he tapped the tree, ...) (WMD 9)

- The house now faced a plot of rubber where each morning Sirisena's mother tapped the trees, ... (BTH 42)

- ... the art of toddy-tapping - the high-wire collection of the palm-flower juice for fermenting into arrack. (SG 109)

- "The man who climbs coconut trees and taps toddy?" (July 140)

- In those days Amare wore a sarong and torn banian and often cut school to help his ailing father tap rubber trees and gather milk. (WCS 45)

tapper

a person who **taps** rubber, **toddy**, etc. (> **rubber tapper, toddy tapper**)

- ... a rubber plantation where it was rumoured a woman tapper was stabbed to death with a tapping knife and her ghost walks at noon-time. (BTH 34)

- Agnes was married to a tapper on Sweena's rubber estate in Kalutara. (CP 110)

tara padre
/tāra padre/ a type of duck curry, a **Burgher** speciality (Sinhala: tara = duck)

♦ ... the *tara padre* curry which was curried duck but cooked with ghee, sugar, coconut milk and - hold your breath - half a cup of whisky! (JFT 186)

tasty
/tēsti/ (of food) good, delicious → In BSE it would be more common to say 'It tastes good' than to use the adjective 'tasty'.

tat
a screen or blind made of bamboo or cane slats, which is rolled down to protect a window, doorway or open verandah from sun, rain, etc. (Anglo-Indian, also 'tatty', from Hindi)

TAT

♦ ... but it needed a fresh coat of paint and some new cane tats. (MM 89)

♦ I sat in the front bay with the bamboo tats half rolled up. (Reef 42)

♦ ... and on the two open verandahs with rolled up tats hanging in front were white-painted rattan chairs, ... (BTH 31)

♦ ... and there was a green tat hanging over the balcony of the Station Master's Quarters upstairs ... (BTH 53)

♦ Its walls were inset with lattice, its verandahs screened with rattan tats that could be lowered against the sun and sprayed with water. (HC 154)

tavern
(= **toddy tavern**) a bar selling **toddy** (archaic in BSE)

tea
(= **milk tea**) tea with milk and sugar (> **plain tea**)

□ tea boutique
(= **thee kade**) a small **kade** serving tea, **short eats**, etc. (> **boutique**)

♦ Even the 'boy' in the tea-boutique I frequented had thrown off his servile manner; ... (WMD 169)

♦ ... then as we took the bend near Manchi Akka's little tea boutique opposite the gate leading to the Village Headman's house, ... (BTH 7)

♦ In the thatched booth of a tea-boutique at the junction with the trunk road, a tot of illegal toddy eased his nausea. (HC 153)

♦ The coconut plantations spread almost to the cross-roads, where a few thatched huts and a tea-boutique squatted beside a paddy field. (HC 175)

♦ "If you could walk up to that tea boutique, you could take food," ... (KCS 119)

□ tea country
the areas in the **hill country** where tea is grown

♦ The dingy shops dwindled behind them and they were soon in open tea country again. (FSD 144)

♦ She is proud of her knowledge which she acquired having been a domestic aid to an English family in the tea country. (KCS 103)

□ tea dust
(= **fannings**) low grade tea; also called **dust** (> **leaf tea**)

□ tea estate
an estate where tea is grown

♦ Best of all, a week on our tea estate, some thirty miles out of Nuwara Eliya, where our bungalow looked out on near green hills and far blue ones, … (HC 81-2)

♦ … and he was back on that tea estate where he had spent the first six years of his life. (SMS 8)

□ tea factory
a building where tea is produced

TEA FACTORY

□ tea leaves
loose tea (as it is bought in a shop)

□ tea plucker
(= **plucker**) tea picker

TEA PLUCKER

♦ We had passed some tea pluckers a few hundred yards back … (RF 174)

♦ How much did the tea-pluckers get out of it? (WMD 96)

♦ … the green of the tea bushes spotted with the brightly clad tea pluckers at work. (CG 211)

♦ If you are driving you turn left and park, near the tea pluckers' shed. (AG 201)

♦ Rajendran ran a thriving bicycle-repair business in a filthy alley that was known to all the tea-pluckers in the district: … (HC 97)

♦ Now there was every chance she would turn out to be a tea-plucker. (HC 249)

teapoy
(dated) a small three-legged table (Anglo-Indian, from Hindi/Urdu)

TEAPOY

♦ There was a teapoy in the middle of the veranda with a tablecloth, white and tasselled at the edges, … (BTH 13)

tear
/tɪə/ (vi) (of the eyes) water, fill with tears ° *My eyes are tearing.* → In BSE, 'tear' is only used as a noun in this sense.

♦ The glare of the sun, reflected from the desert like terrain, was making my eyes tear. (REP 43)

♦ The garbage man dropped half the garbage on the road because his eyes were tearing. (M&P 182)

♦ Our eyes were a burning wound
that teared and blocked our sight.
(M&P 342)

telecast

(n) a TV programme; (v) show, broadcast (a
programme) on TV (also US, but not BSE);
also **teleseries** (TV series), **tele actor/actress**
(TV actor/actress) ° *Attack on tele artistes*

♦ Now the master tapes were ready to
be delivered to client, and the telecast
was scheduled to begin on the ninth of
April. (BTH 2)

♦ The television set re-repeated repeat
telecasts, all of which I had seen.
(M&P 350)

teledrama

a TV series or soap opera; also **teledramatist**
(a person who writes **teledramas**)

♦ He watched for three hours without
moving. Filmi dances, teledramas,
news programmes and comedies.
(Z 26)

♦ The other houses were shuttered for
the night although muted sounds of
teledrama dialogue filtered onto the
road. (FSD 268)

♦ "Nonsense. I've seen the tele-dramas.
... That's how it is in the tele-dramas."
(GC 236)

tell

(coll.) say ° *He told he will definitely come.*
° *Did you tell this to your father?* ° *Tell
you're sorry!* → In BSE, you 'say something
(to somebody)' or you 'tell somebody
something'; in SLE, you can 'tell something
(to somebody)'. The examples given would
probably be expressed in BSE as: 'He said
he would definitely come', 'Did you tell
your father this?', 'Say you're sorry!'

♦ "So if you want to marry him you tell
now and we will arrange." (JFT 111)

♦ "As I told before, he can learn quickly
but he cannot live at home any more."
(Reef 17)

♦ "Tell, will you? What's wrong?"
(FB 200)

♦ "Now this chap is telling I don't know
what I am doing on the footplate."
(YY 28)

♦ "Go and tell to come inside."
(TT 146)

♦ "Ah, von Bloss, no? Only yesterday
your aunt was telling about you."
(TT 150)

♦ "Ah yes, I remember now, but he
didn't tell the name." (WMD 127)

♦ "So biased, no? ... They are all just
telling for their side." (WE 101)

♦ "I am sorry about this, more than I can
tell," ... (FSD 55)

♦ "She has been telling it is a skirt, but I
have been telling her it is a trouser, ..."
(M&P 238)

♦ "See sister Beet, what did I tell?"
(M&P 312)

♦ I wished he had remained in India for
us to scold him for leaving without
telling. (M&P 354)

□ I'll tell you

I'll tell you what

♦ "I'll tell you, you get in and pass to
me." (TT 146)

temperadu

/temparādu/ (in cooking) tempered,
sauteed, lightly fried with onions, etc.
(Sinhala) ° *fish temperadu*

♦ "Hmm, that smells lovely." -
"*Temperadu*," I explained. (Reef 125)

temple

the temple ° *Are you going to temple?* ° *They must be at temple.* → In BSE, 'temple' would normally be used with the article 'the'; in SLE it is often used without the article (like 'church' in BSE).

♦ I remember Lucy-*amma* sometimes went to temple and lit incense for *poya* ... (Reef 86)

♦ ... though they only saw each other at temple on festival days. (WMD 30)

♦ "If only he would go to temple more." (WMD 136)

♦ Women and children, all in white, were making their way to temple. ... "It's so long since I've been to temple." (WMD 218)

♦ The following Sunday, and all remaining Sundays for the next few years I was sent to temple to learn the true essence of Buddhism. (M&P 89)

♦ "That is why I never go to temple any more, ..." (M&P 317)

temple flower

(= **araliya**) frangipani flower

♦ I set the table in the dining-room for the eight of them and decorated it with temple-flowers and some left-over Christmas tinsel. (Reef 89)

♦ The scent of temple flowers hung in the evening air. (WMD 218)

♦ "Dor stuck a temple flower in the bark ..." (MiP 299)

temple tree

(= **araliya**) frangipani tree

♦ Later that night I found him staring at the moon kicked high above the temple trees. (Reef 171)

♦ One day she was arranging the white and gold flowers of the temple tree before a bronze figurine of the Buddha when I entered the house. (WMD 180)

♦ "He had a pukka desk by the window. Looking straight at the temple trees." (SG 154)

tender

(of certain fruits, leaves, etc.) young, unripe ° *tender jak* ° *tender coconut leaves* → In BSE, 'tender' usually means soft or sensitive; it is used to refer to meat, but not to fruits, etc.

♦ ... and fine smelling tender jak fruit curry according to the tradition of the highlands. (KCS 49)

terra

/тега/ (coll.) terrorist (army slang)

♦ Commonly known as the Tigers - or simply as terras to the security forces ... (CU 12)

♦ "Surely the terras wouldn't be stupid enough to use the passports of known hijackers?" (CU 29)

thaachchi

/tāchchi/ a team game played in a circle drawn on the ground (Tamil)

♦ But for now it was alive, with *thaatchi* and rounders and cricket, singing contests and *kool* parties, ... (WMD 141)

thaachchiya

/tāchchiyə/ a small bowl-shaped pan used for deep frying and to make **hoppers**; also a larger circular tray used to carry and measure sand, stones, cement, etc. (Sinhala; Tamil thaachchi) (> **aappa thaachchiya**) ° *You'll need at least 5 thaachchiyas of sand.*

THAACHCHIYA

thaaththa, thaaththi

/tātta, tātti/ father, Daddy, Dad (Sinhala); grandfather (Tamil)

- Father - *Thaththi* - died on this coast road. (MM 101)

- "Thatha, ... this is not your concern." (FB 66)

- "You know, I have not seen your mother for more than twenty years, since your *Thaththi's* funeral," ... (SG 213)

- She used to call him Thaththi when she was a little girl. (July 300)

- "Thaathi never loses. You know that, don't you?" (FSD 53)

- "I can go to Thathi's village and apply for university." (M&P 304)

Thai Pongal

/tai pongǝl/ a Hindu festival held in January (Tamil)

- They had risen early in honour of the Hindu harvest festival of Thai Pongal, when barefoot pilgrims crowd into temples to offer up rice and vegetables to the god of the sun. (HC 127)

thala

/talǝ/ (= gingelly) sesame (Sinhala)

thalagoya

/talǝgoya/ (= land monitor, iguana) (Sinhala) (> monitor lizard, kabaragoya)

- The thalagoya ... is also a great climber, and can leap forty feet from a tree to the ground, breaking its fall by landing obliquely with its chest, belly and tail. In Kegalle the thalagoyas would climb trees and leap onto the roof or into the house. The thalagoya has a rasping tongue that "catches" and hooks objects. ... But as children we knew exactly what thalagoyas and kabaragoyas were good for. ... We used the thalagoya to scale walls. (RF 73-74)

THALAGOYA

- No telling, but he could bag a thalagoya - the iguana - and Daddy liked thalagoya flesh. (TT 114)

- The thalagoya was motionless, the three huge statues of the Buddha a backdrop for its immobility. (Z 124)

- The meat of the thalagoya was tough as leather but palatable, rather like country chicken. (REP 206)

thalaguli

/talǝguli/ a sweet made with sesame seeds (thala) and jaggery (Sinhala)

thalana batu

/talǝnǝ baʈu/ a type of brinjal (small and round with a bitter taste) (Sinhala)

thalapa

/taləpə/ a traditional dish made with **kurakkan** flour (Sinhala)

thalapath

/taləpat/ a type of fish (Indo-Pacific sailfish) (Sinhala)

thali (1)

/tāli/ a gold necklace given to the bride in a Tamil wedding (also India, orig. Tamil)

THALI (1)

♦ I noticed that Amma has removed her thali and gold bangles. (FB 293)

♦ "And I don't even have money for her *thali*." (WMD 266)

♦ … and then her mother had pawned her gold *thaali* to buy the medicine. (WE 27)

♦ In the middle of the garlands was a twenty two carat gold Thali, sacrificed only that morning by a young Hindu woman … (M&P 109)

thali (2)

/tāli/ a vegetarian rice meal usually served on a metal plate with separate compartments for different curries (also India, orig. Hindi)

THALI (2)

thamai

/tamai/ (coll.) indeed (for emphasis) (Sinhala) (> **itself, only**)

♦ "Spending *thamai*, spending on whom? Five mouths to feed, no?" (TT 145)

thambi

/tambi/ (= **malli**) younger brother (Tamil)

♦ "You are still one of us, *thambi*," … (WMD 13)

♦ "… and he was not Commander, then, but *thambi*, everybody's younger brother …" (WMD 394)

♦ The words themselves were innocuous, things like "Ah here comes, thambi," "Good health to you, thambi," "thambi is looking well today." (CG 233)

♦ "Murugasu thambi and I have been urging her to return to Colombo …" (CG 256)

♦ "This must be such a hard time for you *thambi*," … (WE 95)

thambili

/tæmbili/ (= **king coconut**) (Sinhala)

THAMBILI

♦ He called out for his boy to bring some *thambili* - king-coconut - to drink. (MM 91)

♦ "Let's go in and see whether we can't get a drink of *thambili* from your aunt." (WMD 52)

- Louisa sent Ramu to the kitchen for a glass of thambili. (CG 145)

- She would dress his nakedness with thambili leaves that were part of the decoration for death, ... (AG 106)

- At that moment, Siri made an entrance, carrying a tray with a few glasses and a pitcher of thambili. (July 122)

- ... sleeping on the beach and drinking thambili just fallen from the tree. (Z 178)

- "Haven't you offered your cousin a glass of thambili, yet?" (SMS 110)

- ... I was assaulted - no other word for it - by a woman in a thambili-orange trouser suit. (CP 51)

thambiya
/tambiya/ a derogatory term for a Muslim (Sinhala)

- "Just like a *thambiya*, never there when you want him." (WMD 247)

- "Walk into the US embassy and demand they bomb Jaffna jus' because we found two *thamby*-buggers' passports with the Tigers?" (CU 30)

- "We're running the major part of the op, as you know, with the *thambies*, but DFI and the STF are running the Tamil side of it." (CU 423)

thambun hodi
/tæmbun hodi/ a spiced medicinal broth (Sinhala)

than
rather than ° *He is of the opinion that the LTTE should be dealt with militarily than through political negotiations.* ° *... renewing hopes that the government and the LTTE will meet for talks sooner than later.*

thangachchi
/tangachchi/ (= **nangi**) younger sister (Tamil)

- "*Thangachi*," he said and brought the palms of his hands together in respectful greeting. (WMD 338)

- "I have some distressing news for you, thangachi." (CG 356)

thanking you
(in letters) thank you, with thanks

that and this
this and that

that day
the other day

that is what!
(coll.) that's the thing! (expression of agreement)

the
(coll.) his/her (with family members) ° *Just like the father!* ° *You think she's odd - you should see the sister!*

theatre
cinema (also US)

thee kade
/tē kaɒe/ (= **tea boutique**) (coll.) a small **kade** serving tea, **short eats**, etc. (Sinhala) (> **kade**)

thel dala
/tel dāla/ (a dish) fried with onions, chilli and **Maldive fish** (Sinhala: thel = oil) (> **ala thel dala**) ° *karola thel dala*

- Martin had parceled their afternoon meal but supplemented it with a splendid dry fish *thel dala*. (FSD 85)

thera, thero
/tērə, tēro/ Buddhist monk (Sinhala) ° *Injured Thero dies in hospital*

Theravada

/tērəvādə/ the form of Buddhism practised in Sri Lanka, Thailand, etc. (comp. Mahayana) (orig. Pali)

there

in/at another place (assumed though often unspecified), e.g. in your country ° *How is the situation there?* → In BSE, 'there' is only used if the place referred to has already been mentioned or is clear from the context.

□ ... is there / are there

there is / there are ... ° *Lot of problems are there.* ° *That of course is there!* → In BSE, 'there' either refers to a specific place, in which case it is pronounced in its strong form /theə(r)/ and often comes at the end of a sentence: 'He's standing over there'. Or else it acts as a 'dummy subject', in which case it comes at the beginning of a sentence and is pronounced in its weak form /thə(r)/: 'There are going to be a lot of problems'. In SLE this distinction 'is not there': the dummy subject is pronounced strong, and can also come at the end of a sentence.

thereafter

after that, from then on (formal in BSE) (> **hereafter**)

- ♦ The window was closed thereafter and Carloboy would remark on this. (TT 16)

- ♦ And you didn't buy gram for days thereafter, or cast the shadow of a glance at me. (WMD 152)

- ♦ There was a tea kiosk and a banana shop, thereafter a couple of stalls selling vegetables. (REP 75)

- ♦ "Once we find Kalivillu, I have a rough idea of the tracks and water holes we might head for thereafter." (REP 96)

- ♦ The traffic built up thereafter slowing their pace, ... (FSD 69)

- ♦ The road thereafter runs along the western border of Yala, ... (GC 296)

- ♦ Thereafter Kapila was to inform the principal of Sumanasiri's absence from school that day owing to a "family emergency". (WCS 28)

- ♦ Thereafter I mixed Signal toothpaste with a glass of salt water and drank that too. (M&P 73)

- ♦ Life was not particularly pleasant thereafter. (M&P 280)

- ♦ They race down the steps thereafter, ignoring all distractions. (PMS 130)

therefore

so ° *It was raining therefore we couldn't come.* → In BSE, 'therefore' carries greater emphasis, and usually comes at the beginning of a sentence, or after a comma and 'and'. In SLE it carries less emphasis, and often joins two ideas which do not necessarily have a strong logical connection.

- ♦ He could not be bothered buying a ticket and entering, therefore, he drove around the car park while I bought a ticket ... (M&P 360-1)

Thesavalamai

/dāsəvaləmē/ the traditional Tamil legal system, one of several systems still in operation in Sri Lanka (Tamil) (> **Roman-Dutch law**) ° *Thesavalamai pertains to land-owners in Jaffna no matter what race they belong to, and Jaffna Tamils of Malabar origins.* ° *Women under Thesavalamai Law cannot sell, transfer or gift their property without the written consent of their husbands.*

thevaram

/dāvāram/ a Hindu devotional song (Tamil)

◆ We sang two short *thevarams* and my father called me to him and placed holy ash on my forehead. (WMD 120)

◆ He still got me to recite my *thevarams*, though, and go to temple on a Friday, … (WMD 147)

thibbatu
/tibbɑtu/ a type of **brinjal** (Sinhala)

thick
thick-skinned, insensitive, indifferent; adverb: **thickly** ° *He's so thick he just came without an invitation.* ° *I'm very thick about my in-laws.* ° *You should just thickly go in without telling.* → In BSE, 'thick' is a colloquial word for 'stupid'.

think: to think to do something
to think of doing something → In BSE, to 'think to do something' (usually in negatives and questions) is to remember to do something at a particular time ('I didn't think to ask her name'); to 'think of doing something' is to intend to do something in the future ('We're thinking of going abroad').

◆ For an instant I thought to refuse her, but, seeing the warning look in her eyes, I finally acquiesced and went up the porch steps. (FB 32)

◆ I thought to get up, go into the garden and thus interrupt this mortifying conversation. (FB 166)

◆ He had thought to spend his sixteenth birthday with her, … but that day had come and gone without his having seen her at all. (WMD 250)

◆ Yet every time he thought to do so, he kept deferring it. (CG 133)

◆ "I thought to just boil the whole lot with a bit of salt." (REP 113)

◆ Our next leg was a long one, so I thought to turn in early. (REP 116)

□ **I don't think**
I don't think so

thirikkale
/tirikkǝle/ (= **hackery, race cart**) (dated) a small **bullock cart** used for carrying people (Sinhala)

thirty-first night
New Year's Eve

◆ He got very drunk and spent 31st night in an armchair. (YY 214)

this one
(coll.) he/she, this person, what's-his-name

◆ "I thought people go to America to find something. *This one* seems to have lost it all." (SG 60)

◆ "We are a migratory people, you know, but this one won't even move an inch now." (SG 68)

this thing
(coll.) thing, whatsit, what-d'you-call-it (plural **this things**); also used as a verb ° *Did you remember your this thing?* ° *It would have been this-thinged earlier.*

◆ "Your father was … *this thing* … right?" (AG 26)

Thomian
/tōmiǝn/ a student or former student of St. Thomas' College, Mount Lavinia (> **Royalist**) → Pronunciation note: In BSE, there are a few words (Thomas, Thailand, Thames, Anthony) which, though spelt with 'th', are pronounced as if spelt with 't' (Tomas, Tailand, etc.); in SLE they are pronounced the same way as other 'th' words.

thoppi
/toppi/ (= **hat**) (coll., dated) problem, trouble, disaster (Sinhala)

- "*Apoi*, if head priest in temple hears about this, *thoppi* (literally 'big hat' - a colloquial Sinhala expression meaning that it will be a disaster) for us also." (JFT 55)

- "*Thoppi** for me then." (* Thoppi - hat. This Sinhala expression indicates 'trouble'. To put a hat on something is to cause trouble. This was Anglicized to the extent that boys would also say: 'Hell of a hat' meaning a sticky situation or big trouble.) (TT 55)

thora

/tōra/ (= seer) (Sinhala)

- "There is some *thora-malu* - seer-fish for lunch," ... (MM 91)

- Vijay sank his teeth into a piece of *thora*. (WMD 379)

Thora

/tōra/ (= Thomian) (coll.) (Sinhala)
° *Thoras in line for victory*

thorana

/torənə/ (= pandal) a temporary structure erected for religious festivals (esp. **Vesak**); also a temporary decorated archway erected for festive occasions (Sinhala; Tamil thoranam)

thosai

/tōse, dōse/ (= dosai) a type of pancake made with slightly fermented batter made of **rice flour** and **ulundu** flour (also India, orig. Tamil) (> **paper thosai**) ° *masala thosai*

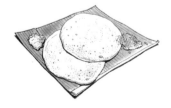

THOSAI

- "And still the *kadé* is there with our *thosai* and sweet tea. Unbelievable, no?" (MM 83)

- In the morning, at first light, the sea lay like a Madras pancake. *Thosai* flat. (Reef 123)

- "What are you cooking? Some of your fabulous thosas?" ... "Actually, I made extra thosa mix for tomorrow, ..." (July 44)

- They giggled while the thosa pan heated. (July 46)

- She decided to invite them for a thosa dinner the next day. (July 314)

- ... while she helped her stir the thosai mixture for their dinner, ... (Z 32)

- "You must stay for dinner - I'm making *thosai*," ... (WE 94)

- Halfway between the toothpastes and the thosai mixes ... (CP 51)

□ thosai kade

/dōse kaɒe/ a small Tamil restaurant serving thosais, etc. (> **kade**)

- ... and then retire to a *thosai-kaddai* for a 'feed'. (WMD 318)

those days

in those days, at that time, in the past (exact time unspecified) ° *He had a beard those days.* ° *Those days the fields were muddy, now they are dry.* (BSE: He used to have a beard, The fields used to be muddy.) → In BSE, 'in those days' refers to a specific time in the past which has already been established.

- "Now not like those days, no?" (JFT 109)

- "How people suffered those days." (TT 148)

- It was my joy those days to watch the white sugar being stirred into the golden brown tea with a little silver spoon. (CM 11)

♦ ... those days trousers ... had two buckles of white nickel on the sides to hold them tight at the waist. (BTH 12)

♦ "Those days you didn't know who was killing who." (AG 48)

♦ Those days, when he was growing up he remembered the horrendous foreign exchange restrictions ... (Z 35)

♦ "I've carried you when you were a baby, back home, those days, you don't remember." (WE 93)

♦ "Didn't you come to the Golf Club those days?" (FSD 9)

♦ Those days you could do things like that. (CP 80)

♦ "Look at the prices of things those days." ... "Don't I know! Those days I did not have to ruin my eyes looking for stones in the rice and the dhal." (M&P 95)

thousand

a thousand, one thousand (> **hundred**) ° *I paid thousand rupees.*

♦ "If you have to go to Purgatory for thousand days ..." (TT 151)

♦ The title of the essay had been 'MY COUNTRY'. Not exceeding thousand words, hand written. (M&P 67)

thovil

/tovil/ a traditional exorcism ceremony, including a **devil dance**, to drive away evil spirits (Sinhala) ° *Problems indicated in Chaturanga's horoscope had led the family to conduct several thovils for him.*

♦ "... we tried everything: doctors, *vedaralas, thoils* ... And I finally became pregnant." (WMD 78)

♦ So she took him to a Buddhist priest to do a *thoil* and drive away the devils. (WMD 148)

thraada

/trāda/ (= **rum**) (coll.) useless, rough, unsophisticated (Sinhala)

♦ "Who would be so interested in this *thraada* business?" (SG 115)

three-wheeler

(= **trishaw**) a small three-wheel taxi (India: 'auto-rickshaw') → Foreigners often refer to this vehicle as a 'bajaj' or a 'tuk-tuk'; Sri Lankans tend to say 'three-wheeler' or 'trishaw' or 'put-put'.

THREE-WHEELER

♦ ... as the three-wheeler struggled through the traffic. (AG 282)

♦ "Don't waste time trying to get buses. Take a three-wheeler." (July 336)

♦ As his van had been out of commission all month ..., they had arrived by three-wheeler. (MiP 9)

♦ She slung her workout bag over her shoulders and dashed to the top of the road to hail a three-wheeler. (Z 40)

♦ "Appa came. Someone brought him home in a three-wheeler." (REP 92)

♦ A three-wheeler took Ravi to the World Trade Centre in the Fort. (FSD 26)

♦ I move to the edge of the pavement and wave at every passing three-wheeler. (GC 241)

♦ I shared a three-wheeler into Fort with my fellow creditors. (CP 15-16)

♦ Every time the three-wheeler drivers got drunk they would sexually harass or assault one. (WCS 34)

thrice

three times (archaic in BSE) ° *I met him twice or thrice.* (BSE: two or three times)

♦ … Father Romiel emerged only after the mission house bell had been rung thrice, … (JFT 55)

♦ And when the sherbet man did it twice and thrice she was smiling on and on … (KCS 35)

♦ In spite of the cigarettes, he was to be seen at the police gym thrice a week. (CU 26)

♦ Stepping up gingerly, Dayan noted that the Tiger had been hit at least thrice in the back, … (CU 304)

throatlet

(dated) choker, a close-fitting necklace worn around the throat ° *Beautiful throatlet she was wearing.*

throw

/trō/ throw away, waste ° *Please don't throw my letter.* ° *Don't throw your food!* → In BSE, you 'throw' a ball, etc., and you 'throw away' rubbish, etc.

♦ "What else to do; nowadays can't throw money, no?" (JFT 205)

♦ "I think it's broken, … Shall I throw it?" (Z 188-9)

♦ I hated throwing my wristwatch but I knew that alone could cost me my life. (REP 23)

□ to throw out

to throw up, to be sick ° *He threw out all over the back seat of the car.*

thug

a politician or other influential person who is prepared to threaten, beat up or murder his opponents, or one of his henchmen hired to do the dirty work (also India, from Hindi) → In BSE, 'thug' is used more loosely to refer to any violent person.

♦ A member of parliament arrived with his thugs, held the voting officials at gunpoint, and then proceeded to stuff the ballot boxes with false ballots. (FB 207)

♦ The family in the car were simply staring out at the thugs as if they didn't realize what was going on. Now one of the thugs began to ask around for a match. (FB 291)

♦ "It would lead to A.E. Goonesinha and his Labour Union thugs running the country," … (CG 70)

♦ "A group of thugs attacked the shop that night, they looted the goods, then burned it down once they had locked the family inside." (CG 218)

♦ "We are not surprised that Comrade Nimal met his death at the hands of these police thugs who are the watchdogs of the exploitative class." (OD 47)

♦ Whenever the rebels had shot a thug who enjoyed the patronage of a minister, he had defended the killing. (WCS 47)

thuggery

the practice of **thugs**

♦ It stank of thuggery, and although Stanley knew that part of the blame lay with Hemantha's street friends, he still acknowledged with a heavy heart that his son had become a thug. (July 169)

- "Our politicians are only interested in lining their pockets, driving expensive cars and thuggery." (Z 65)

- "All the government MPs are resorting to thuggery." (FSD 71)

- Those politicians' sons who lacked brains to study, resorted to thuggery. (M&P 368)

thula

/tulə/ a long pole balanced on a forked stick, with a bucket attached, used for drawing water from a deep well (Sinhala/Tamil)

- … against the horizon we could see the men walking the *thulas* of their wells to eke out the water for their fields. (WMD 137)

thumba karawila

/tumbə karəvilə/ a variety of **karawila** (Sinhala)

thumbing

(in **carrom**) playing with the thumb (in order to hit pieces which are behind the line) (> **carrom**)

thunapaha

/tunəpahə/ a type of **curry powder** used in Sinhala cooking (Sinhala)

thuppahi

/tuppahi/ half-caste (the term implies being westernised and uncultured); (coll., derogatory) cheap, common, lowly (Tamil/Sinhala)

- "*Thuppahi* (half caste) Burgher." (JFT 38)

- Visit his wife's relatives? The people who had looked down on him as a '*thuppai* postmaster' all these years? (WMD 175)

- "Akka, … this is not one of Aunt Philomena's usual types, not some thuppai government clerk." (CG 87)

- "Those 'tuppahi' fellows who spout Marxism with their full stomachs have no right to it." (OD 134)

- "Why should we, Sinhalese people who are heirs to this land, have to learn western *thuppahi* ways to get a job?" Another new word! Am I *thuppahi* then, because I can read English? (GC 74)

tiffin

(dated) a light mid-morning or mid-afternoon meal (Anglo-Indian)

- "Go and tell Soma to make some tea and cut some bread for tiffin." (JFT 110)

- Only at afternoon tea, tiffin she called it, would I come regularly face to face with her, … (WMD 125)

- … reorienting the country's talents and the whole economy towards tea and tiffin. (SG 32)

- That afternoon, a visitor would have found the Kandiah family at tiffin on the front verandah, their white wicker chairs pulled around a matching table, Louisa presiding with the teapot. (CG 14)

- He had taken tiffin at the Hill Club. (HC 94)

- And Juliet was munching her allocation of two biscuits, her tiffin. (KCS 151)

□ **tiffin carrier**
a metal container with different compartments for carrying a meal

TIFFIN CARRIER

♦ ... the stacked aluminium tiffin carrier with its film of greasy curry. (HC 245)

♦ ... his lunch was sent to the office in a tiffin carrier; ... (SMS 9)

♦ ... the clang of tiffin carriers being opened up, the smell of rice and curry in the air. (SMS 26)

♦ Each family brought their own tiffin carrier with one portion of rice and different curries, to share with each other. (M&P 90)

Tigers
(= **LTTEers, the Boys**) militant Tamil separatists, members of the Liberation Tigers of Tamil Eelam (LTTE)

tight: to give somebody tight
(= **cut**) (coll.) to put somebody in their place, cut somebody down to size, give somebody a hard time

♦ "I gave her tight." (JFT 10)

♦ "I heard a big row there. Must have given the bugger tight." (TT 106)

♦ Hitler was, as Edema had said, "getting it tight from all sides, ..." (TT 174)

till
piggy bank, or any container for collecting coins, usually made of clay or plastic → In BSE, a 'till' is a box or drawer where cash is kept in a shop.

♦ Caroline ran into the place where she kept her till and dropped her coin into it. (CM 67)

♦ She had spied on his possessions and knew of the clay till, painted to resemble a tomato and weighty with coins, that he kept in a drawer. (HC 226)

time: in time
on time ° *Please try to come in time for the meetings.* → In BSE, 'on time' means at the correct time (e.g. for a meeting), while 'in time' suggests coming early, e.g. for something which doesn't have a set time, like 'in time for dinner'.

☐ in two days' time
in two days (see note) ° *The work will be finished in two days' time.* → In BSE the expression 'in two days' time' can only have one meaning: The work will be finished two days from now. But in SLE it can also mean: The work will take two days to complete (with no indication of when it is going to start). In BSE 'in two days' (without the word 'time') would be ambiguous in the same way.

time to come
in the future ° *Time to come there won't be any small kades left.*

tin cutter
tin opener

♦ "... aspirin, Burnol, bandages, a tin-cutter, ..." (HC 178)

tin fish
(= **salmon**) tinned fish

tinker
a skilled worker who repairs the bodywork of vehicles, etc.; noun: **tinkering** → In BSE, 'tinker' is an archaic word for an itinerant craftsman who repaired pots, kettles, etc. In modern BSE, 'tinkering' suggests messing

around with something, trying to repair it in a casual or amateur way. In SLE, a 'tinker' is a skilled workman.

tin kiri
/ʈin kiri/ condensed milk (Sinhala; Tamil tin paal)

Tissa
/tissə/ (coll.) Tissamaharama

to
than (> **elder to**) ° *He is three years younger to me.* ° *My wife is two years older to me.*

♦ Eric de Mello worked in the General Post Office too, and was a mite lower in rank to Cecilprins ... (JFT 14)

♦ Here the High Level Road ... is on a lower level to the old road which runs over the ridge. (BTH 17)

♦ ... he was much older to me even then ... (BTH 51)

♦ "One, she is much younger to me, perhaps you would know her." (WE 113)

today morning/evening
this morning/evening ° *They arrived today morning.*

toddy
a sweet white drink extracted from the flower of the coconut, **kitul** or **palmyrah** tree, which is drunk slightly fermented, or distilled to make **arrack**; also used to make **honey** and **jaggery** (also India, from Hindi) (> **coconut toddy, kitul toddy, palmyrah toddy**) → In BSE, 'toddy' is a mixture of whisky, brandy, etc. with sugar and hot water.

♦ ... like the necessary sleep in the afternoon with dreams blinded by toddy. (RF 71)

♦ Joseph should be stuck up some palm tree, high on *toddy*, keeping

the demons happy like the rest of his people. (Reef 39)

♦ The toddy joint had some excellent cuttle fish wrapped in a chilli sauce. (YY 63)

♦ Then again the man started coming to her mat at night, once in a while, usually smelling of toddy. (OM 29)

♦ From early dawn she boiled sweet toddy in an outsized cauldron stirring well all the time. (CM 42)

♦ Lali picked up a coconut shell, blew the ants out of it and poured herself a bit of toddy. (WMD 216)

♦ "Maybe drink some toddy before it gets too late." (AG 9)

♦ The little toddy stand that Sepalika ran was not there. (July 266)

♦ Toddy was cheaper than arrack but produced a more sickening aftermath. (HC 207)

♦ Later in the day, the pale nectar of the palmyrah flower would grow heavy and sour with fermentation, its alcohol content rising, slices of onions and green chillies spicing the pre-lunch toddy. (CU 331)

□ **toddy tapper**
a person who climbs palm trees to **tap toddy**

TODDY TAPPER

♦ Above the small roads of Wattala, Kalutara, the toddy tapper walks collecting the white liquid for tavern vats. (RF 88)

♦ "And as if that is not enough you have to go and lend money to the toddy tapper. How is that cripple going to pay you back? By tapping toddy with his broken arm?" (WMD 145)

♦ "It's that toddy-tapper, ... You can never trust these low-caste fellows." (WMD 410)

♦ He was Ruwan Kumara and he had been a toddy tapper. (AG 269)

♦ "They're for toddy tappers, ... You know, men who climb coconut trees to collect the sap from the flowers to make toddy." (July 116)

□ **toddy tavern**
(= **tavern**) a small bar where **toddy** is sold and drunk

♦ They finally stopped at what looked like an abandoned old toddy tavern, tucked illicitly away in a palmyrah grove, ... (WMD 326)

♦ ... and even at the end of the town where the toddy taverns are. (KCS 129)

toe ring
/ᴛōring/ a ring worn on the toe (esp. by Tamil women)

toffee
a sweet → In BSE, a 'toffee' is a specific type of sweet made with sugar and butter; in SLE it is any type of sweet.

too (1)
(coll.) very, really ° *I was too hungry during the class!* ° *You're too bad teasing me like that!*

too (2)
(word order) (> **also**) ° *Mrs Dharmasena too was there.* → In BSE, 'too' usually comes at the end of a sentence ('Mrs Dharmasena was there too'), while in SLE it often immediately follows the word it refers to.

♦ He too seemed to be floating in the air. (Reef 164)

♦ I, too, was angry when I heard this. (FB 189)

♦ ... but John began to accept that this too was part of the business of getting on in life. (YY 36)

♦ ... because she too came from a poor background, ... (WMD 190)

♦ "If I had been in the village I too would have done the same, ..." (OD 11)

♦ "I actually thought that Nimal too had escaped along with all of us." (OD 78)

♦ We stood as though we too were waiting for the bus. (REP 302)

♦ The roads too are filled with hurrying pedestrians and flashing headlights. (GC 81)

♦ When visitors came Achi would take out the silver cutlery, but the visitors too ate with their fingers. (M&P 92)

□ **too ... not**
(= **also ... not**) not ... either ° *She too didn't turn up.* → In BSE, 'also' and 'too' are not used with negatives, 'either' is used instead: 'She didn't turn up either.'

♦ I too don't talk much. (RF 198)

♦ ... like Vijay he too was not a fully-fledged member of the PLF ... (WMD 248)

♦ "I too don't think that keeping a diary is common among Sinhala people." (OD 72)

too much
(coll.) forward, pushy, cheeky ° *He's too much!*

♦ "One thing, you girls nowadays are too much!" (JFT 134)

too much of
(coll.) too much ° *He's drinking too much of arrack.* ° *I won't take up too much of time.*

toper
/tōpə/ drinker, drunkard (archaic in BSE)

♦ Joseph was a toper, nothing else as far as I could tell. (Reef 86)

♦ "I thought all Burghers are great topers." (FSD 172)

♦ The old toper knocked the shot back with one huge swallow ... (FSD 242)

topping
excellent (dated in BSE) ° *car for sale, topping condition*

tourer
convertible (car)

tourney
(in newspaper headlines) tournament (rare in BSE)

TP
tel., telephone

tracker
a ranger or guide in a national park

♦ The bungalow's cook and the tracker watch from the doorways of the house ... (RF 141)

♦ He instructs one of the trackers to remain with us till we leave; ... (GC 166)

traffic time
(coll.) rush hour

traffic warden
a parking attendant (usually female); also a schoolboy or schoolgirl directing traffic at a pedestrian crossing outside their school → In the UK, a 'traffic warden' is a professional officer, mainly responsible for enforcing parking laws.

tree tomato
a small red fruit used to make jam

Trinco
(coll.) Trincomalee

♦ I am once again in Trinco, without you this time. (Z 127)

Triple Gem
(in Buddhism) the Buddha, the **Dhamma** and the **Sangha** ° *the blessings of the Triple Gem*

♦ "May the triple-gem bless him," ... (M&P 301)

triposha
/tripōshə/ a nutritious type of food given to children (Sinhala)

trishaw
(= **three-wheeler**) a small three-wheel taxi (India: 'auto-rickshaw')

♦ The Fort was overrun with trishaws, and for the first time he noticed that their drivers had a dress code. (MiP 258)

♦ ... and she hopped in and thought nothing of the trishaw careening down the road weaving in and out of traffic, ... (Z 40)

♦ Ravi knew very well the bastard would get a trishaw driver to drop him for free and pocket the money anyway. (FSD 37)

♦ A trishaw drops me outside Food City a few minutes before eleven. (GC 239)

♦ "Sorry I'm late, boys. My trishaw man took forever to come and pick me up." (SMS 47)

♦ The trishaw hurtled off down the road, dodging traffic, stray dogs, cyclists, pedestrians and potholes with equal abandon, ... (CU 35)

♦ A job as a trishaw driver in Colombo barely made him enough money to feed himself and his elderly parents. (CU 313)

♦ The sun flashes off his spectacles, ... when he alights from a trishaw. (PMS 65)

trouser

(a pair of) trousers ° *I need to buy a new trouser.*

♦ "Never mind you bathe in that trouser." (TT 139)

♦ The Bombay sweet seller wore his cloth like a trouser. (CM 55)

♦ The bottom was a baggy trouser tapering to a tight circle at the ankle. (REP 58)

♦ That was when he caught a sight of a victim's faded denim trouser. ... This was his own son's trouser, he was sure of it. (WCS 27)

♦ A burly curly-haired man in a khaki shirt and trouser was already poking his metal rod into a helpless hut. (WCS 51)

♦ "Now tell me, ... this thing you are wearing, is it a trouser or a skirt?" (M&P 238)

♦ "Apo Podian, don't throw the trouser away, you look smart in it," ... (M&P 334)

true

(coll.) that's right; (as a question) really? ° *Her father's sick. – True?*

♦ "It is the Asian style, true, no?" (Reef 146)

TT

table tennis; **TT board**: table tennis table ° *Kalpani bags TT triple*

tubelight

fluorescent light; also used to refer to someone who is slow to catch on ° *He's a bit of a tubelight.*

tuition

/ˈtyūshən/ extra tuition given at a tutorial college (> **tutory**) ° *tuition classes* ° *She's going for private tuition.* → In BSE, 'tuition' - especially 'private tuition' - suggests 'individual tuition' by a private teacher. This is not necessarily the case in Sri Lanka, where tutorial colleges often have large classes. Note also the pronunciation: SLE /ˈtyūshən/, BSE /tyuˈishən/

♦ She still went home with him after tuition and he still went to her house almost every day. (July 167)

♦ The children ... went to a normal free education school during the morning, and paid heavily for tuition classes in the afternoon. (M&P 276)

tuition master

a teacher of **tuition** classes (> **master**)

♦ Father caught and hammered the tuition master also. (TT 195)

♦ ... the posters of the tuition masters, ... (KCS 80)

turn from

turn at (a junction) ° *Turn from the next junction.*

tusker

an elephant with tusks ° *Tusker runs amok before start of perahera*

- ♦ The baby grew into a magnificent tusker. Tuskers are quite rare in the wild today, having been hunted almost to extinction. (REP 140)

- ♦ … as the old tooth rocked on the back of the temple tusker … (M&P 252)

- ♦ … he sees that it is the temple tusker that stands there, tethered by chains to the mighty tree. (PMS 246)

tute classes

/ᴛʏᴜ̄ᴛ/ (coll.) **tuition** classes

tutes

/ᴛʏᴜ̄ᴛs/ (coll.) handouts, tutorial notes

tutory

tutorial college (> **tuition**)

TVP

soya meat (textured vegetable protein)

two three

two or three; also with times ° *Come there at three thirty four* (BSE: three thirty or four)

- ♦ "Two three rooms, I think." (JFT 13)

- ♦ "Maybe two-three months." (JFT 17)

- ♦ … the two, three weeks we all spent in Jaffna once a year, … (WMD 137)

- ♦ "It was only recently, about two, three years ago," … (WMD 159)

U

udekki

/ᴜᴅækki/ a small traditional drum (Sinhala)

uguduwa

/uguᴅuwɑ/ (= **polecat**) (Sinhala)

uguressa

/uguræssə/ a small red fruit (Sinhala)

UGURESSA

- ♦ There were *bakini, kirala, sweet melon, gira amba, uguressa,* woodapple, *jambu, naminam,* olives, oranges and guavas. (CM 77)

UK, US

the UK, the US ° *I'm hoping to go to UK next summer.* → In BSE, the article 'the' is used with the names of certain countries, e.g.: the United Kingdom, the United States, the Maldives, the Philippines, the West Indies, the Netherlands, etc. The article is often omitted in SLE.

ulama

/ulɑmɑ/ (= **devil bird**) a mysterious bird with a loud screeching cry (forest eagle owl) (Sinhala)

- ♦ The Ulama, disgusted at this breach of etiquette, rose into the air, gave its imitation of a lorry with sand in the gear box, and winged away. (YY 175)

ulema

/ulēmə/ a council of Muslim scholars (Arabic)

ultimately

finally, in the end, at last, eventually ° *He had to wait over a year, but ultimately he got the visa.* → In BSE, 'ultimately' is rather formal in the sense of 'finally'; it is more commonly used in the more abstract sense of 'basically' or 'fundamentally': 'Ultimately, it's not my problem'.

uluhal

/uluhāl/ fenugreek (Sinhala)

ulundu

/ulundu/ (= **black gram**) a type of pulse used to make flour for **vadais, thosais,** etc. (Tamil; Sinhala 'undu')

♦ Sanji complimented Chitra on the *vadais* and marvelled that she could still get the ingredients. "Ah-ha, that's not *ulundu* you are eating," retorted Chitra triumphantly. (WMD 399)

♦ ... as she measured out the ulundu to be soaked overnight for the morning's thosais. (CG 6)

□ ulundu vadai

/ulundu vaɒe/ a soft **vadai** made with **ulundu** flour and shaped like a doughnut (Tamil) (> **parippu vadai**)

ULUNDU VADAI

umbalakada

/umbələkaɒə/ (= Maldive fish) (Sinhala) ° *umbalakada sambol* ° *umbalakada vadai*

umbrella couple, umbrella lovers

a young couple sheltering from public view behind an umbrella

UMBRELLA COUPLE

♦ In the evenings, they were dotted by umbrella lovers, young couples who met illicitly at the beach and whispered and kissed behind their umbrella shields. (July 10)

♦ It was deserted now, in the blazing mid afternoon heat. Except for the umbrella lovers! ... Young couples seated on the cement benches, crunched up against each other, and protected from the sun and the eyes of the public, by a single unfurled umbrella balanced on their shoulders. (REP 343)

♦ The umbrella lovers were out in force even in the blazing heat of the early afternoon. (FSD 248)

umma (1)

/umma/ (= **amma**) mother (Muslim Tamil, from Arabic); also grandmother (short for **ummamma**)

♦ "Why discordily Umma?" interrupted the middle grandchild ... (Z 179)

♦ "Ummi," one of them shouted, "who is Karima? And who is Sameer?" (Z 190)

umma (2)

/umma/ kiss (children's word) (Sinhala) ° *Give your thaaththi an umma!*

uncle

a term of respect/affection used by a child to a man or by a younger person to an older man ° *Mohan Uncle*

- Sena Uncle, Chithra Aunty, and Sanath came along in their own car. (FB 102)

- "Really, Uncle? I hope there is no problem." (July 320)

- "How are you uncle?" (Z 26)

- She looked up and saw Raja uncle waving her towards him. (Z 32)

- "Uncle, we need some petrol for our motor bicycle," ... (REP 77)

- "Uncle, what has happened? ... Is anyone hurt?" (GC 255)

- ... but he relaxed enough to start calling them Aunty and Uncle. (SMS 114)

- "Can we at least speak to uncle?" (PMS 161)

- "But, uncle, we have come to help you," ... (PMS 172)

uncleared areas
(in the North and East) areas controlled by the LTTE, not by the Sri Lankan Army (> cleared areas) ° *Uncleared areas a haven for stolen vehicles*

- It was, as arranged, an ID issued by the LTTE to people living in 'uncleared' areas administered by them. (REP 11)

underemployed
doing a job (e.g. a government job) for which one is over-qualified ° *Underemployed graduates threaten fast unto death* → In BSE, 'underemployed' means not having enough work, not fully employed.

undergrad
(coll.) undergraduate (also US, less common in BSE) (> grad)

undermentioned
mentioned below (more formal in BSE) (> above mentioned) ° *Please forward payment to any of the undermentioned.*

undersigned
(dated and formal in BSE) ° *Please feel free to contact the undersigned.*

unduvel, undu walalu
/unduvæl, undu valəlu/ a type of sweet consisting of deep-fried strands of batter twisted in circular coils and sweetened with **honey** (Sinhala; similar to Indian 'jalebi') ° *A special delicacy of the Kandyans is unduvel - deep-fried outpourings from a cloth pouch filled with a mixture of rice flour and undu flour into hot oil in loops and circles. The cooked configurations are dropped into a chatti of treacle and left to soak for a minute or two so that treacle oozes into the tunnels of spaghetti-like twisted coils. It is crisp outside and soft and oozy inside - altogether a delight!*

UNDUVEL

unknown: an unknown person
someone I/you don't know, a stranger, an unidentified person (> known) ° *Better not talk to unknown people.* → In BSE, 'unknown' means not famous, not well known.

- "And what if the Nagendras hear that you're galavanting around with an unknown Sinhala boy?" (FB 58)

- If an unknown car or bicycle made its way down the road, Mr Munasinghe ... would go up to them and ask them to state their business. (July 13)

♦ ... no more than a few crackers lit by some unknown prankster. (FSD 182)

♦ It was the prospect of being ragged, of being physically in thrall to unknown men and women that had terrified me. (GC 7)

♦ Transactions between schoolgirls and unknown males were not permitted during school hours. (M&P 83)

UNPer

a member of the United National Party

unpolished

(of rice) **raw**, wholegrain (> **red rice, country rice**)

♦ Sam hadn't troubled to telephone ahead, so ate unpolished country rice, fried snake beans and coconut *sambol*, like the servants. (HC 239)

until, till

while ° *Offer valid until stocks last!* (BSE: while stocks last)

♦ The food the neighbours brought must have been only for the previous day, till the corpse was in the house. (OD 59)

unwanted

unnecessary, unjustified, unwarranted (> **want**) ° *Remove the unwanted pins.* ° *Don't say unwanted things!* → In BSE, 'unwanted' means 'not wanted' ('an unwanted pregnancy', 'to feel unwanted'). In SLE it tends to mean 'not needed' or 'unwarranted'.

♦ Unwanted memories flit through my mind like thieves in the night. (GC 201)

♦ The poster devil of the municipality that stands on four wheels and pumps water on all unwanted posters pasted on the walls. (KCS 80)

up (1)

(adv.) upstairs, above, on top (> **down**) ° *My room is up.* → In BSE, 'up' is used as an adverb in the sense of 'out of bed' ('Is he up yet?'), but otherwise it is normally used as a preposition ('up the hill'), or with a verb: you can 'go up' or 'come up', but you can't 'be up' unless you specify where: upstairs, up the ladder, up on the roof, etc.

up (2)

awake ° *They're still up.* ° *I was up for a long time before I got out of bed.* → In BSE, 'up' means 'out of bed', not 'awake'.

up and down

return (ticket) ° *How much is an up and down ticket?*

up-country, upcountry

(= **hill country**) (n/adj./adv.) the central hills of Sri Lanka (> **low country**) ° *They went up-country for the weekend.* ° *the upcountry Tamils*

♦ Rich Sinhalese families go up-country during April. (RF 79)

♦ "... and you know those up-country roads." (RF 173)

♦ ... the milkfood company asked Viva to handle distribution and sales of its products upcountry ... (JFT 70)

♦ The morning he was due to leave for up-country I was allowed to serve breakfast. (Reef 34)

♦ ... my carefully brewed up-country tea ... (Reef 138)

♦ He reported fit and was, for a change, given the upcountry run to Kandy and Nawalapitiya. (YY 91)

♦ Nothing like good, fatty upcountry beef, he would say. (YY 102)

♦ Why had he come all the way from up-country? (WMD 29)

♦ The station-master came up to Saha and told him that the up-country train was delayed. (WMD 94)

♦ ... with pear trees and plums, carrots, cabbages, rhubarb and runner beans and all sorts of up-country vegetables and fruit. (WMD 119)

♦ "For the last thirty years he has been up-country," ... (SG 119)

♦ In those days, when the motor-car was a rarity, we travelled up-country by train. (HC 82)

♦ The heady aroma of fine upcountry tea filled the room as appu returned with a tray. (FSD 137)

upon
(in addresses) over, stroke, slash; e.g. 7/15 ° *seven upon fifteen*

uppuma
/uppumā/ a dish made with roasted semolina, vegetables and spices (Tamil)

♦ His mother ... re-created the food of his childhood: uppuma in the morning, ... (CG 209)

upstair house
two-storey house ° *They're living in an upstair house.* ° *Turn left at the upstair boutique.* → In BSE, an 'upstair flat' or 'upstairs flat' is a flat which is upstairs, i.e. not on the ground floor.

♦ "... nice upstair house and all." (TT 171)

♦ The Railway offered him a larger, upstair bungalow into which the family moved. (YY 139)

♦ ... an abandoned rubber plantation with an old upstair house set deep inside. (BTH 13)

♦ Four children, a husband and a servant who all lived in the upstairs part of the upstair house. (M&P 99)

upto
up to (2 words) ° *It's upto you to reply.*

□ upto date
so far, till now ° *I had no reply upto date.*

up train
the train going up from Colombo to the hills (> **down train**)

usher
usher in ° *They declared their support to President Mahinda Rajapaksa to overcome terrorism and usher peace.*

uttappam
/ūttappəm/ a type of thick **thosai** (Tamil)

V

vadai

/vaɒe/ a small, deep-fried savoury snack (also India, orig. Tamil) (> **parippu vadai, ulundu vadai, short eats**) ° *prawn vadai* ° *curd vadai* ° *masala vadai*

♦ ... waiters would serve lobster tails, prawn *vadai* and devilled eggs ... (Reef 134)

♦ Vijay ate the *vadais* slowly, ... He washed the *vadais* down with a cup of tea ... (WMD 320)

♦ Chitra ... handed round a plateful of *vadais*. "Remember the first time you came, Vijay? We had *vadais* then too." (WMD 399)

♦ She made thosas and coconut chutney and masala vadas ... (July 190)

♦ "Rani," he called out to his wife, who came in carrying a plate of *vadais*, ... (WE 93)

♦ Families clustered around vendors who manned little wheeled stalls that sold everything from roasted peanuts to prawn *vadai* - a spicy ring of fried dough, similar in looks to a doughnut. (CU 39)

vain: in vain

/vēn/ unnecessarily; (as an exclamation) what a shame! what a pity! what a waste! ° *In vain we bought a ticket.* → In BSE, if you do something 'in vain', it means you try to achieve something but get no result: 'All our work was in vain'. In SLE, it means to do something which turns out to be unnecessary, a waste of time. Note also the word order: in SLE 'in vain' usually comes at the beginning of the sentence; in BSE it usually comes at the end.

♦ "Only for one day? In vain, no, men." (YY 162)

♦ "It's nice, Mummy, in vain he spoilt it, no?" (TT 173)

Valsatian

a humorous term for a **pariah dog** (a combination of Sinhala 'vul' = wild, and Alsatian) (> **vul**)

♦ Mrs. Adonis had an Alsatian, we had a Valsatian (a Pariah). Valsatians were pedigree-less dogs found by the roadside. ... We did not have one valsatian but three. (M&P 155)

vamban

/vambən/ rascal (Tamil)

♦ "Come here, you vamban," she said to me sharply. (FB 37)

vambatu

/vambətu/ (= **batu, brinjal**) aubergine (US eggplant) (Sinhala)

vangediya

/vangeɒiyə/ a large stone mortar used with a **molgaha** for pounding rice to make **rice flour** (Sinhala)

VANGEDIYA + MOLGAHA

Vanni

/vanni/ an area of thick forest in the Northern Province (Sinhala/Tamil)

varai
/varei/ a Tamil dish similar to a **mallung**
(Tamil) ° *suraa varai (shark varai)*

♦ ... his mouth full of shark *varai*.
(WMD 60)

varsity
university (> **campus**) → In BSE, 'varsity'
is normally used only in a sporting context,
especially with reference to Oxford and
Cambridge ('the varsity match'). It is also
used in the US in the same way.

♦ Dias had become a government officer,
following in his father's footsteps, after
varsity. (Reef 56)

vatadage
/vaтədāge/ a circular relic house consisting
of a **dagoba** surrounded by stone pillars,
originally covered with a conical roof
(Sinhala)

VATADAGE

vatakolu
/vœтəkolu/ (= **ridged gourd**) a type of
gourd used as a vegetable (Sinhala)

VATAKOLU

vedamahatteya, vedarala
/vedəmahattəya, vedərālə/ (= **native
physician**) **ayurvedic** doctor (Sinhala)
(> **ayurveda**)

♦ They will tell you, the neighbours,
their faces dark with fear, how Malini

and Ranjit did not take heed of the
Vedamahaththaya's words and went
ahead and got married. (OM 23)

♦ Mother was worried, and when the
Veda Mahathmaya, our village doctor
came visiting us, mother would
complain, ... (CM 18)

♦ Lucky's father was a *vedarala* whom
my father would go to see every time
he fell out with Western medicine.
(WMD 116)

♦ There he began to practise some of the
craft of the native physician which he
had picked up from his father-in-law,
a *vedarala* famed for his techniques in
bone-setting and in treating ulcers and
kidney complaints. (WMD 243)

♦ He had been bitten by a snake but
saved from death by Weerawansa
Vedamahaththaya, the ayurveda
specialist living near the bridge.
(FSD 255)

Veddah
/vœdda/ a member of the aboriginal
community of Sri Lanka, the earliest
inhabitants of the country (Sinhala; OED
Vedda)

VEDDAH

♦ "... we have a pinch of everyone in us,
from the Veddah to the Scot, like most
people." (SG 80)

◆ Thathi received a new job. He was to build a road to the Veddha regions. (M&P 201)

vee bissa

/vī bissə/ (= atuwa) a traditional storage bin or silo used for keeping paddy (Sinhala)

VEE BISSA

veena

/vīnə/ a traditional Indian stringed instrument (also India, orig. Sanskrit)

◆ His wife would have furniture and a sewing-machine and a veena and bring jewellery ... (YY 45)

vehicle

/vehikəl/ car, van, etc. ° *I parked my vehicle outside.* → In BSE the word 'vehicle' is much less common, except in an official context or when talking about vehicles in general. People would normally refer to their own vehicle as their 'car'. The pronunciation is also different: SLE /vehikəl/, BSE /viyəkl/.

vela

/vælə/ a variety of **jak fruit**, with softer and shinier flesh when ripe (Sinhala)

vel cart

/vēl/ a decorated chariot which is pulled through the streets during the **vel festival** (Tamil)

◆ Achi saw him, running from shop to shop looking like a two-legged Vel cart which travelled the city with

coloured trinkets in honour of Lord Kataragama. (M&P 109)

VEL CART

vel festival

/vēl/ an annual Hindu festival in which a **vel cart** is pulled through the streets carrying the 'vel' or trident of the god Skanda (Tamil)

◆ ... the night before the celebration of the Tamil Vel festival in honour of Lord Kataragama, ... (M&P 326)

veli aatha, veli anoda

/væli āta, væli anōda/ (= **custard apple**) a type of fruit the size of a large apple, with a green skin and white pulp (Sinhala)

vellakaran, vellayan

/velləkārən, velləyən/ (= **suddha**) (coll.) a white man; female **vellakari** (Tamil)

◆ "Whose government, Saha? Not ours, is it? It is the *suddha's* government, the *vellayan's* as you say in Tamil, the white man's." (WMD 38)

◆ "They can't stand the heat of Colombo at this time, the *vellayans*." ... - "But they are not just *vellayans*," I said. - "No, our people too, but they think that by coming up for the season and playing golf and going to the races they become *vellayans* too, ..." (WMD 126)

◆ "And I thought that when the *vellayans* were gone, we'd be free of all that. ... They are worse than the *vellayans*, *aththan,* our rulers, worse. They are the *vellayans,* now. They even kill our people like the *vellayans.*" (WMD 175-6)

♦ "There is something you must do. Go to the vellakari." He stared at her in astonishment. "Miss Adamson?" (CG 238)

vellala, vellalan

/vellālǝ, vellālǝn/ the 'farmer' caste, considered the highest caste (Tamil) (> **govigama**) ° *Jaffna Tamil Hindu Vellala divorcee 35 years no children ...*

♦ ... the high-caste *vellalans,* the so-called landed gentry, ... (WMD 215)

♦ "We are high-caste *vellalas,* you know, ... manual work is beneath us." (WMD 332)

venerable, ven.

(in the names of Buddhist monks) reverend, rev. ° *Ven. Anandatissa Thero*

venivelgeta

/venivælgœtǝ/ a type of plant used in **ayurvedic** medicine (Sinhala)

♦ She dosed Carloboy with Venivalgata,* ... (* The stems and bark of the Calumba wood shrub - a spiky medicinal plant which makes a strong antiseptic infusion....) (TT 41)

veralu

/verǝlu/ a small green fruit with a large stone and a bitter taste, also known as Ceylon olive or sometimes 'olive' (Sinhala)

VERALU

♦ ... the lacy tangle of the upper foliage of the weralu (*Eleocarpus serratus*) tree. (TT 114)

♦ The veralu trees were in full bloom, and the canopies were flecked with white ... and the air was heavy with that strange scent of veralu flowers ... (BTH 10)

verti

/vāti/ a garment worn by men, consisting of a length of material tied around the waist (Tamil) (> **sarong**)

♦ To demonstrate the Tamilness of his character he would always change into a verti in the evenings ... (YY 156)

♦ He wore a white *verti* and *banian* and had thrown a cream woollen shawl over his shoulders. (WMD 99)

♦ "... and that time that Roy came home my father had put on a shirt over his *verti* to come out and meet him." (WMD 163)

♦ The men were unusually dressed. Instead of suits and ties, most of the men wore sarongs or vertis, clothes that were usually worn at home. (CG 376)

♦ For his encounter with authority the pawnbroker wore a tweed jacket above his *verty,* ... (HC 97)

♦ An elderly man dressed in a white verti walked up to the barrier, had his papers scrutinized, and was allowed to pass. (REP 7)

♦ ... an old person from the bridegroom's side, clad in a chalky vetti and a shirt and his forehead painted with sacred ash and a red dot. (KCS 54)

Vesak

/vesak/ the most important Buddhist religious festival, on the May **poya day**, which commemorates the birth, death and

enlightenment of the Buddha (Sinhala)
° *Vesak cards* ° *the day following Vesak*

♦ *Vesak* that year came soon after Nili left, a week before the elections. (Reef 171)

♦ ... memories that came alive at Poson and Wesak and New Year's Day, ... (WMD 199)

♦ Each year during the April season a giant wheel would be constructed in Depanama and it would be there till after Wesak; ... (BTH 32)

♦ Somaweera had not been able to participate in the alms giving Mr. Gunatilaka had organised for Vesak. (OD 26)

♦ When paper lanterns glowed in the village for Vesak, the fisher huts were holes of briny darkness. (HC 152)

♦ The coloured bulbs on a string that illuminated the petti kade during *Vesak*, were arranged along the edge of the coffin. (WCS 63)

♦ It had been *Vesak*, the biggest Buddhist festival of the year, when the followers of the Buddha celebrated the day of his birth, enlightenment, and death. ... The people of the cities thronged the streets in their millions, "going to see *Vesak*," as it was called. (CU 85)

□ **Vesak lantern**

a lantern made out of coloured tissue paper, a popular **Vesak** tradition (Sinhala: Vesak kuduwa)

VESAK LANTERN

♦ He was also a skilled maker of Vesak lanterns. On Vesak night people from far and near came to see his marvellous creations. (CM 72)

♦ ... the colours of the *Vesak* lanterns dotting the streets ... (CU 47)

vidyalaya

/vidyālǝyǝ/ college (in the names of schools) (Sinhala; Tamil vidyalayam) (> **MMV**) ° *Ananda Vidyalaya*

vihara, viharaya

/vihārǝ, vihārǝyǝ/ (= **pansala**) Buddhist temple (Sinhala; also India, from Sanskrit) ° *Residents against construction of viharayas*

♦ He had accompanied Auntie Prema to the Vihara a few times ... (WMD 28)

♦ Other invaders would be repelled in the millennium to come, and other *stupas* and *viharas*, more illustrious perhaps and beautiful, be erected, ... (WMD 199)

♦ "... and have every church, vihara, mosque and synagogue buzzing with prayer for him." (SG 144)

♦ "It has to happen before a statue or a painting in a *vihara* can become a holy thing." (AG 97)

♦ I saw to the restoration of viharas, temples and public places ... (Z 167)

village

(= **gama**) native place, the place where a person originally comes from ° *At New Year all take a week off and go back to their village.*

village headman

(= **headman**) (dated) an administrative officer at village level; now called **grama sevaka** or **grama niladhari**

♦ The Portuguese even took the humble village headman and called him a Mayoral, which made the said headman think no end of himself, ... (TT 11)

♦ ... and his mother's grandfather had been a village headman. (WMD 98)

♦ The first Bandara was a village headman from the Kandyan district ... (WMD 243)

♦ ... new ration books from the village headman's office ... (BTH 11)

♦ "The thugs were employed by the village headman who wanted to start up a shop of his own." (CG 219)

♦ "She is my father's older sister; her husband is the village headman." (GC 260)

♦ A message was sent to the village headman but he was fast asleep after having liquor. (KCS 104)

♦ "I heard cousin Gamini tell someone that he must have bribed the village headman," ... (PMS 225)

village side
in the country (i.e. not in the town or city)

villu
/villu/ a natural pond (Tamil)

♦ Fortunately the park authorities had created rough tracks to connect the villus, since they were the best places to see our wild fauna. (REP 47)

♦ This villu was really a marsh covered with patches of tall reeds. (REP 127)

♦ And a herd of elephants on the far side of a villu, ... (GC 148-9)

voile saree
/voil/ a saree made of voile, a thin cotton material

♦ It was the white voile saree with clusters of purple flowers Mother used to wear ... (BTH 21)

♦ Priyanthi came out of her room wearing a simple blue voile sari, her hair braided casually. (July 286)

♦ They bought one piece of hand luggage for both of them and secured one urn between two voile saris. (M&P 360)

vomit
be sick, throw up (more formal in BSE) ° *I think he's going to vomit.*

vomitish
(coll.) feeling sick, nauseous ° *I'm feeling a bit vomitish.*

vul
/val/ (coll.) dirty, obscene, vulgar (Sinhala = wild) (> **Valsatian**) ° *Don't be so vul!* ° *He gave me a vul look.*

W

wadiya

/vāɒiyə/ a camp or small **cadjan hut**, e.g. one occupied temporarily by fishermen, farmers, etc. (Sinhala/Tamil) ° *Three wadiyas were set on fire by an unidentified gang.*

wait

/wēT/ hang around, do nothing ° *He spends the whole day sitting in a chair and waiting.* ° *They're just looking up and waiting!* ° *He just sat on his back and waited.* → In BSE, to 'wait' suggests waiting for something, or for some specific purpose; in SLE it can just mean hanging around with nothing to do.

wakf

/wakf/ the board of trustees of a mosque (Arabic)

wala

/valə/ (coll.) (adj.) wild, riotous; (noun) an informal party or gathering of friends, a fun time (Sinhala = hole) ° *a wala party* ° *We had a wala time.* ° *Shall we have a wala at my place tomorrow?* ° *Let's put a wala!*

walauwa

/valauwə/ a large old house, originally the **ancestral home** of a land-owning family in the traditional feudal system (Sinhala) ° *a walauwa girl* ° *In the walauwa house I lived in as a girl, there were different sized stools for people to sit on according to their castes.*

WALAUWA

♦ "There is a place we can stay, a *walawwa*, an old family estate - ..." (AG 153)

♦ "Well, his father is dead now, but Stanley inherited the walauwwa and half the money." (July 247)

♦ Mrs. Herath had been born to a Kandyan *walauwa*, with all that that entailed, ... (CP 84)

waleema

/walīma/ a Muslim marriage feast similar to a **homecoming** (Arabic)

wallam

/valləm/ dugout canoe (Tamil)

wallop

(= **whack**) (coll.) eat greedily, gobble up, guzzle ° *She walloped the whole lot!* ° *I bought 25 rambutans yesterday and walloped them all.*

wandu aappa

/vandu āppə/ a sweet steamed cake made with **hopper** batter and **jaggery** (Sinhala)

♦ Steamed honeyed dumpling known as *vandu arppa.* (CM 76)

wappa

/wāppa/ (= **appa, thaaththa**) father (Muslim Tamil)

wappamma

/wāppamma/ (= **appamma**) grandmother (father's mother) (Muslim Tamil)

waraka

/varəka/ ripe **jak fruit** (Sinhala)

ward

(v) take to hospital, send to hospital (not used as a verb in BSE); **to be warded** (passive): to be in hospital (> **admit**) ° *She was warded for three weeks.* ° *He is warded at the General Hospital.* ° *Ten children warded with dengue fever*

- Both engines had been warded there for a general overhaul. (YY 75)

- Having warded his wife and after earnest consultation with a lawyer, ... (YY 207)

- "Your wife is badly sick. And we had to ward her." (KCS 161)

warrant
a permit for free rail travel by **government servants** → In BSE, a 'warrant' usually means an official authorization to arrest somebody.

- ... with second-class railway warrants courtesy of the Ceylon Government Railway ... (JFT 113)

- ... with his warrant to travel to Trincomalee, ... (YY 38)

- "How about next week if all of us go to K.K.S.? I'll get the warrants." (YY 151)

- ... entitled to one week's leave in the year and a free railway 'warrant'. (WMD 12)

- ... as he now had two railway warrants a year. (WMD 18)

washed off
washed away ° *The potholes are filled with sand and tar, but soon as it rains it all gets washed off.*

wasted
/wēstəd/ worn, worn down/out/away ° *The tyres are completely wasted.*

- "Feel like asking for a pair of shoes. Mine getting wasted by coming up and down like this." (JFT 96)

watalappam
/vaтəlappam/ a popular dessert made with **jaggery**, eggs and **coconut milk** (from Malay)

- He had gone straight to Sohani ... and given her a big tray of Wattalappam as a part of the funeral feast contributed by the neighbours of the deceased. (M&P 292)

watcher
guard, security guard

- "There is a small bungalow there. ...The watcher could do the cooking." (SMS 168)

water cutting
a traditional ceremony, marking the end of the Kandy **perahera**

water monitor
(= **kabaragoya**) the larger variety of **monitor lizard**, which lives in the water (> **monitor lizard**)

- A large yellow-speckled water monitor was savaging the carcass of the baby elephant ... (YY 159)

- De la Motte shot a very large water monitor which he dragged along by its tail ... (YY 192)

- A water monitor, dark, scaly, was cutting through the water, splitting it, ... (WE 119)

- "My sister had skin trouble once; made her look like a water monitor." (PMS 91)

wattakka
/vaттakka/ pumpkin (Sinhala); the smaller pear-shaped variety ('**batana**') is commonly called 'rata wattakka' or 'Dubai wattakka'

WATTAKKA

- ... a vattacka being fried ... (RF 76)

- "And if we're there a few months, what do we live on? Wattakka?" (CP 157)

watte
/vaṭṭə/ shanty, slum (Sinhala = garden)
° *They come from the watte.*

- He went back to being quiet obscure Raja Selvadorai who lived in one-room quarters in the watte. (Z 31)

- Sometimes he could hear the clear voices of families ring through the watte and it made him wish for a different life. (Z 36)

- "There is no one to look after them in the *watte*." (WE 41)

- "I think those men will watch the roads round our *watta*." (FSD 217)

watti
/vaṭṭi/ a shallow woven basket (Sinhala)
° *stringhopper wattis*

- There were several sizes of rattan trays called *vattis*. (CM 14)

wear
put on (clothes, etc.) ° *I'll wear my shoes and come.* → In BSE, to 'wear' something is a habit expressed in the simple form ('He always wears a sarong') or a temporary state expressed in the continuous form ('She's wearing a saree'); in SLE it also refers to the action of putting on clothes.

- And while all these delicious titbits were tossed around and Anna wore a pale-blue silk and Maudiegirl charged in ..., the drinks had begun to circulate with a vengeance ... (JFT 57)

- ... but the girl had twisted away as she wore her cloth. (TT 5)

- I then wiped myself with my sarong and wore it, depending on the night air to dry it later. (REP 113)

- Tanya had worn a flimsy pair of shorts with a loose T-shirt. (FSD 86)

- He wore the belt and looked at himself in the mirror. (FSD 213)

- When his son had seen the trouser he had been so excited that he ... had immediately gone to the bathroom to wear it. (WCS 27)

- "Thereafter you will go to your room, have your hair combed, wear the jewellery I have kept on the dressing table and come to the dining room." (M&P 235)

- Then I wore the peach half sari and went into the world outside the toilet. (M&P 236)

weaver bird
a small bird which weaves an elaborate hanging nest

- Once she saw a weaverbird with a scrap she recognised in its bill, and recalled the legend that says the weaverbird studs its nest with fireflies to light it up at night. (HC 203)

- Velaithan spotted a tree festooned with Weaver bird nests. (REP 208)

wedding hall
a reception hall usually hired out for weddings and **homecomings** (also India)

- ... the stray dogs at the backyards of the wedding hall ... (KCS 50)

wedding house
a house where a wedding is taking place

- The little flower girls never thought that they would be crying at the wedding house, ... (KCS 56)

weedicide
weedkiller

welcome speech
welcoming speech

Wella
/vælla/ (coll.) Wellawatte

well bath
a bath at a well (> bath)

- "Come, ... I'll find you some towels and you can have a refreshing well-bath." (WMD 331)

- "I'd like a well bath," ... (AG 90)

- On the same page, they were both in bathing suits having a well bath, flinging pails of water at each other. (SMS 31)

wet zone
the south-west part of Sri Lanka and the central **hill country**, where the rainfall is highest (> **dry zone**)

- We were now well into the wet zone. (REP 319)

- The people of the dry zone are thriftier than those of the wet zone. (M&P 220)

wewa
/vævə/ (= **tank, kulam**) (Sinhala) ° *the programme for the construction of thousand wewas* ° *I would hurry down to the wewa to watch the crocodiles come ashore.*

- Nothing like a bath in the Wewa. (YY 145)

- ... drag in the biggest catfish from the wewas or tanks. (TT 117)

- ... that age when falling in love was as easy as falling, like Ivor, into the wewa. (TT 142)

whack
(= **wallop**) (vt/vi) (coll.) eat greedily, gobble up, guzzle ° *Now don't whack that whole cake, leave some for me to take to office also.*

° *I of course didn't think about my diet, the food was tasty so I whacked.* ° *We stopped at Pilawoos on the way home and whacked.*

- "Well sir, it's hard to get beef in Buttala sometimes, so I thought I'd whack a deer or pig ..." (GC 306)

what ...
(coll.) what do you mean ...

- "You are not even fifty no?" - "Apo what fifty, thirty-eight!" (M&P 14)

what and what?
(coll.) what? (plural) ° *What and what have you been doing?*

- Though from time to time Megawathi would ask him what-and-what acts he did along the railway tracks with that dirty woman, ... (KCS 141)

what the hell?
(coll.) what? (expressing surprise or anger) → In BSE, 'What the hell?' by itself normally means 'So what?'. To express surprise or anger it is normally part of a longer question: 'What the hell are you talking about?', 'What the hell does he want?'

- "What the hell, men, you don't know when to stop?" (YY 224)

what to do?
(coll.) what can be done?, it can't be helped (see quotes for other similar expressions) (> **how to?**)

- "Sir, what to take?" (Reef 62)

- "But what to say if he wants it?" (Reef 81)

- "Where to put them?" (Reef 113)

- "Which to buy?" (Reef 128)

- "What to do? One has to be realistic." (FB 190)

◆ "So what to do? No trains could come or go." (WMD 229)

◆ "My God ... Now what the hell to do." (July 160)

◆ "Say something," ... "What's to say?" (July 284)

◆ She stretched herself out and stared up at the ceiling. What to do? What to do? (Z 40)

◆ "What to do? That's life." (CU 566)

◆ "What to do?" replied Achi, "that was the poor man's karma." (M&P 16)

whatnot

(dated) an item of furniture like a sideboard, consisting of shelves with or without a cupboard and drawers

WHATNOT

◆ "See, child, if have a candle in the whatnot." (JFT 11)

◆ ... and Elsie would take the long rattan cane from the top of the whatnot ... (JFT 165)

when you say

(coll.) (expression used to define or add emphasis to the word preceding it) ° *Chronic when you say!*

◆ Room when you say, three plywood partitions reaching up to about shoulder height that separated me from the common herd. (CP 47)

where and where?

(coll.) where? (plural) ° *Where and where did you go?*

◆ "What, child, two hours in the meat queue and don't know where and where I walked to get some milk." (YY 133)

white

(of curries) mild, made with **coconut milk** and green chilli but no other spices ° *a white curry* ° *We usually make the fish white.*

◆ The rice was overcooked, the beef was tough and the white potato curry, which usually had a creamy gravy, was dry. (July 270)

who and who?

(coll.) who? (plural) ° *Who and who were there?* ° *She wants to know who and who have come.* ° *Whose and whose are these?*

whom, to whom, from whom

who, who to, who from (> **from where?**) ° *To whom did you give it?* ° *From whom did you buy it?* → Though considered more correct by many people, 'whom' is now restricted to formal contexts in modern BSE, and is normally replaced by 'who' in colloquial contexts: 'Who did you give it to?' 'Who did you buy it from?'

◆ Vijay liked it there, and the young couple with whom he lodged treated him as a member of the family. (WMD 277)

◆ But for whom would he write? (WMD 291)

◆ "Whom have you got here?" (WMD 387)

◆ To whom could he tell this news in barracks? (OD 23)

♦ "Whom will I see in Intelligence?" ... "It will depend on whom I can reach in my Division." (REP 319)

♦ "Whom should I see in head office?" (FSD 101)

♦ "Whom are you living with now?" (GC 68)

♦ "Went for a shot." - "All this time? With whom?" (CU 41)

♦ "Whom are you talking to?" (M&P 64)

who's who

(coll.) who someone is related to (see quote)

♦ She asked them who's who they were. Meaning, who their mothers were, who their fathers were and who their uncles and aunts were. (M&P 296)

why

(coll.) because ° *Can't go there tomorrow, why Gamini is coming for lunch no?*

why?

(coll.) what do you want? what's the matter? what are you doing? → In BSE, the question 'Why?' cannot normally stand alone unless the context has already been established, e.g. 'I have to leave early today' - 'Why?' In SLE it can be used to open a conversation.

why not?

(= **otherwise?**) (coll.) of course! (as the answer to a question) ° *Are you coming for the trip? - Why not?*

♦ "Everything all right?" - "Why not?" she yelled back. (MiP 375)

wicked

/wikəb/ mean, cruel, nasty ° *Don't be wicked!* → In BSE 'wicked' is a strong word, meaning 'evil'. In SLE it is used in a more light-hearted way. Note also the difference in pronunciation: SLE /wikəb/, BSE /wikɪb/

will

would (> **would**) → In BSE, 'would' is used in reported speech where the main verb is in the past tense ('He said he would be late'), and in conditional sentences where the verb in the 'if' clause is in the past tense ('She would come if you asked her'). In both cases, 'will' is more likely in colloquial SLE.

♦ ... and I knew the paddy field will soon come into view just round the bend ... (BTH 44)

♦ I knew the car will be there, and sure enough, it was, ... (OD 128-9)

♦ "I never believed that such a situation will ever come about in this country." (OD 140)

♦ "We will be surprised if such things did NOT happen, ..." (OD 142)

♦ "If they also started personal vendettas, when will this war ever end?" (REP 116)

♦ "Do you think I will send you away if there was any other way?" (REP 357)

♦ "Father Basil said that I will find out, ..." (GC 207)

Willard mango

a small, sweet, reddish variety of mango

will you!

(coll.) (with imperative) please (also used for emphasis where there is no imperative) ° *Tell what happened, will you!* ° *I'll see you tomorrow, will you!* → In BSE 'will you?' is used as a question tag as in the first example, but not as in the second example.

♦ "You leave the bread, will you." (JFT 9)

♦ "You try, will you and see what will happen." (JFT 36)

♦ "My God! Look, will you, who's coming." (JFT 136)

♦ "See, will you, the price of things now." (JFT 184)

wine biscuit
a type of thin, hard biscuit

wine stores
drink shop, (US) liquor store, (UK) 'off-licence' (selling **arrack**, beer, etc., but not necessarily wine)

♦ ... the Dematagoda Wine Stores. (YY 4)

winged bean
(= **dambala**) a type of vegetable (Sinhala)

winkle
(= **bicycle repair shop**)

winnower, winnowing fan
(= **kulla**) a shallow fan-shaped basket used to winnow rice

♦ Attamma collected the *goraka* rind into the kitchen winnower to sun dry till it became black. (CM 16)

♦ They chatted quietly with Sepalika, helped her to toss the rice in her winnowing fan to disperse whatever tiny husks remained in it, ... (July 157)

wish (1)
congratulate, wish somebody well ° *I forgot to wish him.* → In BSE, you must 'wish somebody something', e.g. 'I wish you a happy birthday'.

♦ "Must go and wish Papa, no?" (JFT 177)

♦ "Yes, men. Have to wish the old lady, no?" (JFT 187)

♦ That day was Daddy's birthday and of the friends and relations who had come to wish him, only ... a few close relations stayed for dinner. (OD 88)

wish (2)
hope (tenses) ° *I wish I can go.* ° *I wish he will come.* ° *I wish I don't have to go.* ° *I wish we can win the toss and put them into bat.* → In BSE, there is a sequence of tenses after 'I wish' and after 'if' (and in all conditional/hypothetical sentences): present tense becomes past tense, past tense becomes past perfect, can becomes could, will becomes would, etc.: 'I wish I could go', 'I wish he would come', 'I wish I didn't have to go'. This sequence of tenses is less strictly applied in SLE. On the other hand, 'hope' is used in BSE with present and future tenses: 'I hope I can go', 'I hope he will come'.

with: to be with something
to have something ° *He was with a long face.*

withering
the first stage in the process of producing tea

woodapple
a type of fruit with a hard brown shell and rich brown flesh, which is usually made into a drink or a jam (Sinhala 'divul') (> **divul kiri**) ° *woodapple jam*

WOODAPPLE

♦ ... and offered them wood-apple for dessert. (MM 36)

♦ I offered him everything - even wood-apple cream - but nothing interested him. (Reef 169)

♦ "See the woodaple trees," (YY 179)

♦ ... thorny woodapple, spreading margosa, ... (TT 117)

♦ When we walked under the tall spreading woodapple tree my head turned skywards. (CM 8)

♦ ... wood-apple pickle, ... (WMD 126)

♦ She had been known to breakfast on curried sardines and woodapple jam on the morning they struck camp, ... (HC 178)

♦ The elephants who yearn to swallow woodapple. (KCS 97)

♦ Wood-apple grows wild in the forest near their village. (PMS 127)

work off, work out
(in newspaper reports) hold, play out (e.g. a tournament) ° *The annual inter-schools netball tourney will be worked off next month.* ° *The finals were worked out at the Sugathadasa Stadium yesterday.*

worry
/wori/ (vt) pester, hassle, harass (dated in BSE) ° *Don't worry me men, can't you see I'm busy?* ° *You'll have to worry her if you want to get anything done.*

♦ "Only knows to worry, that's all he knows to do." (TT 200)

worship
(vt) kneel at somebody's feet as a sign of respect (e.g. children to parents) ° *At New Year all children must worship their parents.* ° *When I was at primary school, we had to worship our teacher every morning.* → In BSE, 'worship' is normally used only in a religious context.

♦ After the New Year meal mother worshipped father offering him a sheaf of betel leaves. (CM 67)

♦ I want to kneel on the floor and worship them because their appearance compels the seniors to move off. (GC 10)

♦ He first went up to my grandmother and fell down at her feet and worshipped her. (M&P 331)

worst comes to worst
(coll.) if the worst comes to the worst

worth
worthwhile, worth it, worth doing, good value (cannot stand by itself in BSE) ° *It's fully worth!* ° *Not worth!*

would
will (> **could, will**) ° *We would inform you as soon as we hear.* ° *The memorial service would be held on June 25th.* ° *This is to inform you that this email address would not be valid from next week.* ° *The promotion period would be from 17 March to 10 April.* ° *We believe that the President would give an ear to what we say even if he fails to listen to others.* ° *If we do not hear from you by 5th April we would presume that you will not be available.* → In BSE, 'would' suggests an element of doubt which is not there in SLE.

♦ "Devi would have finished cooking by the time you are done." (WMD 331)

would have
must have, should have ° *They would have arrived by now.* → In BSE, 'would have', although it can be used in the same way, usually suggests a conditional clause: 'They would have arrived ... if they hadn't got a puncture'. When making deductions, 'must have' or 'should have' are more likely: 'They must have arrived by now'.

♦ ... giant mara trees which would have slowly matured over more than a century. (BTH 17)

♦ "Did I say that? ... I'm sure you'd have misheard me." (REP 271)

wound

cut ° *I have a wound on my finger.* → In BSE, a 'wound' suggests a more serious injury.

wristlet

watch, wristwatch → In BSE, 'wristlet' is a dated word for a bracelet.

Y

yak bera

/yak berə/ (= **devil drum**) a drum used in a **devil dance** (Sinhala)

yakka, yakkha

/yakə/ devil, demon (Sinhala)

♦ From the well a *yakkha*, a demon, bit him when he lifted the bucket to bathe. (MM 115)

♦ ... and we were left with this spoiled paradise of *yakkhas* - demons - ... (Reef 94)

♦ ... a hydraulic system that required our *yakkha* engineers to measure a half-inch change of water-level in a two-mile stretch of water. (Reef 95)

♦ He had the paint and the tattered clothes of a *yakka* on him, ... (AG 210)

yakko

/yæko/ (n/adj.) (coll., dated) a derogatory term for a peasant or low-class person (Sinhala) ° *He's a yakko fellow.* ° those JVP *yakkos*

♦ "Those Balapitiya *yakkos* ..." (YY 82)

♦ I headed straight for the middle thinking who are all these *yakkoes*? (SG 3)

♦ "Anyway she doesn't approve of nice Burgher girls getting involved with Sinhala *yakkos*." (FSD 160)

♦ "There'll be nice boys there, not these university *yakos*." (GC 125)

yala

/yalə/ one of the two annual paddy harvests (Sinhala) (> **maha**)

y'all, you all

(coll.) you (plural), all of you (also US)
° *What are y'all doing?* ° *Where are y'all's books?*

- ♦ "What did you all do?" (FSD 187)

- ♦ "I don't care. ... You all are not my family." (SMS 178)

- ♦ "How long were y'all standing there?" (CU 44)

- ♦ "Ah? Then what're all'f y'all doing here?" (CU 557)

- ♦ "So y'all all came together? Like going on a pilgrimage?" (M&P 22)

- ♦ "Then why don't you take the pumpkin preserve for you all to eat?" (M&P 117)

- ♦ "Don't even look at me, y'all keep on dancing, ..." (M&P 293-4)

year: an year

a year ° *It happened about an year back.*

- ♦ ... in 1951, which was an year after we came to Egodawatta ... (BTH 42)

- ♦ "For an year and a half in Australia I tried to forget you," ... (GC 232)

year end

the end of the year ° *They expect to be finished by year end.* ° *Year-end exams were disrupted.*

years

years old ° *She's 13 years.* (BSE: She's 13, or: She's 13 years old.)

yellow rice

(= **kaha bath**) rice cooked with turmeric, spices, etc., and normally served on special occasions

- ♦ ... great bins of yellow rice studded with cashew nuts, plums and stoned French olives; ... (JFT 60)

- ♦ For the poker lunch I made the usual yellow rice and chicken curry. (Reef 150)

- ♦ I had just walked back home to my yellow rice and chicken curry when they called, ... (CP 200)

- ♦ In one expansive gesture she had told an astonished waiter to bring yellow rice, both chicken and fish and three other curries. (WCS 18)

yeoman service

sterling service, faithful and devoted service (dated in BSE) ° *retiring after thirty years of yeoman service* ° *She has rendered yeoman service to the department.*

yet

still ° *I can yet remember.* ° *He is yet not finished.* ° *Child employment yet rampant* ° *The strategy is yet the same.* ° *That huge tree is yet standing.* ° *Tsunami victims yet waiting for houses* → In BSE, 'yet' is used more often in questions and negatives: 'Have they arrived yet?', 'I haven't finished yet'. Note also the word order: in BSE 'yet' tends to come at the end of the sentence, while in SLE it can come before the verb (like 'still' in BSE).

young coconut

(= **kurumba**) the young green coconut, before it matures, containing a sweet water which can be drunk; different from the **king coconut** or **thambili**, which is orange in colour and comes from a different tree

- ♦ ... when Siri reappeared carrying a bunch of young coconuts. (July 107)

- ♦ It had a sweet, milky taste, much like the meat of a young coconut. (REP 265)

Z

zipper man
(= **showman**) (coll.) flasher, exhibitionist, a man who exposes himself in public ° *They are called 'zipper men' because they open their zippers and expose themselves.*

Z-score
A level marking system used to determine university entrance ° *Revised Z-score cut off marks released* → Pronunciation note: the letter z is commonly pronounced /ized/ in SLE.